What Readers Are Saying About *Business Pl*

"This is much more than a business planning handbook; it is a tutorial on how to launch and manage a business."

DENZIL DOYLE
Chairman, Doyletech Corporation and Author of *Making Technology Happen*

"All team members came to this project with very limited experience with the ideas and vocabulary of business planning. The RoadMap™ is quite simply the most well-written, clear nearly fool-proof guide that we have seen for the novice business planner. By breaking the tasks down into so many small steps and providing good summaries of how these are to be done, Mr. Boudreau has made the whole process less intimidating and yet comprehensive."

NORMAN DALE
Project Manager, Wood-bee Business Planning Team.

"When I began to investigate starting my own home-based business, I wanted to maximize my chances of success by doing appropriate research and using effective business planning tools. Having reviewed a fairly wide array of materials, programs and services, I highly recommend the products produced by Macrolink Action Plans Inc. – namely, the RoadMap™, the Biz4Caster™ and the RiskBuster. As I work on my business plan, I am finding that these tools are comprehensive, user-friendly, and very effective at providing me with a complete view of my business planning needs. The practical, step-by-step guide to producing a business plan is very valuable — the best I've seen. I expect to produce an excellent business plan, and my confidence in securing a successful business is greatly increased."

DAVID LEMAN
Consultant, Internet Mapping and Land Use Planning

"After working through the RoadMap™ with the help of the RiskBuster™ CD I completed my business plan much sooner than I had originally anticipated. There was still a great deal of work to be done but these tools made the work much more focused and easily completed. I have since used my business plan to secure funding and to have a viable plan for my business's future. I would highly recommend any or all of these tools to anyone who is serious about getting into business for him or herself. Thanks Dan."

BRAD J. GRANTHAM, B.SC.
Practical Tactical & Martial Arts Supply

"Your writing is warm, truthful and at times, funny. The candle shop feasibility study had me laughing out loud. You have a gift, Dan, of coming across the pages and being right there in the room while I was reading your book."

BARA-DAWN LEWIS
Business Counselor and Analyst

Business Plan or BUST!

Dan Boudreau

Happy trails
Dan Boudreau

TRAFFORD
PUBLISHING™

www.trafford.com

Note for Librarians: A cataloguing record for this book is available from
Library and Archives Canada at www.collectionscanada.ca/amicus/index-e.html
ISBN 1-4120-9285-x

Printed in Victoria, BC, Canada. Printed on paper with minimum 30% recycled fibre.
Trafford's print shop runs on "green energy" from solar, wind and other environmentally-friendly power sources.

TRAFFORD
PUBLISHING

Offices in Canada, USA, Ireland and UK

Book sales for North America and international:
Trafford Publishing, 6E–2333 Government St.,
Victoria, BC V8T 4P4 CANADA
phone 250 383 6864 (toll-free 1 888 232 4444)
fax 250 383 6804; email to orders@trafford.com
Book sales in Europe:
Trafford Publishing (UK) Limited, 9 Park End Street, 2nd Floor
Oxford, UK OX1 1HH UNITED KINGDOM
phone +44 (0)1865 722 113 (local rate 0845 230 9601)
facsimile +44 (0)1865 722 868; info.uk@trafford.com
Order online at:
trafford.com/06-1039

10 9 8 7 6 5 4 3 2 1

Dedication

This book is dedicated to my parents, Clarence and Olga Boudreau.

Acknowledgements

I am thankful to so many who, knowingly or unknowingly, made this book possible.

For their friendship, wisdom and unwavering loyalty I thank Maxine Koppe and Richard Duval.

A special warm thank you goes to Shirly Prokopchuk for her love and support. My deepest gratitude is to Julia Cameron, author of *The Artist's Way*, for leading with courage and for creating a process that led me to writing this book. Thank you to Carol Whetter for the kick in the seat of the pants that got me to pull *The Artist's Way* off the bookshelf and actually go through the process.

I wish to thank Brenda Koller for her persistence in editing and answering my many questions. A special thank you goes to Mike Carr for his patience with my thousands of adaptations to the Biz4Caster™! And a further thank you goes to Shawn Petriw for not bolting when he realized how many pages the individual chapters added up to ("the book will be how many pages?!").

I am thoroughly grateful to the entire team at Community Futures Development Corporation of Fraser Fort George (CFDC). Special kudos go to Don Zurowski for sharing his acute business savvy and for his commitment to efficiency; Eric Bennett for bouncing ideas back and forth with me; Laurie Hooker and Tandra Masse for their strong support. A heartfelt thank you goes to all of the members of the CFDC Finance and Lending Committee and to all of the participants of the CFDC Entrepreneurial Development Series for showing me the need for this book and teaching me what needed to go into it.

Thank you to Graham Stanley, Eric Bennett, Don Zurowski and Rab Kooner for reading my business plan and to Dianne Fowlie for editing the Biz4Caster™.

I wish to acknowledge and thank those who pioneered the RoadMap™ and RiskBuster™ Business Planner and offered their feedback and encouragement: Danny Panya, Krista Fick, Glenn Singleton, Jody Hunter, David Leman, Gary McIntyre, Debi Dowd, Danielle Peloquin, Norman Dale, Deryl Seymour, Conrad Jaye, Alan Dixon, Andrew Tejero, Bonnie Mercedes, Brad Grantham, Charlene Cruezot, Debbie Peever, Dolores Bazil, Michelle Brundige-Hess, James Liddle, Roseann Blackburn and Larry Cadieux.

Finally, I wish to express my sincerest thank you to the busiest group of all for taking the time to read and comment on the entire draft book: Clarence and Olga Boudreau, Denzil Doyle, Ray Gerow, Maxine Koppe, David Leman, Bara-Dawn Lewis and Don Zurowski.

The list of those who helped bring this book into existence could go on and on. Although it was me slumped over my laptop writing at peculiar hours (complete with low brow, the drool, and the knuckles dragging on the floor), the true development and inspiration took place out in the world, interacting with real customers. This writing is not really an independent work; it is drawn from and feeds back into the communities and the world in which I live, play and work. My sincerest apologies if I've missed anyone.

Contents

Introduction

This book is comprised of parts of my story and the lessons I have learned as an entrepreneur making my way in the world. For me, entrepreneurship has been an adventure that has led to a better understanding of myself and my environment.

I didn't start down my entrepreneurial path with a lot of money; my businesses have all been started with minimal investment. Some of my enterprises have sustained me for years. I have been in one form of business or another since 1980 and I will likely be in business for many years to come. If I took snapshots of my business life, you would be able to see that each snapshot looks different than the previous one - it continually evolves. In 1983 you would have seen a profitable reforestation business, having just captured $1.6 million in sales. In 1987 I was just emerging from a dreadful bankruptcy. The 1990s brought an awesome period of growth for my training business and 2003 saw the layoff of our last eight special employees with me headed back to being a home-based, single operator business.

Business hasn't always been easy for me, but I believe it to be my best chance to work at something I enjoy and my best opportunity to succeed financially. Regardless, owning and operating a business is my choice as an entrepreneur and free spirit.

My mission is to provide practical and affordable business planning solutions for do-it-yourself entrepreneurs. If this book helps you achieve your dream, you will be helping me to fulfill my mission. If you win, I win. That is good business.

If you're hoping to start a small business to sustain yourself this book is for you. I wish you great success in your entrepreneurial adventures.

What is an entrepreneur?

I have been called an entrepreneur. I've been nominated as "Entrepreneur of the Year." Many people have labeled my actions and achievements as entrepreneurial.

My Oxford Paperback Dictionary defines an entrepreneur as "a person who organizes and manages a commercial undertaking, especially one involving commercial risk."

What makes me an entrepreneur? I own and operate a small business. I innovate and create solutions that I call products and services and I market and sell those products and services. I serve customers. Sometimes I collaborate with others to get massive amounts of work done: contractors, employees, partners, customers and advisors. Some of the time I am comfortable with leading or following yet other times I am very uncomfortable with both. I take calculated risks. I enjoy innovating, solving problems and serving customers.

In setting out to provide this book for entrepreneurs, I began to seek ways and means to measure how many entrepreneurs might need my book. This led me down a slippery path. How do I define entrepreneurs and determine how many there are? How do others quantify and categorize the fuzzy term "entrepreneur"?

As with anyone who sets out to research a market, I encountered uncertainty. The process of researching one's market can be an agonizing roller coaster ride before clarity prevails. Perhaps the most daunting aspect of market research is the challenging of our own assumptions and learning new things.

This book is for entrepreneurs who want or need to develop a business plan, including those who want to start the simplest business.

So, what is an entrepreneur? I define an entrepreneur as anyone engaged in providing products or services to others, including those who are:

- Starting a business
- Growing a business
- Buying a business
- Motivated to entrepreneurial activity either by opportunity or by necessity

One More Crazy Idea — New Years Day 2003

How many people, at any given moment, are either in business, starting a business, or considering starting a business? Let's consider Canada and the United States for starters:

- My local Chamber of Commerce has more than 950 member businesses.
- My home city reports having between 4,800 and 5,000 businesses licensed.
- There are many network marketing opportunities with many, many down-line entrepreneurs grinding a few shekels from their surroundings.
- The British Columbia Chamber of Commerce claims to represent 25,000 businesses throughout the province.

In my role as business planning facilitator, I am aware of at least 100 people each month who invest in themselves by taking training or attending workshops.

The city I live in has a population of 84,615, according to the 2001 census. Of those, 45,925 are between the ages of 20 and 54. This I consider to be the age group most likely to be considering starting a small or home-based business.

I have a strong hunch there at least 4,592 people in my city who are thinking about starting a business, or planning to start a dream business one day. That figure is 10% of the 45,925 people in the ideal age group for starting a business.

British Columbia has a total population of 3,907,740. According to the 2001 census, of those, 2,018,545 are between the ages of 20 and 54. Using 10% as a benchmark, this means there might be 201,854 people either planning or starting a business.

Canada has a population of about 31 million people, of which 13.5 million are in the ideal age group. Ten percent of 13.5 million places the number of entrepreneurs in Canada at about 1.3 million people.

In Canada, we live next door to the United States. The US has a population of about 284.8 million, of which 122.7 million are in the ideal age group. Ten percent of 122.7 million people puts the potential number of entrepreneurs in the US at about 12 million.

I believe there is a need for a realistic, yet entertaining book that helps entrepreneurs wade through the business planning process. I believe my entrepreneurial "trail of terror" has many valuable lessons to offer entrepreneurs.

There are plenty of books already available on the topic of business planning. Many are written by academics, accountants, lawyers or seasoned business people holding MBAs. There are many wonderful resources that help a great number of people.

I am not an academic, an accountant, a lawyer, nor do I have an MBA. Like any other entrepreneur wishing to start a business, I must develop a business plan in order to avoid losing my investment or wasting my time. To me, a business plan is my best defense. I believe I can make a positive difference for many other entrepreneurs who also need business plans as their defense.

To me, a business plan is my best self defense. I believe I can make a positive difference for many other entrepreneurs who also need business plans as their self defense.

Based on my hunches, I will write a book on business planning for entrepreneurs and use my business plan as a sample, detailing how I will sell enough books to survive and thrive.

At this pre-business planning juncture, I hope the book will sell for about $35. When I get to it, my sales forecast will demonstrate survivability selling as few books as possible, maybe a few thousand. But imagine this – if I can sell one million books my business will capture in excess of $35 million. That, to me, is an impressive potential market.

The short story is that I have an idea that is born out of a hunch. The idea has been percolating for a few years. In the past 20 years I have owned and operated seven businesses and coached hundreds of others through the business planning process. As well, I have provided business planning workshops for more than 5,000 entrepreneurs.

So, here is my proposition. I will write the book, create the business plan, and then live with the results. If my business plan proves there is no market or that the market is less than I believe, I will lower my expectations or make changes to increase the market for my book.

I'm putting my butt on the line. By the time you read this book I will be well into my business plan. I urge you to read on to learn what the plan is or was. The rest will be measured by my results in the marketplace.

What a crazy idea! It makes me smile to think you could be studying this book to determine where I went wrong or analyzing it to learn what I did right. I hope it provides you the benchmarks you need to get out there and make a few mistakes of your own. Most importantly, I hope this work inspires you to follow your dreams and gives you the confidence to convert some of your own crazy ideas into a thriving business. May you get as much enjoyment out of reading this as I have in writing it and implementing my business plan.

I hope this work inspires you to follow your dreams and gives you the confidence to convert some of your own crazy ideas into a thriving business.

Dan Boudreau

Business Plan or BUST!
Book at a Glance

Chapter 1: Discovering Entrepreneurship

A series of snapshots of the author's journey into the world of entrepreneurship. It is not a rant about the successes, the fast track to riches, or early retirement. It is focused on the realities of owning a business; the disappointments and pitfalls, and some of the lessons learned along the way. This chapter is about the potential downside of business ownership and what it's like to lose everything you own.

Chapter 2: Your Personal Toolchest

The toolchest is a collection of tools for organizing your personal affairs, from financial and personal goals to listing your successes. If a business is to serve your needs and move you closer to the lifestyle you desire, it is important to know what those needs and desires are. In reference to this line, I always like the saying "If you don't know where you are going, how will you know when you get there"?

Chapter 3: So You Want to Start a Business!

Perhaps the darkest chapter of the book, with descriptions of the people and the forces you will deal with once in business. If you're not suited to business ownership, it is better that you know before you invest. The lessons in this chapter might just save you a lot of time and energy, and even help you avoid bankruptcy.

Chapter 4: Business Planner's Primer

An assortment of informative articles, encouragement, and business planning tips. This chapter is intended to be a pre-business planning read and serve as a reference at any time.

Chapter 5: Business Planner's RoadMap™

A comprehensive 99-step business planning process for any business. The RoadMap™ is an integrated market research and business plan development process for shepherding your business from the first idea to opening day. It is also effective for growing an existing business, or for business counselors and coaches to use as a client development tool.

Chapter 6: Sample Business Plan

This chapter is a real life example of the author's business plan for Macrolink Action Plans Inc. The examples used throughout the RoadMap™ in the previous chapter are taken from this business plan.

Chapter 7: The Fast Track Business Plan

A second, shorter example of the author's business plan for Macrolink Action Plans Inc. This shorter business plan can be scaled down from the longer plan in Chapter 6 or developed by existing businesses, using the Fast Track method in this chapter.

Glossary of Terms

Definitions for over 500 business and technical terms.

Appendix

Business startup checklist, suggested reading and several different RoadMap™ checklists, including 4-week, 12-week and open variations.

Quick Start Guide

Business Plan or BUST! is more than a business planning handbook, it is a complete reference guide and tutorial for anyone wishing to start or grow a business. The book is a smorgasbord of lessons, methods and solutions for entrepreneurs and business counselors. Some people may read the book cover to cover, but most probably won't. The important thing is for you to know where to find the tools you need when you need them. I hope you recognize the powerful reference you hold in your hands and come back to it again and again. The suggestions in the table on the next page will help you easily find what you're looking for.

This book is more than a business planning handbook, it is a complete reference guide and tutorial for anyone wishing to start or grow a business. One way to gather business wisdom is to learn from your own mistakes, another way is to learn from the mistakes of others. In today's business environment, you don't have the luxury of enough time to make all the mistakes yourself.

YOU ARE HERE	QUICK START SUGGESTIONS
If you have no previous business experience and are considering starting a business	· Read the first three chapters before proceeding to the business planning · Complete Step 9 in Chapter 5 – Write Your Business Vision in an Hour · If you're still determined to move forward, read Chapter 4 and then follow all 99 of the RoadMap™ steps in Chapter 5 · Use the glossary in the back to clarify any confusing terms
If you have no previous business experience and are definitely starting a business	· Go directly to the RoadMap™ in Chapter 5 and work through the steps · Use all other parts of the book as a reference
If you have prior business experience and wish to start a business	· Use the Fast Track method in Chapter 7 to create a brief business plan · If the Fast Track method proves to be unworkable, follow the 99 steps of the RoadMap™ in Chapter 5
If you own a business and want to create a business plan for growth or change	· Read any of the articles that appeal to you in Chapter 4 · Use the Fast Track method in Chapter 7 to create a brief business plan · For any areas of your business plan requiring more detail, refer to the relevant RoadMap™ steps (noted in the Fast Track) · Use all other parts of the book as a reference
If you want to buy a business, or if your market is relatively proven (for example, you have already secured sales through a contract or agreement)	· Read any of the articles that appeal to you in Chapter 4 · Use the Fast Track method in Chapter 7 to create a brief business plan · For any areas of your business plan requiring more detail, refer to the relevant RoadMap™ steps (noted in the Fast Track) · If the Fast Track method simply proves to be too difficult, try following the RoadMap™ steps, skipping the market research steps 11 to 30 · Use all other parts of the book as a reference
If you are a business trainer, coach or counselor	· Use the entire book as a reference · Clients can be coached using the RoadMap™ in Chapter 5 as a process · The RoadMap™ can be purchased separately, in hard copy or e-book format, to use as a workbook for your clients · Downloadable worksheets and the Business Plan Shell™ are available free from www.riskbuster.com · For detail on other products or services available through Macrolink Action Plans Inc., see the last six pages at the end of this book or visit www.riskbuster.com

Tip: The RoadMap™ in Chapter 5 is a 99 step business planning process that works for a broad range of business planners and situations. Rarely will anyone need all 99 steps. If you are in a hurry to get your business plan done, you might try the Fast Track method in Chapter 7. Designed for experienced business owners, this method offers a quicker way to pull together a business plan. If the Fast Track method doesn't work for you, or if the result doesn't satisfy your banker, you can always revert to the RoadMap™.

Tough Love for Entrepreneurs

If you dream of owning a business, this book provides you the opportunity to make your dream a reality.

I must tell you, right here at the beginning, that business ownership is not for the weak or weary. It is risky to own a business; it is not easy and it is not for everyone.

This is not a "Rah, Rah, Get Rich Quick & Easy" book. It *is* intended to give you a sense of what it's *really* like to own a business. Though the pages are sprinkled with glowing encouragement and helpful tips, there are many places for you to fall off the path.

In 2005 there were 111,807 new business and consumer bankruptcy cases filed in Canada and 1,794,795 in the US. When you consider the families and friends of those involved, that is a lot of lives impacted negatively. Your strongest self-defense against bankruptcy carnage is the *increased knowledge you will gain* as a result of doing a business plan.

Tip: Business planning is a large and complex project. At the beginning, it can appear to be a formidable wall. Unless you have previous or similar experience, such as researching and writing a university level report, it can seem like an insurmountable wall. The RoadMap™ is arranged in small, manageable projects that make it possible for the novice to scale that wall. You can do it.

I wrote this book to help those who want to help themselves. It's not yet clear to me how I will penetrate the market and get the RiskBuster™ tools to the right customers. As a seasoned entrepreneur I am prepared to push forward knowing that the road ahead is littered with speedbumps and detours. I am determined to do my best to get this book into your hands.

Reading is a very inexpensive way to learn. If you are put off by the fact that this book is over 400 pages, I offer no sympathy. Instead I urge you to also read a number of the books in the *Suggested Reading* Section at the end of this book. I suggest that you read 4,000 pages and learn all you can!

If you are intimidated by the 99 steps, I challenge you to explore each of the steps to learn what you can. You may be relieved to learn that some of the steps are very brief while others are not necessary for your business. Be discerning; I'm not suggesting you do any more than is necessary for your situation. I suggest you start at the beginning and don't stop until you get to the end.

If you are troubled that it might take as many as two-hundred hours or more to build your business plan, don't be. I say roll up your sleeves and get busy! This is truly a tiny investment of your time and energy when compared with the mountain of effort it can take to dig your way out of a bankruptcy.

Alternatively, if you're prepared to reach out for what you want, the world of business is a playground awaiting your participation. Envision what you want, plan it, and go get it. Imagine working each day at something you enjoy, a workplace designed by you for you. What could it be like to actually choose the people you work with? Do you want to *make a difference* with your work? You can be, have, and do whatever you want in this world, but *you* are the one who has to step up to the plate. You hold in your hands the means to take control of your work life. It's up to you to decide whether or not you will follow through and do it.

My passion for business has endured the test of time. After 25 years I still believe that owning a business is the ultimate path for those who have what it takes to succeed; it is our best chance to do work we enjoy, to shape our contribution to the world, to make a difference, and to achieve our desired level of financial comfort.

Chapter 1

Discovering Entrepreneurship

Table of Contents

Sandburn in the Baha

I've always had a high degree of faith in the Creator. It was about 1978 when I headed down the Baha Peninsula with my buddy Brian Doyle. It was a fun adventure for us both. Brian had officially quit drinking and I was in one of my rare life snippets when it seemed healthier to abstain. For the entire one-month journey, we lived in the canopy on the back of Brian's brown GMC pickup.

Somewhere north of Cabo San Lucas we pulled off the highway into the darkness. We drove on a short, dead-end sandy road toward the Baha side of the peninsula and camped. Just beyond the huge sand dune that stopped us, we could hear the waves thundering persistently against the shore.

The following day was the fulfillment of a dream I didn't even know I had. The sun was hot. The sand was pure white and it rolled and dipped for miles to the north and south. The blue-green water of the Baha was wildly alive, full of fish and sea life. From our viewpoint at the top of a dune it was obvious there was no human form of life within miles. We had this wondrous natural playground to ourselves. To these two Canadian adventurers the surf was both alluring and daunting. Neither of us really knew about surf or how to navigate it. What we did know was that it was February and back in Canada our friends and family were shoveling snow from their driveways while we basked in this lush Mexican paradise. We had time and a yearning to learn. A skinny dip just seemed like the right thing to do.

I'm a kinesthetic learner - I learn by doing. I will gleefully do all nature of things in the interest of learning, knowing I will need to learn from any mistakes on the run. I calculate the risk and then leap. That's how I operate.

I had never seen surf like this. The beach was quite steep, indicating that the water depth went from zero to deep within a very short distance from shore. The waves arose from the calm blue sea about 100 meters from the shoreline and inflated themselves quickly to scary height, then crashed onto the hard sand. It was thunderous, invigorating and compelling.

The surf rolled into the shore in sequence, building from lowest to highest. The smallest wave was just a couple of feet high while the largest was mountainous. Each wave got progressively higher until the biggest thundered in, quickly followed by the second biggest one. The waves and the intensity would increase and subside like this time after time. I love the sea.

If you don't have the guts and the will to cool yourself off in the water, the Creator will cheerfully fry you on a Mexican beach.

We baked in the sun for awhile, studying the surf. If you don't have the guts and the will to cool yourself off in the water, the Creator will cheerfully fry you on a Mexican beach. We knew we had to give it a try. Kinesthetic learners; fun loving adventurers. Clad only in the swimsuits we were born with, we waited for the smallest wave and waded in.

Once we got through the initial thrashing and a short distance from shore, the water was calm, nurturing. Of course we got tossed around a bit on the way back to shore, but for the most part it was pure fun and we always arrived back on shore with a minimum of lacerations and most of our pride intact. Some landing positions are not really flattering when you're swimming starkers.

We spent most of the morning fumbling our way in and out of the waves, playing in the warm blue water, just beyond the clutches of the surf. We bobbed up and down, swam, played and laughed. We wondered aloud how many of our friends actually comprehended the stark contrast between Canadian and Mexican winter. My life changed forever that day in the cozy waters of the Baha. Of course I'll never know how close it came to ending.

On one of these forays into the waters beyond the thundering surf, Brian decided to head back to shore ahead of me. "Hasta Luego Amigo," I bid him as he headed toward shore.

"Si," he said. Add "bano" to this and you had our entire five-word Spanish vocabulary encapsulated in one dialogue. As neither of us was drinking alcohol, we hadn't yet added "cerveza" to our list.

I watched as he disappeared over the top of the wave, reappeared on the sand and meandered up the knoll to flop on his towel. I frolicked a while longer in the deep water, then decided to head to shore.

One of the challenges to getting back out of the surf was the fact that, from out on the water it was difficult to see how high the waves were. It was impossible to know if we were cruising in on the lowest or highest waves. Up until then we had lucked out by arriving completely by chance on the smaller waves.

As I approached the shore I could see the crest of the wave breaking away and down, behind it the high sandy knoll and Brian lying on his towel squinting in my general direction, shielding his eyes with his hands.

I rolled in toward the shore on my wave of choice. After a bit of a tumble I hit the sand on hands and knees and began fighting the fierce thigh-deep back current. I was home free again... or at least so I thought.

It was Brian suddenly sitting upright that first got my attention. I think he was yelling something to me, but there was no hope of hearing his voice over the roar of the surf. Something behind me had aroused his interest. I turned to see what it was.

Towering over me, backed by the clear blue sky, was the menacing frothy crest of the biggest wave. The sky disappeared instantly. I sucked in my breath, threw my arms out wide and embraced the force of the Baha.

The wave smacked me onto the hard-packed sand and thrashed me, tumbled me, tossed me where it pleased. I'll never forget the ferocity of the point where the sea meets the packed sand.

The goddess of the sea chewed me up and pummeled me along the unforgiving hard packed sand like a crab on a hot tin roof. Just about when breathing the water seemed more viable than waiting for air, she spewed me out into a vicious knee-deep back current.

I was now quite eager for this segment of my adventure to end, longing to be set down on dry land.

Somewhat dazed, I struggled to my feet. Brian was now at the water's edge about thirty paces away, yelling and pointing behind me. I had come to respect his angle on the proceedings. Struggling with the irrefutable current, I glanced over my shoulder just in time to greet the second biggest wave.

> *The sky disappeared instantly, I sucked in my breath, threw my arms out wide and embraced the force of the Baha.*

Wave number two threw its arms and legs around me, slapped me about wildly, and then tossed me like a flaccid jellyfish onto the sand. Brian was now at my side, helping me up, looking very concerned.

"I thought I'd lost you there," he said with a relieved chuckle.

I thought so too. Aside from a severely sand-burnt butt, multiple lacerations and a wounded bravado, I was OK. The Creator had chosen to teach me a cheap lesson and leave me to adventure another day.

That was my introduction to the fury of the surf. As loud as it sounds from the shore, it's much louder inside the water mill.

That was my introduction to the fury of the surf. As loud as it sounds from the shore, it's much louder inside the water mill.

I was to learn sometime later on that trip, by watching local Mexican boys playing in the surf, a more effective way to manage approaching waves. It's really quite simple. You dive straight into the oncoming wave and pop out on top. How was a boy from the mountains of Canada to know this? By doing it, of course.

This story is a glimpse of my life and how I learn. It is how I learned about the surf, how I have splashed into and out of business and how I approach each new adventure.

My life is a trail of continuous innovation, trying things until either they succeed or I drop them and move on to something else. This applies to customers, products, services, employees, investments, bankers, marketing strategies, business planning, business systems, and partnering. I am immersed in the wild surf of life, virtually powerless except for my ability to listen, learn and innovate.

I have a high sense of trust and a very close relationship with the Creator. I know the Creator has a plan for me. I am led to learn what I need to know, when I need to know it. Being led, I mostly follow; sometimes I appear to lead.

I'm not always comfortable in my learning; it is sometimes very difficult for me, and at times it is downright painful. Yet I continue to trust and to surrender my future to the Creator.

In life, in business, as in the surf, I embrace each swell as an adventure and I strive to learn what it teaches me. I innovate until I can do it no more. This, to me, is the business of life and the life of business. It's thrilling and fulfilling. I wouldn't trade it for anything.

In life, in business, as in the surf, I embrace each swell as an adventure and I strive to learn what it teaches me. I innovate until I can do it no more. This, to me, is the business of life and the life of business. It's thrilling and fulfilling. I wouldn't trade it for anything.

I never found a job that excited me quite like getting into business. From that first leap in 1980, the change, the creativity, the achievement and the successes have thrilled me. Failures are just opportunities vying for attention so I can innovate my way to yet more success.

Later that day in Cabo San Lucas, a local told us that particular stretch of surf is called "the head-cruncher."

Life Before Business

I was born in 1952 in my grandmother's house in Penny, British Columbia, the first of five children. My childhood was an adventure, but a different world than the one in which I live. Penny apparently had more than 500 residents the year I was born. It was a thriving sawmill town with a lot of pioneer types roaming around carving their sustenance from the forest.

Sawmills came and went in Penny and occasionally burned down. Then a large company bought all or most of the smallmills along the railway between Prince George and McBride. Once the last mill closed, my home town slid quietly into the status of ghost town.

There were very few people left in Penny by the time I was ten years old. From that time period I remember only a couple of friends my own age. The two-room school employed a couple of teachers who taught all the subjects to the handful of kids ranging from Grades 1 through 7.

One of my fondest childhood memories was playing cowboys and Indians. My preferred role was that of a Lone Ranger or Maverick type. We played away many hours that way, must have killed thousands of Indians, back when it seemed politically correct to do so. The rules were simple; the Indians always lost and you couldn't hit a *running target*. I could run like a deer. It wasn't until years later that I came to realize how thoroughly racist was the preferred game of my childhood. It was the culture of my pre-10 years, cloaked in cardboard buckskins and a thick shroud of ignorance.

When I was 11 years old, I was sent off to the thriving metropolis of Prince George, British Columbia to attend high school. In my small-village mind I had just been plopped into the biggest, scariest city in the universe. At the time Prince George was a little logging town of a few thousand people, some of whom were a little rough around the edges. I was cut loose from the safety of my tiny town cocoon and cast into the sea of life to sink or swim.

For my eighth grade, I boarded out with friends of our family. For my ninth grade I lived with my Dad's oldest sister, Aunt Isabelle. For grade 10 I moved into the high school dormitory in Prince George... both years. I remained there for a couple of attempts at grade 11. Apparently 20% attendance was not enough to earn passing grades. I managed to pass a few of the courses required for grade 11 and then quit high school forever... at least as far as I know at this time.

I suppose the dormitory brought an opportunity to conform to some sort of group. The kids were all displaced like me, staying away from home for most of the school term, visiting on the major holidays or the odd weekend. But by then I was already hopelessly alone. I don't recall making a decision to become a lone wolf. Sometimes I really wanted to fit in, but there was no escaping the fact that I was as different from the mainstream folks then as I am now.

By Grade 11 I was turned off the academic stream – partying held far more intrigue and complimented the badass image I had begun to cultivate. Although I couldn't see it at the time, being different from the crowd has turned out to be a valuable strength for me. It has forced me to be innovative at times when status quo just wasn't an option.

I don't recall making a decision to become a lone wolf. Sometimes I really wanted to fit in, but there was no escaping the fact that I was as different from the mainstream folks then as I am now.

My work life has been like riding an endless array of waves where the wind meets the water. On good days I have one eye on the horizon while surfing the rollers in front of me. At other times the horizon is engulfed by frothy darkness and I am left to my instincts and the grace of the Creator.

As if by magic, every phase of my work life seems to have been built on past jobs and experiences. My life is simply different than most doctors, lawyers and accountants. I haven't really planned the next steps; more likely I roll into the next steps because of where I've been. It's like a life-long string of projects woven together in some divine way that I have no pressing need to understand. I really can't claim to have much control over the weaving. The Creator looks after that. It seems that my responsibility is to embrace and handle each step, each project as it is placed in front of me. I just am, my career just is, yesterday's job just was. Today I'm working on this book. Tomorrow, who knows?

My job history, prior to starting my first business, would induce a serious bout of heartburn for your neighborhood career counselor. It goes something like this:

My job history, prior to starting my first business, would induce a serious bout of heartburn for your neighborhood career counselor.

Age	Job
14	My parents got me a summer job working as a laborer with the section crew for the railway. That was my introduction to the workplace, the land of drudge. It felt kind of cool to be one of the boys riding up and down the railway line on the Speeder. There was a lot of waiting around for trains to arrive and when we did work, the work was hard.
15	I quit school and went to work in Mackenzie, British Columbia for Findlay Forest Industries. I was a laborer in the planer mill there for a very short stint. Two things stand out in my mind from that time period; It sucks to work in -56°F weather and Otto was a butcher from Germany with a vision. He had spent some time in Mexico, had married a Mexican lady and was working at the planer mill long enough to save money to get back to Mexico and start his own butcher shop. He used to muse about how easy it is to operate a business in Mexico, not as complicated as Canada.
16	I got a job with Palm Dairies, helping the delivery guys load their trucks with dairy products. The pay was great, I would work for a brief vigorous early morning stint and then it was off to school. For my teen years, this was about as close as I ever felt to mainstream; I had a great job, enjoyed a wonderful girlfriend, owned a car, I was doing reasonably well at my second hack at grade 11. I had it made and I was enjoying life. This was very short lived however. One day I drove to the junction of Highways 97 and 16 and flipped a coin. It was heads; a long day later I ended up in Prince Rupert, British Columbia.
16	I worked for a very brief stint at a local sawmill in Prince Rupert. It wasn't a complicated job. I was hired at the same time as a guy who I shall refer to as Norm. I don't remember much about Norm, but he was a tad unstable. He and I wandered around the mill cleaning up stuff. I don't recall exactly what ticked the supervisor off; possibly it was when Norm threatened to kill him. We both got fired a week later. I rarely use this as a reference in my bio.
17	Got a fabulous summer job as a part of an initial attack crew, a joint effort between the Ministry of Forests and Northwood Timber Ltd. Under this arrangement the employer provided three teenage reprobates with a hot, spitting new, fire-engine-red pickup truck and turned us loose in the Aleza Lake Forest District to fight fires, build trails and picnic areas.

17	I was hired to supervise a tree planting crew for the Ministry of Forests. It was short-term and I got to drive a forestry truck. The paycheck was incidental and took a back seat to the privilege of driving the truck. Had they only known, they wouldn't have had to pay me.
18	Worked in Prince George on a cruising crew, dream job for a young single man. We got to travel throughout the forest region visiting pristine forests and mountainsides. It held a lot of what I really needed in terms of job satisfaction; variety, excitement, travel and adequate pay. After a few months I quit that job because I was now married and wanted to spend more time at home with my wife Milly.
19 to 24	Milly and I moved back to Penny with a dream of living off the land. During this time we spawned a couple of beautiful baby girls, Dawn Michelle and Melanie Tamara. For work I took on whatever jobs came along in order to put food on our table; fire fighting, tree planting, falling and bucking, cone collection and slash burning. One of my fondest memories of this time period was running compass lines and carrying trees for tree planting crews. What I loved was the autonomy and the varied types of work. I worked fairly much on my own yet served the needs of the team. Although it wasn't a job there was one significant project I worked extensively on during this time. Milly and I cleared a patch of forest and built a log cabin in Penny. We were living our dream, wild and free in our log cabin in the forest. It was a rough piece of construction but it was home for a time.
24	I was accepted into a six-month carpentry pre-apprenticeship program at Pacific Vocational Institute in Burnaby, BC. We packed up our two children and all the worldly belongings we could cram into our vehicle and journeyed to the thriving metropolis of Vancouver. I reckon we must have looked something like the Clampett family in the Beverly Hillbillies.
25	I passed the carpentry course and got a non-union job building houses in North Vancouver. After about a year I quit and went to work on my first union job. My pay rate went from $5 per hour to more than $9 per hour. Life was grand and I became a believer in unions, at least until I understood more about them.

During the last half of my four-year carpentry apprenticeship, I worked on several commercial construction projects, hi-rise office buildings. I had chosen carpentry because I love to work with wood – in reality I actually spent very little time working with wood. I found myself spending far too much time assembling and dismantling concrete forms.

Once I acquired my journeyman carpentry ticket, I ventured back up to the Prince George area to run a tree planting crew for a friend for the season.

This was a defining season in my so-called career. I was drawn to the wild fun times, the variety and the freedom of reforestation. I was now able to see more of the opportunities and found myself quite unexpectedly contemplating owning my very own business.

Who would have imagined?

I was now able to see more of the opportunities and found myself quite unexpectedly contemplating owning my very own business.

Crossing the Slippery Slope from Employee to Employer

I remember when I crossed the great divide, from employee to business owner and employer. An almost imperceptible feeling deep inside me told me I had shifted to some sinister dark side. I felt like a traitor. I felt I was betraying the millions of working people who were my peers, to become a businessman. Up to that point I had never really put much thought into such things but it played heavily on my mind for the first year in business. I felt a nagging sense of guilt for trying to succeed, as if it were evil to be successful or wealthy.

I felt a nagging sense of guilt for trying to succeed, as if it were evil to be successful or wealthy.

I have come to realize that I was feeling the loneliness of leadership as I stepped away from the crowd. Unknowingly, I was casting off the tentacles of poverty mentality and stepping into the stream of abundance. This can bring about isolation, particularly when most of your friends are headed down a different path. It wasn't until after my bankruptcy that I began to learn about the devastating power of poverty consciousness and how it has saturated my view of the world.

Poverty consciousness is what some refer to as the crab-pot syndrome. If you observe a bucket of crabs, every time one attempts to clamor up and out of the bucket the others pull it back in. The analogy is that when one person appears to be getting ahead, the others pull them back into the norm, whatever that happens to be. I now recognize poverty consciousness as one of the most pervasive evils on this planet.

I recall when I shook loose the last threads of guilt for being in business. It was at the end of the first year in business, facing the taxman, alone. No employees, no peers, nor any friends or family were there to help me pay the taxes. I knew then there was ample justification for any benefits I might reap. How robust are the seeds of poverty in our upbringing and how seductively they permeate our lives.

My First Voyage into Business

When I plunged into my first business in 1979, you could have scratched everything I knew about business onto the back of a beer cap.

For the first couple of years I operated as a proprietorship under the name of Sundance Reforestation. I had an opportunity to compete for a few tree planting contracts, won a couple and started planning my attack. For me the business offered a living, a fresh new adventure, a chance to work at something I enjoyed, and an opportunity to party – to dance in the sun.

I started Sundance with less than $400 and grew it to $1.6 million in sales within three years. By 1983 and '84 Sundance's payroll included more than 300 seasonal workers. Is that impressive? I was impressed with my achievements; I was having a ball and felt pretty much unstoppable.

I started Sundance with less than $400 and grew it to $1.6 million in sales within three years.

I was overwhelmed but continually pushing straight forward. I was caught up in the "bigger is better" trap. The reforestation industry was drifting toward larger contracts and contractors who could move in and bang in huge numbers of trees in short work windows. I thought I was invincible and loved the challenge. Rapid, unchecked growth just seemed like the right thing to do.

As one can readily imagine, there were always problems to be solved. Here are a few of the challenges I encountered during Sundance's six-year adventure.

1. From the start the business was undercapitalized, which means there never seemed to be enough cash to operate the company properly.

2. Reforestation had a low entry requirement, which meant that any idiot with a truck, a planting shovel, and a case of Budweiser could jump in. This means continual low-ball competition from new contractors; I was one of these.

I re-read the beer cap; there was nothing written about management and training.

3. Competitive low bids can mean unhappy workers some days; I navigated a few of these.

4. Rapid growth meant building crews and supervisory teams from zero to full-tilt in very short time frames.

5. My lack of management skills led to inadequate training for supervisors and employees.

6. Often my planters were more seasoned than I at dealing with complications such as the employment standards, labor relations and union issues – which meant I got my butt kicked a few times as I learned the ropes and each costly lesson meant a reduction in profit.

7. Some folks felt it was their right to screw the business (in other words, to screw me) in various creative ways, from theft of equipment to stashing trees under stumps instead of planting them properly. Another favorite was to abscond with half a dozen of my best planters to start their own company.

8. With the increasing number of employees I eventually hired full-time office staff; this brought another realm of management and training challenges for which I was thoroughly unprepared. I re-read the beer cap; there was nothing written about management and training.

9. An increase in the amount of equipment meant keeping some staff employed all winter for maintenance and preparation for the next season. The characters I hung with while skipping high school classes had never spoken of maintenance or sustainability.

10. The profit was never enough to counteract the high risk. After six years in business, one two-day contract garnered me a $40,000 loss which led to the eventual demise of the company. I still think we did most things right, but collectively we blew it. At the end of the Sundance path, it didn't matter who was right or wrong. Nor did it matter how many people contributed to its demise – I was the captain of the ship; I owned the business; it went down; I blew it.

That business died a fiery death in 1986 and propelled me into personal bankruptcy in 1987. On July 17, 1987 I received an absolute discharge from bankruptcy – a date I remember well. I partied. My sense of self worth bottomed out for a time. No longer did I feel quite so invincible. I vowed never to go back into bankruptcy, no matter what the conditions.

Not the Glorious Success I'd Envisioned

I had always hoped to be a success, to make a positive difference to those around me, and to be a valuable asset to my family. The day I declared bankruptcy, nothing could have been further from the truth.

The real heartbreaker was the day my daughter, barely into her teenage years, asked me, "Daddy, one of my friends told me you're going bankrupt. Is that true?" Although she didn't intend it to be, that was a crushing moment. I hadn't yet admitted defeat to myself, and certainly hadn't announced it to others. After all, I *was* invincible. If my daughter was hearing it, perhaps I was in denial.

When I told my mother I was about to go bankrupt, she was shaken and concerned for me. My father asked if, upon declaring bankruptcy, my name would be published in the local newspaper. The good old *Notice to Creditors* – not the kind of publicity one strives for when starting a business. Oh yeah, I was making the family proud now!

It seems that many others suspected I was going broke before I accepted it myself. Of course, there are always forecasters of doom lurking in nearby shadows. Ever the optimist, I clung to the belief that I could pull another rabbit out of the hat. At the time I didn't know whether this was because I was a dummy or because I was tenacious and believed in my ability. I had pulled off so many miracles over the life of the business I mistakenly thought I was invincible. While I helplessly groped around for the next star performance the truth crept up behind me and whacked me on the side of the head. For a while I opted to feel like a dummy. Now I believe in my ability and I'm more passionate than ever about erring on the side of optimism.

Tenacity is a tremendous strength, but we all have our limitations. It's important to know when to throw in the towel. There came a desperate day when my towel was drenched in tears and it was time to end the craziness.

> *While I helplessly groped around for the next star performance the truth crept up behind me and whacked me on the side of the head.*

> *There came a desperate day when my towel was drenched in tears and it was time to end the craziness.*

Wrath of the Banker

There are at least two chairs that ought to infuse the entrepreneur's heart with fear, the electric chair and the banker's chair. With the electric chair, someone else gets to clean up the mess; a bout in the banker's chair is guaranteed to leave you scrubbing the excrement from your bruised self-image.

I'm not down on bankers. It's just that I realized a long time ago that the banker is not necessarily an entrepreneur's best friend. A banker is not really the best friend of any new business owner, unless and until that entrepreneur already has more collateral than the amount he or she wishes to borrow.

Bankers have a tough, pitiable job some days. It was on one of these sad days I found myself planted in *the chair*. The banker and the banker's boss were sitting across from me. I owed their institution more than $100,000 on an operating loan they had graciously extended to me at the cheery beginning of the year. They were a little choked because the nice folks over at the taxation office had slapped a garnishee on my bank account. They had called me in for this meeting.

The banker's boss is someone you don't see unless there's serious bad weather on the horizon. In this case, my business was going down and I was already well acquainted with the dynamics of bad weather. I felt as though I had just touched down from the heart of the hurricane and I'm sure I looked a little wind-torn.

A bank is in business to make a profit. They profit when you pay them back the money you borrowed plus the interest. From the interest they pay their expenses; whatever is left over after the bank's expenses is their profit. They often earn huge profits, far more than your business will likely ever earn. For most of us borrowers, this means they are big and we are little. If you get in a pissing match with a bank, you had best have a change of clothes handy.

Early in my business life I was privileged to have a wonderful banker named Marty who invested some time and energy in me. He was very patient with me in my state of absolute ignorance about banking, business and anything to do with money. I liked Marty. Of course I never tested him quite to the extreme to which I had pushed the two sinister looking rascals sitting across from me that day. I was about to learn that few things in life cause a banker's orifices to contract quite like the demand-to-pay slapped on my bank account by the tax collectors. The boys were wired pretty tight that day… and I was in the chair.

The big guy said, "Dan, tell us in your words, what went wrong?" If they called their loan, I was dead.

I was shaking as I struggled to find the right words. I needed a bit of financial support to pull off the miracle of the hour. I was hopeful that they would give me more room to move, but I intuitively knew better. The look in their eyes said it all. They were there to protect their assets. The horizon was getting very dark and I could hear the surf thundering in on top of me.

I had fumbled the ball. I hadn't taken a lot of time to think about what went wrong – I was more focused on how to make things right. I hadn't really formulated a rationale. I hadn't really prepared for this fateful moment in the chair. I wonder if anyone ever really does.

They left the office that day knowing that they had done their job, I left knowing I needed to survive and pay some bills. They called their loan, I was dead.

> *If you get in a pissing match with a bank, you had best have a change of clothes handy.*

> *If they called their loan, I was dead.*

Down in a Ball Of Fire

Shortly after the roughing-up in the banker's chair I declared personal bankruptcy. I realized that the problems were multiplying at a faster rate than I could create solutions. Up to that point I pushed the business with raw energy. As I wore down, the problems seemed larger. Eventually I burnt out and gave up, and the problems swallowed me like an oyster. I ran out of innovative steam.

I learned that there is a time to get out of business. That time is likely when you get tired of the customers, internal and external. When you find yourself getting bitter, when it turns from play to hard grinding work, it's most likely time to move on. A couple of years prior to the bankruptcy I knew the business had lost its luster, but it didn't seem practical or plausible to just quit the business at the time.

When you're the boss, it's impossible to quit even though some days you may want to. There were too many times in the autumn of that business when I pleaded with the Creator for someone to fire me, cut me loose. I should have been more careful about what I asked for. The Creator sent me a malicious tax collector, a bitter banker and a throng of pissed-off employees.

Two years prior to the bankruptcy, my office manager told me that we had a $30,000 shortfall to cover employee payroll deductions. Oddly, that shortfall didn't surface as an immediate problem. It took two full years to manifest itself as a life-threatening factor. In the meantime, it was business as usual. I learned that there is almost always more than one solution to a problem and that I could pull solutions to almost any problem out of my magic hat - almost any problem.

I should have been more careful about what I asked for. The Creator sent me a malicious tax collector, a bitter banker and a throng of pissed-off employees.

Then a nice lady telephoned from Canada Revenue Agency to inform me that it was time to pay the debt. I was cooperative, but very busy. We still had a number of contracts in progress and more than 100 workers out in the field. I believe there are times when the tax collectors should take a back seat to customers and employees. Perhaps I have an attitude problem. I naively thought that the world should respect that I was frantically busy, back off and let me work. In reality, Canada Revenue Agency and the bank held the power and they both placed their own agendas ahead of mine.

The lady at Canada Revenue Agency had a job to do, a long overdue receivable to collect and a file to get off her desk. She wasn't overly concerned whether or not my work got done; she simply wanted to be placed higher in the payable shuffle. I promised her I would bring the account up to date and we worked out a plan to pay it out. The plan required that I borrow more money from the bank. I was about to be introduced to the long-term hate relationship between banks and tax collectors. I wasn't able to get the necessary money from the bank and missed the first Canada Revenue Agency payment I had committed to.

The next call from the tax lady was just a titch less congenial. Apparently, I had somehow urinated in her cornflakes. She said, "I'm going to bankrupt your company, you're going down!" I told her to go screw herself, and challenged her to give it her best shot. I never followed up to determine whether she took my advice on the first point, but she certainly lined up her ducks and went to work on my second suggestion. In fact, she turned out to be a fairly good shot. I wasn't nearly the illusive running target I had envisioned. She placed all of my receivables in collections through the Ministry of the Attorney General. If you ever want to see your business gear down to a hopeless, faceless, grinding inertia, just have the Ministry of the Attorney General collect your paychecks for you. The universe knows no slower form of life. The tax lady knew the collection game, had the clout, used government agencies to do the dirty work and collectively they ran over me like a rodent on a busy highway. In no time at all I was roadkill.

By now the bank had cheerfully called its loan, Canada Revenue Agency fervently desired its money and WCB raised its ugly head and waded into the donnybrook, calling for a payroll audit. To add to the fervor I was enjoying a parade of angry, unpaid employees and their pathological parents at my office door, zealously seeking their overdue paychecks. My tales of woe were not of great interest to these single-minded vigilantes. This was beyond unpleasant; my health and my life were now threatened. After dealing with this snaggle, there simply weren't enough hours left in the day to run the business.

By then I was on a first-name basis with most of the staff at the local Employment Standards office. I called one of them to explain my situation. I asked if they could collect the monies owed to me and to get my employees paid *ahead* of the tax collectors and the bank. The lady said, "You bring me the employee files and records and I will get your employees their money." I got the files to her and she did.

At the end of my bankruptcy story, the bank and the employees got paid in full; the tax piranhas did not. I have no regrets. As far as I'm concerned, the tax collectors are an army of predatory, legalized thugs. Intoxicated with their power, they have grown out of control and have no regard for those of us who tough it out in the world of business. They are not friends of the entrepreneur and never will be.

When you're late with payments, creditors are rarely enamored with your stories, they simply want you to pay your debt and go away. My expectation was that people might be more compassionate when someone is having difficulties. It was during my lowest times I saw some of these folks at their worst. By their actions, I'm certain some of the people I dealt with believed they were dealing directly with the devil. I went broke because I made some mistakes, not because I'm evil. In the years prior to the bankruptcy, I contributed a lot to the world around me. Since then I have continued to contribute and I have a great deal more to add as long as I'm still around and productive. I genuinely want to serve.

> *As far as I'm concerned, the tax collectors are an army of predatory, legalized thugs.*

Lessons from Hurricane Bankruptcy

Though I haven't read a single book on the topic, I know about bankruptcy from the inside out. Alas, I learn best by doing — a bona fide wild-eyed kinesthetic learner and, as it turns out, a lousy surfer some days. My heart aches for anyone who is tossed into bankruptcy. This is about the horrid reality of losing everything you have worked for, and how to surf your way through the eye of the bankruptcy hurricane.

What did I learn from bankruptcy? While it does nothing to quell your intrinsic turmoil, it does stop the external madness. Up to the point I declared bankruptcy, a mob of creditors howled and hissed at my door. Most people are not all that patient about collecting their money. They quite rightfully hope to get paid ahead of all other creditors and display little concern for others when attempting to collect. Bankruptcy stops the craziness and gives you an opportunity to have a life again.

From the bankruptcy I learned to feel compassion for those in financial trouble. I remember those who treated me like dog shit during that time; I remember those who grabbed what they could while the ship was sinking. I also vividly remember those who treated me with respect and I appreciate them for it.

I now believe bankruptcy is almost always avoidable - but only if we start listening soon enough. Unfortunately, we don't always acquire the ability to listen in time to avoid the storm.

Far too many businesses live just a couple of bad blows from bankruptcy. If your business is currently keeping the sharks at bay, my hat's off to you. As a business owner, I know what it takes for you to stay ahead of the game and you are to be commended. If you're experiencing rough financial times, I want you to know there is life after bankruptcy and that there *is* some silver lining in all those dark clouds.

I offer these lessons, gleaned from my turbulent surf through the heart of the hurricane:

1) Bankruptcy begins a long, long time before it surfaces publicly.

In my case, it was the culmination of a long and nasty trail of terror. Open any Business Management 101 book and read the *top ten boo-boos made by business owners* and I guarantee it will read like a list of my mistakes made during the first years in business. The seeds of bankruptcy actually begin taking root years before you see it coming.

Lesson: *The information is always readily available and we can choose to start listening and learning at any time.*

2) There is always more than one solution to a problem.

I learned that there are always solutions to problems, far more answers than I initially thought there were. Solutions are always there, we simply have to get to where we can see or hear them. It begins with listening. I learned what an obnoxiously persistent character I can be when put to the test. We can all use a blast of tenacity from time to time.

Lesson: *Problems always arrive with solutions; we just have to free up the headspace to be able to see those solutions.*

> Alas, I learn best by doing — a bona fide wild-eyed kinesthetic learner and, as it turns out, a lousy surfer some days.

> I learned what an obnoxiously persistent character I can be when put to the test. We can all use a blast of tenacity from time to time.

3) The system is big and we are small.

If you spark the wrath of the system, it will chew you up and spit you out on the sand. Sprawled on the sand, you will lose control of your business. The system is my label for all the players who deal with the dark side of business life, from the plethora of private businesses to the layers of government and legal agencies that live off the avails of the bankrupt. I also include other heavyweights such as tax collectors, banks and major creditors in this group. In my case, once the heavyweights were cheerfully duking-it-out for the receivables that I naively thought were owed to my business, I truly began to glimpse my insignificance. I was chewed up and spat out before I knew what had hit me.

Lesson: I am stronger and wiser than I was. I am deeply grateful for every day I do not incur the wrath of the system.

4) Bankruptcy is a lonely journey.

I learned who my real friends were. However, the abuse I took from others paled when compared to the thrashing I laid on myself. When it comes down to the crunch, there is only one person responsible and he or she is the one who signs the cheques. Some of the most empathetic people I encountered during that dark time were others who themselves had weathered rough financial waters. The most unsympathetic and abusive people were those who had always been rather comfortable and never had to grapple with financial challenges themselves.

Lesson: I learned to be more responsible and to be a better friend to myself.

5) Everybody is affected when a business goes broke.

A 360-degree ripple goes out to touch even the most arms-length stakeholder. The ripple rolls through the life of the gas station owner who slugs his guts out every day to earn his pay cheque and who trusts you by extending a $500 trade account. It caresses the employee who has heat, rent and gas bills to pay and who devoted time and sweat working for you. It ruffles family, friends and employees.

Lesson: Nobody wins when a ship goes down. Those who think they have a leg-up on those who are tumbling in the storm simply haven't learned this yet. We are all in this world together.

6) Poor financial management is different than bankruptcy.

Poor financial management is an issue that is very different from bankruptcy and as such it needs to be dealt with separately. In other words, the bankruptcy wasn't quite enough of a slap on the side of the head. I cheerfully continued to go more and more broke afterward until I finally changed the habits that led to the difficulties. Poor financial management is just one of many challenges that can lead to bankruptcy. One day after I changed the habits that led to the bankruptcy I began to see positive results.

Lesson: You don't have to go bankrupt to learn how to manage your finances.

> *The abuse I took from others paled when compared to the thrashing I laid on myself.*

7) Lenders can be obtusely unenthusiastic about loaning money to a sinking surfer.

The time to go looking for financial help is long, long before you're overwhelmed with the flood of 120-day overdue payables. No mainstream lender wants to loan money to pay overdue debt. It is critically important that you communicate with your creditors. Anyone who loans you money is a business partner who, in my view, deserves all the integrity and honesty expected of a partner in a marriage.

Lesson: If you go to lenders soon enough, you will likely increase your chances of getting the loan and reduce the likelihood of going broke.

8) Credit is a privilege.

A bankruptcy causes you to lose credibility and "credit-ability" with the financial community. If you need to use other people's money to operate your business, and you abuse that privilege by not paying bills, you will lose the privilege and reduce your ability to operate. In short, no credit equals a very limited ability to do business!

Lesson: The daily choices you make determine your future. Ask yourself whether your choices are leading you to where you wish to be.

9) The gloves come off in a bankruptcy situation.

You may be tempted to do things that are unethical or illegal. I can only suggest that you take the high road and stay on the right side of the law. Bringing on the wrath of the legal system is unlikely to make your bankruptcy hurricane more enjoyable. You have to live with yourself long after the bankruptcy has come and gone.

Lesson: You are the boss and you have control.

10) Creditors tend to get emotional about collecting their money.

We all conduct business on the faith that we will get paid for our service and when we don't get paid most of us tend to get angry and take it personally. Wherever there are unpaid bills, there is bound to be some turbulent air and stress. Bankruptcy is a very precise law that creates a path to dry land for anyone who slips through the cracks in this free enterprise system.

Lesson: Bankruptcy is the safety valve that stops the insanity and allows the individual to live his or her life out of the reach of the screeching, snapping creditors.

A business plan is your best weatherproofing against a bankruptcy. A business plan will not reduce the need to think on your feet once in business, nor will it guarantee your success. It will, however, help you identify problems and develop solutions earlier than you otherwise might; it will force you to think through problems before they actually happen.

There is life after bankruptcy. The storm eventually calms and when it does, you will be stronger, wiser and hopefully wealthier. The sun always shines after a storm. The only true failure is the one who doesn't get back up on his or her feet and try again. Like the young man on the shore of the Baha after getting thoroughly trounced by the wave, I may have been scratched and bruised but it wasn't terminal. Once again the Creator had chosen to let me live to play another day. It wasn't long before I was plotting my next business adventure.

> A business plan is your best weatherproofing against a bankruptcy.

> Like the young man on the shore of the Baha after getting thoroughly trounced by the wave, I may have been scratched and bruised but it wasn't terminal. Once again the Creator had chosen to let me live to play another day.

Catching the Next Wave

Somewhere part way through my troubled waters, an acquaintance approached me and asked if I would coach a small group of people on how to start businesses. I entered the world of training and soon found myself at the helm of Macrolink Administration Ltd.

Back then I had a huge vision for Macrolink. I was going to provide all types of training to all nature of people. Anyone with a modicum of business knowledge will immediately recognize that I hadn't yet learned the ills of attempting *to be all things to all people*. There was another difficulty with my mission to be the world's hottest training business. I was terrified of public speaking. When I started out in the training game, I would have cheerfully thrown myself onto a bed of hot spikes rather than speak to a group of people. I needed to learn public speaking skills.

When I started out in the training game, I would have cheerfully thrown myself onto a bed of hot spikes rather than speak to a group of people.

In the late 1980s I joined a Toastmasters club and proceeded to grind my way toward the Competent Toastmaster (CTM) level. Allow me to shamelessly promote the Toastmasters organization. Toastmasters International is the most effective system available for learning to deal with the jitters and acquire public speaking skills. If you or anyone you know wishes to enlist in one organization that will change the course of your life and career, I highly recommend doing a stint in your nearest Toastmasters club.

I participated diligently in Toastmasters for more than six years. During that time I embraced all of the duties in the regular weekly meetings, served at least a term in most of the club executive positions, helped to start a new Toastmasters club and competed in speech competitions at club, area, division and district levels. Along the way a miracle took place: I actually began to enjoy speaking to groups.

During that time Macrolink plugged along, losing money. In the early 1990s I took a full-time job as Entrepreneurial Training Coordinator with a not-for-profit organization. I was responsible for creating, coordinating and facilitating a ten-month training program to assist entrepreneurs to start businesses. For five years I awoke at 4:00 am to work on Macrolink duties until 8:00 am, when I switched over to my day job. At 4:30 pm I put my Macrolink hat back on and worked until bedtime.

In the early 1990s I wrote Macrolink's first business plan. I was able to access an operating loan and the business began to grow. In fact, it averaged about 35% growth per year for the following five years.

In mid-1996 I left my job to devote myself full-time to Macrolink. In August the business went from a home based office and two full-time employees to a 3,200 square foot facility and eleven full-time employees. My business life once again became a turbulent reactive adventure. Apparently I hadn't learned the ills of rapid expansion well enough. It seems I had to take one more run at it to get the lesson.

In the early 1990s I wrote Macrolink's first business plan. I was able to access an operating loan and the business began to grow.

Time for a Cool Change

In the beginning of Macrolink's life, I had a huge vision. My dream for the business was that it would become a large training company that served great numbers of people in a variety of topics. The vision was impressive.

Macrolink grew. It emerged from its fledgling years to a thriving business offering more than two hundred courses and programs in a variety of sectors and on a broad range of topics. In the meantime, the network grew to a high of 22 employees and more than 30 trainers. The original vision was materializing, but it wasn't as satisfying as my partner and I had hoped.

In 1999 my partner and I agreed that something had to shift. We both wanted to get away from the program work and into a more sensible business model. In a courageous, brash move we re-engineered the business concept, stopped competing for the government funded contracts, and began marketing our new concept throughout western Canada. Essentially, we cut our main revenue source in the belief that we might get our new product to market quickly enough to thrive. By July 2003 we could no longer sustain the financial loss. That was when we decided to stop the bleeding, lay off the remaining eight employees and call it a day. We changed the corporate profile alright; from making sales to losing $30,000 each month. By August 2003 I was once again Macrolink's sole employee, operating from a home base.

Thinking about how I felt between 1999 and 2003, I would equate it to what it must feel like to get hit by a train. For a time I felt like I was lying on the side of the tracks, numb and semi-conscious.

I want to make a difference for entrepreneurs who wish to sustain themselves doing types of work they love.

Every adventure seems to be followed by some downtime. I receive encouragement most days, either from friends and family or from customers who appreciate the service I provide. All bursts of energy are applied to completing this book, to consolidating my new business concept, and to getting my newest products to market. I am thankful for the freedom to write. It excites and motivates me to think that someday, at a time that is right for you, you will sit and read these words and know that I understand where you are at in your life and what you are up against.

A vision can morph. The Macrolink vision is shifting as I write this. I'm plotting the next leg of my journey. The vision was once a huge almost unattainable climb involving vast numbers of people and massive quantities of energy, now its waters have calmed considerably. Now I work toward a quieter, more manageable vision. The old Macrolink vision served its purpose, which was to provide me with the drive to grow and excel at certain skills. As I moved through it and past it, it stepped aside to make way for the new vision. I now want to reach entrepreneurs world wide with a few well planned products and services. I want to make a difference for entrepreneurs who wish to sustain themselves doing types of work they love.

A vision can morph. An entrepreneur can flex. I have survived the surf once again to catch the next wave.

Onward and Upward

I'm excited about my newest business concept. I have designed the products and services to meet my customer's needs and I've shaped the business to meet my needs. It is a good business designed for the betterment of the world around me.

One might think that my negative encounters would cause me to be disillusioned, but I'm thankful that my plate has cleared enough to allow me to see the next steps. Armed with the lessons of past adventures and strengthened by the experiences, I gain more confidence with each update of my business plan. As I turn my face to the wind I am optimistic about the future.

I have provided you with snapshots of the dark side of business ownership. There are a few more warnings and splashes of gloominess sprinkled throughout this book. It hasn't been easy for me to be in business, but I wouldn't change a single thing. Each lesson is a gift. Each moment is an opportunity to serve. Each challenge is a chance to learn, to innovate and to become stronger. Each day is a treasure to be savored and experienced to the fullest. This chapter presents you with the reality. If you're going to go into business, I want you to remove your rose-coloured glasses and begin your business plan development with your eyes wide open.

After everything I have been through in the past 25 years, I believe more than ever that business is my best option. Self-employment gives me the most freedom, the ability to sustain myself through work I love doing and the best opportunity to fulfill my definition of success.

I developed my business plan and I hope my experience helps you to build yours. It is a real business plan, not the fictional fabrication you will find in most business planning books. You can read it and measure for yourself whether it has value.

I'm pushing onward and upward.

Let's wish each other luck!

If you're going to go into business, I want you to remove your rose-coloured glasses and begin your business plan development with your eyes wide open.

Chapter 2

Your Personal Toolchest

Table of Contents

Dear Creative Entrepreneur

Y ou, entrepreneur, are the raw energy that fuels the economies of the world. Do you realize how powerful you are? Can you see the impact you have on the world around you? Does your vision include making a difference to your community, to your family, to your world?

Entrepreneurs have fueled economies with their energy since the beginning of time. A humble tailor taking care of business in feudal times had many of the same dynamics to attend as a home-based web-site designer of today. Whether using a barter system or the currency of the day, he or she had to acquire equipment, purchase raw materials and produce and provide products or services. They produce goods, pay bills, market, negotiate, sell, fend off rent seekers, pay taxes, sweep the floor, and take out the garbage. Somehow they manage to feed, clothe, shelter and nurture their families.

As an entrepreneur, you are a worker bee with a vision. You are motivated to serve others, to solve problems and to make a difference. You need to be productive and you love to win. You pull miracles out of nothingness in the stillness of night while others sleep. You are a conduit for the raw energy that binds all people together. You help to feed, clothe, shelter and nurture the people around you.

Your vision elevates you above the masses of workers who simply work to survive.

Sound a bit lofty? Consider this. You may work with a team or by yourself; you might work full-time, part-time or double-time. You might be a carpenter, a doctor, a house cleaner, a teacher, an artist, a mechanic or an inventor. Whatever the nature of your business, your work makes the lives of others better in some way. You take pride in your work and in doing so, you set yourself apart from the mundane. You are accountable and responsible. You continually make improvements because you are passionate about your work and you care about yourself and those you serve. Your vision elevates you above the masses of workers who simply work to survive. Your vision includes goals beyond survival, perhaps abundance, enriched lifestyle and autonomy. Whatever you do, you will make a positive difference in the world around you.

Affirmation

I am a creative entrepreneur. I am privileged to be able to serve others. I love to serve others. I am rewarded for serving others. I am in service to the world around me. I am successful in my business venture. I know why I am in business and I gain from it what I need every day.

Dream Big and Bright!

Whenever I got in trouble during my school years, it usually had something to do with dreaming. Apparently I spent too much time daydreaming, gazing out the window, cruising somewhere out there, light-years from the topics our instructors were trying to teach. I managed to get myself into enough hot water that I eventually came to view dreaming as a waste of valuable time. The culture I was born into insisted that I adopt a more mechanical, left-brained approach to life. This was all facilitated with my best interests at heart. By the time I reached adulthood, I had buried my dreams somewhere deep inside of me.

It wasn't until my mid-thirties, during a workshop, that I attempted to write a list of my dreams. While others in the group vigorously scribbled out their lengthy lists I sat dumbfounded. At the end of the exercise my mind and my page were blank. I realized that I had subdued my dreams for a very long time.

I was shocked that I had somehow drifted from black-belt daydreamer status to complete inertia. That experience, though painful at the time, was pivotal in my life. It inspired me to revive my dreams. I determined then to build my list of dreams. It was like rekindling a fire. As I fanned the flame with more and more oxygen it grew, and one by one I began to remember the tiny precious elements of my passion. Over time my list grew to more than 50 core dreams that continue to shape my life to this day.

Whenever I review my list of dreams I am amazed at how they just seem to materialize over time. There is power in the simple act of writing the dreams down. I see this power with written goals as well... and with business plans.

I encourage you to dream big, bright full-colour dreams... and write them down. After all, everything starts with a dream.

> *There is power in the simple act of writing the dreams down. I see this power with written goals as well... and with business plans.*

Tip: You don't have to be perfect to start a business, but having your personal affairs in order will help.

Opportunities Abound

An abundance of opportunities drift through our lives at an astonishing rate. Each moment brings new opportunities in vast quantities. Yet there lives within us a daunting scarcity consciousness that compels us to believe there are only a few opportunities to be generously bestowed on the chosen few, leaving most of us commoners to serve that sparkling elite. Why do some people embrace their opportunities and succeed while others park on the riverbank of life?

Most of us fill our plate to overflowing. While living in Penny in the 1970s, I used to work at seasonal jobs. While one might think I would be less active during the jobless periods, the opposite was true. In fact, I always seemed to be far busier while unemployed.

Time fills up with activity.

There is a difference between those we might label winners and the poor sots we refer to as losers. Winners tend to fill their time with meaningful, focused activities while the less fortunate appear to exert less will over their time. What does this have to do with opportunity? The key to getting where you want to be is to begin by knowing where that is, and then to invest your time and energy in the activities that take you there.

The starting point to filling your time with purposeful action is knowing what you want.

> "You are an investor poised on the brink of the most important investment of your life – putting your time, energy and money into your own business."

There are some big picture items that should be addressed before you hunker down to planning your business. If you want to succeed, to achieve your dreams, to experience fulfillment – it will be more efficient to begin with a clear idea of what these things are to you. After all, if you don't know what you're chasing, how will you know if you catch it?

Purposeful action is that which takes you toward your vision.

Is it fair to say that an opportunity is anything which might enable you to get closer to fulfilling your vision? If so, then clarifying your vision is the starting point to selecting the right opportunities for you.

You are an investor poised on the brink of the most important investment of your life – putting your time, energy and money into your own business. You have a finite amount of time and energy to invest in your business. Invest wisely and your investment will grow and bring you what you want from life. Clarifying your vision now will enable you to choose your opportunities wisely and channel your energy into actions that are right for you.

Clear Your Personal Space

So you are considering starting a business or thinking about shifting gears in your existing business. It's time to make room for the business planning process. Prepare yourself by clearing your space.

Time fills up with stuff. If we do not exercise some control over what that stuff is, we can easily waste a lot of time on things that are not important to us. A quick scan of your life will reveal areas, projects, time wasters and habits that you might consider clearing from your plate to allow time and energy to pursue your dreams. Unless I've somehow overlooked a fundamental energy source, we all have twenty-four hours in each day. If you're anything like me, you feel more positive about yourself when you are able to focus on the things most important to you; less positive when you are not able to do so.

Time fills up with stuff. If we do not exercise some control over what that stuff is, we can easily waste a lot of time on things that are not important to us.

The following tasks will help to clarify where you spend your time and identify potential areas for personal improvement.

Task List

1. Determine where you invest your time. Choose a one-week period to monitor what activities fill your time. Make a list of the activities and how much time you devoted to each. Be honest and as accurate as you can without burying yourself in detail. For example, you can record your activities in 15-minute, 30-minute or 1-hour segments.

2. Use the following worksheet to complete a personal reality check and determine the areas you might wish to improve or need to improve in order to start your business. Rate yourself 1 to 5 for each of the items in the following table (1 = definitely needs attention, 5 = excellent).

Tip: Throughout the book you will find worksheets. These worksheets can be downloaded free from our website at www.riskbuster.com. Downloadable worksheets are identified by this icon in the top right corner: 📄

Tip: For an excellent detailed work on goals, refer to Zig Ziglars video, Goals: Setting & Achieving Them. Learn more about this resource at the www.nightingale.com website.

WORKSHEET: PERSONAL REALITY CHECK										
Rate yourself 1 to 5 for each of the items below. (1 is low, 5 is high)	Where I Am Now					Where I Want To Be				
	1	2	3	4	5	1	2	3	4	5
1. Physical										
Medical Check-up										
Nutrition										
Exercise										
Weight Control										
General Health										
2. Family										
Good Role Model										
Effective Listening Habits										
Forgiving Attitude										
Supportive of Others										
Respectful										
Loving										
3. Financial										
Earnings										
Savings										
Investments										
Budget										
Insurance										
Credit Management										
4. Social										
Sense of humor										
Self-confidence										
Manners										
Caring										
5. Spiritual										
Inner peace										
Sense of purpose										
Prayer / meditation										
Study										
6. Mental										
Imagination										
Attitude										
Learning										
Reading										
Curiosity										
7. Business/Career										
Satisfaction										
Effectiveness										
Training										
Competence										
Opportunity For Growth										

Develop Your Strategic Plan and Inspiration

Strategic objectives are broad in nature and provide overall direction or intention rather than specific detail. They are also typically long term in nature. Strategic objectives deal with *what* you plan to do, while goals deal with the *how* you plan to achieve your strategic objectives.

Goals are more detailed than strategic objectives. Goals are strongest when they:

- Are written out in detail
- Are specific enough to be measurable
- Are realistically achievable
- Have deadlines

For example, if your strategic objective is *to be physically fit*, one of your goals might be *to exercise one hour, three to four times each week.*

The simple act of writing your goals down gives them a life of their own. Try it and prove it for yourself.

Example: Strategic Plan

---

1. Physical

Strategic Objective: I will maintain fitness and health by eating nutritious foods and exercising regularly.

Goals:

- Exercise for at least 1 hour, three to four times each week.
- Eat at least 2 healthy meals each day, with nutritious snacks whenever I'm hungry.
- Participate in at least 1 adventure each month that requires physical exertion.

2. Family

Strategic Objective: I demonstrate love and support for my family through an appropriate investment of time and by encouraging a healthy level of intimacy with each individual.

Goals:

- Enjoy at least 1 fun activity with my daughter every other week.
- Surprise at least 1 family member per week with a phone call.
- Communicate weekly with my parents and siblings.

3. Financial

Strategic Objective: I maintain a healthy attitude toward money by devoting my energy appropriately to earning, spending, saving, investing, growing, safeguarding and contributing.

Goals:

- Earn a minimum of $3,600 each month.
- Save a minimum of 10% of each paycheck.

Strategic objectives deal with what you plan to do, while goals deal with the how you plan to achieve your strategic objectives.

4. Social

Strategic Objective: I foster a healthy social life by spending time with those I love and appreciate.

Goals:

· Participate in a golf tournament each August.

· Arrange to visit with at least 1 friend per week.

· Invest 4 hours each month learning to cook.

5. Spiritual

Strategic Objective: I maintain a healthy spiritual life and enjoy an intimate relationship with the Creator.

Goals:

· Journal for a minimum of 30 minutes each morning.

· Take time to revere the spirituality in the people I interact with each day.

· Foster positive thoughts and feelings toward others.

6. Intellectual

Strategic Objective: I regularly exercise and grow my intellectual capacity through a healthy balance of reading, movies, audiotapes, workshops and discussion with intelligent people.

Goals:

· Read 1 new book each month.

· Watch a minimum of 1 stimulating movie each month.

· Engage in a dinner or lunch date with at least 1 new person every two weeks.

7. Career

Strategic Objective: My career is a life-long learning adventure. Each job or task I complete prepares me for the next steps, whether or not I can see what those next steps are. I do work I enjoy and I do my very best at each task or project placed in front of me.

Goals:

· Write for a minimum of 2 hours each day.

· Publish my book by my next birthday.

· Complete the business planning CD and prepare it for distribution by April.

8. Adventure

Strategic Objective: I foster an interesting and healthy lifestyle by engaging in thrilling adventures. Each adventure is a project I do purely for enjoyment, learning and fun.

Goals:

· Go kayaking every couple of weeks while weather permits.

· Climb a mountain before the end of September.

· Go on a holiday to a hot sandy beach in February.

Task List

1. Develop your *personal strategic plan.* Reflect on the eight categories and then write out at least one strategic objective and a couple of goals for each. This can be done in your scrapbook, on your computer or using the Personal Strategic Plan Worksheet that follows this page. You can have more than one strategic objective in any category. Succinct is better; this exercise is intended to help you focus, not mire you in detail.

   1. Physical
   2. Family
   3. Financial
   4. Social
   5. Spiritual
   6. Intellectual
   7. Career
   8. Adventure

2. Create your *personal inspiration lists.* In your scrapbook or on your computer, create lists under the titles below. Be sure to leave some space in each category so you can come back and enter items you think of later. Any or all of these lists will provide you with a powerful source of motivation. This can be done in your scrapbook, on your computer or using the Personal Inspiration Worksheet that follows this page. Place the lists somewhere convenient so you can review or add to them as you feel the need to.

   - Strengths
   - Successes
   - Areas of Excellence
   - Contributions I Wish To Make
   - Dreams
   - Purpose
   - Definition of Success

Tip: This activity doesn't need to be done all at once. More likely you will come back to it again and again to update your lists. Over time, this document will become a powerful source of inspiration to you.

WORKSHEET: PERSONAL STRATEGIC PLAN
Physical Strategic Objective *Goals:*
Family Strategic Objective *Goals:*
Financial Strategic Objective *Goals:*
Social Strategic Objective *Goals:*
Spiritual Strategic Objective *Goals:*
Intellectual Strategic Objective *Goals:*
Business/Career Strategic Objective *Goals:*
Adventure Strategic Objective *Goals:*

WORKSHEET: PERSONAL INSPIRATION
Strengths
Successes
Areas of Excellence
Contributions I Wish To Make

Dreams

Purpose

Definition of Success

Get Your Personal Finances in Order

There are a number of things you can do to tidy up a messy personal financial situation. Personal financial management habits cascade into an owner's business like a thundering waterfall. If you are one who has a messy personal financial situation, you may be frustrated that a banker places so much emphasis on your credit record. It's really not that complicated.

The habits we employ in one situation often spill over into other areas of our lives. Once we take the leap into business, two areas of our lives that are very closely woven together are our personal and business finances. For better or worse, the habits we exercise in our personal financials extend into the business financials. It is safe to extrapolate from a war torn personal financial panacea that one will create a similar landscape once in business. You can take a look at your personal net worth and figure it out for yourself. You don't need a banker or a priest to tell you how you will manage your business finances. If you need to change how you manage your financial life – just do it.

> *Personal financial management habits cascade into an owner's business like a thundering waterfall.*

For anyone experiencing financial challenges, I highly recommend reading *The Richest Man in Babylon* by George S. Clason. It is a quick, easy read that spells out a simple, effective recipe for financial success. This tiny book can cause a positive shift in your financial life. Here are the seven fundamental rules for acquisition of money, adapted from Clason's book.

1. Save a portion of your earnings.
2. Control your expenses.
3. Invest your savings to grow.
4. Protect your assets from loss.
5. Make your residence a profitable investment.
6. Ensure a future income.
7. Increase your earning capacity.

The earlier you get started, the sooner you will see the results of your actions.

Example: Personal Financial Management Strategy

STRATEGY	GOALS
Save a portion of my earnings.	Save 10% of the gross amount of each paycheck.
Control my expenses.	Eliminate junk food from my diet.
	Ride bike to work for summer months instead of driving.
Grow my savings.	Keep $2,500 in my savings account for emergencies.
	Each time my savings account reaches $5,000 I will reinvest $2,500 into tax shelters or real estate.
Protect my assets.	Insure any assets I can't afford to replace.
Make my residence a profitable investment.	Purchase a house in a suitable location, with room for my home office and 250 square feet of storage.
Ensure a future income.	Pay the maximum allowable pension premiums.
Increase my earning capacity.	Invest in my business to increase book and CD sales.
	Complete marketing courses at college or university.

Tip: Throughout this book I will refer to a number of books on a variety of topics. For further detail on Clason's and many other excellent resources, please refer to the Suggested Reading section on page 379.

Task List

1. Scan your personal financial situation and list any goals you wish to set. If appropriate, use the *Personal Financial Management Strategy Worksheet* below.

2. Use the *Owner's Drawings Worksheet* on the following page to list all of your personal expenses and income.

3. Take the necessary steps to get your personal finances in order.

WORKSHEET: PERSONAL FINANCIAL MANAGEMENT STRATEGY	
STRATEGY	GOALS
Save a portion of my earnings.	
Control my expenses.	
Grow my savings.	
Protect my assets.	
Make my residence a profitable investment.	
Ensure a future income.	
Increase my earning capacity.	

WORKSHEET: OWNER'S DRAWINGS

Personal Expenses Paid Monthly	Totals
Rent or Mortgage Payment	
Food	
Telephone	
Fax	
Internet	
Heat, Air Conditioning	
Electricity	
Clothing	
Entertainment	
Medical Expenses	
Cable	
Satellite TV	
Newspaper, Other Subscriptions	
Child Support, Expenses	
Automobile Expenses (payments)	
Automobile Expenses (repairs, gas and oil)	
Hobbies, Memberships	
Gifts, Charity, Religious Contributions	
Education	
Investments	
Lottery, Gambling, Tobacco, Alcohol	
Loan Payments	
Credit Card(s)	
Subtotal	

Expenses Paid Once a Year	Month Due	Yearly	Monthly
House Insurance			
Vehicle Insurance			
Life Insurance			
Property, Water/Sewer Taxes			
Personal Income Taxes			
Holidays			
Other			
Subtotal			

Total Expenses (monthly)	
Minus: Income you will get from sources other than your business	
Plus: Desired discretionary cash (extra spending money)	
Desired earnings from business	
Variance between desired earnings and minimum requirement	
Minimum Monthly Owner Drawings Required	

Total Expenses - Income from Other Sources + Desired Discretionary Cash =
Minimum Monthly Owner's Drawings Required

Embrace Uncertainty

How comfortable are you with uncertainty? Some people tend to get frustrated by the uncertainty in the business planning process, while others are naturally more comfortable with it. If you like to have everything organized and clear, I suggest you sit down right now and have a little chat with yourself. If you feel the need to have all of the answers in advance you may never go into business because we never have all of the answers in advance. If you are starting a business and think you already have all of the answers, you're likely in more trouble than a business plan can hope to clear up.

Knowledge is power. In business and in life, it's what you don't know that creates the most risk. Most of us can draw examples from our own lives where something unknown snuck up from behind and whacked us on the head.

Whether you think you have all of the answers or not, I suggest you warm up to the idea that there is different and critical information out there and open your mind to receiving that information. It may save your house or whatever other investment you are putting on the line. It can be unsettling to put forth your assumptions only to discover you were totally wrong.

Here are some tips on dealing with uncertainty:

- Accept that you do not know everything about your business.
- Know that you will become the expert on your business.
- Ask questions and listen to the answers.
- Be open to new ideas and information.
- Be flexible and adaptable.
- Incorporate new information into your business concept, as you deem appropriate.

Whether you think you have all of the answers or not, I suggest you warm up to the idea that there is different and critical information out there and open your mind to receiving that information.

Affirmation

I am not alone. I work and play in a world rich with interesting, knowledgeable people. I keep my mind open for new information. I listen to the words and thoughts of those around me and continually assess whether the input is valuable or not. When I hear information I do not understand, I ask for clarification and keep asking until I am satisfied that I understand the topic. When I learn new information that I consider to be important to my life or my situation, I write it down in a convenient place where I can easily review it. I review the new information until I internalize it. I am vigilant for nuggets of information that will help others, friends, family, customers. When I find important information for others, I share it with them. I thank the Creator often for bringing me the information I need, when I need it.

Befriend Change

Most things change. As an entrepreneur, change will affect you in many ways. Change occurs while you develop your business plan. Even a simple statistic, like the population of my country, changes every minute. The longer you take to develop your business plan the more changes you will likely have to make to your plan. Everything changes the minute you move from planning into operating your business. Your business will change daily, weekly, quarterly and annually.

You will work hard to develop positive relationships with customers, only to discover your key contacts get new jobs, transfer, quit, get fired or die. Then you begin all over again building your business relationship with a new entity. You will strive to build credibility with suppliers, only to have them disappear from your radar – mergers, acquisitions, bankruptcies, phasing out of old products, new management and new policies. You might build a segment or even all of your business on a platform of government policy or political direction, only to have it change or a new politician voted into power. It changes. You may work your tail off to build a product or service, only to have a competitor scoop you by innovating, lobbying, bribing or simply adapting yours to build a better one. Change tends to be disruptive; more so for those who prefer stability or for those who are less comfortable with uncertainty.

As a customer, have you ever dealt with someone who places your satisfaction second to their own need to avoid change? I have, and I don't like it. As a customer this is one feeling that will cause me to shop elsewhere, to go out of my way to spend my hard-earned money at a different business. Being open to change strengthens our ability to serve customers. When we are open to change we are better listeners.

The only thing that does not change is change itself. If you cannot embrace change, don't go into business.

When your energy is high, change is easier to manage. When your energy is dwindling, change can really bring you down. In fact, change can be an endless energy drain. In your business, it is critical to understand those things that should not change and leave them alone. Change for the sake of change is a disease.

Embrace change in the same way you would greet waves when playing in the surf. Use the power of change to your advantage, surf while your energy is high – when fatigue overtakes you, get out of the surf and rest a while.

Pace Yourself

Your energy ebbs and flows like the tide. Energy is different at the age of 50 than at the age of 20. When energy is low, small problems appear bigger than they really are. When energy is up, large problems become smaller. Tackle big projects when your energy is up – rest or take on smaller, achievable projects when your energy is down. Match your workdays and hours to the amount of energy available. Nurture yourself. Look after yourself, physically, mentally, emotionally and spiritually.

Have Faith

I recall a meeting with several other business owners. In one of our conversations we discussed how long each of us had been in business and whether or not we would do it over again. The general consensus was that if we had known how much work there was to starting and building our businesses, we might have chosen to do something else. Though we were all surprised at the amount of time and money we had invested, I seriously doubt that any of us would want things differently.

I enjoy the challenge of being in business, the thrill of doing work I enjoy, the privilege of playing with people of my choosing and the opportunity to serve customers. I have loved it from the first moment I scrambled onto the entrepreneurial path. When I started my first business I had faith that the rewards would outweigh the risks in the long run. After more than 25 years in business I know this to be true and it's easier now for me to move forward with business activities because of this knowledge. For someone going into business for the first time it takes a lot of courage... and it takes a lot of faith.

Recently I listened to a business owner speak about how much faith it takes to launch a new business. We take on a huge load with no guarantee of return. In fact, the only sure thing is that you place yourself in the line of fire when you go into business. Each new day brings more exhilarating opportunities to lose everything you own. Am I cheering you up yet? Have faith.

Why would someone subject themselves to the risk of being in business? Why do I do it? Well, it doesn't take much of a crumb in the way of a reward to rekindle my entrepreneurial fire. All it takes is a positive comment from a satisfied client, a new lead in Manitoba, a sale in Thailand, a call from a friend with money to spend on a new project. Treats like these fuel my engines.

As a volunteer for the local lending agency, I review many business plans prepared and submitted by entrepreneurs wanting to borrow money. I sometimes marvel at how little the fledglings know as they venture into their business. Some will get bloody noses and lose their homes, others will blossom. In order to take the leap they all need to have that initial measure of faith.

When I think about my first business venture, I'm amazed that it took as long as six years to go down in a blazing ball of fire. When I first launched, I knew nothing about business. A real kinesthetic learner, I didn't take a course or write a business plan. I just did it. I had faith.

My first business plan might have looked something like this:

1. Give and you will receive.
2. Give more and you will receive more.
3. Ask and listen and the answers will appear.
4. Those who work hard will be rewarded.
5. Be courteous – say please and thank you.
6. Believe in people and they will continually amaze you.
7. Serve customers well and they will pay you, tell their friends and return for more.

Ah, there you have it – Boudreau's 1980 business plan, all seven lines. The seven points above are as valid today as they were then and they are still principles I live by, but you will find that my current business plan has a tad more detail.

Faith – don't leave your day job without it.

I enjoy the challenge of being in business, the thrill of doing work I enjoy, the privilege of playing with people of my choosing and the opportunity to serve customers. I have loved it from the first moment I scrambled onto the entrepreneurial path.

Chapter 3

So You Want To Start a Business!

Table of Contents

Why a Business Instead of a Job?

Many people start planning their business, only to discover that they are better suited to work for someone else. It's important to keep the rewards front and center. There are many great reasons to start your own business:

- To be your own boss
- To work at something you enjoy
- To work at something you are good at
- To serve customers
- To contribute a positive service to your community
- To make money
- To enjoy a lifestyle
- To have more freedom
- To create a job for yourself
- To support your family
- To get away from a deadbeat boss
- To take advantage of an opportunity
- To create retirement income for yourself

What's In It for You?

Do you have other reasons for starting your business? List them here.

WORKSHEET: WHAT'S IN IT FOR YOU
•
•
•
•
•
•
•
•
•

Myths

1. **A Business Is a Get-Rich-Quick Scheme.** It is more accurate to say that most overnight successes take at least 25 years of hard labor. An entrepreneur is a twisted individual who will work 15-hour days at minimum wage to avoid taking a real job at $20 per hour.

2. **Bigger is Better.** Be careful what you ask for. The sweet little enterprise you grow might become a treadmill trap just like the drudgery you attempted to shed by leaving your old job. Millions of small and micro businesses survive and thrive and meet all the owner's needs without growing into large companies.

3. **You Need a Lot of Money to Start a Business.** While it's true that some types of business have a high start-up price tag, many do not. As a tradesperson who owns all the necessary tools to work for someone else, you probably already have most of what you need to start your own business. Many single operator service businesses require minimal investment to get started.

4. **Owning Your Business Is Easier Than Working for Someone Else.** If you view business owners as being on easy street, there is probably more to the picture than meets the eye. Most business owners work far longer hours and endure far more stress than many of those who work for others.

5. **"Kicking Your Boss's Butt" is a Valid Reason to Start a Business.** First of all, that boss is in business because customers pay for his or her products or services. Secondly, kicking his or her butt will never be enough of a reward to warrant the risk and stress of operating a business. You had best dig a bit deeper and get into a business you are passionate about.

6. **Someone Needs to Lose In Order for You to Win.** Occasionally, I encounter folks who believe they win at the expense of others. This is 180 degrees off the real reason to get into business: to serve. In my opinion, the only real win is when all stakeholders win; owners, investors, employees and customers.

7. **Most People Are Not Suited To Own and Operate Their Own Business.** I don't buy this. I believe most people ARE suited to own and operate their own business. It's just that many folks never get to the point where they realize they can do it and take the leap of faith!

8. **You Need to Get Into a Business You Know.** Most people will change careers several times during their work life. It's never easy to shift from one career to another, but folks are doing it all the time. Getting into a different type of business has all the challenge and thrill of changing careers, and even more risk. As a business start-up it will be difficult to get others (bankers, lending agencies) to buy into your entrepreneurial career shift. If you're leaping into unfamiliar waters you had best be prepared to finance your own adventure.

An entrepreneur is a twisted individual who will work 15-hour days at minimum wage to avoid taking a real job at $20 per hour.

9. **Existing Revenue Sources Abruptly Stop and You Suddenly Begin Depending On Your Business.** I equate business start-up to weaving threads together to form a fabric. Those successful owners earning six-digit incomes most likely didn't start out drawing a huge salary from the business. More likely, they held a part time job or depended on a trusted spouse to pay some or all of the bills while the business built its base. While it's true there is a magic day called opening day, you will be weaving the threads of your business fabric long before and long after opening day.

10. **You Don't Need a Business Plan**. From the moment you step into business, you will be surrounded with 360 degrees of liability. In my world, there are simply too many details to leave entirely to chance. Even if you do decide to wing it without writing a formal business plan, you will fly further faster by going through the planning process.

Before You Launch

So you want to start a business... You have a spectacular business idea and are about to launch into the business planning process.

Not knowing about a problem does not entitle us to any protection from the effects of that problem. It's often those things "we don't know we don't know" that can be most threatening to the health of our business. Our best strategy to deal with the traps is to get to know them.

Negative credit history follows and affects the entrepreneur. Most of us encounter financial challenges at some point in our lives. Personal financial management is a full-time job and it is easy to drift into financial trouble. I have come to accept that many perfectly healthy, hard working people have a "financial black eye" somewhere in their credit history. Those shiners can make it difficult to outstare the banker and swing into a bank loan. What does this mean to you? It means you must correct the original problem. Your business plan might show that you need to borrow $50,000, but if your credit history motivates your banker to quaff a couple of Rolaids you are headed for certain disappointment and a couple of Rolaids for yourself. You are better off to recognize and deal with any credit challenges before any visits to bankers. While sporting a poor credit rating doesn't necessarily mean you can't start your business, it may require you to take a different path to start-up. Don't give up on your dream business because of financial complications. Instead, consider different options such as reducing the size of your desired loan, reducing the size of your start-up business or seeking money from some source other than a bank.

A murky credit history is just one of many challenges illustrating the importance of doing a reality check early in the business development process.

Rate yourself from 1 to 5 for each of the following statements. Give yourself a rating of 5 if the statement is all or mostly true and 1 if it's all or mostly false. The lower your number for any of the points, the more work you might need to do to prepare yourself for business.

> It's often those things "we don't know we don't know" that can be most threatening to the health of our business.

WORKSHEET: BUSINESS READINESS										
Rate yourself 1 to 5 for each of the items below. (1 is low, 5 is high)	Where I Am Now					Where I Need To Be				
	1	2	3	4	5	1	2	3	4	5
1. I have enough money of my own to invest in my business										
2. I have access to money from others (family, friends)										
3. My credit rating is excellent										
4. I have assets or equipment to invest in the business										
5. I have enough time to work on my business										
6. I have enough energy to work on my business										
7. I know how to run a business										
8. I know my business										
9. I have experience at running a business										
10. I understand the industry that my business is part of										
11. I have the necessary certification and accreditation										
12. I have the necessary credentials for my business										
13. I have strong trade skills (negotiating, selling, sourcing)										
14. I have a strong network of contacts in my industry										
15. I am persistent										
16. I use technology (computer, internet, email)										
17. I have an adequate tolerance for risk										
18. I feel I can control the risk for my business										
19. I am confident about starting my business										

This list of items can be daunting. I urge you to use it in a positive way and to view each "lower rating" as an opportunity to improve. Invariably, when I use this activity in a business planning session, there are one or two people who get stumped on something in this list, stopped in their tracks. That is not the desired outcome.

The reality check is designed to alert you to some of the common factors that stop many aspiring business owners from getting their business off the ground. Ultimately, you are the best judge of how ready you are to start your business.

Here is one way to get some mileage out of this activity; pick the three areas you wish to improve and set goals to improve each area. Write the goals into your journal or scrapbook. For example, if you rated yourself a 1 for question number 15, you might set a goal that goes something like this: "Purchase a used computer and printer by June."

In medicine, it is said that "identifying the problem is 50% of the cure." In business, being clear about your weaknesses is critical to survival. If you choose to embrace each insight as an opportunity to learn and grow, you're well on your way to starting that dream business and making it successful. The choices are yours to make.

Wrestling with Risk

The moment you step into business, you surround yourself with 360 degrees of liability. If you arrive at the other end of this chapter still motivated to start your business you may have what it takes to succeed.

This chapter is not intended to discourage you. Instead I hope you will fully realize the risks you are facing and embrace them knowingly, rather than getting bludgeoned on the rocks like a caught fish.

It has become more and more difficult to start and operate a micro-business over the past twenty years. This is definitely true in Canada and I know it is also true in many other parts of the world. I encourage you to open your eyes to the complexity and rigors of doing business and to consider my words very carefully before putting your investment on the line.

We live in a litigious society, one in which many folks will deplete your resources for their own personal gain. A growing number of individuals and groups have increasing amounts of time to seek out ways and means of extracting your energy from you. I call these leeches *rent seekers*. I'm talking about the real enemies; thieves of your time, money and energy.

You will invest time, money and energy to get your business up and running. Whatever you invest is placed at risk. The threats I speak of are:

1. Predatory government agencies cloaked as friends of the great unwashed;
2. Individuals desperately plotting to make their own lives easier;
3. Hostile competitors bent on eliminating you to enhance their own survival;
4. Rent seekers shoring up their residual income; and
5. Plain old fashioned acts of God.

1. Predatory Government Agencies Cloaked as Friends of the Great Unwashed

Small business is the target of a thick incestuous web of government agencies, all vying to extract rent from the owner under the guise of offering to protect the poor helpless consumer from the evil business owner.

They all begin with a motherhood issue, such as safety, protection from loss, protection of human rights, protection from employer abuses like harassment, low pay, etc. Like gangsters, they offer the illusion of protection, except they are also backed by all the power of government legislation, laws, regulations and a police force. You won't be in business five minutes before they creep around the corner and into view. After a couple of cruises around the block they begin extracting their pound of flesh. What the small businessperson really needs is protection from the parasites themselves.

These flesh eaters tend to be funded by your tax dollars. They are narrowly differentiated from gangsters by the erroneous notion that their government sanction somehow makes them right and just. Many are hatched through legislation and given the power to begin inventing their own policies and regulations. They are provided with authority to regulate, levy fines, and enforce.

They hire seasoned bureaucrats as managers, the employees tend to be unionized and carry benefits packages that you are unlikely to enjoy. Their workplace reality is starkly alien to yours as a small, single operator, start-up business. They are not remotely concerned with your needs as a small business owner or with the survival of your business.

The job of the managing bureaucrat at the helm is to ensure the health and growth of their prized domain, their fiefdom. They grow, create more rules and regulations, hire more people, and sit on more boards and committees. They infiltrate brother and sister organizations and market their services in all the right places. They have the appearance of being productive members of our economy and in some cases they employ thousands of people. They are all parasites paid for by the tax dollars that are extracted from you by one of the largest and most ruthless brothers, the tax collection agency.

I am not criticizing the many good people who manage and work in the parasite organizations. They are simply doing their jobs. The more effective they are at fulfilling their job descriptions, the more powerful their organization, and the better they are at surviving and thriving – which is really the goal of any great business. The problem is not usually the people who work at these agencies, it's the fact that any large organization tends to grow its own culture and focus inward. The larger an agency or organization becomes, the more distant is its day-to-day reality from the fledgling business start-up. Organizations don't have a conscience or a soul – they can roll over top of you without really even knowing you're there.

Organizations don't have a conscience or a soul – they can roll over top of you without really even knowing you're there.

If you or I were hired to manage a parasite agency and charged with the responsibility to fulfill its mandate, we would likely conduct ourselves as follows. We would:

1. Learn the mandate and scope of the agency.
2. Research the market and learn how the customer's minds work.
3. Set about to create and publicize successes.
4. Hire the best people and build the strongest team possible.
5. Build clientele, create satisfied customers – return customers if possible.
6. Fortify our position by expanding laws, regulations, mandate, scope and profile.
7. Discredit those who complain about the organizations power and actions.
8. Label as scumbags those who don't play by the rules.
9. Grow the organization.

If this sounds like the core of a great business plan, it is. The good people that work in these organizations are simply doing their jobs.

As an example, consider the Workers' Compensation Board. Who in their right mind would argue that worker safety is not important? Of course it is. Worker safety is a huge motherhood issue. Now empowered to extract monies from employers, WCB has taken on a life of its own over the past few years. The organization is now completely out of control and running over businesses like a steamroller. They have distanced themselves from the government enough to protect the politicians that initiated them in the first place and they're growing.

Here is a snapshot of some of the luxuriant network of the agencies you will face, along with their illustrious motherhood issues:

FRIENDS OF THE GREAT UNWASHED	
ORGANIZATION EXTRACTING RENT	MOTHERHOOD ISSUE
Gangsters	Protect us from the other bad guys
Workers' Compensation Board	Protect workers from hazards, bad employers
Employment Standards	Protect workers from bad employers
Canada Revenue Agency	Protect us from our own greed
Human Rights Commission	Protect us from each other
Legal System	Protect us from wrongdoing
Firearms Control	Protect us from protecting ourselves
Freedom of Information and Privacy	Protect us from knowing too much or too little
Psych Ward	Protect us from ourselves

The secret to dealing with any of these agencies or fiefdoms is to get to know them and their rules. Understand that the moment you first click on that website or open that information package, you are beginning the process of a long-term extraction of your time, money and energy. Learn where you need to register and where you don't. Know which rules apply to you and meet any of the required deadlines. Don't draw their attention to yourself or your business unnecessarily. They have more time and money than you will ever have for protracted entanglements and they most often seem to recruit and attract people who enjoy a good fight.

The secret to dealing with any of these agencies or fiefdoms is to get to know them and their rules. Don't draw their attention to yourself or your business unnecessarily. They have more time and money than you will ever have for protracted entanglements and they most often seem to recruit and attract people who enjoy a good fight.

2. Individuals Desperately Plotting To Make Their Own Lives Easier

Thankfully, most people are well intentioned and good at heart. I'll say this as politely as I can: in business you are sure to encounter a few conniving, ruthless, selfish, unscrupulous, cunning sons of bitches. These delightful specimens can take on a variety of personas.

Tommy Time Waster

Tommy Time Waster telephones whenever it suits him, whenever he has a need for which you might have the answer. He will suck up your time, in spite of any hints or suggestions that you might be busy. He never calls to offer you anything; he's not really that sophisticated. He calls to ask endless detailed questions about your product or service. No amount of information is enough. Just when you think you are closing a deal or about to do business with Tommy, he finds a cheaper vendor, or a blood relative or something, but always someone else walks away with the money for your endless efforts. Another quality peculiar to Tommy is that he is mysteriously absent or busy whenever you call him.

How do you deal with Tommy? Flag him in your database as a time waster. Treat him politely. Quote him very high prices and do it verbally rather than agonizing over lengthy written proposals or quotes, and don't lose any sleep over him. Your time is better spent serving real paying customers.

Litigious Lucy

Litigious Lucy makes one trip to your facility, slips on a patch of water that nobody else seems to be able to see, somewhere almost in sight of one of your staff. She visibly and audibly hobbles out of your facility and a short while later you are blindsided by a huge lawsuit. In the words of my lawyer, you cannot stop anyone from taking a run at you in court.

Lucy is a study. It's worth investing a little time in identifying at least some of the ways she may come at you. Lucy could be a customer, an acquaintance or a friend of a friend. You might actually employ her unknowingly. At first she appears to be as sweet as honey, but once inside your sphere the true colors spring forth and you soon realize a poison has penetrated your firm. One thing is for certain; Lucy doesn't give a rat's ass about you, your business or your well being. She's out for herself and only herself. If there is a way to pry money out of your pocket, Lucy will figure it out and stick it to you, staring you in the eye and grinning all the way to the bank.

Lucy has a number of favored tricks up her sleeve. It could be the good old tendonitis claim with the Workers' Compensation Board or a lawsuit for damages caused by your product or service. It could be the Human Rights charge du jour, including anything from harassment to racial or gender prejudice.

If there is a way to pry money out of your pocket, Lucy will figure it out and stick it to you, staring you in the eye and grinning all the way to the bank.

How do you deal with Lucy? For starters, don't commit the indiscretions mentioned above and be vigilant for anything that even remotely smells like them. Without becoming a paranoid schlock, take notes, keep accurate records and communicate all important items in writing, save copies of everything including all of your email messages. When you deal with situations that might put you at risk, be sure to include one or more credible witnesses.

Peter Proposal Eater

Peter calls you and befriends you. He then requests a proposal for a program that sounds almost too good to be true. You write the proposal on your own time, thinking you might land a lucrative contract. You are back to Peter several times to collaborate on the proposal. Peter positively affirms your idea, applauds your solutions, and encourages you all the way to completion of your proposal. You proudly deliver the bound proposal in triplicate to Peter's office and head back to work to wait for word on his acceptance... which never comes.

By the time you get back to dear Peter, he has a sad story for you. Dang, the contract went to a local organization and your "travel and accommodation" costs just weren't acceptable to the board or the boss or whoever. The reasons don't much matter at that point – you have already loved, labored and lost.

Beware. Peter doesn't love you in the morning. Peter just scooped your proposal for one of his buddies and there isn't much you can do about it... unless you want to spend a lot of money in court fighting a battle that you really can't win.

How do you recognize and manage Peter? Unfortunately this type of person is initially hard to tell from a real customer; at least until after he has diddled you out of your time and energy a couple of times. Stay alert and don't allow too many unsuccessful proposals with any given agency before calling and asking a few probing questions. There is one indication that you are dealing with a Peter. He will usually ask for more and more detail, to the point of driving you to distraction. Another protection against this type of theft is to interact with others in your industry; you are unlikely to be the first sucker Peter has burned.

It's important to trust your customers and to treat them with respect. Don't allow yourself to become jaded or mistrustful of your customers; you will simply chase them away. If you impose restrictive rules on them they simply move on to another service. It is probably most important to meter out your energy in smaller dosages when it comes to writing proposals for free.

> *The reasons don't much matter at that point – you have already loved, labored and lost.*

Agenda Annie

Sometimes folks have an agenda that we can't begin to imagine or understand. This is market savvy and I'm not convinced it's something that can be taught. Some people are just ahead of the game when it comes to reading the waters and understanding what others are up to. I'm sort of serendipitous about this and tend to get shafted occasionally for my approach. I have others in my network who are more discerning, more vigilant. I am thankful for their presence and their acute awareness. They save me from the occasional heartbreak.

What does Agenda Annie look like? She is always watching out for herself and doesn't mind gaining at the expense of others. She's cunning, cavalier, calculating and a cutthroat.

How do you deal with Annie? Be yourself, be fundamentally fair and don't compromise your values. Annie will watch for anything that smells remotely of weakness. When you are most vulnerable, she will move in and pick you off like a bug on a barn wall. She will cunningly contrive whatever story works best and make you look bad. She will tell all of her friends and bad mouth you until she moves on to her next victim.

Bait 'n Switch Billy

This handsome specimen waves a big flag in front of you to get your attention. Billy's trick is to ask for a quote or proposal for a sizeable project, which motivates you to pull all of your tricks out of the hat to provide them with your best prices based on economy of scale. Once he has your rock bottom prices, he then scales the project down and asks you to rewrite your proposal to provide a smaller amount of product or service at the same low prices. This process can lead to several proposal re-writes and waste a lot of your time. By the time you get to the second or third revision, you should be aware that Billy is either telling you to go away or using the bait 'n switch to get your prices down. At a minimum, he is wasting valuable time.

Once he has your rock bottom prices, he then scales the project down and asks you to rewrite your proposal to provide a smaller amount of product or service at the same low prices.

How do you deal with Billy? If you find you're subjected to the bait 'n switch technique:

- Assess whether or not you seriously need the work.
- Know your bottom line, the minimum price you can work for.
- Keep your prices high enough to enable you to provide excellent customer service.
- Limit the amount of time you put into rewriting your proposals.

That is usually the last you will see of Bait 'n Switch Billy.

3. Hostile Competitors Bent on Eliminating You to Enhance Their Own Survival

One of the most concerning strategies is the use of other agencies to attack a business. In 1999, we got a call from an audit tag team authorized by the provincial government, announcing that they would arrive within a couple of days to perform an audit on one of our programs. I arranged to meet them, thinking that they might be on-site for a few hours and go away happy. You could have heard a ferret fart when, at the end of two hours of what appeared to be a set-up phase, one of the auditors announced that the audit would take somewhere in the order of six weeks... if all went well. All went well, and the audit took six weeks.

The audit was initiated by a nameless person who apparently alleged that we were mismanaging the program. It was all rather misty and apparently untraceable. Even though the complaint proved unfounded, the audit process cost us at least $5,000, six weeks of downtime for two key staff, lost energy, and the time spent not serving clients.

The sad truth is that you cannot prohibit anyone from malicious, unfounded attacks or from using the power of regulatory agencies to erode your effectiveness in the marketplace. Here are some preventative suggestions:

- Avoid drawing negative energy by being on your best behavior always.
- Don't allow yourself to be drawn into unnecessary squabbles.
- Choose your battles carefully – fight when you have to.
- Focus on serving your customers.

The sad truth is that you cannot prohibit anyone from malicious, unfounded attacks or from using the power of regulatory agencies to erode your effectiveness in the marketplace.

4. Rent-Seekers Shoring Up Their Residual Income

Your local tax collectors are the primary example of this group. However, it doesn't stop there. There are rent seekers on all fronts and you are well advised to get to know them well enough to recognize and avoid them. My definition of rent seeker is anyone or any organization that strives to set itself up as a recipient of a monthly payment from your bank account. The simplest and most visibly beneficial form of this is your landlord, who collects rent for allowing you to reside in his or her quarters. You pay rent for the privilege of having a place for you or your business to live.

Beyond the landlord relationship, it quickly gets more complicated. Here are a few rent seekers to watch for: insurance agents; all nature of tax authorities; Workers' Compensation Board fees; equipment lease payments; water dispenser lease agreements; telephone accounts; internet accounts; employee benefits packages; bank fees. The list is endless.

Here are some things you can do to keep the rent seekers to a minimum:

- Don't engage or commit to a payment unless there is a clear benefit to you.
- Be frugal, bargain intelligently, don't pay more than you need to.
- Review your payables monthly to ensure you are getting value for your money.

At the end of the day, rent seekers don't care how much money is left in your bank account – that is your responsibility. It is said that "a fool is soon parted with his money." Don't be a fool.

5. Plain Old Fashioned Acts Of God

If you live in hurricane country, plan for hurricanes. If you live in a high-risk fire zone, plan for fires. If you play on the freeway, plan to dodge traffic. If you get into a high-risk business of any kind, know you will have to contend with that risk sooner or later no matter what it is.

How to Embrace Risk and Sleep at Nights

Many first-time business owners tend to believe that the myriad of threats might be integrated, coordinated and fair – I'm sorry to say they are none of these. They are independent from each other. You can be in angelic compliance with all the government agencies and still be cheerfully sued by a disgruntled employee. And here is the juiciest part of all: you can get nailed by several of them simultaneously. Am I cheering you up yet? Are you still thinking about going into business?

Here are some strategies to help you embrace risk:

1. Know the rules for each of the agencies that impact your business.
2. Follow the rules to the best of your ability. Pay the remittances on time. Don't draw attention to yourself by paying late or having irregularities, certainly not by doing anything illegal.
3. Protect your assets. Use insurance where it makes sense to do so.
4. Hire a competent bookkeeper and accountant. Clarify what they need to do to keep you in the clear. Be decisive if you discover you have hired an incompetent bookkeeper or accountant; immediately get a good one.
5. Don't allow your business to grow any larger than you absolutely need; bigger is not always better when it comes to managing a business or employees.
6. Develop a business plan and review and update it regularly.

Forces You Will Encounter

There are a number of forces that affect you in business, whether or not you know about them or believe in them. They are as real as the seasons, as pervasive as the weather. Early in my business life I was oblivious to these forces. Eventually they penetrated my awareness, at times gently and sometimes like thunderbolts.

Force One: Galloping Growth

Organizations and processes grow. They begin with basic needs and a birth, and then they proceed to take on lives of their own. For example, the simple act of organizing a workshop seems innocent enough when you first begin doing it. After we organized a few workshops, we learned a few tricks and discovered how to be more efficient. Because we are diligent, we wrote down our learning and it grew into a process with its own checklist. Our checklist grew to approximately three typewritten pages and then got divided into several segments, which we then further tweaked and refined until they became efficient and effective. Next, the fabulous checklist acquired a Table

You can be in angelic compliance with all the government agencies and still be cheerfully sued by a disgruntled employee.

Early in my business life I was oblivious to these forces. Eventually they penetrated my awareness, at times gently and sometimes like thunderbolts.

of Contents so we could locate the various segments... which is actually a subset of a much larger Table of Contents that helps us navigate our entire operating manual. Do you see what I mean?

You have only to look at any large corporation or government organization to see this in effect. They begin with a basic need, take on a life of their own and unfold like a shamrock into the world. The stronger the leadership, the more entrenched, far-reaching and forceful the organization becomes. Next, along comes a new management team or a new government with a new mandate. They typically kick the living crap out of the "old way" things were done, and proceed to create their own brand of monster and make it grow. The downsizing is often far more painful than the growth because nobody enjoys what appears to be a step backwards. It seems there's nothing particularly macho about becoming smaller.

Where there are people, there will be politics.

As a business owner, understand that you have control over many of the internal growth forces but very little impact on the external forces unless you begin to play politics.

Force Two: Plundering Politics

No matter what type of business you get into, you will encounter politics. Where there are people, there will be politics. The most pervasive and obvious politics is all around us in the form of the many layers of government. But politics doesn't start or stop with government. It's a force that is alive and well on every front.

On a smaller political scale, businesses often form associations. The associations spin their own little political webs and then begin to grow. This is a likely first brush with politics for most micro-entrepreneurs.

The main point about politics: it is a force that lives and affects your business life. Whether or not you actually become involved in the politics, you will enhance your chances for survival by understanding those that affect your business.

Force Three: Rampaging Regulators

Regulators abound. From the moment you step into business, you are subjected to a daunting glut of regulators and lawmakers. In what we erroneously refer to as a *free country*, we are regulated to the point that the life is often squeezed out of businesses before they even have a chance to build a foundation.

In fact, many businesses tend to operate illegally for years before taking the leap into legal business status. Called the *underground economy*, they accept only cash payments and don't report to the authorities. Underground businesses don't normally advertise through regular channels; they attract their customers through word of mouth.

Regulators, armed with all the power and financial backing of the government, keep on creating more and more laws and regulations in an effort to confine and control. It seems that once they grow to a certain point they focus inward and get so caught up in their own world they become insensitive to the needs of the businesses around them.

Most new micro-entrepreneurs do not understand that regulators, for the most part, are not aligned with each other. In many cases they are not knowledgeable about the rules and regulations of the other agencies. You can play perfectly by the rules of one agency and be completely at risk or liable to another. For example, in Canada you can honor and obey the rules of Canada Revenue Agency and be in trouble with Workers' Compensation Board and/or Employment Standards and/or Human Rights.

If you're going to survive and thrive in business you will need to surf your way through these gluey matrixes and get to the business of serving customers. If you find that the regulation restricts or eliminates your ability to serve customers, you may wish to consider plying your trade in some other jurisdiction.

You can play perfectly by the rules of one agency and be completely at risk or liable to another.

The thing to remember about regulations is that they are rife with and propelled by the other forces, growth and politics. Together these forces create a formidable wall for the entrepreneur to scale.

Force Four: Obnoxious Overhead

Whatever business you're in, you will encounter *Obnoxious Overhead*.

You may be familiar with the term "overhead," used in business to represent "business expenses not directly related to the goods and services produced." Some of the more obvious overhead expenses are: ongoing rent, utilities, advertising, insurance premiums and paper clips.

Obnoxious Overhead is the term I use to represent all those costs that are hidden from you when you begin a project or a business but materialize as real as taxes along the way.

I spoke to a realtor who had done business in Latin America. Her comment about her experience with Honduran employees caught my attention. She said, "We were surprised when we no longer needed the services of the caretaker of our property; there was an expectation that we would look after him for a considerable time beyond the employment arrangement." She was referring to a cost of doing business that I would call *obnoxious overhead*. It exists everywhere.

Here is a surprising array of delights that can blindside you and relieve you of time, energy and equity:

OBNOXIOUS OVERHEAD	
Audits and fines by government or regulatory agencies	Wrongful dismissal lawsuits
Government agency requests for information on employees	Employee buyouts
The cost of marketing and selling	Natural disasters
Non-productive or subversive employees or contractors	Political & bureaucratic whims
Human rights allegations or charges	Legal battles
Professionals without clear directions or controls	Insurance
Non-payment for goods or services	Theft

Force Five: Formidable Fatigue

Formidable fatigue makes all problems loom up larger than life. When our energy is down, challenges tend to look bigger than they do when we're charged and energetic. Fatigue makes problems appear larger than they are.

When I speak of fatigue, I'm talking about the kind that drains the life from your veins. I'm not referring to good old-fashioned tiredness that results from a hard day of work; that's healthy. *Formidable fatigue* is not healthy, it slowly kills you.

One of the most dangerous aspects of fatigue is that it creeps up on you. It is possible to drift into a deep state of burnout unaware, even though it might be visible to those around you. The fatigued person can be the last to know he or she is burned-out.

Force Six: Devastating Dependency

This force is huge. In my part of the world there appears to be two major doctrines: right wing and left wing. It seems the flow of human sentiments has a rhythm comparable to the ocean; the doctrines ebb and flow like the surf. Certain snapshots in time will reveal right wing on the rise and others will show waves of the left wing rolling into shore. The waves come in, higher and higher, and then subside. One moment my world is permeated with socialism; the next year or term capitalism cascades into view. To and fro the pendulum swings.

In between the two systems we have a whole lot of hangers on, leeches, rent seekers. There are a lot of folks who understand and work the systems to their advantage. The Employment Ensurance (EI) trap is only the tip of the *devastating dependency* iceberg. The welfare trap is where the real devastation sets in. I am in favor of a safety net for those who truly need it, those who cannot work. Unfortunately, once the door is open all manner of lizards slide in to feed off the system. They become adept at playing the games required to stay in the system and they are fully complimented by a number of well-paid folks whose job it is to process, manage and manipulate them - a well-oiled bureaucratic machine that rolls out each morning to administer the welfare crowd. This is big business in Canada; you will have to assess for yourself how prevalent it will be in your part of the world and how much influence you want it to have in your life.

When you step toward operating your own business, it is important to take a close look at the effects of *devastating dependency* in your life. Entrepreneurship and business ownership require that you take massive action. When you allow yourself to become dependant on a system such as employment insurance or welfare, you hand over much of the control to that system.

Force Seven: Spongy Supply and Demand

Life and business are acutely affected by the forces of *supply and demand*.

Let's imagine you are selling potatoes. You are the seller, the supply. When you get to the store, if the store needs potatoes, there is demand and you are in business. The store is the buyer, the demand. If your early bird neighbor has already been by and filled the store's bins with his potatoes, then there is no demand and you are either off to the next store or headed home to conjure up a new use for your potatoes. Supply has now overbalanced demand.

The forces of supply and demand will affect your business every day of its existence. It's not so much the level of demand that controls the market, it's more the relationship demand enjoys with supply. No matter how much demand, if there is one dollar in value more than the demand the force on the market price is down. If there is one dollar less, the force is up, a complete reversal in the energy. When demand for your product or service is higher, you will likely feel more like you're paddling with the current. When supply is abundant, you will have to work harder to stay in business.

Those on the demand side of the equation will always want to ensure an abundance of supply. Those on the supply side of the equation will always aspire to more demand.

Interesting dynamics can happen with supply lines. Imagine the effect on your business if your supply is cut off. Imagine the effect on your business if there is suddenly no demand for your goods or services. These are important considerations, whether you are a plumber serving your neighbors or importing crafts from India. Larger businesses will often purchase their suppliers in order to secure their supply lines.

Force Eight: Master Money

In business, money rules. The esoteric side of me resists this, but that fact is no money, no business. It's fairly straightforward. Pour money into a business, ideally from customers, and the business thrives. Stop the flow of money into the business and it dies. In business terms, money is life. Cash flow, sales, down payments and loans. Stop the flow of these things and the business dries up. This leads to a discussion about the power of money.

If a major customer wants something, he or she can demand it based on the power they wield with the money they spend in a business.

As a business owner your main job is to ensure enough money remains, after all the rent-seekers have had their drink, to fill your own tin cup.

If a major supplier wants something, he or she can demand it based on cutting off the supply. In this case, your control is the money you pay them. If the money is important to them, they are more negotiable. If it is not, you are more negotiable.

A wise friend once described his fiscal management plan to me this way. He said, "You have to scrimp and save as many pennies as possible every day. That gives you a small financial buffer for those little emergencies that tend to arise. If the emergency never happens, that's your gravy. But don't worry – the emergencies almost always happen."

In your business life, imagine money as a waterfall that spews from somewhere high on the side of a mountain. Planted at strategic places all the way down the mountainside are people holding out tin cups of various sizes and shapes. Some of the people have large buckets (tax collectors?). They are all siphoning off portions of the flowing money. As a business owner your main job is to ensure enough money remains, after all the rent-seekers have had their drink, to fill your own tin cup.

Chapter 4

The Business Planner's Primer

Table of Contents

Congratulations on Getting Started!

Congratulations for launching on a very exciting journey… starting your own business! And hats off for starting with a business plan.

Over the past couple of decades I have coached thousands of people along the path to business start-up. Of the millions of people who aspire to operate their own business, too few succeed. Too many potential business owners back off when they realize how much work goes into developing a business plan. If fear of hard work is the only reason people abandon their business ideas, then we could safely say that the business plan does its job early in the process. But that is not the full story.

Many people fail to complete a business plan because of the confusing array of business planning systems, books, software applications, web sites and consulting services. Is it any wonder that many business dreams end up in the owner's top dresser drawer or worse, in the trash bin? What's more amazing is that some aspiring entrepreneurs actually figure their way through this bewildering matrix of systems, structures, terms and demoralizing roadblocks… complete a business plan and start their business.

Do You Fit This Profile?

The planning process can be fun and educational, but even more importantly, it can help protect your house, your parents' retirement fund, or whatever else you intend to put at risk.

- You are excited about your business idea.
- You are afraid of failing.
- You wonder if your product or service will sell.
- You want to push ahead, but don't want to risk losing your investment.
- You have a limited amount of money to risk.
- You may be pushed toward business or self-employment out of necessity or you might be desperately attempting to take advantage of an opportunity.
- You may simply aspire to be your own boss or to create a better lifestyle for yourself and your family.
- You most likely have some of the core skills to work in your business but you probably have little experience to operate the business.
- You have never developed a business plan.

If any of the above points describe you, I urge you to accept my encouragement. If you really want to start your business, you will do it! Even if this is your first business plan, you will succeed. The planning process can be fun and educational, but even more importantly, it can help protect your house, your parents' retirement fund, or whatever else you intend to put at risk.

Congratulations! You are launching on an exhilarating learning adventure.

Why Develop a Business Plan?

You have decided to start a business and are now poised to develop one. Why would you set out to complete such a project?

There are many sound reasons to begin your process by creating a business plan.

- So you know where you're going.
- To have a roadmap or blueprint for your business.
- To have a document to look back on in order to measure your progress.
- To protect your investment and equity from loss.
- To find out if your idea will work.
- To build confidence about your business.
- To get a loan from a lending agency.
- To access funding from government.
- To reveal and solve problems before starting the business.
- To learn more about / become the expert on your business.
- To create a document to use to communicate with others: family, partners, investors, and bankers.
- For your own peace of mind.

Do you have other reasons for developing your business plan?

Perhaps it would be more appropriate to ask: *"Why would you not develop a business plan?"*

Tip: The shortest form of business plan can be referred to as an Executive Summary, Business Brief or Opportunity Document. As an example, refer to the 2-page Executive Summary of the business plan in Chapter 6. It's important to understand that a brief plan or summary can necessitate as much background research as a longer, more detailed business plan.

What is a Business Plan?

What do you want your business plan to be?

Those who control the money generally suggest or require their own business plan format. If you're hoping to get a loan from a lender, I recommend you review their format and ensure your business plan meets the criteria.

Business plans can:

- Be detailed or brief
- Be long or short - 50 pages or 5 pages
- Include detailed financial information or no financial information at all

The range is broad, depending on the needs of the writer and the reader. As a volunteer for the Finance and Lending Committee for a Community Futures Development Corporation, I might review as many as four business plans for a meeting. In this situation, the readers of the business plans appreciate brevity. The business plans come to us as summaries prepared by the business analysts who present them to the committee.

When I worked as Community Outreach Officer for the Softwood Industry Community Economic Adjustment Initiative (SICEAI) the projects were much larger, sometimes several million dollars. To successfully garner SICEAI funding, the applicant's business plan or proposal had to survive the scrutiny of up to 40 different reviewers. Those business plans and proposals required a tedious balance between providing enough detail and being brief – they were often longer.

For the novice business planner, I hope there is some comfort in knowing that plans can be short or long, brief or detailed. As a rough guide, your first business plan should be for yourself; as *your* business plan, the first one can be as lengthy and detailed as you need. I'm not suggesting this plan be unnecessarily wordy. I recommend you use your first plan to create a blueprint or roadmap to guide you in your business and to build your confidence in your business idea.

Once you have completed your first business plan, you can then use it as the *raw material* to create shorter, more targeted business plans for specific readers. In applying to a bank for a loan, for example, you might create a loan application comprised of a few selected elements of your business plan and then attach the main business plan as one of the Appendices. I can almost guarantee the banker will never read the entire business plan, but he or she will know you've done your homework.

The body of your plan, not including the Appendices, will most likely be between 15 and 30 pages. This is a rough guide, not a firm rule; for a variety of reasons your plan might be shorter or longer.

Read Some Business Plans

The body of your plan, not including the Appendices, will most likely be between 15 and 30 pages.

Have you ever read a business plan? There are many different business plans available from various sources. There is a business plan in Chapter 6 and a shorter version in Chapter 7; read them both. Note the language and the tone, observe the use of tables, bullets and graphs. What appeals to you when reading a business plan? Which formats make it easier or more difficult to read?

Business plans come in all sizes, shapes and forms. One of the most confusing things to the new planner is the array of different terms, titles and formats. While most business plans have commonalities, it seems that no two formats are exactly the same. This invites many questions by those new to the business planning realm. How is a new entrepreneur to decide which to use and which to avoid? What does your banker wish to see? What should you NOT be communicating in your plan? How many pages should your business plan be?

The questions above and many more will be answered as you work through the business planning process. I recommend you use the RoadMap™ in Chapter 5 to develop your plan and use whatever the target agencies use as their preferred format when submitting your plan for financing.

Tip: Use any of the search engines to locate other business plans or visit www.riskbuster.com.

Locate some other business plans and read them. Note aspects such as:

- Balance of text and financials tables
- Use of bulleted lists
- Use of tables or graphs
- Language
- Use of summaries to present financial information
- Clarity of communication

Conquer Fear of Writing

Many people fear speaking in front of groups, but many people also fear writing.

When we speak in front of a group we feel as though we are naked. We open ourselves up to the scrutiny of those in front of us. Once we make a mistake we can't take it back; it is immediately visible to our audience and irrevocable. At the core of the fear of public speaking is fear of failure. To many, this fear is limiting. In fact, some people never get past the fear and consequently never speak to groups.

The fear of writing is similar to the fear of public speaking. When we write our thoughts for others to read, we are as exposed as those who stand and speak in front of groups. We open ourselves up to the scrutiny of those who read our writing, our mistakes forever visible to our audience. Fear of writing stops many people from writing their business plan. In fact, many would rather leave the writing of the business plan to a professional. This diverts the potential fear of failure to the consultant. If the business plan fails it's the consultant's fault. While there are situations that warrant hiring a consultant, most of the entrepreneurs I encounter benefit greatly by writing their own business plan. I strongly urge you to develop your own business plan, along with all its blood, sweat and tears.

The process of developing your own business plan offers a tremendous opportunity to learn and grow. The skills and knowledge you take away from the experience are forever enriching. Even if you never start the business, you will exit the adventure a wiser, more marketable person.

Here are some pointers to help you along the path:

1. Embrace the business planning process as an adventure.

2. View mistakes as opportunities to learn and to build your business acumen.

3. Seek the opinions and suggestions of others.

4. You can always correct written mistakes. Be patient and persistent and adjust errors as they are revealed to you.

5. Recognize business planning as a process that does not end; your business plan is a document that lives for the life of your business.

6. If you are able to see a mistake or an improvement, you are learning – that is positive.

7. The way to get past the fear factor is to face the fear. Just do it!

8. Read the next few segments of this chapter. The information that follows has been developed in response to the many questions business planners have asked me over a number of years. By the time you arm yourself with the tips that follow, you are certain to feel prepared to tackle the task of writing.

9. Get busy writing your business plan today.

10. If you get stuck, email me at **danb@riskbuster.com**

Tip: If you have difficulty getting your ideas out of your head and onto paper, here are two ideas that might help.

1. If you find talking easier than writing, have someone interview you to get you talking about your business. This will help reveal what you know and alert you to missing knowledge and information. Have the other person record your dialogue either by taking notes or by using a tape recorder.

2. If you are working alone, it can be helpful to record yourself as in #1 above, without the help of another person.

Climb Inside Your Reader's Head

A variety of people are likely to read your business plan. In writing your business plan, it is important to create a clear image of your ideal reader. This will help you write directly to your audience.

As indicated in the Task List, you should choose an ideal reader relevant for your business or situation. I have used a banker for the following example.

Example: Your Ideal Reader

My name is Gerry Tightwad and I am your banker. I am your *special business plan reader*. I have the ability to lend you the money you need to make your dream come true and I hope to be able to serve you in the future. I wish to take a few moments of your time to describe what's important to me in order that you do the best possible job of writing the plan for me.

First, I'd like you to know that I am fiercely busy. Time is important to me. Your job is to organize your information and present it to me, complete, readable and accurate. Please don't waste my time. Every hour you invest in organizing your information and in communicating clearly will save me two hours in frustration. When I'm frustrated, I don't lend money. If your plan is confusing or unorganized I won't even take the time to read it. On the other hand, I truly appreciate everything you do to make it easier for me to say *yes* to your request.

I like:

· A business plan that is brief, but not so brief that it's missing key information

· To see an idea that is well thought out, logical

· To see you invested in the idea; cold hard cash and assets are strongest

· That you can interact with and listen to others

· That you are the expert on your business

· A clear, well written text section with any relevant detailed information in the Appendices

· A meaningful Financial Section that supports all claims made in the text portion of the plan

I dislike:

· Dishonesty

· A messy personal financial picture

· Inaccuracy or miscommunication

· Long rambling sentences that just go on and on and on and on and...

· Ineffective or meaningless market research

· Unrealistic, pie-in-the-sky forecasts

I worry about:

· Making a decision to finance you and then having you default on the loan

· Being taken for a ride, financially speaking, and looking like an idiot to my peers

· Making a poor decision on your file and losing my job

· Missing my scheduled tee time

When I'm frustrated, I don't lend money. If your plan is confusing or unorganized I won't even take the time to read it. On the other hand, I truly appreciate everything you do to make it easier for me to say yes to your request.

I need:

· To know that your business idea makes sense

· To know that you have the ability to interact with real people, especially your customers

· To know that your business will pay back the loan

· To know that you have the ability to make and keep a deal, to honor a contract

· To know that you are invested to the point that you will stay committed

· To know that you tell the truth, you say what you mean and you mean what you say

· Security, probably your house or your most prized possessions – sorry, business is tough

· You to succeed in order that I succeed

I will have made 90% of my decision within three minutes of opening your business plan. When I'm finished reading it, I will want to be confident that:

· Your business idea will succeed

· You have the ability to implement the business plan

· You can and will pay back the money I loan to you

When business gets tough, I need to know that you will be the one laying awake at night in a cold sweat solving problems, not me. Then I might lend you money.

I recommend you do this exercise, even if you're not planning to borrow money. It will help you capture an image of the person you are writing for and make it easier to focus your thoughts and words.

When business gets tough, I need to know that you will be the one laying awake at night in a cold sweat solving problems, not me. Then I might lend you money.

Task List

1. List all the potential readers – your audience. Some suggestions to get you started: you, family, friends, investors, bankers, business acquaintances, members of your business planning team, business analysts, consultants, accountants, bookkeepers, employees, loan review committees, lawyers.

2. Choose one reader from your list who will represent (in your mind) the entire group. Keep that reader at the top of your mind while you write your business plan. In other words, write your business plan directly to and for your special reader.

3. Now, imagine you are that reader. Take 20 to 30 minutes and write what is important to you as the reader: wants, needs, concerns, likes, dislikes.

Hitch a Ride on the Shoulders of Giants

There is a force that kicks into play when you get a team of people working together to solve a problem. It's one of the most powerful options we have at our fingertips and it doesn't have to cost a lot of money.

A business is a complex series of processes. In any business, many processes are group activities. Stated differently, most of the activities that lead to serving customers involve different combinations of members of a team. No task is completely separate or divorced from the other.

As an example, a letter will often be stronger if someone other than the writer proofs it and provides feedback. This applies to every written document, be it an article, a manual, advertising copy, a contract or an important email message.

Brainstorming is another way to work together in teams. Brainstorming is a tremendous way to solve problems or to generate ideas. If you have ever participated in a brainstorming session, you were probably amazed at the power of focussing more than one brain on a problem. Effective brainstorming is always fun and it usually brings forth creative and unforeseen solutions.

As with the day-to-day operations of a business, teamwork plays an important role in the developing of a business plan. If you've never developed a business plan, it can be daunting. You can help yourself by organizing a team to help you through the process. What would a business planning team look like? It could be as little as three or four respected friends who wish to see you succeed enough to invest some of their time and perspective.

If you've never developed a business plan, it can be daunting. You can help yourself by organizing a team to help you through the process.

There are several ways you might use a business planning team.

1. They can provide you with encouragement and moral support.
2. They can serve as sounding boards by providing feedback on your ideas.
3. You can have one or more people proof your draft business plan.
4. You can ask them to help you source information or direct you to where to find information.
5. They can help you network with important contacts for your business.
6. They might actually write or help you write certain parts of your plan.
7. They can give you their perspective on your business concept or plan.

My business planning team includes my most respected business-minded friends:

- My friend, who has one of the brightest strategic minds around, is one heck of a skeptic, and has the ability to see further than most people;
- My sister, with her sharp mind, her sensitivity to others, and her ability to pick a small font typo at forty paces; and
- One or two friends from the local business community, with their business acumen, their frankness, their ingenuity and their scope of understanding of many different businesses and the politics that surround them. I choose only people who are supportive to my success, who will speak their mind openly and who have a positive attitude.

Points to consider when setting up a business planning team:

- Clarify what you want from them and pitch it clearly. Ensure that you do not use up more of their time than promised and if you do, be prepared to compensate.

- Be considerate of the amount of time and energy you request; most people are busy.

- Unless you have deep pockets, you probably don't want people who will cost you a lot of money.

- Determine in advance what you can do for them, what the benefits are to them for participating on your business planning team.

- Be sure that all the people you choose are supportive of you and care whether you succeed.

- Keep your commitments; when you promise to have work ready, ensure that it's ready.

- Match the level and type of expertise to the business you wish to start; for example, a café or restaurant business plan would ideally include at least one person who is experienced at operating a restaurant.

It will be easier to sell prospective team members on the idea if you can provide them with your expected timelines. There is nothing scarier than getting involved in a project with no end in sight.

Your willingness to invite others to participate in your business planning process might actually be a measure of how solidly you believe in your business idea. A lack of initiative or reluctance on your part might be your inner voice signaling to you that not all is right with your idea. You will likely have to do enough market research to at least gain some confidence in your business idea before beginning to eat up others' time and energy.

Your willingness to invite others to participate in your business planning process might actually be a measure of how solidly you believe in your business idea.

When setting up your own business planning team, consider: Who are all the stakeholders in your business? If you deem stakeholders to be anyone involved or affected by your business in some way, this includes a very broad range of people. It might include *family, friends, a banker, a bookkeeper, a business analyst, a lawyer, suppliers and customers*. It might even include your competitors or someone who is in the same business in a different city or area who doesn't compete with you. It may also include a friend who is in business already and whose judgement or perspective you trust. You are definitely the number one stakeholder in your business.

You probably know or know of people in each of the groups listed above. Make a list of those you might wish to include on your business planning team and why. What special skill, attribute or knowledge can they bring to your planning process? Don't make this process too formal or cumbersome. Keep it simple.

BUILDING A BUSINESS PLANNING TEAM WORKSHEET	
Person	
Address and Telephone	
Skills, Knowledge	
What role will he or she play?	
Benefits to him or her	

Writing Tips for Wide-Eyed Business Planners

When you are ready to sit down and write, just do it. Some people prefer to write the first draft with a pen or pencil and paper, others are comfortable composing directly into a computer. Choose a method that works for you and a time when you will be left alone without distractions.

The business plan is arranged into a number of small, manageable writing tasks. The following suggestions apply to any of the many steps that include written outputs as well as to the entire business plan.

With any text element of your business plan, the first step is to write your rough draft, concentrating on your ideas and all the information you need to include. Don't worry about grammar and spelling or any form of editing in the rough draft, you can polish and add refinements during the revision process. This first draft is not the place to be concerned with perfection.

Read the following list of suggestions prior to writing your business plan. You might also consider copying this list and hanging it in a visible location wherever you will do your writing.

1. Write in the third person

The business plan is arranged into a number of small, manageable writing tasks.

Write about your business and yourself as though they are separate entities. Rather than stating "I / we expect to bring in $24,000 in sales…" you might write "The business will achieve $24,000 in sales."

2. Lead your reader from general to specific

Make it easy for your reader to understand what you wish to communicate. This *general to specific* suggestion applies to paragraphs, elements, sections.

3. Be thorough

You want to make sure that you have included all the necessary information. Check your notes to ensure you have covered all of the important points. Provide answers for obvious questions. Be sure to cover all of the relevant Elements of the business plan and the key points indicated in each Element.

4. Maintain accuracy

Can you back up your statements with facts? When you quote text or statistics, ensure that you record them accurately. Look for contradictions that may leave your reader wondering. Accuracy is the foundation that enables your reader to build trust in you and your plan; contradictions and inconsistencies are seeds that grow into doubt.

5. Be consistent with names and terminology

To achieve clear meaning in your writing, choose and use your terms carefully. If you wish to make your writing more interesting by varying your terminology, be sure to provide explanations where it makes sense to do so.

6. Use an active voice

Always use the active voice unless there is a good reason to use the passive. Active voice is more direct, more forceful, and often easier for the reader to understand. For example, "The owner will contact the customers" is active voice. "The customers will be contacted by the owner" is passive voice.

7. Write positively

Wherever possible, avoid writing negative statements, unless the negative aspect of the statement needs to be emphasized. It is advisable to extol the benefits of your products and services but highly distasteful to make negative comments about your competitors.

Accuracy is the foundation that enables your reader to build trust in you and your plan; contradictions and inconsistencies are seeds that grow into doubt.

8. Minimize jargon, abbreviations and acronyms

Jargon is language that fails to communicate because it is full of long or fancy words. Most often jargon takes the form of technical terminology or characteristic idioms of a special activity or group. If you use too many words and expressions unique to your industry or business, you might confuse your reader. If you need to use jargon, provide an explanation for your reader. Abbreviations and acronyms, while shortening your text, can often confuse the reader.

9. Be concise

Make all the words, sentences, and paragraphs count by eliminating unnecessary words and phrases. Avoid repeating the same idea using different wording - this tends to tell the reader you are unsure of what you are trying to say. Be careful to remove every word, phrase, clause or sentence you can without sacrificing clarity.

10. Avoid clichés and superlatives

Clichés are timeworn expressions or ideas, such as "the price is right." At best, clichés are obviously borrowed phrases that can be confusing to readers from other cultures. They tend to irritate readers when used repeatedly. Superlatives (such as "biggest," "best," "fastest," etc.) tend to erode your credibility.

11. Choose the right words

Avoid double-edged words; words that can carry an undesired connotation. Also vague or pretentious words, coined words and unnecessary intensifiers should be replaced or deleted.

12. Eliminate awkwardness

Awkward writing can make it more difficult for the reader to understand your message. To smooth your writing, keep the sentences uncomplicated and eliminate excess words.

13. Correct all typos and grammar errors

The errors that result from carelessness have a tendency to stand out to a reader and sabotage the reader's confidence in the writer's ability. Make sure you scour your document for the obvious embarrassing errors like misspelled words. It is wise to have someone proof the plan for you.

14. Create a visual format that is easy to read

Use a mixture of text, tables and bulleted lists. Keep your paragraphs short to break text into smaller bites and make it easier for the reader.

15. Use appropriate pictures and diagrams

Use pictures or diagrams only where they compliment or simplify your message. Avoid using eye candy simply to impress your reader, unless your business plan is for a graphics-related business. Overuse of pictures can dilute your message and create the impression that you're not serious.

16. Include your sources for key information

If you use tables from the local census archives, state the source. If you quote an article from a credible trade magazine, provide the name of the magazine and the article, as well as the date. This helps the reader build credibility and confidence in your research and your business plan.

17. Include important detail in the Appendices

Whereas it is important to include a brief biography in the body of your business plan, it is more appropriate to house your complete resume in the Appendices.

18. Refer the reader to related information

For example, at the end of your biography you might state, *"See complete resumé in Appendix A."*

19. Ensure numerical information matches text statements

A common mistake in business plans is to state conflicting information in different Sections or Elements of the business plan. For example, stating a different sales total in the Executive Summary than that shown in the Financial Section. Go through your plan and double check for this kind of discrepancy – before it gets into the hands of your reader.

20. Build a complete, cohesive communication package

As a business planning coach, I will often write up a list of questions and comments for a business planner. Invariably, the writer of the plan then responds with a list of answers to my questions. Over the duration of the business plan development process, we will sometimes do this half a dozen times or more, resulting in a half-baked business plan and up to four lists of responses filling in the holes. This is the raw material, not the finished product.

A finished business plan is a complete, cohesive communication package, with any important detail attached in the Appendices for reference. Rather than submitting a half-baked plan with a tangle of disjointed responses to others' questions, create a full plan with all the information included.

As you create your business plan you should involve others to critique and provide feedback. As the champion of your business plan, take control of this valuable process. Assess all feedback and questions for their value and relevance and then incorporate the useful information into the plan. View questions and feedback as gifts, as opportunities to clarify and strengthen your business plan.

A finished business plan is a complete, cohesive communication package, with any important detail attached in the Appendices for reference.

Tips for Making Your Business Plan Easy to Read

Here are a few ways to make your business plan easier to read.

1. Use simpler words where you can.

2. Use short sentences.

3. Use short paragraphs.

4. Break up your text with an appropriate amount of white space.

5. Use <u>underline</u> or *italics* to highlight or <u>*draw attention to words or phrases*</u> where appropriate.

6. Use bulleted lists.
   - Did I say – use bullets?
   ◊ There are a few different kinds of bullets
   √ Keep it simple. Be consistent and don't use too many different types of bullets.

7. Use numbered lists.

  1. Numbered lists help us read and remember.

  2. Numbered lists can also help us prioritize.

  3. Numbered lists are easy to refer to.

  4. Use numbered lists mixed with bullets.

    • You can also add indent for effect.

    a. You can also mix lettered lists for detailed sub-lists.

8. Use tables where appropriate.

TABLE EXAMPLE		
I AM A TABLE	**ONE DAY**	**TEN DAYS**
Use tables.	1	10
Tables work great for arranging numbers.	+2	+20
Especially great for totals.	=3	=30
Tables enable us to organize information.	Capital Assets	Small Tools
You can merge cells like this to form larger cells like this one.		
You can left justify like this.	You can right justify like this.	
You can center like this.		
You can use tables with or without borders.	This table uses borders.	

9. The *text box* is another great tool.

This is a text box. Do I draw your attention?

A text box can be used to break out, separate or highlight information. It can also be used for lists like this:

Year 1 Sales = $100,000
Year 2 Sales = $150,000
Year 3 Sales = $200,000

10. Color can be fun, but the more colors you use the more expensive the printing. Some colors are more difficult to see than others.

11. CAPITAL LETTERS can set words or **HEADERS** APART FROM OTHER TEXT.

12. You can use different fonts.

    (**Arial** / Times New Roman / `Courier New`)

13. You can use different font sizes for functions such as **Headers**.

14. Some fonts are easier to read - Some fonts can be difficult to read.

15. For some things a picture is worth a

16. Graphs are great for showing trends.

17. Pie charts work well to show portions of a whole.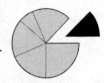

18. Bar graphs are an effective way to show sales.

19. For the tables and summaries in your business plan, round all figures up to the nearest dollar and eliminate any unnecessary zeros and redundant currency signs.

20. Don't overdo it with the "special effects." Keep it clear, simple and professional.

21. A little variety makes it interesting; too much can confuse or irritate the reader.

22. Continually ask yourself, "What will make it easier for my reader to understand my message?

Prepare to Burn the Midnight Oil

It's the extra mile that usually makes the difference. Any noteworthy achievements in my business have been built over and above my day job, beyond the normal energy outputs and expectations.

Once my training business grew to offer more than 20 courses and workshops, I identified the need for a catalog. The absence of the catalog was glaring and the need was pressing, yet there seemed to be no extra hours in the day or night to do the work. I mulled this over for a few days, the idea simmering in my brain. One evening I headed home after working all day, a rough format for the catalog flopping around in my mind, and fired up my computer. At the time, I was working more than fourteen hours each day, seven days each week. There didn't appear to be enough time left over to get the job done. After a couple of late nights and early morning stints I had three-pound bags under my eyes and a draft of our catalog. I had "burned the midnight oil" to pull a critical job together.

I have seen this dynamic at work many times throughout my business life. Here are some important points to consider:

- Clarify what you want or need.
- Ask for what you want and watch it happen.
- Many of the really great achievements take place over and above the regular workday.
- We can almost always do more than we think we can; it's a choice.
- We usually have more time than we think we have.
- We always have enough time to get done what needs to be done.
- We have access to more energy than we think possible.
- Your business plan might be a project that gets done by "midnight oil."

The example I used above, the creating of our first catalog, was a fairly large need, which required a significant burst of energy. The concept of "going the extra mile" can be applied to many different aspects of your business. For example, you can apply this principle to:

- Serving customers
- Serving employees
- Pulling together teams to complete projects
- Marketing your products and services
- Continuous innovation
- Business planning

There is always enough time for miracles; it's simply a matter of desire and focus.

> *There is always enough time for miracles; it's simply a matter of desire and focus.*

Giving Birth to Your Business

As you start the long trek down the business planning path, it's healthy to separate yourself from your business. From this moment forward, I invite you to consider your business to be a separate entity from yourself. What does this mean?

A little investment of energy at this point can reap huge dividends later on in the life of your business. For example, you should set up a business bank account, rather than mixing your business expenses with your personal – your accountant and bookkeeper will both be thankful. You will also enjoy the benefits: less confusion and less cost for accounting and bookkeeping.

It may help if you think of your new business as a separate entity, like having a baby, building a house, or hatching an egg.

I have observed many new and experienced business owners who intertwine their business in their personal lives. There is a tendency to dovetail your personal and business lives. I have done this in the past and it only leads to difficulty.

It may help if you think of your new business as a separate entity, like having a baby, building a house, or hatching an egg.

Here are some ways to separate your business from your personal life.

1. Separate your personal time from your business time.
2. Train your customers to contact you during your business hours.
3. Train your friends to contact you during personal hours.
4. Open a separate bank account for the business.
5. Establish separate telephone and fax numbers for the business.
6. Whether home-based or not, create a separate space for the business.
7. Have a separate entrance for a home-based business.
8. Create a separate Internet and email presence for the business.
9. Consider the business to be a living being with its own economy and rhythms.
10. Even if your business is a proprietorship for which the tax authorities view you and your business as the same entity, set-up your business with its own bookkeeping and accounting systems.
11. Consider yourself to be an employee of your business – pay yourself a wage – a regular paycheck, if this is possible (this is sometimes referred to as "Owner's Drawings").
12. Pay your personal expenses out of your wages and pay business expenses from your business account.

There are some wonderful payoffs for keeping your personal and business affairs separate. You will:

- Have a clearer picture of both personal and business expenses
- Find it easier to establish effective prices, knowing your accurate costs
- Likely have an easier time getting through any government audit
- Foster better relations with your bookkeeper and accountant
- Be better prepared if you decide to sell the business or bring in a partner
- Have more peace of mind and less mental or emotional intrusion of either your personal or business life on the other

One exception to this purposeful separation of personal and business is your mailing address. I recommend using a post office mailbox as your main mailing address. I have done this for more than two decades. During that time I have started, operated or sold more than half a dozen businesses. During the same time period I have moved personally at least a half a dozen times and many of the businesses have either moved physically with me or at other times my home address is stable but the businesses have moved. Having a post office mailbox has saved me a lot of time and money in address changes.

With so much to gain and so little to lose, I urge you (at the start of your business planning process) to consider your business to be a separate entity from yourself.

Tackle Your Deal Breakers

There are some things that will stop your business idea, no matter how wonderful it is. These are the costly rough spots that you would rather conceal from the business analyst or banker. Hiding the information will only bring you and everyone you deal with frustration. Your best strategy is to get any deal breakers onto the table and mitigate them early – the sooner the better. In case any of these apply to you, here they are:

1. **100% Financing.** Sure, you and I have heard about those folks who manage to get it. It doesn't happen that often; more often it's a deal breaker. Would you invest your savings in someone who apparently doesn't have the guts or the capacity to invest in themselves?

2. **Bad Attitude.** There are entire books written on this topic. The real difficulty with this deal breaker is that most polite folks will not tell you that you suck – instead they will go quietly about taking their business elsewhere. It's not the responsibility of bankers, employees or customers to create our approach to others. We are each responsible to manage our own attitude.

3. **Cards & Toys.** Nasty credit card balances and a yard full of unnecessary toys. Owning toys is not the sin; it's the high interest loans with outstanding balances and endless minimum payments that break the deal.

4. **Fantasy Forecasts, Unrealistic Cashflow.** Would you invest your hard-earned savings in a person who can't take the time and effort to build realistic sales forecasts? The cashflow is your opportunity to impress the lender that you know your business. It's got to make sense. Missing or inaccurate expenses will destroy the reader's confidence in your projections.

5. **Getting into a Business You Know Nothing About.** If you are asking a lender to finance you to get into a business you know nothing about, be prepared for the jaundiced eye. Certainly many folks have changed careers or leapt into a business they didn't know anything about. I've done it, but I did it at my own risk. Would you have financed me to get into a business I knew nothing about?

6. **Inconsistencies or Dishonesty.** Would you invest your money in someone who either doesn't know or doesn't make the effort to tell the truth?

Your best strategy is to get any deal breakers onto the table and mitigate them early – the sooner the better.

There are some things that will stop your business idea, no matter how wonderful it is. Your best strategy is to get any deal breakers onto the table and mitigate them early – the sooner the better.

7. **Looming Liabilities.** There's nothing quite like a pending legal action or a recent bitter marital break-up to scare off your potential lender.

8. **Not Fitting the Lenders Priorities.** Lending agencies have different and ever-changing priorities. Know what those priorities are and target the right agency for your type of business.

9. **Outstanding Taxes or Aging Accounts Payable.** If your business hasn't been able to pay its bills, you had better have a good explanation why and a bullet-proof plan for recovery and success. Specifically, you need to show that you can and will pay back the loan.

10. **Overpaying to Purchase a Business.** Your inability to negotiate a reasonable price to buy the business raises questions about your ability to survive once in business. With your credibility in question, the deal is broken.

11. **Security Doesn't Match Level of Risk.** Are you asking a bank to lend you money with no security? Sorry, banks are not in the business of taking major risks.

12. **Ten-Bell Credit Rating.** The kind that gives your banker heartburn!

Build, Buy or Franchise

WILL YOU BUILD, BUY OR FRANCHISE?		
	ADVANTAGES	**DISADVANTAGES**
Starting Your Own Business	More freedom & flexibility in how you design and do things You have control over costs and prices You can usually start and build your own business at a lower financial cost As the owner and designer of your business you will have complete authority and flexibility to adapt the business to suit your lifestyle and needs You reap all of the rewards for your efforts	You are responsible to develop standards, roles, training, managing, mopping floors Isolation can be an issue You will expend more energy because of the need to develop everything from scratch New businesses have a high failure rate As a lone purchaser, you will most likely pay premium rates for goods and services You take all the risk and blame if things go wrong You are responsible to develop your own business plan As a new business, you will not have a financial history to use as a benchmark

Table continued next page

WILL YOU BUILD, BUY OR FRANCHISE? continued		
	ADVANTAGES	**DISADVANTAGES**
Buying an Existing Business	You should be able to negotiate the price You might purchase the solutions to some of the problems of starting a business If the business model is well designed and working, you may benefit You might benefit from goodwill, that is customer loyalty, traffic and cash flow You might be able to interview existing customers and vendors to gain perspective on your buying decision The existing business should be able to provide a minimum of 3 years financial history Existing employees and infrastructure could make your entry easier and faster	You could inherit negative results of past actions (unpaid bills, back taxes, lawsuits) Negative history with customers could follow you Most lending institutions will not recognize goodwill as a financial value In many cases goodwill follows the original owner(s) Where purchasing the assets of a business, you might inherit faulty equipment or surprise repair bills Unless the existing business already has one, you will be responsible to develop your own business plan
Buying a Franchise	With a reputable franchisor you will be purchasing a proven business model Standards, roles and training are pre-developed and provided Ongoing support and training Can benefit from a franchisors marketing, common branding and customer recognition A good franchisor will make your sourcing easier and you should benefit from group or bulk buying strategies A reputable franchisor should be able to provide you with most of the raw material for your business plan Franchising is closely regulated, which should make it easier for you to assess its track record and credibility	In many cases you will pay a costly upfront fee to purchase a local franchise In most cases you will have to pay ongoing monthly royalties and fees to the franchisor The franchisor will control your expansion The franchisor will determine and limit the size of your territory For the most part you will be locked into a franchisor's methods, timelines and processes – you may not have as much freedome to do what you want

Taming the Famous Name

Naming your business can be both exciting and agonizing. It is exciting because the naming makes the business a bit more real – it can be agonizing because you want to get it right.

There are legal considerations when it comes to naming your business. You don't want to infringe on someone else's turf by using his or her business name, nor do you want someone else using your business name.

I view the name as having three important components: the grabber, the descriptor and the legal identifier. As an example, *Macrolink* Action Plans Inc.

The Grabber - I begin with a word I like. I chose Macrolink because to me there are pleasant and positive connotations arising from this word and it said something about the image I wished to create.

The Descriptor –*Action Plans* describes the service offered by the company.

The Legal Identifier – The *Inc* part of the name conveys that the business is registered as a limited company.

Before naming your business, it is critical that you first research to learn what types of business vehicles are available in your jurisdiction. A business vehicle is also referred to as the *form* or *legal structure*. For example, the business above is a corporation or limited company registered in the Province of British Columbia.

Most regions or countries have a range of business vehicles that must be used when conducting business in that locale. In Canada, the simplest form or structure is called a proprietorship. More complex configurations or vehicles include the corporation, partnership and not-for-profit vehicles.

Here are some tips on how to choose a business name.

1. Use the Internet search engines to determine if the name is already being used. Plug your name ideas into any of the popular search engines and see what comes up. If the name draws 457,000 potential links, it's overused.

2. Visit the domain registration websites and plug your name into the search engines to determine if the domains are available. Simply type "domain registry" into a search engine of your choice and try the mini-search function built into the domain registry website. The search results will tell you whether your name is available in the .com, .net, .org, .biz or .info – some of the registry sites will also list a number of suggestions close or related to your name.

3. Have the name searched by the local authorities. In British Columbia you can conduct your research through the government registry. If the name is permitted and available, you can then register it for a fee.

4. Keep the name as brief as possible. Throughout the life of your business, you and others will write, type, think or speak your business name many, many times. If you wish to inspire others to repeat your business name, make it easy for them to do so. The worst names are typically impossible to pronounce or employ so many words you need an acronym to shorten them. Brief is better.

Use the Internet search engines to determine if the name is already being used. Plug your name ideas into any of the popular search engines and see what comes up. If the name draws 457,000 potential links, it's overused.

5. Search copyrights and trademarks to determine if some corporate giant has already cornered the name. You can either hire a trademark lawyer to do this or you can do it yourself by visiting the appropriate government agency or website.

6. Bounce the name off anyone you know and ask them for feedback. How does the name fit the business you are attempting to name? What do they think of when they hear the name? Does the name sound right for the image you wish to portray? Do they know of any other business with a similar name?

The smaller your area of operation, the simpler it will be to name your business. A word of caution: do not assume that you can ignore other jurisdictions simply because you plan to conduct business only in your own town, city, county or province. The following story illustrates this point.

> After being in business for more than five years, Bill got a strongly worded legal letter from a large corporation he'd not previously heard of. The corporation was located in a different part of the world and did not conduct its business within Bill's small marketing area. The letter, written by the corporation's lawyer, demanded that Bill immediately cease and desist from using the business name he had been using since the inception of his business. The name was very similar to his business name and the other company had registered in a different jurisdiction and trademarked the name.

Situations like the one above can lead to a very expensive name change, which is never convenient. Part of the expense arises from hard costs, such as changing letterhead, logos and business cards, but ever more daunting is the marketing cost. You don't want this to happen to you after you have invested time, money and energy into marketing.

Once you have chosen your name, have the appropriate authorities do the necessary search and then register the name in the jurisdiction you intend to operate your business.

The Trademark Tango

There are many pitfalls in the trademark process. The following story should help you avoid them.

> My partners and I decided to trademark the BEST Program logo. We were about to put a lot of money and effort into marketing the program and didn't want anyone else using the logo or name. We contacted a trademark lawyer and started the ball rolling. Some time later, we had the legal right to claim that our logo was trademarked.

> Moments after notification that we were proud owners of the trademark, we received a phone call – someone was marketing a BEST Program right under our noses. I spoke with the offender to bring the infraction to her attention. The lady was quite unapologetic but she assured me they had been unaware of our use of the name and that they were *unlikely* to use the name again.

Over the next few months we discovered several folks using "BEST" as part or all of their title for training programs covering a variety of employment related topics. The message was clear: ownership of our trademark was only the beginning of the journey. It was merely a ticket to the fight. In other words, if we wished to maintain and protect our trademark, we now had to vigorously go after anyone using it and use whatever legal means available to have them back off. This would require time and money – and lots of it.

A few months after reaching what we thought to be a protected legal plateau we received the first of many offers to expand our trademark protection to different jurisdictions of the world. Our first acquisition of the trademark for our part of the world was only the tip of the iceberg. As anyone knowledgeable about trademark law would already know, each new territory requires further protection and more and more money.

The message was clear: ownership of our trademark was only the beginning of the journey. It was merely a ticket to the fight.

We came to realize that acquiring a trademark is only a license to go forth into the market and begin to really invest money protecting it. In our case, it wasn't productive or sustainable.

The world of trademark is segmented. It varies as you move from country to country, continent to continent. It's a quagmire without a great deal of coordination or uniformity throughout the world. The fact is, there are many people in different parts of the world that don't give a damn about trademark or copyright; if you want to market your product in those parts of the world it's seller beware!

If you need to trademark, use a highly recommended trademark lawyer, bring your wallet and prepare to do battle with those who infringe upon your turf.

Use the Internet to Research Your Business Idea

The Internet has brought the world of market research to our fingertips. Yet unless you know at least some of the basics of how to research, it can be a frustrating experience. The following is an introduction to searching for information using the Internet.

Locating an Existing Business on the Web

Sometimes the easiest way to locate a business is to try guessing its URL and then doing a search for it using your favorite search engine. The URL, or Uniform Resource Locater, is the address of a resource or file on the Internet. An easy way to do this is to write the name of the company - or a series of words you're sure of in the search box. If you have trouble locating the business, using different search engines may bring different results.

1. Think of the name of the organization you wish to locate.

2. Often you can locate the website by simply using the full business name and doing a search.

3. Another approach is to precede the business name with www. and to follow it with the most appropriate top level domain, such as .com, .net or .org (For example: www.riskbuster.com).

Here are the most common top level domains.

.com is for commercial websites

.net is for networks, but can be used by anyone

.edu is for higher education

.org is for organizations, often used by non-profits but can be used by anyone

.biz is for businesses

.coop is for co-operatives

.info is open for anyone

.name for personal pages

There are many other domains, such as those for each country, province or state throughout the world. For a more complete listing visit:

http://www.norid.no/domenenavnbaser/domreg.html
or
http://www.iana.org/cctld/cctld-whois.htm

or do a search using the phrase "list of domains."

Doing Simple Key Word Searches

The best way to get familiar with searching is to get out on the Internet and play. Try different searches, words and search engines to learn how information is stored and managed.

It is possible to get results by searching single words using most of the common search engines. Adding more words can help to narrow the search and bring more targeted results. When using multiple words, place the most unique words first.

1. Using phrases can be an effective way of searching. When searching for phrases (using quotations), it is important to understand that the combination of words must be in the correct order. If you're not getting results, try switching the order of the phrase to see what comes up.

2. Use AND or the plus sign (+) to add words. For example, a search for suppliers can be made more specific by adding the area or the type of suppliers you are looking for. Instead of searching for suppliers you could try suppliers AND clothing or suppliers + clothing.

3. Use NOT or the minus sign (–) to subtract words. For example, suppliers NOT turtles or suppliers – turtles.

4. Use OR to broaden your search (OR = more). For example, cats OR dogs.

Almost all portals and search engines will do phrase searching, identified by using double quotes at each end of the phase — "I am a phrase". It's important to know that quotes are used to search for exact phrases only.

The best way to get familiar with searching is to get out on the Internet and play. Try different searches, words and search engines to learn how information is stored and managed. For more detailed information do a word search for Boolean or visit these sites:

http://library.albany.edu/internet/boolean.html

http://library.albany.edu/internet/choose.html

For example here are some ways to narrow a search for suppliers.

- Add more words: suppliers clothing
- Use a phrase search: "Canadian clothing suppliers"
- Use the AND (+): suppliers + clothing + Canada
- Use the NOT (-) to exclude : suppliers – distributors
- Use the AND (+) to add and the NOT (-) to exclude: suppliers + clothing – distributors.
- Use the OR to broaden your search: suppliers OR manufacturers + clothing

Where to Search for Information

Search Engines: Indexing the words on every page in their database, a search engine covers Web pages and can include billions of pages. Different search engines can bring different results.

Portals: Offer search, directory, and many other general services such as email, free home page building, news and popular topics. Yahoo!, AOL, and MSN are popular portals.

Directories: A subject directory includes selected websites and classifies them into hierarchical subject categories. Most portals have one and some specialized directories are available by themselves. They do not index every word on every page included.

Newsgroups: Discussion forums organized around a particular interest, issue or activity. They can be used to share expertise, views, information, and to debate issues. Newsgroups can be a great source of technical information.

Archives: Dated information or even complete websites can be accessed through sites such at **www.faqs.org** or **www.archive.org**.

Message Boards: www.boardreader.com reads forums and message boards from more than 750,000 sites.

Blogs: A short form for weblog, a personal journal published on the Web. Blogs often include philosophical reflections, opinions on the Internet and social issues, and provide a log of the author's favorite web links. Blogs are usually presented in journal style with a new entry each day.

E-zines: E-zines are electronic magazines. Sites such as LISTZ at **www.tile.net** host many e-zines, mailing lists and related information.

The following table has a few links to get you started on your market research.

WEBSITE ADDRESSES	
Search Engines	**Domain Registry Sites**
http://www.google.ca	http://www.domaindirect.com/index.html
http://www.alltheweb.com	http://www.internic.net
http://www.hotbot.com	http://www.register.com/retail/index.rcmx
http://www.altavista.com	http://smallbusiness.yahoo.com/domains/
http://www.dogpile.com	http://allwhois.com
http://www.search.com	http://www.newregistrars.com
http://www.lycos.com	http://www.domainpurpose.com/main.htm
http://www.excite.com	
http://www.yahoo.com	**Census Information**
http://www.metacrawler.com	http://www.statscan.ca
http://www.mamma.com	http://www.census.gov
http://www.gigablast.com	http://www.census.gov/main/www/popclock.html

Researching the Internet

http://www.rbbi.com/links/sengine.htm for a list of useful search engines and tools

http://www.northernlight.com to search special publications for in-depth thoroughness

http://www.completerss.com search and subscribe to thousands of RSS feeds & topics

http://groups.google.com/ search Google newsgroups

http://www.faqs.org/faqs search archived Internet FAQS from A to Z

http://netscan.research.microsoft.com search thousands of newsgroups

http://www.boardreader.com search bulletin boards with Vivisimo's clustering engine

http://websearch.about.com research just about anything, expert articles on A to Z topics

http://websearch.about.com/od/searchingtheweb to learn about searching on the web

http://tile.net search email newsletters, e-zines, newsgroups, vendors, web articles

http://www.lsoft.com/lists/listref.html the official catalog of LISTSERV lists

http://messages.yahoo.com/index.html search Yahoo message boards

http://www.archive.org/web/web.php search 40 billion archived post-1996 web pages

http://www.researchinfo.com for a market researchers goldmine

WEBSITE ADDRESSES

International Research Links

http://www.fita.org is the source for trade leads, news and events and over 7,000 international sites

http://library.uncc.edu/display/?dept=reference&format=open&page=68 Virtual International Business and Economic Sources – over 1,600 international business and economic links

http://www.ita.doc.gov/td/tic US Dept of Commerce market information for countries & industries

http://www.jetro.go.jp Japanese External Trade Organization

http://projectvisa.com links to embassies around the world

http://globaledge.msu.edu/ibrd/ibrd.asp to access international business links

http://www.tradeport.org/countries market reports by country

http://www.hkecic.com/eng/flash_home.html Hong Kong Export Credit Insurance Corporation profiles the credit and sales situation for many major industries

http://www.tpage.com major source of import / export leads

http://www.euromonitor.com international consumer product market research by industry

http://us.yesasia.com/en/index.aspx Japan, Korea, China pop culture, books, magazines, food

Web-based Surveys

http://info.zoomerang.com/

http://www.webmonkey.com/

http://www.websurveyor.com/gateway.asp

Credit and Financing Options

Sources of Financing

The most common sources of money to finance a business are personal contacts, i.e., friends, family, inheritance, mortgage extensions, etc. You should be aware that personal relationships can be jeopardised, unless you set the loan up on a business basis appropriately secured with a principle repayment schedule.

If sufficient financing is not available through personal contacts, you will need to consider commercial lending sources.

Types of Short-Term Credit

The following table lists a number of different credit possibilities and interest rate categories. Also listed are the *ease of obtaining* and the *popularity*, from the very small business start-up perspective.

TYPES OF SHORT-TERM CREDIT			
Type of Credit	**Ease of Obtaining**	**Interest Rate**	**Popularity**
Advance Sales to Customers	Difficult	Medium	Medium
Angel	Difficult	High	Low
Bank Loan	Easy	Low	High
Credit Card	Easy	High	High
Factoring	Easy	High	Low
Government Funded Agencies	Difficult	Low-Medium	Low
Industrial Bank Loans	Difficult	High	Low
Insurance Policies	Easy	Low-Medium	Low
Inventory Loans	Easy	Medium-High	Low
Love Money	Difficult	Low	High
Personal Loans	Difficult	High	High
Promissory Notes	Easy	Medium	High
Trade Credit	Easy	Medium-High	High

Short-term Financing

MATCHING SOURCES TO SHORT-TERM FINANCING	
Sources	**Type of Financing**
Chartered Banks, Credit Unions	Accounts receivable Operating loan Government guaranteed loan
Trade Credit	Usually 15 to 30 days granted by suppliers before payment is due
Factoring Companies	Buy accounts receivable outright without recourse and assume all risks of collection; will advance funds against purchased receivables, less a percentage
Commercial Finance Companies	Funds advanced upon assignment of receivables and warehouse receipts Equipment financing

Long-term Financing

MATCHING SOURCES TO LONG-TERM FINANCING	
Sources	**Type of Financing**
Developmental Lending Agencies	Start-up financing Upgrading or expansion Fixed asset acquisitions Equity financing Refinancing Change of ownership Working capital
Commercial Banks	Capital financing Fixed assets and equipment
Sales Finance Companies	Instalment purchase of equipment and machinery Sales and lease-back options on equipment
Insurance and Trust Companies	Direct loan secured by fixed asset mortgage Open market loan by offering debt security on market
Government Funded or Guaranteed Loans (usually administered by financial institutions)	Product research and development Pre-commercial and commercial product development Development for international markets

Credit is a privilege that increases your capacity. Abuse it and you will lose it.

To Plan or Not to Plan: Assessing Feasibility

Are you sitting on a hot business idea but you're not sure if it's a winner? If you have a limited budget, the feasibility process might just be the tool you need to make the critical go/no-go decision. It doesn't have to cost anything more than your own time, and if you approach it in a thoughtful, inquisitive way you should be able to produce realistic results.

Here are a few points about feasibility studies:

- A feasibility study requires that you research your market enough to decide whether to complete a business plan.
- The information you gather for your feasibility study will be useful should you decide to proceed with a business plan.
- Some feasibility studies can be very quick and inexpensive and some can take much longer and cost thousands of dollars.
- Use round numbers and approximations – round up for expenses and down for sales.
- If you feel like you are guessing too much, you probably are. Research more until you trust your numbers.

The Feasibility Process

If you have a limited budget, the feasibility process might just be the tool you need to make the critical go/no-go decision.

DETERMINING FEASIBILITY	
The ANSWER...	**To The QUESTION...**
Step 1: Total Market Potential	How many people need this type of product?
Step 2: Market Share	How much of this product can I sell?
Step 3: Building, Fixtures and Equipment	What type of building, fixtures, and other equipment do I need?
Step 4: Cost of Merchandise	How much will I have to pay for merchandise?
Step 5: Calculation of Operating Expenses	What cash expenses will I have to meet?
Step 6: Budgeting for Other Expenses	What other expenses do I have to allow for? Will I have to borrow money?
Step 7: Sales Minus Expenses	After paying all expenses, how much do I make?
Step 8: Return on Investments	Is it worthwhile?
Step 9: Go/No-Go Decision	Should I go ahead with the venture?

Let's imagine that you have scrimped and tucked away a small investment fund of $9,850 and you have a growing passion to own and operate a small candle shop. Keep that figure in the back of your mind while we work our way through the following example, the candle shop feasibility process.

The Candle Shop Feasibility Example

THE CANDLE SHOP FEASIBILITY EXAMPLE	
STEP	**RESULTS**
1. Determine Total Market Potential	Our secondary market research shows there are 20,000 people in the market area who spend an average of $100 each on candles and accessories each year. This would mean the total market potential is $2,000,000. Yippee! I don't know about you but I'm already rubbing my hands together.
2. Calculate Market Share	Our research shows us that 1,000 of the people in our market area will buy from our candle shop. This would bring 1,000 X $100 = $100,000 in sales. Woo Hoo! Stand back, we're gonna be rich!
3. Cost Building, Fixtures & Equipment	Imagine that our fixtures, shelving, renovations, counters, display cases add up to $30,500. ...Gulp!
4. Estimate Cost of Merchandise	Suppose we determine that it will cost $30,000 to purchase enough candles, matches, wax and candle-making kits for the first year. Eeek!
5. Identify Operating Expenses	Let's say we have been able to scrounge up a set of financial statements for a similar business and that our utilities, rent, wages, insurance, advertising and all those other trinkets... cost us $35,400 for year one. Hmm... it's getting warm in here - has someone jimmied the thermostat?
6. Budget for Other Expenses	In the spirit of wide-eyed entrepreneurship, let's toss in a slush fund of $1,600.
7. Subtract Expenses from Sales	Breathless... we reach for the calculator and enter our hard-earned data: $100,000 - (30,500 + 30,000 + 35,400 + 1,600) = $2,500 At this point it is not uncommon to see your life, at least all of your worldly possessions, flash past the insides of your eyelids. You might be thinking "all that money passing through my hands for this"? There's more...
8. Calculate Return on Investment	The scenario above is not so bad. At least the print is black instead of red. I have come to cherish black ink as a very good thing, especially in year one. If everything goes according to your plan, it appears you will profit by about $2,500. In Canada where there is profit, there awaits our trusty old friends at the Canada Revenue Agency, with a giant tin tax-cup. That's in the summer, during our seven months of winter they use a large snow shovel for collecting taxes! Let's say that the $2,500 is earnings before taxes of $625 and at the very end of your long stressful year, you are left with blisters on your feet, bags under your eyes, and $1,875 profit. Yikes! Is this a good deal or not?
9. Make Your Go/No-Go Decision	We now must determine whether we will be satisfied with the after tax return of $1,875 on the original investment of $9,850. See the following analysis.

This would mean the total market potential is $2,000,000. Yippee! I don't know about you but I'm already rubbing my hands together.

Assessing Return on Investment

Is it a wise use of funds to invest the $9,850 in the Candle Shop? It seems that the business will bring you a return on investment of 19%.

$1,875 ÷ $9,850 X 100 = 19%

Let's consider some of your other options, beginning with a regular old-fashioned savings account at your local bank. If you figure you could earn 5% ROI in a savings account, you will have $492.50 at the end of the year for no effort and no risk. The calculation looks like this:

$9,850 X 5% = $492.50

If you socked the same amount into mutual funds under a Registered Retirement Savings Plan with a potential 10% ROI, you might net $985 but there is risk and you could make less or even lose part of your investment.

$9,850 X 10% = $985.00

Perhaps the 19% ROI that you will earn with the $1,875 is a reasonable deal after all. If money were your only concern, you might decide at this point to continue with the development of a complete business plan. That completes step nine of the feasibility process.

Have You Hugged Your Gatekeeper Today?

As you venture down the business planning path, you are certain to encounter one or more gatekeepers. "Gatekeeper" is the term I use to describe bankers, business analysts and managers of any government programs that might provide grants to your business. While each gatekeeper is responsible to protect their employers' assets, they also offer you a tremendous learning opportunity.

As a fledgling business start-up, it is natural to feel somewhat defensive as you share your business idea with others. I encourage you to rise above your initial apprehension and realize that gatekeepers are continually seeking to invest in well researched and presented businesses. If you've done your homework, you could be offering just the package he or she is looking for.

The gatekeeper's first order of business will be to perform all the necessary due diligence to determine if your business idea is viable. He or she will also be responsible to assess whether or not you can do all those glorious things outlined in your business plan, before taking it forth to run the gauntlet with his or her boss or the committee that decides whether or not to lend you the money.

A banker once told me that, when meeting a loan applicant for the first time, the first few minutes of the meeting gave her enough information to decide whether or not to lend the person money. Your conduct and personal interaction with the gatekeeper count. I have seen loan applications rejected because the applicant simply couldn't honor commitments as simple as showing up for appointments on time or returning phone calls promptly.

I encourage you to rise above your initial apprehension and realize that gatekeepers are continually seeking to invest in well researched and presented businesses. If you've done your homework, you could be offering just the package he or she is looking for.

If you are a learner and if you are courteous in your interaction with the gatekeeper, he or she can become a tremendous ally in your business planning process. Be thankful for the gatekeeper's involvement in your business planning process. Often, they are highly knowledgeable generalists who perform due diligence on a daily basis for a broad range of businesses. They will easily recognize if you are on or off track. If you work with your gatekeeper, he or she will help you build a stronger business plan.

Tip: The gatekeeper laying roadblocks in front of you is assessing you and your business idea to determine the level of risk. If you meet his or her requirements, you might just win the opportunity of your life!

How to Be Effective When Dealing with Your Gatekeeper

1. Be curious. Be a learner. Be coachable.

2. If possible, communicate with the gatekeeper at the beginning of your business plan development. Learn his or her process and timelines; find out what he or she expects to see in your business plan and determine if he or she wants opportunities to provide input to your draft business plan.

3. Prepare for your discussions and meetings with the gatekeeper and manage the time efficiently.

4. Know your business plan thoroughly but accept that you may not have all the answers. If you don't have answers to questions, commit to finding them.

5. Without being a know-it-all, try to anticipate which questions the gatekeeper might ask and have your answers ready. You have two ears and one mouth; listen twice as much as you talk.

6. Be on time for meetings, return phone calls promptly and honor all promises you make.

7. If the gatekeeper seems to be negative about your business plan, ask why and request more detail until you understand the problem and what you need to do to fix it.

8. If a gatekeeper turns down your application, determine whether the decision is final or if you can fix any weaknesses and reapply.

9. Whether you reapply or not, use the gatekeeper's input to strengthen any weaknesses in your business plan.

10. Thank the gatekeeper for his or her feedback.

Dan's Hot Business Planning Tricks

1. Do your business plan for yourself first and then craft it into a tool for communicating to others.

2. Write for your average reader — don't try to baffle your reader with big words or complexity.

3. Champion your own business planning process — don't give away the privilege.

4. Do your own market research — be the expert for your business.

5. Business planning is a confidence-building process, don't miss it by hiring someone to do it all for you.

6. Engage someone you trust as a sounding board to discuss all aspects of your business concept. This is critical in order for you to process your thoughts and ideas.

7. Ensure the narrative part of your business plan is consistent with the Financial Section.

8. Back up your narrative and financial assertions with supporting information and documentation in the Appendices.

9. Clean up any inaccuracies and inconsistencies yourself — don't leave it to your reader.

10. Be curious — identify and challenge your assumptions.

11. Determine what will prove each Element of your business plan and prove everything you can; ensure that you use conservative assumptions for aspects you cannot prove.

12. When using assumptions, state them for your reader.

13. Keep the body of your business plan brief and refer the reader to detail in the Appendices.

14. Forecast sales conservatively low.

15. Estimate expenses aggressively high.

16. Prove your business case. Leave no stone unturned in leading yourself and your reader to the conclusion that your business can live in the gap between supply (cost) and demand (price). If you can't prove your business case, start a different business or get a job.

17. Focus on your strengths and positives rather than the competitors' weaknesses and negatives.

18. Don't prevail upon your reader to go fishing for information. Create one complete, cohesive communication package that is easy for your reader to read and understand.

19. Go as far as you can see, then you will be able to see further.

20. Remember, you are creating a business plan not building a piano!

21. If you get stuck, re-read this chapter.

Remember, you are creating a business plan not building a piano!

Business is like Fishing

I love fishing. I enjoy it whether or not I catch fish. A good catch makes the fishing trip more than just a visit – it makes it a successful fishing trip. I prefer to catch fish. A memorable fishing adventure begins with a good plan.

What makes a fishing trip successful? For starters you need to gear up. You need to:

• know the right spot to fish,

• have the right vehicles to get to the right spot,

• use the right bait to attract the right fish to take the hook,

• know how to set the hook, and

• how to play and land the fish.

Do all these things properly, and you will have a great fishing trip.

Plan. A successful fishing trip begins long before the first cast. Being at the right place at the right time might look fortuitous to the onlooker, but it's usually the result of research and planning. Someone has taken the time to learn about the fish; habits, patterns, likes and dislikes. It is also critical to know the waterway and have a roadmap to guide you to the spot. You also want to understand weather patterns and have backup plans to deal safely with accidents or disasters.

Preparation. In getting equipped for a great fishing trip, you will want to prepare for all possible situations. You will need survival gear, fishing equipment and the suitable vehicles to get to the right location. Then there's the fishing gear – rod and reel, the tackle box, line, lures, weights. If you're camping you will have a whole other range of concerns and equipment to attend to.

Competition. You will need to be aware of the other fishermen vying for the same fish as you are. Too many competitors will deplete the supply of fish and you might find yourself working much harder than you want. A certain amount of competition is healthy, too much is not. If your business is competing with too many others, you will need to work much harder to capture your share of the market. If you find yourself surrounded by a throng of hungry fishermen and no fish, it might be time to pack up and move to a new location. If you find yourself engulfed by competitor advertising and your sales lagging it may be time to reposition your business.

Location. Success is only possible in both fishing and business by choosing the right location. Ideally you want to place yourself on the bank of a river where the current compels the fish to swim within a few feet of you. Fishing where there are no fish is like trying to sell goods where there are no customers. In business, you must locate yourself where customers can see you and where they can stop to shop. You can do everything else perfectly, but if you are in the wrong place customers and fish won't even know you're in the game.

Presentation. You can pick the right location and do many things well, but if you don't present the right tackle the customers will pass you by. As the fish swim through your location, something has to catch their interest and entice them to pause long enough to inspect your offering. It might be some sort of bait or a shiny lure, or a combination of the two. The bait can be real food; the lure might look like food. The function of your presentation is to get the fish to stop and bite. In business, you must find ways to catch your customers' interest and slow them down long enough to nibble on your lure.

A successful fishing trip begins long before the first cast. Being at the right place at the right time might look fortuitous to the onlooker, but it's usually the result of research and planning. Someone has taken the time to learn about the fish; habits, patterns, likes and dislikes.

Play. Once a fish bites you need to set the hook and reel 'em in. If you blow this part of the process, the fish gets away and isn't likely to take your bait again for a long time. I don't know if fish talk to each other, but customers definitely do. Make sure each encounter is positive. Depending on the type of fish and your skill set, you might have to play a few fish and customers before actually landing one.

Landing. You can play the fish and bring it to the water's edge, but your job is still not done. Many great fish are lost at the point of landing. Part of the trick to a successful landing is to remain calm so as not to spook the fish. With customers you will need to be attentive to the last drop, listening for objections, answering questions, focussing on the benefits. It is also critical to know when your catch is complete, and how to stop selling and start bagging.

Like fishing, your business adventure should begin with a plan. In planning your business you will:

- Prepare yourself to manage and operate your business
- Learn what's working for your competitors
- Research and compare different locations
- Develop and fine tune your presentation

Planning will take you to a certain point and then it's time to get out into the current and fish. Once in business you will have plenty of opportunities to learn the business trade skills of attracting, engaging and keeping customers.

Just Do It!

The prospect of developing a business plan can be daunting. The RoadMap™ in the next chapter is a 99-step business planning process organized into logical, manageable tasks. Business planning can be compared to building a house: both projects can be large and formidable. When building a house, it's easier to break the overall project into smaller tasks. The entire project of building a house becomes easier to understand and manage when broken down into smaller projects such as building a floor, a wall, or a roof. When developing your business plan, consider each step of the process as a unique piece of the overall project with its own task list. Persistently complete each of the steps needed for your business and you will end up with a business plan.

You may have considered hiring a professional to develop your plan. In doing so, you will cheat yourself out of a wonderful opportunity to become *the expert* for your own business. *It is critical that you be the expert for your business. Writing your own business plan is the opportunity to become that expert.*

Are you ready to begin your business planning adventure? Take a deep breath and turn the page. As my kayak trainer says, focus on where you want to go and keep your paddle in the water at all times. **Bon voyage!**

> *It is critical that you be the expert for your business. Writing your own business plan is the opportunity to become that expert.*

> *As my kayak trainer says, focus on where you want to go and keep your paddle in the water at all times.*

Chapter 5

The Business Planner's RoadMap™

Table of Contents

GET EQUIPPED FOR YOUR BUSINESS PLANNING ADVENTURE

You are to be commended for making it this far and still wanting to run the business planning gauntlet. If your business idea is viable and you proceed into business, you are in for one of the most exhilarating adventures of your life!

The RoadMap™ is the process that will lead to completion of your business plan. It includes tasks, worksheets, checklists, samples, tables and tips. It will challenge you to learn and grow. It will be a lot of work and you might even enjoy the process!

Your energy will drive this process. You control the amount of time it will take to complete your business plan. It can unfold quickly or it can be carried out over a longer period of time, depending on your needs and how much time you have available. The time this process takes to get you to opening day will be directly related to the amount of time you invest. You are the boss!

The Transition from Idea to Action

Every business starts with an idea. The idea grows in the mind of the entrepreneur until he or she can no longer ignore it; that's usually when the research process tends to become more formal. Though there are different ways to roll into the business idea, the process of fleshing it out into a business plan is similar for many businesses.

- You might love to work with wood and want to create birdhouses for a major chain of stores.
- You may be skilled at a trade and want to provide your service from your home-based shop.
- You might like to sew things with your industrial sewing machine.
- You might clean houses for busy people, paint wonderful pictures or build a unique line of furniture.
- You may have been laid off by an employer who now wants to hire you as an independent contractor.

You will know when the time is right to research your market. Your business idea will be occupying your thoughts; you will be driving people around you crazy with your incessant ramblings. You will be unconsciously investigating similar products or services. You will be comparing, asking questions, perhaps trying to sell your closest friends on the idea. You might be pointing out weaknesses in competitor products. Your closest network of friends might be encouraging you, or perhaps not. Regardless, there will come a time to get serious about your market research; only you can say when that is.

Regardless of your area of pursuit, the dynamics are the same. You percolate on your idea until one day you simply must move into business planning mode or lose your mind.

Welcome to the Macrolink
Business Planner's RoadMap™

Introduction to the Business Plan Structure: The Shell™

Step 1

The following two pages will provide you with an introduction to the business plan structure and the RoadMap™. It is critical that you understand the difference between the business plan itself (The Shell™) and the process (The RoadMap™) you will follow to develop your business plan. The Shell™ is arranged to be a final presentation to the reader of your business plan, while the RoadMap™ is the 99-step process you will follow to build your business plan.

MUST HAVE
RECOMMENDED
NICE TO HAVE

The following table provides a snapshot of the Business Plan Shell™. Note there are six Sections, 39 Elements and 24 possible Appendices. The outline below shows the Elements <u>in the order in which they will be presented</u> to those who read your business plan.

THE BUSINESS PLAN STRUCTURE: THE SHELL™

1. Introduction
- ☐ Title Page
- ☐ Executive Summary
- ☐ Table of Contents
- ☐ Confidentiality and Copyright

2. Business Concept
- ☐ The Business
- ☐ Products and Services
- ☐ The Industry
- ☐ The Owner(s)
- ☐ Strategic Plan and Goals

3. Marketing
- ☐ Market Area
- ☐ Location: Marketing
- ☐ Profile of the Customers
- ☐ Competition and Differentiation
- ☐ Sales and Distribution
- ☐ Servicing and Guarantees
- ☐ Image
- ☐ Advertising and Promotion
- ☐ Pricing Strategy
- ☐ Marketing Action Plan

4. Operations
- ☐ Description of the Operation
- ☐ Equipment and Methods
- ☐ Materials and Supplies
- ☐ Risk and Mitigation
- ☐ Management
- ☐ Professional Services
- ☐ Employees and Contractors
- ☐ Operational Action Plan

5. Financial
- ☐ Sales Forecast
- ☐ Explanation of Projections
- ☐ Market Share
- ☐ Cost of Goods Sold
- ☐ Labor Projections
- ☐ Cash Flow Forecast
- ☐ Operating Expenses
- ☐ Projected Income Statement
- ☐ Break-even Analysis
- ☐ Pro Forma Balance Sheet
- ☐ Start-up Expenses
- ☐ Uses and Sources of Funds

6. Appendices
- ☐ Resumé(s)
- ☐ Personal Net Worth Statement(s)
- ☐ Certificates and Accreditation
- ☐ Historical Financial Statements
- ☐ Organizational Charts
- ☐ Board or Band Council Resolution
- ☐ List of References
- ☐ Letters of Reference
- ☐ Letters of Intent
- ☐ Contracts or Offers
- ☐ Partnership Agreement
- ☐ Lease Agreement
- ☐ Insurance Documents
- ☐ Price Lists
- ☐ Price Quotes
- ☐ Appraisals
- ☐ Market Survey Results
- ☐ Map of Area
- ☐ Environmental Information
- ☐ Publicity
- ☐ Promotional Material
- ☐ Product Literature
- ☐ Technical Specifications
- ☐ Glossary of Terms

Your completed business plan will be made up of three main parts, narrative, financial and supporting information. Sections 1 to 4 will house the narrative, Section 5 holds the financial Elements and Section 6 contains the supporting information.

Introduction to the Business Planning Process: The RoadMap™

Starting a business can be one of the scariest things you will do in your entire life. There are many reasons for this, including fear of the unknown, fear of loss and fear of failure. I think the transition to owning a business is far more daunting than buying a house for the first time. Somehow the rules seem clearer – at least one will have the advantage of having lived in a house, while most have not operated a business.

Once you understand the high level of fear and stress that accompanies business start-up, you begin to see how important it is to develop a business plan. Equally important, thoughtful people will recognize that you should develop the business plan yourself if at all possible.

Those of us who review business plans know that the single biggest challenge in any business plan that fails to achieve its goal is *incomplete or inadequate market research*. Yet the critical flaw in most of the business planning books on the market is that they shoot over the heads of the largest target group, micro-entrepreneurs. Most of the available books outline their variation of the business plan format and point the reader toward market research, providing little or no direction on how to carry out the market research. Their business planning systems simply expect a higher level of knowledge and skill than many people possess. Most writings on the topic simply do not offer the user an effective roadmap through the maze. As a result, too many business planning attempts neglect the most important objective of all – to prove one's business case – and end in failure.

Note: The Shell™ can be downloaded free and the Biz4Caster™ (forecasting spreadsheet) can be purchased at the Macrolink website at www.riskbuster.com. Both products are also available as part of the RiskBuster™ CD or digital download.

This 99-step RoadMap™ dovetails the market research and business plan writing processes, enabling the user to work methodically from the first idea through to implementation of the business plan.

Here is an overview of the journey you are starting, the business planning process:

OVERVIEW OF THE 99-STEP BUSINESS PLANNING ROADMAP™ & JOURNEY			
	ROADMAP™ STEPS	BUSINESS PLAN PORTIONS	**MACROLINK TOOLS**
Idea to Action	1 to 10		RoadMap™
Embrace Your Market Research	11 to 30		RoadMap™
Write Draft Copies Of Core Elements	18, 20, 29		RoadMap™ & Shell™
Prove Your Business Case – Feasibility	30		RoadMap™
Write the Narrative for Your Business Plan	31 to 53	Narrative – Text	RoadMap™ & Shell™
Forecast Your Financial Scenario	54 to 65	Financial Projections	Biz4Caster™
Add Your Appendices	66 to 89	Supporting Information	RoadMap™
Craft Your Introduction & Final Presentation	90 to 99		RoadMap™, Shell™ & Biz4Caster™

The Slippery Path to Proving Your Business Case

I wish I could tell you that building your business case is a linear process, but it rarely is. More likely you will venture into the various Sections and Elements of your business plan and travel far enough to determine viability or workability and then move on to a different Section. For example, you will need to work far enough into the Marketing Section to gain at least a rough idea of your prices. At the same time you will want a preliminary peek at your operating expenses, your fixed costs, and other Elements of your financial scenario. In reality, you will most likely work simultaneously in at least three different Sections and a variety of Elements of your business plan.

As you work around and around, through the entire business plan, your case will either get tighter and tighter – or it won't. If it begins to show that it can be viable and workable, you may be moving closer to going into business. As viability and workability become clearer, your confidence will increase. If your business case never does reach viability, you will not gain confidence and you won't be starting the business.

You are launching on one of life's most rewarding journeys: to plan and start your own business. The RoadMap™ is the safest way to approach the journey. I wish you great success!

Task List

1. Think about your business idea.

2. Talk to others about your business idea; listen to their comments.

3. Read books or magazines on topics related to your business idea.

4. Watch newscasts or documentaries or any video footage you can find related to your idea.

5. Make a conscious decision to research your market and determine the viability of your idea.

6. Review this step until you have a firm grasp of the following concepts:

   - The RoadMap™ (the 99-step process)
   - The Shell™ (the business plan structure)
   - The Biz4Caster™ (see note to the right)
   - Sections and Elements of the business plan
   - Narrative – Text, Financial and Supporting Information

***Note:** The Shell™, the Biz4Caster™ and sample business plan are components of the RiskBuster™ Business Planner's CD.*

Prepare to Embark on Your Journey

Step 2

| MUST HAVE |
| RECOMMENDED |
| NICE TO HAVE |

Tip: If you find yourself putting off or delaying an activity, perhaps you are faced with a task that you don't understand or that you dislike. Many people find it difficult to get out and talk to customers. Some cannot write while others dislike working with numbers or financials. The task you are avoiding might be something for which you need assistance.

You have begun a journey that will change your world forever.

You may be starting down this path with no business idea at all, with only an idea for your business, or with a business already in motion. No matter what stage you are at in building your business, the RoadMap™ will enable you to take control of your planning process.

Along the way, you may experience doubt: in yourself, in your business idea, or in others. You must begin to gather together a strong support system for your journey. The key to success is to keep working toward fulfillment of your vision, regardless of the obstacles.

One of the most powerful tools in your toolkit is your written personal vision and goals. There is pure spiritual magic in the simple act of writing down what you wish to achieve. You don't always have to be able to see the solutions in order for them to work. When your goal or vision is written, the power of the universe begins to work with you to bring about success; elements of solutions will begin to gravitate toward you. You will find the right people, the knowledge, the skills and the information you are seeking. To prove it to yourself, simply write out your goals and watch miracles blossom before your eyes.

Time Management for the Business Planner

Your business plan will come together more quickly if you invest sufficient time in the process. It is equally acceptable that your business plan will take a lot longer to complete if you're working at a job full-time or have other commitments that tie up your time and energy. The key is to use this process in a timeframe that works for you and your business.

It is up to you to attach your own degree of urgency and to determine timelines that work for you. It is entirely realistic to complete your business plan in one to two months. The development will go more quickly if you come to the process having already done part of the work. For example, many people think about their business idea for years, reading, talking, asking, listening, watching relevant TV programs, buying and/or selling. Obviously those who have invested time and energy on their business idea should progress more quickly than those who have never given business ownership a thought.

External events may affect parts of your journey. Try not to be stressed by this. Keep pushing forward. If any step or task stops or frustrates you, apply your energy to another part of the process. Should you find yourself blocked for any reason - discouragement, disillusionment, procrastination - there's no antidote quite like action – just keep rolling forward!

From the very beginning, split your time between researching, writing and forecasting. The key is to work on each aspect of your process simultaneously. Here is one example of a daily business planning schedule.

ONE WAY TO ORGANIZE YOUR BUSINESS PLANNING TIME		
ACTIVITY	**ESTIMATED TIME**	**TOOL**
Researching	3 hours	RoadMap™
Writing	2 hours	Shell™
Forecasting	1 hours	Biz4Caster™

Use time allocations that work for you but keep pressing forward on all three activities until you complete your business plan.

Task List

The RoadMap™ is laid out in 99 logical steps to provide you with a structure to navigate the business planning process. I suggest you begin by scanning the entire process to get a sense of how it flows. It is a matter of following the steps, which are comprised of one or more bite-sized tasks arranged in an order that enables you to systematically build your plan.

If you come across steps or tasks that do not pertain to you, bypass them. To help you determine which steps you require, refer to the priority box in the margin for each step. If you find the order of the steps awkward, feel free to complete them in an order that works best for you. This is your adventure and you are the boss.

If you have a computer, your business planning process will involve three main tools, the RoadMap™, The Shell™ and the Biz4Caster™. Everything you do in any of the three tools is for the purpose of completing your business plan, which will ultimately end up in The Shell™.

1. Quickly read or scan the RoadMap™.

2. Quickly read or scan the sample business plan in Chapter 6.

3. Set-up a working copy of your business plan. From the RiskBuster™ CD or download menu, select "Start a New Business Plan" to open a copy of the Business Plan Shell™ – use the file-save-as option to save a working copy of the file in which you can begin creating your own business plan. This is the file or document that will house your finished business plan. If you do not have the RiskBuster™ CD, you can download the BP Shell™ free from **www.riskbuster.com**.

4. Set-up a working copy of your financial scenario. From the RiskBuster™ CD or download menu, select "Start a New Financial Forecast" to open a copy of the Biz4Caster™ – use the file-save-as option to save a working copy in which you can begin building your own financial scenario. If you do not have the Biz4Caster™, you can purchase it at **www.Biz4Caster.com**.

5. Begin working through the RoadMap™ steps, writing narrative in The Shell™ and building your financial scenario in the Biz4Caster™.

6. Email me at **danb@riskbuster.com** if you get stuck anywhere or have questions.

Tip: As you work your way through the RoadMap™, you will encounter speedbumps, steps that are difficult to complete. Any one of these challenges could stop you from completing your business plan. It is essential to foster a sense of urgency to reach your goal, which is, to complete your business plan. When you encounter a step that is difficult to complete, carry on to the following steps. Do what you can in each step, make copious notes on what still needs to be done, and continually push forward. It's OK to bounce forward toward completion and backward to make revisions. The key to successful business planning is to keep the end goal in sight and keep pressing forward on all fronts simultaneously.

Chart Your Path

Step 3

MUST HAVE
RECOMMENDED
NICE TO HAVE

In charting your path, there are two things you can immediately do to lighten your workload: eliminate unnecessary steps and use technology.

Eliminate the Steps Not Relevant To Your Business or Situation

Most people are shocked at the first thought of completing a 99-step business planning process. The 99 steps exist in order to make the planning process work for a broad range of business planners and situations. Rarely will anyone need all 99 steps.

Use Technology to Your Advantage

The RoadMap™ can be completed using either low tech or high tech methods, depending on your financial and technical ability. Throughout this process, you will find my clear bias for the high tech method, simply because of the amount of time and energy it saves. A three-year financial forecast is produced easier and quicker using a computer. Regardless, the RoadMap™ has been created to enable you to complete your business plan using simple resources at minimal cost.

Many people still do not have access to computers and Internet technology. You can develop a perfectly good business plan without a computer; it will just take a bit longer. If you must build your business plan using only pencil and paper, be encouraged. You will succeed and your business plan will serve its ultimate purpose, which is to enable you to become *the expert* for your own business.

Many people will use a mixture of low and high tech methods. It is very effective, for example, to forecast your sales, project your labor requirements and develop your cash flow forecast with a paper and pencil prior to keypunching the numbers into the computer.

The 99 steps exist in order to make the planning process work for a broad range of business planners and situations. Rarely will anyone need all 99 steps.

Task List

1. Using the one page 99-Step Checklist following this page or the larger one in the Appendices Section of this book, make note of any steps that are unnecessary for your business plan.

2. Decide whether you will use low tech, high tech or a combination of the two and gather together the tools you will need to complete your business plan. There are essentially three options for this task.

   • **Low Tech:** The low tech path would be to complete the tasks using a couple of lined notebooks, spare paper, a pencil, an eraser and a calculator.

   • **High Tech:** This path will require that you prepare yourself with the items listed above and a computer with Microsoft Office or equivalent software, a printer, Internet, email capability and the

Macrolink RiskBuster™ (including The Shell™, the Biz4Caster™ and sample business plans).

- **Both Low and High Tech:** You may find that you prefer to carry out certain parts of your process using low tech and others via high tech.

99-STEP ROADMAP™ CHECKLIST	
☐ 1: Welcome to the Macrolink Business Planner's RoadMap™	☐ 51: Research and Select Your Professional Services
☐ 2: Prepare to Embark on Your Journey	☐ 52: Determine Your Employee and Contractor Requirements
☐ 3: Chart Your Path	☐ 53: Develop Your Operational Action Plan
☐ 4: Organize Your Work Space	☐ 54: Forecast Your Sales
☐ 5: Establish Your Timelines	☐ 55: Explain Your Projections
☐ 6: Create Your Action Plan	☐ 56: Estimate Your Market Share
☐ 7: Wade Into Your Industry	☐ 57: Present Your Cost of Goods Sold
☐ 8: Start Your Research Scrapbook	☐ 58: Summarize Your Labor Projections
☐ 9: Write Your Business Vision in an Hour	☐ 59: Develop Your Cash Flow Forecast
☐ 10: Set Out to Prove Your Business Case	☐ 60: Identify Your Operating Expenses
☐ 11: Set Up Your List of Appendices	☐ 61: Develop Your Projected Income Statement
☐ 12: Brainstorm Your Products and Services	☐ 62: Determine What Level of Sales You Will Need to Break-even
☐ 13: Prioritize and Select Your Products and Services	☐ 63: Develop Your Pro Forma Balance Sheet
☐ 14: Discover and List Your Assumptions	☐ 64: Identify and Calculate Your Start-up Expenses
☐ 15: Identify Your Market Research Issues and Strategic Objectives	☐ 65: Clarify Your Sources and Uses of Funds at Start-up
☐ 16: Clarify-Write Your Market Research Questions	☐ 66: Build a Resumé
☐ 17: Prove or Disprove Your Assumptions	☐ 67: Develop Your Personal Net Worth Statement
☐ 18: List the Important Information about Your Industry	☐ 68: Organize Your Certificates and Accreditation
☐ 19: Segment Your Market	☐ 69: Produce Your Historical Financial Statements
☐ 20: Write a Draft Description of Your Customers	☐ 70: Create Your Organizational Charts
☐ 21: Assess What You Are Learning About Your Business	☐ 71: Get the Approval of Your Board
☐ 22: Identify and Research Your Competitors	☐ 72: Build Your List of References
☐ 23: Prioritize and Target Your Customers	☐ 73: Request and Include Letters of Reference
☐ 24: Clarify and Write Your Primary Market Research Questions	☐ 74: Gather and Include Letters of Intent
☐ 25: Determine the Best Method to Gather Primary Research	☐ 75: Copy and Include Signed Contracts or Offers
☐ 26: Create Your Market Survey Questionnaire	☐ 76: Create a Partnership Agreement
☐ 27: Survey Your Customers	☐ 77: Copy and Include Lease Agreement(s)
☐ 28: Compile and Analyze Your Market Survey Information	☐ 78: Copy and Include Insurance Documents
☐ 29: Rewrite Your Description of Your Customers	☐ 79: Develop Your Price List(s)
☐ 30: Make a Go / No-Go Decision	☐ 80: Gather and Include Written Price Quotes
☐ 31: Describe Your Business	☐ 81: Build Credibility with Written Appraisals and Estimates
☐ 32: List Your Products and Services	☐ 82: Provide the Right Amount of Market Survey Information
☐ 33: Describe Your Industry	☐ 83: Create a Map of Your Market Area
☐ 34: Write Your Biography	☐ 84: Gather and Include Environmental Information
☐ 35: Develop Your Strategic Plan and Goals	☐ 85: Build Credibility with Free Publicity
☐ 36: Describe Your Market Area	☐ 86: Create Dynamic Promotional Materials
☐ 37: Describe Your Location	☐ 87: Add a Pinch of Product or Service Literature
☐ 38: Describe Your Customers	☐ 88: Add a Titch of Technical Information
☐ 39: Analyze Your Competitors and Differentiate	☐ 89: Explain any Confusing Terms
☐ 40: Describe How You Will Sell Your Products and Services	☐ 90: Create Your Title Page
☐ 41: Clarify Your Servicing and Guarantees	☐ 91: Write Your Executive Summary
☐ 42: Craft Your Business Image	☐ 92: Develop Your Table of Contents
☐ 43: Develop Your Advertising and Promotion Plan	☐ 93: Write Your Confidentiality and Copyright Statements
☐ 44: Present Your Prices and Pricing Strategy	☐ 94: Evaluate Your Business Plan
☐ 45: Develop Your Marketing Action Plan	☐ 95: Have Business Plan Critiqued by Others
☐ 46: Describe Your Operation	☐ 96: Revise and Rewrite Your Business Plan
☐ 47: Determine Your Equipment Requirements and Methods	☐ 97: Complete Your Application for Financing
☐ 48: Source Your Materials and Supplies	☐ 98: Write Your Cover Letter
☐ 49: Identify Your Risks and How You Will Control Them	☐ 99: Put It All Together
☐ 50: Describe Your Management Team	

Tip: Refer to the Appendix (page 369) for 3 different RoadMap™ checklists.

Organize Your Work Space

Step 4

As you research your market you will accumulate information, articles, reports, magazines, newspaper clips and other assorted documents. If you have a computer you will also gather a lot of the information in digital format.

Task List

Get organized. Create places to store your hard-earned market research information, whether electronic or hard copy.

1. **Determine Where You Will Work.** Determine where to locate your work and storage areas. In the physical world, this means setting up an efficient work area and figuring out where to store your books and files. Do you have a file cabinet with space for your business planning files or will you purchase a file box? Determine where you will locate your business plan on your computer and create a main folder called "My Business Planning Project."

2. **Create Your Hard File Storage Area.** Set up a place for your business planning project in your file cabinet or file storage box. At minimum, begin with one folder for your business plan and one for market research documents. Use the categories listed under point number three as a starting point for your filing system.

3. **Create Your Digital Business Planning Folder.** Set up a folder for your business planning project on your computer. At a minimum, begin with one folder for your business plan and one for market research documents. Your list of folders will grow as you begin to develop different Elements of your business plan and Appendices, but here is a starting point for you.

A WAY TO ORGANIZE YOUR FILE FOLDERS, HARD COPY AND DIGITAL	
FOLDER	FILES
Administrative Files	Action Plan, Vision, Goals, Survey Questionnaire Form(s)
Holding Tank	All homeless clips and files, until you find a home for them
Market Research	Completed Surveys, Research Documents, Clips, Quotes, Tables
Business Plan	Your Business Plan, Your Financial Projections
Appendices	Use your short-list of Appendices developed in Step 21

4. **Set up a Binder for Market Research Documents.** Whether or not you gather the market research documents digitally, you may find it easier to read them in hard copy. This is one way to organize the documents so they are easy to locate for reviewing purposes. If you prefer, you can simply store these hard copy printouts in a file folder as indicated above for the digital counterparts. Depending how many of this type of document you collect, you may wish to insert a set of tabs to make it easier to source the information.

5. **Organize a Bookshelf.** If appropriate, you may also wish to make space available for books related to your business studies and planning.

Tip: Arranging all your business planning files and folders into one folder makes it easy to back-up your business planning information.

Tip: Be sure to back-up your digital business planning folder often – daily is not too often when you are actively working on your plan and progressing. Keep your back-up in a safe place, preferably in a separate building than your computer.

Tip: Get started on the actual writing and forecasting as early as you can. Don't feel that you have to wait until your market research is done before starting these two critical processes. Write in your business plan and work on your projections while simultaneously researching your market. Use your business plan and financial projections as a benchmark to measure your progress. When working as part of a business planning team, the text and financial printouts can serve as a communication tool for team meetings. If you're using the RiskBuster, this means setting up and working in copies of The Shell™ and the Biz4Caster™, almost from day one of your planning process.

Establish Your Timelines

I f you are starting a new business, when do you wish to open? If you are already in business, what date will you implement this plan? If you have a start-up or implementation date in mind, write down your goal.

Step 5

MUST HAVE
RECOMMENDED
NICE TO HAVE

Task List

1. Identify and write your goals.
2. Set timelines for each goal.

WORSHEET: BUSINESS PLANNING & IMPLEMENTATION GOALS	
GOAL	COMPLETION
1. Complete market research.	
2. Complete business plan.	
3. Start business.	
4.	
5.	
6.	
7.	
8.	

Tip: Not writing a goal is the same as not setting a goal; it is one of the ways we deceive ourselves into avoiding the commitment. Write your goals.

If you don't know your start-up date, move on to the following steps and come back to set this goal once you have a clear target.

Tip: Throughout the RoadMap™ you will find worksheets. These worksheets can be downloaded free from our website at www.riskbuster.com. Downloadable worksheets are identified by this icon in the top right corner:

Create Your Action Plan

Step 6

One of the most useful skills you can cultivate for your business planning journey is the ability to develop an effective action plan. An action plan is a systematic process for clarifying and targeting your longer term goals and breaking them down into smaller short term goals.

Task List

1. Develop your action plan for success.

   An action plan includes the following eight steps:

   1. Write your goal clearly and in detail.

   2. List all the benefits associated with achieving your goal.

   3. Identify the people, information, actions and anything else you need to make your goal happen.

   4. Describe the biggest hurdle you need to get over to achieve your goal and how you will overcome it.

   5. List those who will support you and what type of support you want from each one.

   6. Set an overall timeline to reach your goal. Break it down into smaller monthly, weekly and daily goals. What will you do tomorrow to bring you closer to your goal?

   7. Describe when and how will you will reward yourself.

   8. Write one or more affirmations that support you in accomplishing your goal. Repeat your affirmations to yourself regularly. Guidelines for writing affirmations are:

      • Affirmations are stated in the present tense. "I am…"

      • Affirmations are stated in the positive.

      • Affirmations are short and easy to remember.

Affirmation Example

I hold a copy of my completed business plan in my hands. I am very confident about starting my business because of the great learning experience it has been to develop the business plan myself.

Use the *Action Planning Worksheet* to write out your action plan to start your business. You can write your action plan into this book or you might choose to do it on your computer. Allow yourself a couple of days before reviewing and revising your action plan.

WORKSHEET: ACTION PLANNING
1. Write out your goal clearly and in detail.
2. List all the benefits associated with achieving your goal.
3. Identify the people, information, actions and anything else you need to make your goal happen.
4. What is your biggest hurdle to get over to achieve your goal? How will you overcome this hurdle?
5. Who will support you? What type of support do you want from each one?
6. Set an overall timeline to reach your goal. Break it down into smaller monthly, weekly and daily goals. What will you do tomorrow to bring you closer to your goal?
7. When and how will you reward yourself?
8. Write one or more affirmations that support you in accomplishing your goal. Repeat your affirmations to yourself regularly.

Tip: Although the steps are laid out in a linear way, know that it will be necessary to bounce forward and backward in order to complete the process. When creating a new business concept, it may be necessary to work through the market research steps (11 to 30) several times before arriving at a viable concept.

Are you too action oriented to take the time to write an action plan? Bypass this step and keep moving.

Wade Into Your Industry

Step 7

Tip: *This task doesn't limit you to hard copy or paper magazines, nor does it have to cost you a lot of money. The Internet is loaded with websites and e-zines on every topic imaginable. The beauty of e-zines is that they are often free. Use any of the popular search engines to locate directories of e-zines.*

This activity is intended to help you become immersed in your industry and your business by subscribing to and reading one or more trade publications and by researching and joining one or more trade associations.

One of the benefits of developing your own business plan is that you become more knowledgeable about your business and your industry. Trade journals are magazines written specifically for a type of business or industry and they can be a wealth of information. Trade associations are groups of businesses that get together for professional development, networking and training opportunities.

What do you want from trade publications or associations? Here are a few suggestions:

- To learn who the leaders are and what they are doing and saying
- To identify networking, educational, marketing and/or advertising opportunities
- To learn about the industry or industries affecting your business
- To keep current on industry issues and events
- To learn about trends or new developments in your industry
- To discover possible leads or ideas for customers
- To keep tabs on your competitors
- To make contact with suppliers or customers

Task List

The main point of this step is to set out to become the expert on your targeted business and industry.

1. In a library or on the Internet, search and <u>locate and read at least one trade publication relevant to your business</u>. If you have access to back issues, scan them as well. Assess the publication for its usefulness and relevance to your situation. If it seems appropriate, subscribe to it. If it isn't useful, search for a different publication until you find at least one or two that meet your needs.

2. Research and <u>select at least one suitable trade association and join it</u>. If you can't afford to join, perhaps you can become an associate member. If you can't become an associate member, determine whether they have an e-zine you can subscribe to.

3. Be curious and get out there and mingle. Identify changes and issues that currently challenge business operators in the industry. Note any current or future trends that affect your industry.

4. Reflect on how this affects your business idea or your business plan.

Start Your Research Scrapbook

A great journey could use a scrapbook. Your research scrapbook can serve as your trusted companion throughout your adventure. It will help you get through the process and provide you with a forum to vent, to store information, and to process your thoughts. It will provide you with a place to jot down contact information, market research, sales leads and important points to remember. It will also serve to hold pictures and those many bits of paper you will collect along the way.

Here are some suggestions as how you might use your scrapbook:

- Write your goals, your vision, your mission
- Record market research information
- Make lists of things to do
- Write affirmations
- Record quotes or clips that inspire you
- Ask questions (and answer them if you wish)
- Identify problems / challenges
- Clarify confusing things or information
- Whine if things aren't going the way you want
- Write down what you are experiencing
- Write what you are learning
- Make general notes on conversations or information gathered
- Paste or clip in business related pictures, articles or information
- Record sales leads, contact information, market research
- Write portions of your business plan
- Jot down creative or innovative ideas
- Congratulate yourself on tasks well done

Step 8

Tip: It's unlikely that you will need all 99 steps. Lighten your load by going directly to Step 11 and selecting the appendices you will need. Each appendix that is not needed drops one step from your process and shortens your journey.

Task List

1. Start your research scrapbook. You can either use a simple lined notebook or you might wish to purchase a fancier book if that appeals to you. Make it something you will enjoy writing in each day.

Write Your Business Vision in an Hour

Step 9

Many entrepreneurs are frustrated by the fact that business planning takes up more time than they wish to invest. That's only true if you take a long time to do it. Some folks manage to create their entire plan at the kitchen table on a napkin and their business plan exists in their head for the life of the business. I don't subscribe to the napkin plan, nor do I believe a business plan should take forever to complete. I suggest you take some time prior to burying yourself in market research to write out your vision for your business idea.

This is a solution that should not take a lot of time or paper. Sometimes it is helpful to simply blast your way through the process and come out the other end with something written, something to build upon. This activity can be healthy and productive for those just starting out with a new business idea — it can be equally useful for those who are already in business.

Allow yourself at least one uninterrupted hour. Have a pen or pencil and a few pieces of paper handy (if you prefer you can do this activity on the computer). Find a comfortable spot where you can be creative, think and write. Stick to this process and within an hour you should have a draft vision to use as a benchmark for creating your business plan.

Before you launch there are a few tips to propel you into "business visioning nirvana":

Write your vision for some point in the future – pick a date, perhaps your opening day, and write how you wish it to be.

1. Write your vision for some point in the future – pick a date, perhaps your opening day, and write how you wish it to be.

2. Don't worry about perfection - that might come later... keep it simple.

3. Holes-lead-to-goals; it's helpful to keep a piece of paper handy to write yourself a list of "things to research" for information that doesn't easily find its way into this writing.

4. Once you have begun, don't stop until you have finished writing the entire vision.

Task 1: Identify your business. (One paragraph)

1. What is the name of your company?

2. What is the legal form or structure of your business?

3. Where is the business headquartered, licensed, registered?

4. When did or when will your business start?

5. What is the nature of your business (home-based, retail, services or products)?

6. What is the scope of your business (local, regional, national, international or global)?

7. What industry is your business in?

Task 2: Develop your mission statement. (One sentence)

1. What business are you in?
2. What product(s) or service(s) do you provide?
3. Who are your customers?
4. What is your competitive advantage?

Task 3: Write your vision statement. (One sentence)

1. What kind of company do you want to be?
2. How do you wish to be viewed by the individuals and communities you serve?
3. How will you treat your customers, both internal and external?

Task 4: Describe your product(s) and/or service(s). (One paragraph)

1. What proprietary features (patents or trademarks) do you hold for your products and services?
2. What are some innovative characteristics of your products and services?
3. What are the benefits and features of your products and services?

Task 5: Describe your industry trends and the niche your business will serve. (One paragraph)

1. What size is your industry in terms of quantity and value of goods sold?
2. Is your industry static, shrinking or growing?
3. What are the main challenges currently faced by your industry?
4. What are the most prominent new developments in your industry?
5. What are the major trends affecting your industry?
6. What gap or niche will your business serve?

Task 6: List your overall business objectives. (Three to five main points)

1. What are your sales projections for year one, two and three?
2. How many workers will you employ in year one, two and three?
3. What major achievements will you accomplish in year one?

Task 7: Describe your customers. (One paragraph)

1. Who will buy your products and services?
2. What are your customers' age, gender, and family status?
3. What best describes the area where your customers live?
4. How many customers are there?
5. How much will your customers spend on your products and services?
6. If your customers are businesses, describe their size and type, number of employees and location.

Task 8: Describe your major competitors. (One paragraph or a table)

1. Who are your main competitors and how many are there?
2. What key product or service characteristics motivate customers to buy?
3. What are your advantages over the competition?

Task 9: Explain why you and/or your team are qualified to operate your business. (One paragraph)

1. Who will own and/or manage your company?
2. What related business, education or experience qualifies you / your team to operate this business?
3. How and why are you qualified to operate this business?
4. If there are weaknesses, how will you compensate for them?

Task 10: Outline your financial requirements. (One sentence to one paragraph)

1. Will you finance your vision yourself or will you need to use others' money?
2. How much money do you need?
3. When do you need the money?
4. If you are approaching other organizations for financing, what type of loan or grant are you seeking?
5. What terms will you request or offer?

Tip: The only difference between your Business Vision and the Executive Summary is a few miles of market research to build your confidence. Steps 11 to 30 guide you through that market research.

Task 11: Describe what security you will provide to finance your venture. (One paragraph)

1. What can you offer to your lender or financial institution to reduce their risk?
2. How much will you invest in your business and what form will your investment be?

That's it! You've just finished your business vision. If you have more questions than answers at this stage, don't worry, that's normal and healthy. If you're learning things you didn't know about your business, this step is doing exactly what it should. If you feel your vision fairly accurately describes the future for your business, your business planning process might be further along than you previously thought.

Further steps might include:

1. Complete your list of things to do, while it's still fresh in your mind.
2. Prioritize and follow-up on your list of things to do.
3. You might choose to use this mini-plan as an Executive Summary and build on each Element to develop your detailed business plan.
4. If you are relatively confident in the accuracy of what you have written, you could copy your vision into the working copy of your business plan as the Executive Summary.

Set Out to Prove Your Business Case

The following steps, 11 to 30, will lead you through the process of researching your market. Hopefully, the market research steps will also result in proving your business case. **This may be the most critical step in the entire business planning process**. It's important enough to take time to understand how to prove your business case.

Step 10

| MUST HAVE |
| RECOMMENDED |
| NICE TO HAVE |

Business Case Explanation #1

In its most simplistic form, the business case formula looks something like this:

> **Demand Price** (Price You Get For Your Product)
> – **Supply Cost** (Cost of Producing & Selling Your Product)
> = **Enough Money to Meet Your Needs**

Business Case Explanation #2

In your financial projections, proving your business case might look like this:

> **Sales** minus **Cost of Goods Sold (COGS)** = **Gross Profit Margin**
>
> **Gross Profit Margin** minus **Operating Expenses** = **Net Profit before Taxes**

In accounting terms this equation is called an **Income Statement** or a **Statement of Profit and Loss**. When you project it in advance it's referred to as a **Projected Income Statement** or a **Proforma Income Statement**.

The most common pitfall with business plans is that they do not prove the business case, which is often the result of inadequate market research.

Business Case Explanation #3

Here are other ways to view the same information.

BUSINESS CASE EXPLANATIONS			
BUSINESS TERMS	FINANCIAL TERMS #1	FINANCIAL TERMS #2	FINANCIAL TERMS #3
Demand Price	Sales	Sales	$100,000
Supply Cost	COGS	COGS	$ 50,000
Enough Money for Your Business to Survive and Thrive	Gross Profit Margin	Operating Expenses	$ 45,000
		Profit	$ 5,000

If accounting or financial terms cause you stress, use the common terms: *supply, demand* and *enough money for your business to survive and thrive*. These terms are more practical for the following discussion on proving your business case because the matter of proof goes beyond financial viability into many areas of market research.

What Is Proof?

When it comes to proving your business case, what may be proof to some may not be proof to others. You will want to keep the following two questions in mind when proving your business case:

1. What is proof to you?
2. What is proof to your reader(s)?

If you prove the business case to yourself, you will have already gone a long way toward proving it to others. Given that you are the one who will put your time, energy and money on the line, how much proof will enable you to sleep at night?

If I tell you I'm planning to sell laptop computers to polar bears, you will likely think I am crazy. If I back my claim up with letters of support from the Northern Polar Bear Association, you might become mildly interested and want to know more about the idea. If I include orders for laptops from 20 polar bears, you might take me more seriously. If I increase the number of orders to 100 and include a couple of long-term contracts with prominent computer distributors in polar bear country, you might consider the case proven.

When it comes to proving your business case, there is no proof quite as sturdy as having a throng of customers ready to purchase your product or service. In other words, a significant part of your proof might be evidence of customers exchanging their money for your product or service. Assuming you've done your homework in crunching your expenses and can sell at profitable prices, sales prove your case to a certain point. Typically referred to as "test marketing," this method is desirable but not always possible prior to starting your business. Too often, the risk is increased when the supply or demand-side necessitates large quantities of the product or service.

If you're doing a business plan for yourself and not concerned about borrowing from a lender, you can simply determine how much money you are putting at risk and then be sure not to risk more than you can lose. In this way you can fine tune your concept on the fly, letting your customers guide your choices by their purchases.

The business plan is entirely concerned with identifying and strategizing how to deal with business risk. By the time you get through it you will either have proven your business case or not. If you have proven your business case you may be ready to start your business. If you have not proven your case, at least to your own satisfaction, you are not ready to start the business.

What is proof? The strongest "proof" might be customers purchasing products or services, but many start-up businesses will not have the luxury of real paying customers until after the business is started. Some will not even have the product or service to offer until after they have proven their case. This elicits a potentially troubling "chicken or egg first" conundrum.

While it may be challenging to achieve absolute proof, there will always be ways to strengthen or weaken your business case. As demonstrated by the following table, proof will often have to be built in various ways. Confidence that your business case is proven will come about as a result of a number of things you do.

Tip: The most important person to prove your business case to is you. Once you have clarified your proof and have confidence in your business idea, you will find it easier to convince others (like your banker) to believe in or buy into your business idea.

Strengthening or Weakening Your Business Case Argument

Here are a number of ways to strengthen or weaken your business case.

STRENGTHENING OR WEAKENING YOUR BUSINESS CASE	
STRENGTHENS Your Business Case Argument	WEAKENS Your Business Case Argument
· Having spoken to real customers.	· Not having spoken to customers.
· Forecasting sales conservatively.	· Pie-in-the-sky sales forecasts.
· Signed contracts or letters of intent from customers willing to buy your products or services.	· A "build it and they will come" attitude and approach.
· Estimating expenses a little higher than you believe they might be.	· Low or incomplete expense projections.
· Demonstrating frugality, smart shopping and sourcing.	· Lazy or sloppy sourcing, paying too much.
· Being accurate, realistic and truthful all the way through your business plan.	· Inaccuracy, half-truths or false statements of any kind.
· Answering your readers' questions in your plan.	· Leaving your readers with unanswered questions.
· Clear, believable language.	· Fuzzy, unclear language of any kind, including superlatives and hyperbole.
· Using accurate, reliable and credible sources of key information.	· Using unknown, inaccurate or unreliable sources of information.
· Providing clear, accurate references for your sources of information and/or attaching backup documentation in the Appendices.	· Leaving your reader wondering where your information comes from.
· A complete set of clear and realistic financial forecasts that you can discuss intelligently with your banker/investor.	· Financial projections too skimpy or too overwhelming.
· Easy for your reader to understand.	· Difficult for your reader to understand.
· Knowing your business.	· Not knowing your business.
· Knowing your industry.	· Not knowing your industry.
· Using common sense.	· Not using common sense.
· Clear explanations of anything that might be confusing to the reader.	· Lack of clear explanations.
· Having experience related to your business or industry.	· Not having experience related to your business or industry.
· Comparisons with similar businesses.	· Absence of comparison to competitors.

IDEAS FOR PROVING YOUR BUSINESS CASE	
AREA TO PROVE	ELEMENTS OF PROOF
1. How will you prove that your customers are real and that there is a strong demand for your products and services?	Surveys, contracts, letters of intent, sales, testimonials
2. How will you prove the size of your market?	Third party write-ups, articles, surveys, credible statistics
3. How will you prove your qualifications?	Certificates, diplomas, degrees, accreditations, licenses, affiliations, work experience, references
4. How will you prove who your suppliers are?	Supplier contacts, price lists, written offers, expressions of interest, letters of intent or quotes where possible
5. How will you prove your pricing will work?	Comparison to competitors, surveys, other business cases, sales, accurately identifying COGS and other expenses, profit margin within industry standards
6. How will you prove your financial case?	Forecast sales conservatively, project expenses higher than you expect them to be, develop an income statement, and use the Biz4Caster™
7. How will you prove sustainability?	Project three to five year forecasts, use examples of existing comparable businesses, show availability of ongoing supply, and prove demand
8. How will you prove that you can mitigate risks and meet all of the applicable regulatory requirements?	Knowing and communicating that you understand the risks and regulations, acquiring any applicable licenses, certifications or approvals
9. How will you prove your business case?	Credible numbers, realistic sales and cash flow forecasts, build credibility all the way through your business plan, tell the truth, accuracy, clarify all assumptions used, use defensible assumptions

Use whatever level of detail you need to prove your business case to yourself and then rework it to suit your target reader.

The first and most important person to prove your business case to is you. You're the one who will live with the business and hopefully benefit from the venture. You are also the one who will be left facing the taxman at the end of the year. Blow it and you will pay the price; get it right and you may prosper. Use whatever level of detail you need to prove your business case to yourself and then rework it to suit your target reader. Once you are confident in your business you will then be in a better position to convince others to finance or invest, if that's your goal. The first step is to prove it to yourself.

Task List

1. Use the worksheet to map out how you will prove your business case.

WORKHSHEET: IDEAS FOR PROVING YOUR BUSINESS CASE	
AREA TO PROVE	ELEMENTS OF PROOF
1. I will prove that my customers are real and that there is a strong demand for my products and services.	
2. I will prove the size of my market.	
3. I will prove my qualifications.	
4. I will prove my suppliers.	
5. I will prove my pricing is workable.	
6. I will prove my financial case.	
7. I will prove my business is sustainable.	
8. I will prove that I can mitigate risks and meet all of the applicable regulatory requirements.	
9. I will prove my business case.	

EMBRACE YOUR MARKET RESEARCH: BECOME THE EXPERT

Market research is the process of educating yourself about your business. It includes everything you do to prove or disprove your business case.

The most common reason for failure in business is insufficient market research. In developing business plans, too many people fall short on their market research. Most unsuccessful business plans fail because of weak or ineffective market research. There are several reasons for this, including:

- Market research is a great deal of hard work.
- Market research is unfamiliar, daunting work for most people.
- The goals of market research are not clear to the novice.
- To be effective at researching your market, you have to get out and talk with real people (who may not agree with your assertions).
- One possible outcome is that your business idea is unworkable, which can seem like failure.
- The research process is a sea of change from start to finish and change can be frightening.
- You need to multitask, keeping your complete business plan in mind. For example, you might be searching for information on your customers and discover a nugget about your industry; you need to be able to manage the information effectively.
- Without exception, those who tackle the market research process are busy. Time and life are typically already full to the brim when we start researching. Many people give up part way through their research.

Tip: A business plan without adequate market research is like a house without a foundation.

Quite naturally, people tend to have a lot of questions when beginning to research their market.

- How much market research is enough?
- Who do I talk to?
- What questions do I ask?
- How do I know when I have proven my business case?
- How do I gather information about my competitors?
- How do I know if people are telling me the truth?

These questions can be intimidating, particularly if you have never developed a business plan. Steps 11 to 30 will bring you the answers to these and many other questions.

As you research your market, your confidence in your idea will either increase or decrease. As you ask your questions and listen to the answers, you will become very knowledgeable about your business. If your research confirms that your business idea is viable, you will eventually reach a stage where you are confident enough to start your business or implement your plan. If the opposite occurs and you decide not to proceed with your plan, the market research has done its job, which is to save your investment for a different venture.

Market research dovetails into many different parts of your business plan. <u>By the time you complete your market research process (Step 30), you will have written draft versions of at least three Elements of your business plan.</u> You will also have revised and rewritten some of those Elements many times.

Affirmations

1. *I realize it's the things I don't even know I don't know that hold the most threat for my business venture. I am a learner. I open my mind to new information and different ways of viewing everything I think I know about my business idea. As I research my market, I spend most of my time formulating the right questions and listening to the answers. I soak up all the information and challenge all of my assumptions about my business idea. Once I've done that, I then chart my business course with confidence.*

2. *I accept that I do not have all of the answers when it comes to researching my market. I know that the information I need exists and that it will come to me easily and quickly if I just write out my goals and questions clearly. I do not let the fear of being overwhelmed stop me. When I feel overwhelmed I revisit my reasons for wanting to start my business. Whenever I experience fear or doubt, I revisit my passion. I have a valuable contribution to make to my customers and to the world.*

3. *Market research is a learning process. As I research my market, I learn more about my business and myself and about the world in general. The more I learn, the more I become an expert for my business.*

Set Up Your List of Appendices

Step 11

Develop a short-list of the Appendices you consider to be relevant to your business.

Now is a good time to take a look at the list of potential Appendices for your business plan and select the ones you will likely use. It is also an ideal time to set up digital and hard file folders to house the information you collect while researching your market.

Task List

1. Go through the list of possible Appendices, determine which Elements are relevant to you and cross out the rest.

2. Create a place to store the information for each category as you collect it. For example, you might choose to use a file box with different files for each category.

3. If you're using a computer and the Business Plan Shell™, go through the Appendices Section and delete each Appendix you will not use, and then update the table of contents using the Table of Contents (ToC) function in your word processor.

4. As you gather the information for each Element of the Appendix Section, store it in the appropriate digital or hard file.

Note: Steps 66 to 89 deal with each of the Appendices in detail. You may wish to review these steps at this time in order to get a sense of what's involved.

WORKSHEET: APPENDICES						
APPENDICES ELEMENT	STEP #	DON'T NEED	DON'T KNOW	ALREADY DONE	PARTLY DONE	NOT STARTED
1. Resumés	66					
2. Personal Net Worth Statement(s)	67					
3. Certificates and Accreditation	68					
4. Historical Financial Statements	69					
5. Organizational Charts	70					
6. Board or Band Council Resolution	71					
7. List of References	72					
8. Letters of Reference	73					
9. Letters of Intent	74					
10. Contracts or Offers	75					
11. Partnership Agreement	76					
12. Lease Agreement	77					
13. Insurance Documents	78					
14. Price Lists	79					
15. Price Quotes	80					
16. Appraisals	81					
17. Market Survey Results	82					
18. Map of Area	83					
19. Environmental Information	84					
20. Publicity	85					
21. Promotional Material	86					
22. Product Literature	87					
23. Technical Specifications	88					
24. Glossary of Terms	89					

The step numbers in column two above will help you locate the information you need to complete the Appendices you wish to include in your business plan.

Tip: Although the Appendices occur much later in the planning process, they are introduced here because you are likely already beginning to gather the relevant information. By establishing your Appendices now, you will have an organized place to store the information.

Brainstorm Your Products and Services

Step 12

Y ou may have started your business idea with more than one product or service in mind. It can be healthy to brainstorm the topic of products and services to see what else might fit in your business idea.

Task List

1. Gather a small group of people together to brainstorm your products and services. Other than organizing your group, the actual session will probably take less than an hour.

   Identify somewhere between four and seven people you wish to participate, set a time for the brainstorming, contact them and explain what you want them to do and invite them to participate in the session. You will require a place where you can brainstorm without interruptions; your living room can work just fine if you unplug the telephones. It can be fun and you can provide beer, although you might like to hold off until you have finished the brainstorming session. Brainstorming is one of the most effective methods for gathering a lot of ideas quickly. I am continually impressed at what can be achieved when you get several different minds focused on a problem or topic.

   Brainstorming works best if all participants follow a few simple guidelines during the session. For example, there are four ways guaranteed to shut down any brainstorming session, and which should be avoided:

   1) Being critical

   2) Evaluating

   3) Negative comments

   4) Lengthy explanations

   When leading a brainstorming session, I find it useful to share these four points with the group prior to starting to brainstorm. Explain to them that you wish them to avoid these pitfalls during the session. Making them aware of these four pitfalls will make it easier for everyone to stay on track.

   Here is a suggested process for keeping your brainstorming session lively, focused and productive.

   A. Share the purpose and objectives of the activity with the group.

   B. Use the following points to explain the procedure:

   • Select someone to record the ideas

   • Clarify guidelines for brainstorming

   • Describe your business concept for the group

   • Brainstorm

   • Review what was recorded

Tip: While brainstorming, play inspirational instrumental music in the background. Be sure to confirm that the music is OK with everyone in the group as the addition of extra sound can make it difficult for some people to focus. Playing the music at a barely audible level can stimulate the brain in a positive way and add to the creativity.

C. Clearly announce the focus or the key question the group will be brainstorming; in this case the goal will be *"To brainstorm all the products and services that could be sold by this business."*

D. Ask for one or two volunteers to record or write the ideas on a flipchart. You can use cards or note paper if necessary, but it is important that the participants are able to see their results as they brainstorm.

E. Clarify the guidelines with the participants.

F. If you're setting a timeline, announce the duration of the session.

G. Ask for and answer any questions regarding the procedure.

H. Start the session.

I. Repeat the key question without variation to keep the group focused.

J. Ensure that the recorders post all ideas for everyone to see.

K. Call "stop" at the designated time, or when ideas stop flowing.

L. Review by going over the completed flipcharts.

M. Feed the participants the beer or pizza or whatever you promised them to lure them out to help you and be sure to thank everyone for their ideas and input.

Tip: Brainstorming is a very powerful tool for creating solutions. By selecting the right people you can bring about amazing results. Consider brainstorming to solve problems, identify potential customers, generate marketing or advertising ideas and discover ways to provide better customer service.

Prioritize and Select Your Products and Services

Step 13

F ocus your market research time, money and effort on the products and services most important to your business. You might wish to provide all the products and services in the world, but time, money and energy require some prioritizing and focus. For most types of business, I recommend you focus on twelve or fewer products, services or lines. Select which ones you will focus on for your market research and file the rest away for future reference.

From the list of products and services you brainstormed, choose those on which you will focus your research effort.

Define Your Units

Tip: In determining units for your business, consider how the same products or services are sold by similar businesses and how they are purchased by customers. The building trades often communicate in terms of square feet of building or linear feet of material. For example, a roof would likely be bought or sold by the square foot, yard, or meter.

Products and services move through the marketplace in units. Units are used in every industry as a way of measuring and communicating about products and services. A unit can be a product, a service or a line of products or services. It can also be a package deal, comprised of either products or services or a combination of both. Examples of units are:

DEFINING YOUR UNITS	
UNIT	EXAMPLE
A product	For my business, a book is one unit.
An hour of service	Each hour your mechanic works on your car is one unit.
A day of service	A training business typically buys and sells training by the day, sometimes by the half-day.
A package or bundle of products or services	The travel industry often groups different combinations of hotel, airfare and food to form a package or bundle.
A product line	In retail businesses where prices, variety and the sheer number of products make it unrealistic to list every item, products are often grouped together and a dollar value can become the unit for measuring purposes. For example, a gift store might consider all of its candles as a line and use the average purchase by a customer as the unit value.

When striving to organize your products and services into units, it makes sense to keep the number of units to twelve or fewer in order to make the forecasting manageable. Although some businesses will have thousands of products, it is not necessary to generate sales projections for each and every one.

Prioritizing Products and Services

How do you prioritize your products and services? There are different views to consider.

PRIORITIZING YOUR PRODUCTS AND SERVICES	
QUESTIONS TO ASK	THINGS TO CONSIDER
Does the product or service fit your business mission and goals?	Your business mission is to serve your customers. If your products or services do not fit your mission, you risk confusing your customers.
Will the product or service earn you money?	If the product or service doesn't earn you money, there has to be some other compelling reason to use it.
How much mark-up or profit will the product or service earn for your business?	It's not that all of your products and services have to be high producers but you definitely want high producers among your offering.
How accessible is the product or service?	Limited accessibility can be a strength or a weakness. A product that is difficult to get can command higher prices.
How much control do the suppliers exert over the product or service?	A supplier who has a monopoly is likely to exert a lot of control over prices and terms.
How much control do the customers exert over the product or price?	Some suppliers will dictate consumer prices; others will give you more leeway. You will want to assess whether you need pricing flexibility in order to satisfy your customers.
Can you build or obtain the amount of product or service your customers are likely to order?	If you are hoping to attract a large buyer, can you ramp up effectively to supply larger orders? Can you maintain profit levels while producing larger amounts?
Can you get the products or services to the customer in a timely, profitable manner?	I might like to sell books in far off countries, but is it realistic? It is not likely that I can get books to someone in Asia in a timely manner until I have made distribution arrangements.

Tip: For retail businesses with hundreds or thousands of products, consider arranging your units into groups or product lines. If this proves ineffective, your best method may be to determine how much the average customer will spend and use those figures to build your sales forecast.

Tip: When arranging your products and services into units, keep two things in mind. First, know how your competitors sell their goods and services to customers and use the industry standard for your type of business. Second, consider how the customer will buy the goods and services from your business. Vegetables are typically sold by the pound or by the bundle. Dinner is sold by the plate. A house is sold by the square foot. Gravel is sold by the truck-load in Canada and by the burlap sack in Honduras. Know your area, know your industry and speak the language. Define your units.

To keep things in perspective, this is only a first cut for your products and services. As you continue to research your market and become more knowledgeable about your business and industry, you may find that you change your thinking many times between now and opening day. Stay curious, keep on listening and keep an open mind. The only constant is change.

I recommend you view this as an exercise to get you started on your market research. You have to begin somewhere. Start with the best list you can concoct and let your customers guide you from this point forward.

Tip: Building a business plan for a proven business concept is very different than creating a new business concept from the ground up. Aspiring business owners can get mired in their attempt to build their product or service offering. What you are really doing in this step is beginning to craft your business concept. You are pioneering, which naturally could lead to some trial and error before you settle on a concept that will work. It is natural and acceptable to spin a few circles at this stage before you settle on your opening day product and service offering. While you're at it you may as well adjust to two more notions; that your concept will change the minute you start the business and that it will continually evolve during the life of the business. Listen to your customers and they will guide you.

Example: Prioritizing Products and Services

My concept began with a desire to serve entrepreneurs. I set out to establish a small business that markets a book, a CD and training resources for entrepreneurs. At this point I believe my business will offer the following products and services to its customers:

PRODUCT OR SERVICE	UNITS
1. Books for Business Planners	Retail, Bookstore, and Distributor Rates
2. Digital Tools for Business Planners	CD and Downloadable from Website
3. Workshops for Business Planners	Day Rate, Half-day Rate, Individual Seat
4. Manuals for Trainers	Retail Rate
5. Consulting and Business Plan Coaching	Hourly and Daily Rates

Task List

1. Review your brainstormed list of products and services from Step 12.

2. Cut all of the most obvious poor product and service ideas from your list.

3. Prioritize which products and services you will focus on for market research purposes. If appropriate, file the rest of the ideas somewhere for future reference.

4. Research businesses similar to yours, then arrange your products or services into units. Keep your short list to twelve or fewer units if possible.

WORKSHEET: PRIORITIZING PRODUCTS AND SERVICES	
PRODUCT OR SERVICE	UNITS
1.	
2.	
3.	
4.	
5.	
6.	
7.	
8.	
9.	
10.	
11.	
12.	

Tip: When you encounter a step you cannot complete, make a list of what needs to be done and move on to the following steps. Keep pushing forward unless your research indicates you should abandon the business idea.

Discover and List Your Assumptions

I t's difficult to discover our assumptions and it's nerve-wracking to change them. Most of us perceive our assumptions to be our reality. We believe things and therefore they are. In business, inaccurate assumptions can cost you your investment.

For a banker or a business analyst, there are few things more frightening than an entrepreneur who has all the answers. We have all met such individuals. Because they already *know everything* they tend to spend a lot more time talking rather than listening. Impassioned about their idea, they assault the marketplace. With fire in their eyes and armed with their bullet-proof rationales, they overpower anyone who might suggest a different view or method. The marketplace has a way of dealing with zealots with blinders on and it's usually messy.

If you are serious about starting your business, classify everything not already proven as an assumption and then set out to *prove or disprove* everything you assume. This is much safer than making a few brash statements and then putting your equity on the line.

Step 14

MUST HAVE
RECOMMENDED
NICE TO HAVE

Tip: As you research your market, be vigilant for assumptions that you missed in your first list. As you discover more assumptions, add them to your list. It may seem difficult to identify and adjust your own assumptions. Consider that any one of your assumptions, should they be wrong, could propel you into bankruptcy. Losing everything you have worked for and bankruptcy are difficult. Humiliation, defeat and feeling worthless are difficult. Market research is a confidence builder!

Example: List of Assumptions

QUESTION	DAN'S LIST OF ASSUMPTIONS
1. Who will buy your product or service?	Entrepreneurs, adults, male and female who need to develop their own business plans
2. What ages are your customers?	Working adults from ages 20 to 55 Hottest markets – 25 to 45 years old male and female
3. How many potential customers are there?	Perhaps 20 to 50% of people of work force age
4. Can you identify different groups or categories of customers?	Those starting businesses, thinking about starting, owners, Canadian, American and other English speaking countries
5. Why will customers buy your products or services?	It is effective for the novice attempting to scale the business planning wall
6. What are they currently buying to meet that need?	All nature of books and digital products that are only partially effective for novices
7. How often will customers buy your product or service?	Once for themselves and perhaps more as gifts for family and friends
8. Will customers come back and buy again?	There is potential to convince customers to purchase products as gifts for friends and family. Also potential to up-sell book buyers to purchase digital products and vice versa
9. Will they send their friends to buy your products and services?	Will have to offer incentives

QUESTION	DAN'S LIST OF ASSUMPTIONS
10. Will customers purchase your product or service as a gift for their family and friends?	Will have to offer incentives
11. What else do they buy?	Computers, business books and magazines, software, food, consumables, cars
12. What magazines do they read?	Business, adventure, sports, hobby
13. What TV programs do they watch?	News, sports
14. What hobbies do they enjoy?	Sports
15. If your clients are businesses, how many are there?	Approximately 90% of small businesses in British Columbia have fewer than four employees
16. What type of businesses are your clients?	Mostly service businesses
17. How many people do they employ?	Fewer than five
18. What products and services do they sell?	All kinds (books, digital, consulting services)
19. What size is your market area?	BC first, Canada second, USA third
20. Who are your competitors?	Other business planning books and digital products. Consultants who write business plans
21. How many competitors are there?	There are many business planning guides or solutions, but this one will work for the broadest group – laypeople
22. Why do customers purchase from your competitors?	In many cases they use whatever product the gatekeeper tells them to use
23. Are customers pleased with the service they get from your competitors? If yes, why? If not, why not?	I don't think so. The path to a completed business plan is too confusing, too many roadblocks, too many places to fall off the path
24. Would your competitors' customers switch to your product or service and what would it take to get them to do so?	It will take strong testimonials from people who successfully scale the wall and start their businesses. My offering will have to stand out in the market

Tip: Your list of assumptions will help you focus your market research. Your assumptions are a starting point to discovering the facts. Don't worry if you don't have all the answers at this point. Subsequent steps will lead you to those answers.

Task List

1. Using the following worksheet or a blank sheet of paper, write out a minimum of twenty assumptions. Don't stop until you have written down every wingding notion you ever had about your business idea. Write a hundred assumptions if you have that many.

WORKSHEET: ASSUMPTIONS	
QUESTION	LIST OF ASSUMPTIONS
1. Who will buy your product or service?	
2. What ages are your customers?	
3. How many potential customers are there?	
4. Can you identify different groups or categories of customers?	
5. Why will customers buy your products or services?	
6. What are they currently buying to meet that need?	
7. How often will customers buy your product or service?	
8. Will customers come back and buy again?	
9. Will they send their friends to buy your products and services?	
10. Will customers purchase your product or service as a gift for their family and friends?	
11. What else do they buy?	
12. What magazines do they read?	

Tip: Your list of assumptions will help you identify what you should be looking for when researching your market. It will also provide you a benchmark to measure your progress as you research your market.

WORSHEET: ASSUMPTIONS Continued	
QUESTION	LIST OF ASSUMPTIONS
13. What TV programs do they watch?	
14. What hobbies do they enjoy?	
15. If your clients are businesses, how many are there?	
16. What type of businesses are your clients?	
17. How many people do they employ?	
18. What products and services do they sell?	
19. What size is your market area?	
20. Who are your competitors?	
21. How many competitors are there?	
22. Why do customers purchase from your competitors?	
23. Are customers pleased with the service they get from your competitors? If yes, why? If not, why not?	
24. Would your competitors' customers switch to your product or service and what would it take to get them to do so?	

Tip: *If you find any of the questions don't apply to your business, skip them or replace them with your own more relevant questions.*

Identify Your Market Research Issues and Strategic Objectives

Step 15

MUST HAVE
RECOMMENDED
NICE TO HAVE

How do you effectively complete your market research? You need to prove your business case. You must prove that your products and services will sell and earn a profit. Keep in mind that the first draft of your business plan will be for you. It is a confidence building process that will result in you deciding whether or not to start your business. Each nugget of research will either increase or decrease your confidence in your business idea. If you discover enough positives you will start your business; negatives should cause you to back off or try different ideas until you get enough positives.

Sources of Secondary and Primary Market Research Assistance and Information

When you set out to research your market, you will be exploring two main categories of research: secondary and primary. Secondary comes first because you will do much of your secondary research before narrowing your focus to primary research. In other words you will likely check out the big picture and then move into the smaller or more localized market research, beginning with a more general approach and moving to more specific.

> **Secondary market research** is the information you will obtain from other sources, such as Statistics Canada or the US Census Bureau, reports, articles in trade or consumer magazines, and the Internet.

> **Primary market research** is the information you gather yourself by talking to customers and by surveying customers, competitors and suppliers. Typical methods for conducting primary market research are observation, personal interviews, focus groups, formal surveys, mail surveys and telephone surveys.

Each nugget of research will either increase or decrease your confidence in your business idea. If you discover enough positives you will start your business; negatives should cause you to back off or try different ideas until you get enough positives.

The following table offers a number of ideas on where to access information and assistance.

SOURCES OF ASSISTANCE AND INFORMATION	
Accountants	Family / Friends
Affiliations	Federal Government Agencies
Associations	Individuals
Audio and Video Cassettes	Insurance Agents
Bankers	Internet
Books	Lawyers
Business Advisors	Libraries
Business Development Banks	Local Government Offices
Business Development Organizations	Newspapers
Census and Statistics Agencies	Provincial Government Agencies
Chamber of Commerce	Publications
Conferences	State Government Agencies
Consultants	Tax Planners
Corporations	The Competition
Courses / Seminars / Workshops	Universities
Economic Development Officers	Yourself

Dan's Strategic Market Research Objectives

After listing my assumptions and reviewing the *Sources of Assistance and Information* above, I wrote the following list of strategic market research objectives:

Example: Strategic Market Research Objectives

STRATEGIC MARKET RESEARCH OBJECTIVES	SECONDARY	PRIMARY
1. Learn more about writing. I know some writers I can take to lunch and ask questions.	Books, Associations	Workshops, interviews
2. Learn more about publishing. I have a great book called *1001 Ways to Market Your Book* by John Kremer. I will read it. Egad, it's thicker than my dictionary! I will search the Internet for information on publishing and search the Statistics Canada and US Census websites to gather statistics on the publishing industry.	Kremer, Associations, Internet, Statscan, US Census	Interview publishers, bookstore owners, distributors
3. Learn more about entrepreneurs. Determine how many are out there. How many are in business, how many are starting businesses, how many are simply thinking about or wish to own a business.	Statscan, UA Census, Government, Internet	Interviews, surveys, focus group
4. Learn more about business books and specifically any that look like competition to my book. I have a few in my library and I will begin gathering more.	Library, books	Read books, use digital products
5. Learn more about every one of the assumptions listed in the previous step. I will have to obtain information from local, regional and federal government and industry sources in both Canada and the United States.	Read trade publications, Internet	Prove or disprove what I think I know
6. Determine how many countries will have a market for my book. My brain thinks globally, even though my capacity lives locally. I will begin my research in Canada and the United States and see where my nose leads me.	Locate existing studies or surveys	Travel to English speaking countries
7. Learn more about business planning. This is my corner of the research. I believe I am already an expert on the topic. However, I resolve to continue my learning in this area. I will challenge my own business planning process and go through it like it's my very first business plan.	Research others systems	Read books, use products, interview bankers
8. Learn more about potential buyers of my book. After ten years spent training others how to build business plans, I know many entrepreneurs who have started businesses. I will create a detailed survey questionnaire to approach a number of these people. Perhaps I will interview them personally.	Find out who buys competitors books, products and services	Listening to questions and comments from participants in my workshops
9. Discover which other products and services might be useful to my customers. Determine a product and service mix that is not only attractive to customers but different from my competitors.	Associations, sublications, Internet	Observe competitors, assess my own skills

My brain thinks globally, even though my capacity lives locally.

Task List

1. Write out a list of your *Strategic Market Research Objectives*, as you understand them at this moment. Don't worry about perfection or missed areas at this point. Write at least five to ten goals, more if you can.

2. Using the *Sources of Information and Assistance* checklist, identify potential secondary and primary sources for each of your strategic objectives.

3. Print or write your *Strategic Market Research Objectives* and hang copies in visible locations (your desk, your fridge, your bathroom).

WORKSHEET: STRATEGIC MARKET RESEARCH OBJECTIVES		
STRATEGIC MARKET RESEARCH OBJECTIVES	SECONDARY	PRIMARY
1.		
2.		
3.		
4.		
5.		
6.		
7.		
8.		
9.		

Tip: Be curious! The trick is to get busy with the goals and questions you create now. As you research, you will discover not only the answers to your existing questions, but hopefully many more questions as well. Keep an open mind and be a learner.

Clarify and Write Your Market Research Questions

Step 16

MUST HAVE
RECOMMENDED
NICE TO HAVE

The quality of your research will be in part determined by the quality of the questions you ask. This is an easy place to get hung up. Don't let it stop you; relax and push on through.

As a general strategy, you will want to glean all you can from secondary market research sources and then narrow your focus to primary. Don't worry whether your questions can be answered through primary or secondary research – it's more important to clarify your questions, then to determine the best method to obtain the answers. If you're confused about what you are doing, re-read Step 10. Clarify what will prove or disprove your assumptions.

The quality of your research will be in part determined by the quality of the questions you ask.

Example: List of Market Research Questions

MARKET RESEARCH QUESTIONS	PROOF	WHERE TO FIND IT
1. How many people, at any given time, are attempting to start a business?	Existing survey, research or poll	Statscan, US Census, pollsters, Internet
2. Are there more men or more women starting businesses?	Existing surveys, magazine articles	Provincial or national studies, Internet
3. How many people, at any given time, are considering starting a business?	University study or paper	Universities, Internet
4. How many existing business owners would develop their own business plan, given the right tools?	Survey, testimonials	Probably have to survey business owners for this info
5. How many existing business owners would contract me to develop their business plan?	Survey, letters of intent	Probably have to survey business owners for this info
6. How many entrepreneurs bypass the business plan and start their business without one?	Survey	Probably have to survey business owners for this info
7. How much will customers pay to solve the business planning challenge?	My personal knowledge and experience will help with this	Interview agencies that pay for business plan development
8. What meeting places do my customers have in common? Where can I get the most bang for my advertising bucks?	Magazine articles from credible sources	Search Inc, Entrepreneur and Profit magazine archives
9. How many of my customers own computers and have access to the Internet?	Statistics showing Internet usage growth	Internet, computer hardware and software magazines and businesses
10. Why do customers buy my competitors' products and services?	Interviews of competitors	Documentaries, videos, competitor advertisements
11. Why will customers pay for my book and digital products when the perception is that the Internet is full of free solutions?	Test marketing, selling samples to customers	Negotiate with existing customers
12. How can I get gatekeepers (bankers, enterprise development agencies, etc.) to recommend my products and services?	Provide sample products, work with clients to create successes	Interview those I know, network to find others willing to test products and services

WORSHEET: LIST OF MARKET RESEARCH QUESTIONS		
MARKET RESEARCH QUESTIONS	PROOF	WHERE TO FIND IT
1.		
2.		
3.		
4.		
5.		
6.		
7.		
8.		
9.		
10.		
11.		
12.		

Tip: Go as far as you can see, and you will be able to see further.

Task List

Write your market research questions.

1. Reread your *List of Assumptions* (Step 14, page 127) and your *List of Market Research Goals* (Step 15, page 131).

2. Write a list of market research questions that you wish to answer. Try to have at least one question for each assumption and each objective. A few questions will get you absolutely busy, but I encourage you to write as many questions as you can.

3. Don't worry about missing questions at this point. If you are truly curious, many more questions will surface as you research. Later, as you think of other questions, add them to your list.

4. Go back and review the list of potential *Sources of Assistance and Information*. Consider where you can find answers to your questions. Make your list.

5. Use either a blank sheet of paper or the table above to list your questions, proof, and where to find the answers you seek.

Prove or Disprove Your Assumptions

MUST HAVE
RECOMMENDED
NICE TO HAVE

This is where the kayak connects with the current. It's time to challenge your own logic. Become a super sleuth and set out to prove or disprove all of your assumptions. This is the work of researching your market. Armed with your *List of Assumptions* (Step 14), and your *List of Market Research Goals* (Step 15), and your *Market Research Questions* (Step 16), get out there and learn.

The key to this step is to avoid taking your misconceptions too seriously. Keep an open mind. Persist in digging up all the information available.

Keep track of your learning by writing in your scrapbook or your business plan. Store the information in your market research files, hard copy and/or digital. Don't worry too much about organizing the information at this point – that is what your business plan is for.

Example: Proving and Disproving Assumptions

I set out to prove or disprove my assumptions. One of the joys of market research is that it compels you to learn more about the world around you. I learned some interesting things along the way.

I want simple and understandable summary population tables and I want them right flipping now!

I get bogged down fairly quickly at the Statistics Canada website at **www.statscan.ca**; it frustrates me and I'm not overly patient when searching. I want simple and understandable summary population tables and I want them right flipping now! I resolve to learn more about searching and fire off an email explaining my project and pleading for direction from a faceless soul at Statistics Canada. The following morning I have a wonderful response from someone whose name I may never know. I print out scads of articles, reports and tables. I wade through the reports and make a few phone calls to learn the information in the table on the opposite page.

EXAMPLE: PROVING AND DISPROVING ASSUMPTIONS		
QUESTION	MY ASSUMPTIONS BEFORE RESEARCHING	WHAT I KNOW OR BELIEVE AFTER RESEARCHING
Population of Prince George	75,000	84,615
Local Chamber of Commerce Members	2,000	950
Number of licensed businesses in Prince George	Hadn't considered	4,800
What % of population considering business?	7% of population 5,250	12% of labor force
Total who could use my book in Prince George	5,000-ish	9,393-ish
Population of British Columbia	3,000,000	3,907,740
Population in ideal business age group in BC	Hadn't considered	2,018,545
Total who could use my book in BC	210,000	201,854
Population of Canada	30,000,000	31,600,000
Population in ideal business age group in Canada	Hadn't considered	16,250,200
Total who could use my book in Canada	2,100,000	3,720,000
Population of United States	300,000,000	288,368,698
Percentage of US population who could use my book	21,000,000	34,604,244
Percentage of population that are entrepreneurs	10%	12%
Total potential book readers in Canada & US	21,210,000	38,333,163
My Confidence In My Business Idea	Less Confidence	More Confidence

Tip: Be curious!

The important thing is not that my initial assumptions are accurate. My increased confidence arises from the fact that my assumptions and knowledge base are becoming more accurate.

Task List

1. Research your market. Read trade journals and books, search on the Internet, review reports, ask questions and follow your nose, turn over all of the rocks.

2. Challenge your assumptions until they are either proven or disproven. Record your findings; adjust your thinking when necessary.

3. As you think of more assumptions and questions, add them to your lists and follow the same process for each.

4. Keep sifting until you have separated the chaff and harvested the purest information for your efforts.

At this point you have gathered a lot of information about your industry. It is time to bring that information together in preparation for writing a description of your industry.

List the Important Information about Your Industry

Step 18

MUST HAVE
RECOMMENDED
NICE TO HAVE

Ultimately this writing will end up in your business plan as the *Industry Element*, but for now don't worry about the business plan, your reader, or getting it perfect. Simply write a list of important points you now know about your industry.

North American Industry Classification System

The North American Industry Classification System (NAICS) is one of three main organizations in the world that deal with industry classification. NAICS was developed by the statistical agencies of Canada, Mexico and the United States. The organization of NAICS followed the North American Free Trade Agreement with a goal of creating common definitions and statistics to facilitate analysis of the three economies.

Here are a number of key points to help you understand your industry:

- Industries are made up of businesses and other organizations that produce goods and services. All businesses produce either products or services or a combination of both.

- The agencies responsible for collecting taxes in each country are primary users and drivers of the industry classification systems, because of their need to classify businesses for taxation purposes.

Simply write a list of important points you now know about your industry.

- As a business planner, it is important to keep one eye on the taxation agency's view as you attempt to clarify which industry you are in.

- In addition to the tax collectors view, it is important to maintain your entrepreneur's view. As an entrepreneur one of your main objectives is to research relevant information and ultimately determine whether or not your business can effectively compete and thrive in your market area. As a business planner you are likely to be less concerned with how the taxation folks wish to categorize your business and are more concerned with the survival and success of your enterprise.

- NAICS analyzes businesses according to their business process to determine what industry they are in. Knowing this helped me to understand why certain types of businesses are grouped in the way they are to make up some of the industries. As a writer I am grouped with artists and performers because my process for doing business is substantially the same as artists and performers.

- Where your business has more than one product or service, tax agencies will use the proportion of revenue to dictate which industry you are in. In other words, if you earn a higher amount of revenue from one product or service they will place you in that industry for taxation purposes.

- Having to know how much of your revenue comes from one product versus another presents yet another conundrum for the business planner. How can you research your industry before you have done your sales forecast, yet how can you forecast sales before researching your industry? This is clearly a situation that demands that you go as far and you can see so that you will be able to see farther. Identify your industry to the best of your ability now and change it after you've done your sales forecast if necessary.

- In the world of NAICS, the hierarchical structure of industries is as follows: sectors (two-digit code), subsectors (three-digit code), industry groups (four-digit code), industries (five-digit code), and national industries (six-digit code).

The following table shows the 20 NAICS industry sectors:

INDUSTRY SECTORS	
11 Agriculture, Forestry, Fishing and Hunting	53 Real Estate and Rental and Leasing
21 Mining and Oil and Gas Extraction	54 Professional, Scientific and Technical Services
22 Utilities	55 Management of Companies and Enterprises, Scientific and Technical Services
23 Construction	56 Administrative and Support, Waste Management and Remediation Services
31-33 Manufacturing	61 Educational Services
41 Wholesale Trade	62 Health Care and Social Assistance
44-45 Retail Trade	71 Arts, Entertainment and Recreation
48-49 Transportation and Warehousing	72 Accommodation and Food Services
51 Information and Cultural Industries	81 Other Services (except Public Administration)
52 Finance and Insurance	91 Public Administration

I determined that the best fit for my business is as follows:

EXAMPLE: DAN'S INDUSTRY	
Sector:	71 Arts, Entertainment and Recreation
Subsector:	711 Performing Arts, Spectator Sports and Related Ind.
Industry Group:	7115 Independent Artists, Writers and Performers
Industry:	71151 Independent Artists, Writers and Performers
National Industry:	711510 Independent Artists, Writers and Performers

"This industry group comprises independent individuals (free-lance) primarily engaged in performing in artistic productions, creating artistic and cultural works or productions, or providing technical expertise necessary for these productions. Independent celebrities, such as athletes, engaging in endorsement, speaking and similar services, are included."

Armed with a meaningful definition of my industry and volumes of research material, I plunged into the task of writing my key industry statements.

Tip: After gathering and listing all the key information about your industry, organize the information from general to specific. For example, you might consider for your readers' sake, beginning with the larger picture (total industry, national or international) and working your way to your more immediate picture, the local industry picture. This will help you and your reader to build a perspective on your industry and how it relates to your business.

Example: Key Industry Statements

LIST OF KEY POINTS ABOUT INDUSTRY	DAN'S LIST OF KEY INDUSTRY STATEMENTS
What industry or industries is your business in?	71151 Independent Artists, Writers and Performers.
What quantities of goods are sold and what is the value of those goods?	The 672 firms active in Canadian book publishing recorded revenues of more than $2.4 billion in the 2000/01 fiscal year, up 9.4% from the previous survey results in 1998/99 and a 20.0% increase from 1996/97. Many new titles entered the Canadian marketplace in 2000/01. Book publishers produced 15,744 new titles and reprinted 12,053 existing titles, an increase of over 13% from 1998/99 and over 47% from 1996/97. Textbooks and trade books each accounted for a third of the production. Sales from exports increased at twice the pace of domestic sales from 1998/99 to 2000/01. For English-language publishers, 78.8% of their export revenues were earned in the United States. The United States continues to be Canada's largest buyer of exported books. In terms of the actual size of the business book market, Kremer states: "More than 1000 business titles are published every year (in the Unites States). In 1996, business book publishers had $666 million in net sales."
What is the industry outlook and growth potential?	Business books are a hot market and they tend to pick up sales momentum as time passes. John Kremer, in his book 1001 Ways to Market Your Books, states: "Between 1991 and 1995, sales of business books (in the United States) increased by 26%. Books about small business are especially hot (Simba Information)." "Business books, like children's books, sell better as time passes. For example, Ingram sold 60% more copies of Service America in 1987 than they did in 1986, and the trend continued in 1988. Business books have a great backlist potential."
What are the industry trends (past, present and future)?	The book publishing industry is growing. E-books are the fastest growing area of the book publishing industry. In Canada, the number of small or micro businesses is growing in four provinces. In the micro-business arena, service businesses are the fastest growing type of business.

Tip: The very best solution to developing your Industry Element is to find an existing description of your industry (for example: trade publications, business books and annual reports of public companies). Failing that take the approach that I did in the tables to the right; pull together key points about your industry and organize them in a presentable, understandable fashion. No one expects you to be a professional economist to start a business, but you do need to communicate that you understand the industry you are getting into.

LIST OF KEY POINTS ABOUT INDUSTRY	DAN'S LIST OF KEY INDUSTRY STATEMENTS
What key points about your industry help to support your business case?	The Canadian book industry saw substantial growth in 2000/01, with increases in revenues, sales and the number of new titles issued. In the United States, 10.1 million adults are engaged in trying to start new firms at any given time. Men are twice as likely to start a business as women. Entrepreneurship substantially involves adults at all ages, except people over 65 years old. The most active group are young men ages 25-34.
What population shifts and/or consumer trends affect your industry?	Population figures for my target customer groups are generally increasing. I believe there is considerable migration from underdeveloped parts of the world to the developed areas – Canada and United States.
What are the main challenges faced by the industry?	The Canadian book publishing industry is challenged by a dependence on government grants and lower profitability.
What are the main barriers or incentives to entry by new businesses?	There are two main barriers to a new independent writer entering the industry · Building of credibility and name recognition, and · The high cost of marketing to penetrate the market.
What significant new developments have or are taking place in your industry?	According to Kremer - "In 1970, there were about 3,000 independent small presses in the United States. In 1997, that number had grown to 60,000 (American Bookseller). This rapid growth has been fuelled by four major changes that occurred in the fifteen-year period." Short-run printing technology enables competitive pricing of books even in runs fewer than 2,000 copies. Computers and desktop publishing programs have cut the cost of designing and typesetting books by as much as 90%. Computers have also cut the costs of order entry, fulfillment, list maintenance, targeted publicity and many other marketing functions. Bookstore distribution has opened up as more distributors and wholesalers actively court smaller publishers. The growth of the superstores has also increased demand for a variety of titles, a demand that the larger publishers cannot satisfy. Increased knowledge has been made available to new publishers by many local and national publisher associations, new books and newsletters have cut the learning curve for novice publishers."

Tip: It's critical that you can support your key industry statements with credible, verifiable sources.

Tip: Don't allow yourself to get hung up on defining the precise industry your business is in. If you're confused I recommend you email or call the help contacts at your local census office. It is more important that you take time to learn generally about the overall industry dynamics that will affect your business. Unless you are already very knowledgeable about your industry, this step will be a much needed learning process for you. Don't be surprised or discouraged if it takes some time.

Tip: Learning about your industry is an ongoing activity. This is one important reason to join associations and subscribe to trade publications and e-zines.

LIST OF KEY POINTS ABOUT INDUSTRY	DAN'S LIST OF KEY INDUSTRY STATEMENTS
What is the size of the total market and how is it divided up and served by your competitors?	There is a history of growth and strong growth forecasted in business book sales for Canada and the United States.
	According to the GEM 2002 study, about 286 million people, or 12 percent of the 2.4 billion labor force in the 37 GEM countries analyzed, are involved in new business formation.
What is the size of your local market?	From what I can now see, this will be a global business, with sales targeted for many English speaking areas in the world. My primary market will be North America.
	There were a total of 344,500 businesses in BC in 2001. Of these, 337,400 (98 percent) were small businesses. Over half (54 percent) of all businesses in the province were operated by a self-employed person without paid help.
	The overwhelming majority of small businesses in BC are micro businesses with less than five employees. In 2001, there were 279,800 small businesses of this description, representing 83 percent of all small enterprises. Over half (55 percent) of all small businesses were comprised of self-employed individuals without paid help. Only a small portion (four percent) of small businesses had between 20 and 49 employees.
	75 percent of small businesses in BC are concentrated in the service sector.
Describe the opportunities your business will take advantage of?	Market and sell books and digital business planning solutions to the largest potential customer group – those considering or starting a business.
	E-books appear to be an interesting prospect.

Task List

To complete this task you must complete your secondary market research and then:

1. Determine what industry or industries your business is in.

2. Research to find existing reports, articles, tables and/or descriptions of your industry or industries.

3. From your market research, identify and list the key points you wish to include in your Industry Element.

4. Using the checklist on the next page, review your list of key points to ensure it is complete; identify any missing information and add it to your list.

5. Organize your list of key points in preparation for writing your Industry Element.

WORSHEET: KEY INDUSTRY STATEMENTS	
LIST OF KEY POINTS ABOUT INDUSTRY	**YOUR LIST OF KEY INDUSTRY STATEMENTS**
What industry or industries is your business in?	
What quantities of goods are sold and what is the value of those goods?	
What is the industry outlook and growth potential?	
What are the industry trends (past, present and future)?	
What key points about your industry help to support your business case?	
What population shifts and/or consumer trends affect your industry?	

Tip: Get in the habit of "Googling" for words, terms and concepts you don't understand. www.google.com

WORKSHEET: KEY INDUSTRY STATEMENTS Continued	
LIST OF KEY POINTS ABOUT INDUSTRY	**YOUR LIST OF KEY INDUSTRY STATEMENTS**
What are the main challenges faced by the industry?	
What are the main barriers or incentives to entry by new businesses?	
What significant new developments have or are taking place in your industry?	
What is the size of the total market and how is it divided up and served by your competitors?	
What is the size of your local market?	
Describe the opportunities your business will take advantage of?	

Segment Your Market

I dentify different parts of your market to use as building blocks for researching your market, forecasting your sales and developing your marketing action plan.

As you learn more you will become either more confident or less confident about your business idea. Stronger confidence will lean you toward start-up while lack of confidence will beckon you away from it, but either result is to be considered a success. That is the purpose of your business plan – to get to start-up or get out prior to start-up. Either way, you win.

Too often I encounter inexperienced business planners who state that they plan to sell their product or service to a generic group called "all people." Aside from my gut instinct that this statement may never be completely accurate, it's not very useful for researching, planning, forecasting or marketing purposes. It will be more effective to describe your market in more detail in order to arrive at a business and marketing plan that you can take to the bank. Dig deeper and strive to define your market and your customers as accurately as possible.

Here are categories of variables, different ways to segment or break your market into manageable groups. The categories are geographic, demographic/socioeconomic, psychographic, behavioral and business.

Step 19

MUST HAVE
RECOMMENDED
NICE TO HAVE

Tip: To "segment your market" means to identify different groups of customers or buyers for your products and services.

SEGMENTING YOUR MARKET	
Geographic Variables	**Segments**
City Size	Under 5,000; 5,000-20,000; 20,000-50,000; 50,000-100,000; 100,000-250,000; 250,000-500,000; 500,000-1,000,000; 1,000,000 And Over
County Size	A,B,C,D
Density	Urban, Suburban, Rural
Region	Maritimes, Central Canada, Western Provinces, Midwestern States, Northern, Southern

Demographic/ Socio-economic Variables	**Segments**
Age	Under 6; 6-11; 12-19; 20-34; 35-49; 50-64; 65+
Education	Grade School Or Less; Some High School; High School Graduate; Post-Secondary; University; Graduate School
Family Life Cycle	Young, Single; Young, Married, No Children; Young, Married, Youngest Child Under 6; Young Married, Youngest Child 6 Or Over; Older, Married, With Children; Older, Married, No Children Under 18; Older, Single; Other
Family Size	1-2; 3-4; 5+
Income	Under $2,500; $2,500-$5,000; $5,000-$7,500; $7,500-$10,000; $10,000-$15,000; $15,000-$20,000; $20,000-$30,000; $30,000-$40,000; $40,000-$50,000; $50,000+

Demographic/ Socio-economic Variables cont'd	Segments
Nationality	Canadian, British, French, German, Scandinavian, Italian, American, Middle-Eastern, Japanese, Chinese, Other
Occupation	Professional and Technical; Managers, Officials and Proprietors; Clerical, Sales; Craftsmen, Foremen; Operatives, Farmers; Retired; Students; Housewives; Unemployed
Race	White, Aboriginal, Inuit, Oriental, Indian, Other
Religion	Catholic, Protestant, Jewish, Buddhist, Other
Sex	Male, Female

Psychographic Variables	Segments
Lifestyle	Upscale, Urban, Rural, Suburban
Personality	Compulsive, Gregarious, Authoritarian, Ambitious
Social Class	Lower Lowers, Upper Lowers, Lower Middles, Lower Uppers, Upper Uppers

Behavioral Variables	Segments
Benefits Sought	Quality, Service, Economy
Readiness Stage	Enthusiastic, Positive, Indifferent, Negative, Hostile
Usage Rate	Light User, Medium User, Heavy User
Use Occasion	Regular Occasion; Special Occasion
User Status	Non-User, Ex-User, Potential User, First User, Regular User

Business Variables	Segments
Number Of Employees	1-4, 5-9, 10-19, 20-99, 100-499, 500 or More
Employment Status	Self-Employed Non-Employer, Self-Employed Employer
How Long In Business	Nascent Entrepreneurs, Start-Up, New Firms, 1-2 Years, 2-5 Years, Etc.
Industry Sector	2-digit codes – 22 Utilities, 23 Construction, 31-33 Manufacturing, 41 Wholesale Trade, 44-45 Retail Trade – see list of 20 sectors in Step 18
Industry Subsector	3-digit codes – search for "N.A.I.C.S." at Statistic Canada or US Census websites
Industry Group	4-digit codes – search for "N.A.I.C.S." at Statistic Canada or US Census websites
Industry	5-digit codes – search for "N.A.I.C.S." at Statistic Canada or US Census websites
National Industry	6-digit codes – search for "N.A.I.C.S." at Statistic Canada or US Census websites
Method of Operation	Wholesaler, Distributor, Designer, Seller, Manufacturer
Operating Hours/Wk.	0-9, 10-19, 20-29, 30-39, 40-49, 50-59, Get a Life

Tip: If you haven't already done so, this is a good time to set up a working copy of the Business Plan Shell™ to do your writing. The Shell™ can be found either on your RiskBuster™ CD or from the Macrolink website at www. riskbuster.com. To set up your working copy, double click on "Start a New Business Plan" to open The Shell™. From the main menu, select "File," "Save as" and then follow the procedure for storing the file on your hard drive. Rename the file to your name or your business name followed by _working copy. For example, "Macrolink Action Plans Business Plan_Working Copy."

Example: Statements Describing Customers

> **My customers will be:**
>
> · Entrepreneurs who need business plans.
>
> · Entrepreneurs in Canada and the United States (primary).
>
> · English speaking entrepreneurs in all other parts of the globe (secondary).
>
> · 10.1 million adults in USA attempting to create a new business at any given time.
>
> · 300 million people in 40 countries, who are involved in entrepreneurial activities.
>
> · Two-thirds of individuals voluntarily pursuing a business opportunity – one third getting into business because it's their best choice for work.
>
> · Males and females, mostly in the 25 to 54 age group (which totals more than 136 million in Canada and USA).

Task List

1. From your market research and the tables above, write out a number of statements describing your customers.

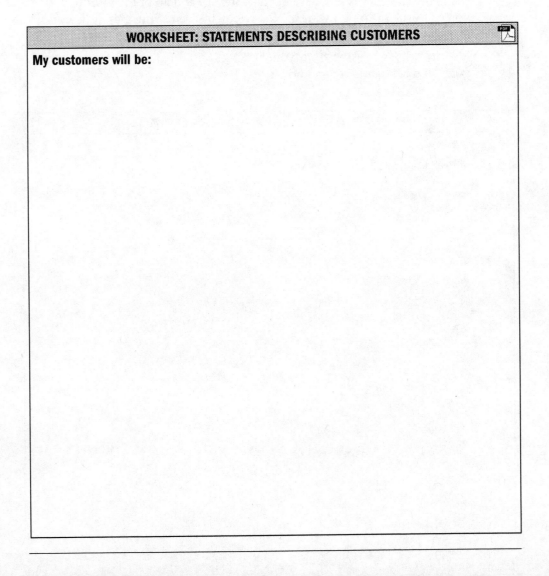

WORKSHEET: STATEMENTS DESCRIBING CUSTOMERS

My customers will be:

Write a Draft Description of Your Customers

Step 20

Bring together what you have learned about your target market and write a draft description of your customers.

When it comes to determining customer wants and needs, part of your market research may come from secondary sources, but ultimately you will need to survey real live customers in order to get the answers you need. At this point you have completed enough research to tackle the first draft of the Business Plan Element called *Description of the Customers*.

A part of the objective with this step is to reveal what you still need to learn about your customers. Don't worry if you feel as though you don't have all of the answers at this point; if you have not yet done your primary market research, you probably still have much to learn about your customers.

Task List

1. Using the statements you developed in Step 19 and all of the information you've learned through your market research so far, write a draft description of your customers.

2. Identify what's missing from your description and clarify the questions you still need to answer and how to get those answers.

Don't worry if you feel as though you don't have all of the answers at this point; if you have not yet done your primary market research, you probably still have much to learn about your customers.

Tip: If you have not already begun to use The Shell™ or other business planning templates, you should set up your own business planning file and start using it. For example, this step could be done in your draft business plan.

WORKSHEET: DRAFT DESCRIPTION OF CUSTOMERS

Assess What You Are Learning About Your Business

Compare what you know now with what you previously thought to be true. This will provide you with a benchmark to identify missing information and next steps.

Step 21

MUST HAVE
RECOMMENDED
NICE TO HAVE

Example: Assessing What You Have Learned About Your Business

PRE-RESEARCH ASSUMPTIONS	WHAT I'VE LEARNED SO FAR
1. My label for my customer will be an entrepreneur.	There are many different segments within this large group; employed, self-employed, start-ups, incorporated, unincorporated, thinking about starting.
2. I think any entrepreneur over the age of 20 would read my book.	More clear now about common statistical groupings such as ages 20 to 54, my most likely readers.
3. After asking more than 200 people their opinion, I assumed that at least 7% of the population, at any given time, was considering starting a business.	I have shifted to 10% of those between the ages of 20 and 54; then further shifted to 12% of the total population. I'm not confident in either of these yardsticks yet, need to dig deeper.
4. The city I live in, Prince George, has about 75,000 residents.	According to 2001 Census it is actually 84,615, of which 45,925 are between the ages of 20 and 54.
5. The local Chamber of Commerce had about 2,000 members, all existing businesses.	Actually 950 in March 2003, however, the City has issued 4,800 to 5,000 business licenses.
6. The province I live in, British Columbia, has approximately 3 million people in it.	According to 2001 Census it is actually 3,907,740 with 2,018,545 between the ages of 20 and 54.
7. Canada has approximately 30 million people in it.	Actually 3,100,000 of which 16,250,200 are in the target age group of 20 to 54.
8. Our closest neighbor, the United States, has a population of approximately 300 million people.	July 2002 Census reports 288,368,698.
9. Of 300,000,000, approximately 7% or 21,000,000 people are potential readers of my book.	I now assume that my potential market is a minimum of 12% of 288,368,698 which is 34,604,244 people.

Tip: This can be a daunting, but healthy part of your growth. On the one hand it's not flattering to be confronted with your ignorance; on the other, knowledge can help to build your confidence in your business idea. You might stumble across information that stops you from going into business or simply helps you avoid losing your investment. Either way, you win.

Task List

1. Reflect on what you've learned so far about your business.

2. Go back to step 14 and re-read your original assumptions.

3. Review the market research steps 11 to 19 and add any points that come up, such as new assumptions you have identified, questions that need to be answered and key things you have learned.

4. List a minimum of ten things you have learned about your market and your business.

5. Make a list of any points that you still need to learn more about.

WORSHEET: ASSESSING WHAT YOU HAVE LEARNED ABOUT YOUR BUSINESS	
PRE-RESEARCH ASSUMPTIONS	WHAT I'VE LEARNED SO FAR
1.	
2.	
3.	
4.	
5.	
6.	
7.	
8.	
9.	

Key Points I Still Need to Learn About

1.

2.

3.

4.

5.

6.

Identify and Research Your Competitors

R esearch and create a profile of your competitors. This may be one of the most daunting yet most revealing and rewarding steps in your market research.

> MUST HAVE
> RECOMMENDED
> NICE TO HAVE

Customers Buy for Their Reasons, Not Yours

Customers purchase products and services from competitors for their own reasons. You must understand those reasons in order to determine why customers will buy from you. Your competitors can be your greatest source of valuable information about the wants and needs of your customers. If you miss this step you could be in for a rough ride.

Do not underestimate your competitors' ingenuity. They are in business because they understand their customers' wants and needs and they know how to sell their products and services to customers. No matter how many things your competitors might be doing wrong, they must be doing many things right to be in the market. You need to understand the good and the bad, the positive and the negative.

Do not underestimate your competitors' ingenuity. They are in business because they understand their customers' wants and needs and they know how to sell their products and services to customers. No matter how many things your competitors might be doing wrong, they must be doing many things right to be in the market.

Direct and Indirect Competition

There are direct and indirect competitors. A direct competitor sells the same products and services as yours. An indirect competitor might sell an entirely different product or service that competes for the same money as yours. You will need to consider all of the competitors in your scan and then determine the impact of each on your potential sales.

Who Are Your Competitors?

Do you know who the competitors are in your market area? If you know who they are, make a list of them. For some businesses this can be as simple as going to the telephone directory, for others the information can be more difficult to dig up.

If there are too many competitors to list, perhaps it is time to ask yourself if you're doing a wise thing by jumping into the marketplace. Is the market large enough to support another competitor? More importantly, why should customers buy the products or services from your business rather than the others?

How Will You Research Your Competitors?

Don't be timid when it comes to researching competitors. This is a task that must be taken seriously if you're going to succeed.

Here are some suggestions on how to research your competitors:

- Survey your competitors.
- Search for them on the Internet.
- Telephone them.
- Pretend to be a customer – call or visit and ask questions.
- Buy and analyze your competitors' product(s) or service(s).
- Join a trade association whose membership is made up of your competitors.
- Contact a competitor located outside your market area and ask if he or she will help you.
- Get a job with one or more of your competitors.
- Interview your competitors' customers.
- Read books, magazines, newspaper articles.
- Watch TV or other media coverage about your competitors.
- Obtain information from market research businesses, for a fee or free.

You must become a master sleuth – an expert at gathering market intelligence. For those new to the game, don't worry about the ethics of masquerading yourself in order to gather information pertinent to the survival of your business; it's OK to snoop.

How Will Your Competitors React?

Tip: Business is not for the faint of heart — get sharp or don't start.

This is also a time to consider the reaction of competitors to your entrance into the marketplace. For example, large businesses can lower their prices to squeeze out smaller competitors. Will your competitors change their products, services or prices to match yours? Will they be hostile toward your presence or will you be different or small enough not to attract their animosity? Businesses survive and thrive because people labor over such issues. Competitors react in the best interest of their own survival, not yours.

Differentiation and Positioning

Differentiation is the term used to describe how you are different from your competitors.

Do you wish to be the cheapest, the fastest or the most convenient? Will you aspire to be the best in your arena and command the highest prices?

Your study of competitors will bring you the information you need in order to differentiate your business from theirs. This will lead to positioning your business in the marketplace, which in turn will lead to positioning your business in the minds of your customers.

Example: Competitive Analysis

My research of competitors' books included a much broader range of topics (and many more books) than those listed here, but this will give you a glimpse of the process involved. All of the books below are well worth reading; I learned something from each and recommend them all.

Business Planning Books & Authors	**Features**				
	Solves the Business Planning Challenge?	Price (CAD)	Author Credentials	Includes Sample Business Plan(s)	Includes Business Planning CD
1. Business Plan or BUST! – Boudreau – 400 pages	For non-academics, For small / micro-business, home-based 99-Step Process	$36.58	Business owner, Business Planning Coach	2	Optional or add-on
2. The Successful Business Plan, Secrets and Strategies – Abrams – 400 pages	For academics & larger projects / investor focused Great worksheets	$43.50	Not stated	1	No
3. Building a Dream – Good – 421 pages	For academics Doesn't really solve the business plan challenge	$24.99	Head of Marketing, U of Manitoba	1	No
4. Business Plans for Dummies – Tiffany and Peterson – 354 pages	Great advice but doesn't solve the business plan challenge	$26.99	Both Ph.D.	1	No
5. Business Plans Made Easy – Henricks and Riddle – 365 pages	Very useful, but doesn't solve the business plan challenge	$19.95	Not Stated	5	No
6. The Business Planning Guide – Bangs, Jr. – 242 pages	For a moderately skilled user, heavy financial analysis	$36.95	Banker	3	No
7. The Total Business Plan – O'Hara – 316 pages	A very difficult read, lots of text, good information	$69.95	Ph.D.	7	Yes
8. Preparing a Successful Business Plan – Touchie – 137 pages	Great introductory book and worksheets, a bit thin	$14.95	B.Comm., M.B.A.	1	No

Tip: I could not have positioned this book without the market intelligence gained by studying these and many other excellent resources. For more detail on the titles to the left please refer to the Suggested Reading section on page 379.

At this stage, I am able to make the following observations:

1. I will need to do this analysis for each major product or service I offer. For now my book is my main focus, so the above exercise teaches me enough to proceed.

2. I have a heck of a lot of work to do (Boudreau wipes sweat from brow)!

3. My competitive edge is that my book and digital products solve the business planning challenge for the non-academic, novice business planner.

4. I wonder how many of those who wrote the books listed above have actually attempted to set out and create their own business plans using their own systems.

5. My target book price is in the higher end of the Canadian market. A quick visit to FXConverter on the Internet reveals that my price of $36.58CAD equates to $31.35USD today. I visit Rhonda Abrams' website and see that her list price is $29.95USD but she is actually selling her book at $23.96USD today. That would be $27.97CAD without shipping or taxes. I think Abrams might also have come down in price since I purchased the book a couple of years ago for $43.50CAD. I also recall that I had to order that book from the US as it wasn't stocked at the local bookstores. Hmm...

6. Competitor number five makes an unrealistic promise; business plans are not easy for most people.

7. I had been puzzling over whether or not to include the CD in an envelope at the back of the book; competitor number seven's price indicates this may not lead to a competitive price; I think it better to give the buyer options (book, CD or both).

8. My product mix – book, CD, downloadable digital products, instructor's manual – differentiates me substantially from most of the competitors. It doesn't hurt that my products and services are totally integrated while also being independent, stand-alone items.

9. I definitely need to get a life.

Example: Positioning Statements

The study above enabled me to begin to differentiate my business from the competitors and to make the following positioning statements:

• Macrolink Action Plans Inc. will serve ordinary, down-to-earth entrepreneurs who will develop their own business plans. The service will not include developing business plans for customers.

• Books will be in the medium to high price range and in the high quality category.

• CD and digital downloads will be in the lower price and high quality category.

• Books and digital products will be stand-alone, as well as integrated and offered in package deals.

• Customers will be male or female entrepreneurs, either considering, starting or growing a small or micro-business. The highest concentration will be in the service sector.

Task List

Here is one simple method for establishing how your business might be different from the others. Create a form or table like the one below. Determine what features or characteristics are most important to your customers. This information can be sourced from secondary sources, but it can also be determined from a market survey of your potential customers. It can also be learned through informal questioning and discussion with those who are knowledgeable about your products or services.

How to use the table below:

1. List your product or service in the first row.

2. List your top six competitors, more if you think it useful or necessary. Rank the competitors *according to their importance to you*, beginning with the most important.

3. List the features from left to right *according to their importance to the customer*. Research to determine where each of the competitors is positioned with regard to each feature. For example, is the competitor's product high, low or medium quality?

WORKSHEET: COMPETITIVE ANALYSIS					
COMPETITORS (in order of their importance to you)	**FEATURES** (In order of their importance to the customer)				
1.					
2.					
3.					
4.					
5.					
6.					
7.					

Prioritize and Target Your Customers

Step 23

At this point you should know your competitors quite well. You have learned how they serve their customers and gleaned what you can about what their customers and yours need.

Now it's time to target your customers. Targeting your customer means deciding which market segment or segments to prioritize in order to focus your researching, selling and marketing efforts.

Criteria for targeting:

- How attractive is the segment in terms of size and growth rate?
- How many competitors are serving the segment?
- Is there a threat of substitutes?
- What is the bargaining power of the buyers and suppliers?
- Is the segment a fit for you in terms of your businesses resources, capabilities, skills and competitive advantages?

At this stage in my own research process, I found that I was using many different terms or labels to describe my potential customers. I recognized that I must somehow move away from the huge (albeit enticing) group described as "12% of the labor force in 40 countries," toward smaller, more definable, more reachable and manageable customer groups.

After some vigorous digging at the Statistics Canada and US Census websites I developed the following table:

Example: Prioritizing and Targeting Your Customers

	UNITED STATES 2000	CANADA 2001	POTENTIAL MARKET
Total Population 2000 Census	281,421,906	30,007,090	
Males & Females 25 to 34 years	39,891,724	3,994,935	
Males & Females 35 to 44 years	45,148,527	5,101,620	
Males & Females 45 to 54 years	37,677,952	4,419,290	
Total Male and Female 25 to 54 years	122,718,203	13,515,845	136,234,048
Total in Labor Force	139,252,000	12,128,700	151,380,700
Estimated 12% of Labor Force Starting Businesses	16,710,240	1,455,444	18,165,684
Conservative Estimate Starting Businesses	10,100,000	900,000	11,000,000
Existing Firms with no employees	16,529,955	1,496,200	18,026,155
Existing Firms with 1 to 4 employees	2,697,839	918,282	3,616,121

Example: Description of the Customers

The table below is a more targeted definition of the customers for Macrolink Action Plans Inc.

TOP PRIORITY	SECOND PRIORITY	THIRD PRIORITY
1 Million Workforce Age People Starting Businesses in Canada Male and Female	Economic and Enterprise Development Agencies In Canada and USA	18 Million Non-Employer Business Owners in Canada and USA
10 Million Workforce Age People Starting Businesses in USA Male and Female	Independent Distributors Bookstores, Colleges and Libraries Chains That Sell Books	Workforce Age People Starting Businesses Not in Canada or USA

At first glance it might look like my third priority targets should be my top priority because of the size of the target market. One sale with a wholesaler or distributor would easily overshadow sales to my top and second priorities. However, my strategy is shaped to my situation. I plan to implement an aggressive but inexpensive, self-driven marketing strategy. I need to get busy with the resources I have at my disposal, now! The bigger fish will have to wait until I have sold a lot of books to my first two priorities. This will give me time to iron the wrinkles out of my business processes in preparation for doing larger volumes of business. From experience I know I could easily starve to death chasing bigger deals. I know I need to build my sales one unit at a time; larger sales will come later and when they do I will be ready for them.

Task List

1. Identify and prioritize your most important target markets or customer groups.

WORKSHEET: TARGET MARKET PRIORITY		
TOP PRIORITY	SECOND PRIORITY	THIRD PRIORITY

Clarify and Write Your Primary Market Research Questions

Step 24

MUST HAVE
RECOMMENDED
NICE TO HAVE

With a clearer idea of who you're targeting, it's now time to clarify what you want to learn about your customers. This might entail looking back through your assumptions and what you've learned. What you are looking for is to identify missing information; what would you like to ask or confirm when speaking directly to potential customers? I've compiled this list of need-to-know questions to get you started. Feel free to delete any that don't apply to your business or add a few of your own.

Need-to-Know Questions for Your Market Survey

1. Who are your customers?
2. What age category best describes them?
3. How many are male and how many are female?
4. What level of education do they have?
5. Where do they live?
6. Where do they work?
7. Do they purchase the products or services you will provide?
8. How often do they purchase these products or services?
9. How much money do they spend on these product or services?
10. Where do they currently purchase these products or services?
11. Why do they currently purchase the products or services where they do?
12. What do they like or dislike about the products or services they currently purchase?
13. How much are they paying now?
14. Do they prefer to pay cash, credit card, debit card or trade account?
15. Do they think their need for these products and services will be increasing or decreasing in the future?
16. Will they buy this product or service in the next year? How often?
17. Will they buy this product or service from you? When?

Tip: If your market surveying is going well, it should be revealing customers to you. Don't get buried in the academic exercise of surveying to the point that you forget to ask for the sale if it seems appropriate to do so. In attempting to prove your business case, keep this in mind – there's no proof quite as strong as a customer who is willing and able to pay for your product or service.

Task List

1. Identify, clarify and write out a list of questions to ask your customers.

Determine the Best Method to Gather Your Primary Research

Primary market research is the information that you collect yourself as opposed to data you might gather from other sources.

Here are some points to consider in deciding which method or methods to use.

Step 25

MUST HAVE
RECOMMENDED
NICE TO HAVE

METHODS FOR DOING PRIMARY MARKET RESEARCH		
RESEARCH METHOD	PROS	CONS
Observation	· Inexpensive if you do it yourself · First-hand learning	· Time consuming · You may feel like you're spying
Personal Interviews	· Inexpensive if you do it yourself · You can learn things you might otherwise miss · Creates an opportunity to develop relationships · Can lead to sales · People might share more information	· Time consuming · You may feel awkward the first few attempts · People may be less frank because they don't want to hurt your feelings
Focus Groups	· Can gather a lot of information · Can benefit from the interaction between people with different backgrounds and perspectives	· Takes some time to organize · Can be more costly to conduct · Requires some skill to facilitate
Mail Surveys	· Inexpensive to get to target market · Can survey remotely · Can reach targets otherwise not accessible	· Low return rate, mailed surveys are easy to discard · Many people are sick of being surveyed · Might get less honest responses
Internet Surveys	· Once it's set up this type of survey can be very inexpensive to conduct · If your customers are computer and Internet savvy, you will automatically narrow your focus · Can be very efficient to manage · You can reach a very broad customer base	· Need some Internet savvy or hire someone to set it up · Once established you still need to invite or attract people to participate · You limit your survey to those with access to a computer and the Internet
Telephone Surveys	· Can reach a lot of people	· Takes some skill and a thick skin to get through the negativity · Many people are tired of intrusions on private time
Personal Experience or Job	· Can view first hand how things work · Earn while you learn	· Can take a long time · You might draw some negativity from an ex-employer once you begin to compete

There are many different methods for gathering primary market research, including talking to customers and surveying customers, competitors and suppliers. Typical methods for collecting primary market information include observation, personal interviews, focus groups, formal surveys, mail surveys and telephone surveys.

Task List

1. Decide which methods you will use to gather your primary market research.

Create Your Market Survey Questionnaire

Step 26

Build a questionnaire that brings you the answers you haven't already gleaned from your secondary market research efforts.

By now you have gathered a few pounds of secondary market research and have reached that terrifying moment when it's time to talk to people. Your business is to serve real people; the sooner you get to talking and listening to those people the more accurate your business assumptions will be. This is your primary market research, and you will likely need to create a survey questionnaire.

Tips for Creating Your Market Survey Questionnaire

Here are tips to help you stay on track with your market survey.

1. Keep the tone friendly.
2. Include an introduction at the beginning and a thank-you at the end.
3. Keep the overall form brief and easy to use.
4. Keep questions short, clear and understandable.
5. Determine what you need to know first then design the questions to get the right information.
6. Everyone is busy – be sensitive to using others' time.
7. Beware of asking for sensitive information.
8. Give choices so the customer can either circle or pick a number.
9. Allow space for the customer to write comments.
10. Make it optional for the customer to include their name and contact information.
11. Keep it simple, but not too simple.
12. If appropriate, be sure to ask if he or she would purchase your product or service.

You will want to test your survey on a few clients before launching. This will give you an opportunity to get some feedback and make minor adjustments before the main thrust of your survey.

Surveying is a very complex topic and I do not mean to make light of it. The main thing is that you embrace the interaction with your customers and listen to what they say – they will tell you what they need.

Your business is to serve real people; the sooner you get to talking and listening to those people the more accurate your business assumptions will be.

Market Survey Questionnaire: Imported Handmade Giftware

1. Have you ever purchased or received as gifts any imported handmade giftware?

   Yes _____ No _____.

2. Have you ever purchased or received as gifts handmade giftware from India or Pakistan?

   Yes _____ No _____

   If yes, what type of giftware?

   Wooden _____ Marble _____ Brass _____

   Copper _____ Cotton _____ Other _____

   Please specify: _____

3. Would you be interested in purchasing the above mentioned handmade giftware from India or Pakistan?

   Yes _____ No _____

   If yes, would the item be used:

   a. In your home for you or your family's enjoyment? _____

   b. As a gift? _____

   c. Other? _____ Please specify: _____

4. Do you know where to shop for such giftware?

   Yes _____ No _____

5. When buying foreign handmade giftware, what do you value the most?

   (On a scale of 1 to 4, list in order according to preference, where 1 is your most valued choice)

   Craftsmanship _____ Cost _____ Uniqueness _____

   Other _____ Please specify: _____

6. How much money would you spend on the above products?

   Monthly _____ Yearly _____ Other _____

Tip: Offering a gift in exchange for a completed survey can often increase the return rate.

Market Survey Questionnaire: Stitches Fabric Store

Do you sew? No _____ Yes _____
If No, please answer questions to Part A. If Yes, please answer questions to Part B.

A. Please check reasons for not sewing.
Lack of interest _____
Lack of knowledge _____
Poor availability of fabric selection _____
Other_____

B. Check type of sewing you do.
Children's wear _____
Ladies' wear _____
Home decorating _____
Other _____

Which patterns do you use?
McCall's _____   Simplicity _____   Kwik Sew _____
Butterick _____   Vogue_____

Check your age group:
10-18 _____   19-29 _____   30 & over _____

Where do you buy your material?
In town _____   Out of Town _____

How far do you live from our town?
In town _____   10-15 miles _____   Out of Town _____

Do you think our town needs a fabric shop? Yes _____ No _____

Would you be interested in sewing classes? Yes _____ No _____

What classes would interest you?

Basic Sewing_____   Lingerie_____
T-Shirt_____   Infant wear_____
Pants_____   Men's wear_____
Tailoring_____   Other_____

How much money would you spend on the above products?
Monthly _____   Yearly _____   Other _____

Market Survey Questionnaire: Sudsy Car Wash

We are interested in knowing what you think about our service. Accordingly, we have prepared a brief questionnaire that we would appreciate you answering while your car is being washed. Your candid comments and suggestions are important to us.

Thank you, SUDSY CAR WASH

1. Do you live / work in the area?
   (Circle one or both)

2. Why did you choose to come to SUDSY CAR WASH today? (Circle all that apply)

   - Close to home
   - Close to work
   - Convenience
   - Good service
   - Full-service car wash
   - Other

3. How did you learn about us?
   (Circle one)

   - Newspaper
   - Mailing
   - Drove by and stopped
   - Recommended by someone
   - Received coupon at work
   - Other

4. How frequently do you have your car washed during the winter months (November 1 to April 30)?
   Please estimate.
   _____ times per month
   Other _____

5. How frequently do you have your car washed during spring and summer months (May 1 to October 31)?
   _____ times per month
   Other _____

6. Which aspect of our car wash do you think needs improvement?

7. Our operating hours are 8:30 am to 6 pm weekdays & Saturdays and 9 am to 2 pm on Sunday. We are closed on holidays. What changes in our operating hours would be better for you?

Weekdays	Saturday	Sunday
Open 8 am	Open 8 am	Close 3 pm
Close 7 pm	Close 7 pm	Close 4 pm
Close 8 pm	Close 8 pm	Close 5 pm
Close 9 pm	Close 9 pm	No Change
No change	No change	

8. Approximate age: Circle one

   Under 25   26-39   40-59   Over 60

9. How much money would you spend on the above service?

   Monthly _____   Yearly _____   Other _____

Comments:

Market Survey Questionnaire: Charlie's Commercial Warehouse

1. Are you presently renting any commercial warehousing space?   YES ____   NO ____
    If NO, go to question 2. If YES, continue with questions 1a. to 1f.

    a. Where do you presently rent your warehouse space (name and address):

    b. How many times a month do you enter the warehouse or use it?

    c. Is your warehouse space heated?   YES ____   NO ____   DON'T KNOW ____

    d. Approximately how much warehouse space are you renting? _____square feet

    e. Do you think you will need additional space in the future?   YES ____   NO ____

    f. Are there any changes or improvements you would like to see made with your
       present warehousing arrangements?   YES ____   NO ____   DON'T KNOW ____
       If YES, what improvements would you like to see?

       _____

       _____

2. Are you planning on using any rented storage or warehouse space?
    YES ____   NO ____   DON'T KNOW ____

    If NO, end interview. If YES or DON'T KNOW, continue to questions 2.a. through 2.d.

    a. If you are planning to rent warehouse space or may rent such space, how far
       in terms of time would you be willing to travel to use your space? _____
       minutes

    b. What would be the approximate size of your storage space needs? _____ sq ft

    c. How much monthly rent would you be willing to pay?
       $ _____ per square foot / month

    d. Would you require heat for your rented warehouse space?
       YES ____   NO ____   DON'T KNOW ____

NAME:_____ TITLE: _____

BUSINESS NAME: _____

BUSINESS ADDRESS: _____

Thank you for your cooperation.

Market Surveys FAQ

What am I trying to achieve by surveying my customers? You are trying to learn more about your customer and your business. You can pick up general knowledge from secondary sources but it is really your primary research — communicating directly with customers — that brings the specific knowledge about your customers in your market area. Ultimately, you are attempting to prove or disprove your own assumptions about your customers, your products and services and your market.

Tip: Don't underestimate yourself as an important source of market research. If you are getting into a business you know a great deal about, you are potentially one of the best sources of market research. Your time working in the industry counts – be sure to use it!

How many surveys should I do? How do I know when I've arrived? This will be different for each situation. A business that has only a few potential customers does not require the same number of surveys as a business with a market of thousands. I recommend getting a few questionnaires out, perhaps ten or twenty, followed by a revision of your survey as feedback dictates. Once you are confident that you are getting the information you need, you can then have another 50 people complete the survey. Assess the information you are getting, and do this again. I suggest doing 50 at a time until you find your results level off or the information appears to provide you with a consistent message. One hundred surveys generally bring a 10% chance of error while five hundred can give a 5% chance of error.

When does my surveying stop? As you do your surveys your confidence level in your business idea will likely increase or decrease. Perhaps the time to stop is governed by when you cease to learn new information from them.

When should I survey? You certainly must survey potential customers prior to starting your business. Your customer service surveys will go on for the life of your business. You should survey for each new product, service, division or business. You can survey to determine pricing, client preferences, changes in the marketplace and competitor characteristics.

Tip: Be sure interviewees understand your product and its advantages. This can be a big problem in the technology realm.

Task List

1. Review the four sample questionnaires in this section.
2. Select which method or combination of methods you will employ to gather your primary research.
3. Develop a list of questions to include in your survey questionnaire.

Survey Your Customers

Step 27

It's important to learn first-hand knowledge about your customers. This is the step most newbie's fear and forego. Get out there and mingle.

Task List

1. Review your business start-up goal in Step 5 and your Action Plan in Step 6.

2. Determine when you must complete your surveying in order to meet your overall business planning goals.

3. Identify those you wish to complete your survey.

4. Plan your approach. Will you telephone, speak in person, mail or email?

5. Contact the customers and determine whether they will participate.

6. Be clear about your expectations and timelines. If possible, arrange in advance a time and place to pick-up the completed survey form.

7. If you plan to follow-up with a personal interview, make those arrangements.

8. Deliver the survey form to the customer; hand deliver if practical.

9. Pick up the completed form at the agreed time and place.

10. Meet with the customer to complete the personal interview.

11. Follow up with a thank you card, message or gift.

Tip: If you're comfortable using the internet, you could try web-based survey options such as www.webmonkey.com and www.zoomerang.com. However, this is only advisable if your customers are comfortable with and have access to the internet.

Compile and Analyze Your Market Survey Information

This is a step that you may repeat, depending how much surveying or how many different surveys you do. Consider compiling the data in a spreadsheet. You will want to look for trends, patterns, and commonalities. If your survey questionnaire is well designed, this step should be relatively simple.

MUST HAVE
RECOMMENDED
NICE TO HAVE

Example: Clarifying Statements about Your Customers

- All those surveyed are busy - short of time
- 96% of those surveyed state that they do not have enough money to hire a consultant
- Most do not have business planning skills
- Most have a limited understanding of market research
- All those surveyed have a desire or need to be involved in entrepreneurial activity
- 87% of those surveyed own computers and have access to the Internet

Task List

1. Create an electronic or hard copy form in which to record the information you've collected through your surveys.
2. Review the information to determine what the surveys are telling you, or teaching you, about your business.
3. Using key points learned from your surveys, write a few clarifying statements about your customers.

Tip: If you are not getting clear answers or direction from your surveys, consider changing your questions. Remember, the quality of your questions determines the value of the answers.

WORKSHEET: CLARIFYING STATEMENTS ABOUT CUSTOMERS
·
·
·
·
·
·
·
·

Rewrite Your Description of Your Customers

Step 29

MUST HAVE
RECOMMENDED
NICE TO HAVE

Pull out the draft description of your customers written in Step 19. Consider whether the profile of your customer has changed because of what you've learned from surveying your market.

What you're striving for is to describe at least your primary and secondary customers. Don't get too bogged down with detail. At the same time, don't make it so light that you can't have confidence in the sales forecast. Your confidence level is one way for you to measure how realistic your figures are. If your forecast makes you nervous, imagine what it would do for a banker.

Yes, this can be difficult. If it were easy, everyone would own a business.

Task List

1. Beginning with your draft description of your customers written in Step 19, and using relevant information learned to date, rewrite the description of your customers. Do this only if you feel it necessary. Your first draft might be just fine.

Make a Go / No-Go Decision

D ecide whether or not to complete your business plan.

Regardless of what order you complete the RoadMap™ steps in, there will come a time to assess whether or not you have reached your main market research destination. That destination is to reach a go or no-go decision, also referred to as proving your business case.

Step 30

Choosing the Right Business Opportunity for You

Aside from financial considerations, there are numerous other factors that could affect your decision. Work through the following list of questions to assess how comfortable you are with the proof you have gathered so far. List any areas that need further market research or strengthening, and carry out those tasks. Work with this step until you have enough information to decide whether or not to complete your business plan.

- Will the business pay you enough to survive financially?
- Will the business generate the amount of profit you wish to earn?
- Is this a life-style choice for you?
- Do you enjoy the work you will be doing?
- What impact will your health have on the business?
- What impact will the business have on your health?
- If you wish to employ family members, will the business enable you to do it?
- Has it been a life-long dream that will preoccupy you until you pursue it?
- Will it enable you to locate and live in a desirable area?
- Are there more attractive opportunities for your investment?
- Can you afford to lose your investment if the business doesn't succeed?

Tip: There are so many possible aspects to deciding whether or not to start or grow a business, and hence whether to complete a business plan. This step provides three different angles, including the list of personal considerations to the left, the Proving Your Business Case Worksheet on page 170 and the Feasibility and Return on Investment Worksheet on page 171.

Task List

1. Using the following worksheet, list the ways you have proven the nine different aspects of your business case.

2. Using the following Feasibility and ROI worksheet, determine if your business idea is viable or feasible and calculate the return on your investment.

3. Compare the return on your investment with other investment opportunities.

4. Decide whether or not to complete a business plan for this venture.

WORSHEET: PROVING YOUR BUSINESS CASE	
HAVE YOU PROVEN...?	HOW?
1. Your customers are real and there is a strong demand for your products and services?	
2. The size of your market?	
3. You're qualified to run your business?	
4. You can supply your products and services?	
5. Your pricing is acceptable to your customers?	
6. Your business is financially viable?	
7. Your business is sustainable?	
8. You can mitigate risks and meet all of the applicable regulatory requirements?	
9. Have you proven your business case?	

Feasibility and Return on Investment (ROI)

The following table provides you a process to determine whether or not your business is viable. It also guides you to consider the return you will earn on your investment. By the time you reach this step, you should have gathered the necessary information to complete this task – any missing information points to a need for more market research.

WORKSHEET: FEASIBILITY AND RETURN ON INVESTMENT	
FEASIBILITY STEP	RESULTS
1. Determine Total Market Potential	
2. Calculate Market Share (Sales)	
3. Cost of Building, Fixtures, Equipment	
4. Estimate Cost of Merchandise	
5. Calculate Operating Expenses	
6. Budget for Other Expenses	
7. Subtract Expenses from Sales	
8. Calculate Return on Investment	
9. Make Your Go/No-Go Decision to Complete a Business Plan	

Tip: *Are you still committed to developing a business plan? This is probably a good time to review your personal goals and purpose to ensure that your business idea is still a fit.*

Calculating Return on Investment

To calculate your return on investment (ROI), divide your profit after taxes by your total investment (times 100), as follows:

Profit After Taxes ÷ Total Investment X 100 = ROI (expressed in percent)

The following worksheet will help you to compare your return with potential returns on other investments:

WORKSHEET: RETURN ON INVESTMENT COMPARISON				
	PROFIT	INVESTMENT	X 100	ROI
Your Business Idea	$	$	X 100	%
Bank Account	$	$	X 100	%
Tax Shelter	$	$	X 100	%
	$	$	X 100	%
	$	$	X 100	%
	$	$	X 100	%

Encouragement for the Weary Business Planner

Are you discouraged at this point because you are only at step 30 of 99? Consider the following. If you have arrived at this point and determined that your business is not feasible, you might have just saved yourself a lot of heartache. If you have determined that your business is feasible and feel confident it can succeed, you have probably completed the most difficult part of the business planning process, your market research. The next steps should go quite quickly. Consider the following:

1. You have already written draft copies of the three most difficult Elements: Products and Services, The Industry and Profile of the Customers.

2. Steps 31 to 53 are devoted to writing various elements of your business plan. For the most part this entails writing information you will have gathered while researching your market.

3. Steps 54 to 65 are devoted to the Financial Section. If you have done your market research effectively, you should now have the raw material needed to build your financial scenario. If you use the Biz4Caster™, it could take as little as a couple of hours to complete your financials.

4. Of the remaining steps, you have likely already eliminated a number of the appendices (steps 66 to 89).

5. If you are using The Shell™ as your business planning template, the structure is provided and most of the Elements of your Introductory Section are already crafted for you.

6. You're a lot closer to completion than you might think!

Tip: If you do not feel that you have enough financial information to reach a decision, go to the Financial Section and work through it until you have produced a financial scenario you can live with. I urge you to use the Biz4Caster™ for this task; it will make your financial calculations much easier. Providing you use solid building blocks, the Biz4Caster™ will show whether or not your business is viable.

BUILD YOUR BUSINESS CONCEPT SECTION

In order to create an introduction to you and your business, in this Section you will clarify who you are, where your business is positioned, and what you are selling.

Here are the five Elements in this Section and the corresponding RoadMap™ steps:

BUSINESS PLAN ELEMENT	ROADMAP™ STEPS
The Business	31
Products and Services	32
The Industry	33
The Owner	34
Strategic Goals and Objectives	35

To prepare yourself to tackle the next few steps, I suggest you read the Business Concept Section of the business plan in Chapter 6. This will give you a sense of what you are trying to achieve in creating the Elements of this Section.

If you have not already done so, I recommend that you begin to do your writing *directly into a draft copy of your business plan.* If you are using the RiskBuster, you can open the Business Plan Shell™ and save it under your business name. You can also download a free copy of The Shell™ from **www.riskbuster.com.**

If you have Microsoft Excel I suggest you use Biz4Caster™ to forecast your financials. From the RiskBuster™ CD or download menu, simply click on "Start a New Financial Forecast" and save a working copy of the file in which to do your projections.

Here is a brief description of each of the Elements of the Business Concept Section.

Tip: Keep your reader in mind when writing the Elements of your business plan. What do you want your reader to know about your business? If you are reading someone's business plan, what do you want to know about the person, the business and the industry?

BRIEF INTRODUCTION TO THE BUSINESS CONCEPT ELEMENTS	
ELEMENT	DESCRIPTION
The Business	The purpose of this Element is to provide a "snapshot" of your present situation, the current condition of your business. ***Key points:*** identity, mission, vision, description, legal and regulatory.
Products and Services	The purpose of this Element is to develop a short, general description of the products and services your business will offer, and a detailed list of the products, services, features, and benefits. ***Key points:*** products and services, purpose of products and services, features and benefits, proprietary features, advantages, standards and legislation, protection (patent, copyright, trademark, industrial design, working drawings).
The Industry	The purpose of this Element is to provide an overview of the industry in which your business will compete. ***Key points:*** businesses are grouped into industries, such as, agricultural/forestry/fishing, construction, manufacturing, mining, retail, services, transportation and storage, and wholesale; industry profile, quantity and value of goods sold; outlook and growth potential; past, present and future trends; key points that support your business case; challenges faced by industry; barriers or incentives to entry; new developments; size of total market; description of the opportunity.

Tip: You are making the transition from market research to the actual writing of your business plan. The business plan is made up of six Sections, each of which contain several Elements. The chart to the left describes the Elements of the Business Concept Section.

Tip: Each of the following steps (31 to 53) lead to completion of a narrative Element of your business plan. Keep pushing forward; you may have to revisit many of the steps in order to complete your business plan.

ELEMENT	DESCRIPTION
The Owner(s)	The purpose of this Element is to provide a brief introduction of yourself. This is your opportunity to toot your horn. Here you must step forward and display your achievements in a positive way, without bragging. **Key points:** educational or business achievements; relevant achievements and successes; your strengths and what you feel you can contribute to the business to make it successful. A detailed resume in the appendices of your completed business plan will support this Element.
Strategic Plan and Goals	The purpose of this Element is to outline your short-term personal and business goals and explain how these increase your chances of success. **Key points:** mission statement, including vision and purpose; goal areas (gross revenues, net profits, number of units to be sold, number of employees, location, new marketing, franchising, new products and/or services, diversification, quality, customers, growth, return on investment, training and professional development); activities, priorities, responsibilities, deadlines; personal and corporate goals must support each other.

Decide Whether You're Using High or Low Tech

As you work your way through steps 31 to 65, your goal is to write the elements of the body of your business plan. You can navigate the path using either low tech or high tech methods. Regardless of which method you choose, here is a suggested four-part process for completing each Segment or Element:

    A. Respond

    B. Organize

    C. Write

    D. Revise

The following describes how the above process might work for each of the two methods.

1. Low Tech: Pen and Paper Method

No computer required for this method, just a supply of sticky paper or small 3" X 5" cards and some blank paper.

    A. Record your responses to each of the questions on separate cards (beginning with the Identity Statement, tasks 1 to 7).

    B. Organize the cards in the order you will write your sentences and paragraphs.

    C. Write the segment non-stop from the cards until you have finished the rough draft.

    D. Revise what you have written until you are pleased with your results.

Follow the same procedure for each Segment or Element.

2. High Tech: Computer Method

Providing you are comfortable writing with a word processor, the high tech method is much more efficient than the low tech method, particularly when it comes to revisions and projections. For this method open the file you will use to write your business plan. To save setup time, you can download The Shell™ free from **www.riskbuster.com**.

A. Record your responses to each of the questions (beginning with the Identity Statement, tasks 1 to 7).

B. Organize your responses in the order you will write your sentences and paragraphs.

C. Write the segment non-stop from your organized list of responses until you have finished the rough draft.

E. Revise what you have written until you are pleased with your results.

Follow the same procedure for each Segment or Element.

Four Vital Benefits to Writing Your Business Plan

Four highly positive things will occur as you write your business plan.

1. You will begin to understand your business more clearly. The more you write, the better you will understand your business.

2. The writing will begin to shape the business. After scrawling out the rough draft and then referring to it later to make revisions, you will find you can identify weaknesses and pick out the holes in your description and in your thought process.

3. The process of writing will help you to identify and set goals. Incomplete tasks or missing information may indicate a need to research further.

4. You will find that you are able to communicate your business more clearly to others.

Describe Your Business

Step 31

The Business Element is a snapshot of your present situation — the current condition of your business.

By now you will have researched your competitors and should have an understanding of how they position themselves in the market. As you explore each business, search for their identity, mission, vision and positioning statements.

This activity requires that you have completed a substantial amount of your market research, that you understand your business well enough to write a description of your business.

Although you can develop your positioning statements by yourself, it is healthy to put the results in front of others for feedback. If you have partners, investors, customers, employees or a business planning team, consider involving them in the creation of the following statements.

I recommend you go all the way through this process to create a draft, whether you have all the information or not. As you prepare to launch, here are six suggestions to help you get organized.

1. Many topics covered briefly in this Element will be dealt with in greater detail in other parts of the plan. The *Business Element* is intended to be a short description of your business. It's OK to be brief.

2. Don't worry if the first draft is too wordy or poorly written. You can trim later or use excess information in different parts of your plan where more detail is required. Throw perfection out the window for the rough draft. Just blast through all of the steps and write what you can at this time. There will be plenty of time later to fuss over things like grammar, accuracy and detail.

3. Keep a blank sheet of paper or a designated goal list handy on your computer. This is to write down the goals and tasks that arise as you work through the process.

4. You may stumble across terms or items that you don't understand or tasks that you haven't completed. Some of the following steps will require research; others will demand time, energy and money.

5. Some of the steps may require that you involve other people - your family, employees, partners or professionals.

Writing the Business Element

The Business Element is comprised of the following five segments:

1. **Identity Statement**
2. **Mission Statement**
3. **Vision Statement**
4. **Description of the Business**
5. **Legal and Regulatory**

Make yourself comfortable and have a couple of pads of sticky notes handy. I encourage you to have some fun with this.

Tip: Respond as though you are at your opening day or the day your plan will be read by the target reader.

1. Identity Statement

Your identity statement should be simple and factual (70 words or fewer) and it must communicate the answers to the following questions:

1. What is the name of your company?
2. What is the legal form or structure of your business?
3. Where is the business headquartered, licensed, registered?
4. When did or when will your business start?
5. What is the nature of your business (home-based, retail, services or products)?
6. What is the scope of your business (local, regional, national, international or global)?
7. What industry is your business in?

Tip: Consider writing your plan in the third person. Write about your business and yourself as though they are separate entities. Rather than stating "I / we expect to bring in $24,000 in sales..." you might write "The business will achieve $24,000 in sales." If you're uncomfortable writing in the third person, it is OK to write in the first person.

Example: Identity Statement

Macrolink Action Plans Inc. is a privately held corporation headquartered in Prince George and registered in the Province of British Columbia. Founded in 1987, the business has focused mainly on delivery of training throughout northern BC. This business plan is the owner's roadmap to reconfigure the business and implement a new marketing strategy for growth. The owner and principal shareholder is Dan Boudreau.

Task List

1. Using the questions and example above as a guide, write your identity statement (70 words or fewer) and enter it into the working copy of your business plan.

2. Mission Statement

Your mission statement should be clear and factual (20 words or fewer) and it must answer these questions:

1. What business are you in?
2. What product(s) or service(s) do you provide?
3. Who are your customers?
4. What is your competitive advantage?

Example: Mission Statement

Macrolink provides practical and affordable business planning solutions for do-it-yourself entrepreneurs.

Task List

1. Using the questions and example above as a guide, write your mission statement (20 words or fewer) and enter it into the working copy of your business plan.

3. Vision Statement

Your vision statement should be brief (20 words or fewer) and it must answer these questions:

1. What kind of company do you want to be?
2. How do you wish to be viewed by the individuals and communities you serve?
3. How will you treat your customers, both internal (employees) and external (customers)?

Example: Vision Statement

Macrolink Action Plans Inc. is the resource of choice for entrepreneurs, ensuring customer satisfaction every time.

Task List

1. Using the questions and example above as a guide, write your vision statement (20 words or fewer) and enter it into the working copy of your business plan.

4. Description of the Business

Your description of the business should address these questions and main points:

1. Briefly describe your customers.

2. Describe your office.

3. Describe any other facilities (plant, warehouse, storefront, field operations).

4. Describe your method of operation. Do you create products or purchase them from suppliers? Do you go to your customers, or do they come to you?

5. What equipment do you need? (Currently own or will have to acquire.)

6. What are the outstanding characteristics (price, quality, selection, etc.) of your business?

Example: Description of the Business

Customers are entrepreneurs, business counselors and trainers. This includes clients from many areas of the globe, encompassing all range of start-ups, new firms, economic development organizations and business financing agencies. The primary market will be entrepreneurs from Canada and the US.

Macrolink is a home-based business, with the majority of client interactions taking place either at the customer's location, by telephone or via email and the Internet.

Tip: Keep this Element brief. You will be going into much more detail in other Elements of your business plan.

Task List

1. Using the key points and example above as a guide, develop a description of your business and enter it into the working copy of your business plan.

5. Legal and Regulatory

Keeping your reader in mind, this topic should cover any important legal and regulatory considerations. Answer the following questions:

1. Have you checked the zoning for your location to ensure that it is appropriate for your business?

2. Have you researched the taxation requirements and taken the necessary action?

3. Have you researched the Workers' Compensation Board requirements and taken the necessary action?

4. Which other regulatory agencies will affect your business and what action have you taken?

5. Write out your contact information; this includes your street address, mailing address, Internet address, email address, telephone number, cell phone number, fax number, etc. If you're using a computer, this information should go into your header or footer.

Example: Legal and Regulatory

> Macrolink's mailing address is Box 101, Prince George, BC V2L 4R9. The phone number is 250-612-9161. The company hosts a website at www.macrolink.bc.ca. Boudreau can be reached via email at danb@macrolink.bc.ca.

Task List

1. Using the questions and example above as a guide, write your legal and regulatory segment and enter it into the working copy of your business plan.

Putting Your Business Concept Together

If you have completed each of the segments above separately and now have five parts of The Business Element, it's now time to bring them all together to create a cohesive snapshot of your business. Your next task is to write a draft copy of your Business Element, using the following process:

Example: The Business

> ~ "Practical & Affordable Business Planning Solutions for Do-It-Yourself Entrepreneurs" ~
>
> Macrolink Action Plans Inc is a privately held corporation headquartered in Prince George and registered in the Province of British Columbia. Founded in 1987, the business has focused mainly on the delivery of training throughout Northern BC. This business plan is the owner's blueprint to reconfigure the business and implement a new marketing strategy for growth. The owner and principal shareholder is Dan Boudreau.
>
> The Macrolink vision is to become the resource of choice for entrepreneurs, ensuring customer satisfaction every time.
>
> Customers are entrepreneurs, business counsellors and trainers. This includes clients from many areas of the globe, encompassing all range of start-ups, new firms, economic development organizations and business financing agencies. The primary market will be entrepreneurs from Canada and the US.
>
> Macrolink is a home-based business, with the majority of client interactions taking place either at the customer's location, by telephone or via email and the Internet.
>
> Macrolink's mailing address is Box 101, Prince George, BC V2L 4R9. The phone number is 250-612-9161. The company hosts a website at www.macrolink.bc.ca. Boudreau can be reached via email at danb@macrolink.bc.ca.

Task List

1. Start with a clean page in the working copy of your business plan.
2. Ink or copy in your Identity Statement.
3. Insert your Mission Statement and Vision Statement.
4. Write or copy in your Description of the Business.
5. Enter your Legal and Regulatory segment.
6. Read it out loud to yourself or have someone read it to you.
7. Revise until it accurately communicates the message you wish to convey.

Assess Your Business Concept

Here is an intelligent set of questions to ask about any product, service or business venture. If you answer yes to most of the questions, you may have a winner. Answering no to any or some of the questions doesn't necessarily mean your idea is a bad one, but it may point you to areas of potential difficulty.

ASSESSING YOUR BUSINESS CONCEPT		
Is this business idea new to the marketplace?	Yes	No
Are there customers for this product or service?	Yes	No
Will buyers part with their money for this product or service?	Yes	No
Will the product or service sell for enough money to make a profit?	Yes	No
Can the business sell enough units to meet its profit goals?	Yes	No
Will the product or service encourage or create repeat customers?	Yes	No
Is there enough money to sustain the venture?	Yes	No
Is it difficult for someone else to copy?	Yes	No
Is it difficult for someone else to substitute or replace?	Yes	No
Do you have more control than buyers and suppliers over the idea?	Yes	No
Do you have more control than buyers or suppliers over the prices?	Yes	No
Can you control any uncertainty or risk?	Yes	No

Tip: The more time and energy you put into your writing, the less effort it will take for your reader to understand your business.

Summary

One of the greatest benefits of creating a business plan is that you can use the information in various ways to operate your business. The information in this Element can be useful for:

- Building a brochure
- Assembling sales letters and other communication tools
- Copying over to other Elements of your business plan as starting points
- Communicating with employees
- Developing proposals

The first writing of your business plan is for you - part of its purpose is to ensure that you have covered all the bases. When it comes to producing your business plan you will likely want to trim this to create a shorter version for your reader. People who review business plans (bankers, investors, analysts, etc.) will appreciate any effort you make to keep your plan as succinct as possible, while communicating enough information to get your message to your reader.

This Element usually ranges from as few as a couple of paragraphs to as much as two or three pages, depending on the size and scope of the business.

List Your Products and Services

Step 32

escribe the products and services your business will sell.

Example: Products and Services

PRODUCT OR SERVICE	UNITS
1. Books for Business Planners	Retail, Bookstore, and Distributor Rates
2. Digital Tools for Business Planners	CD and Downloadable from Website
3. Workshops for Business Planners	Day Rate, Half-day Rate, Individual Seat
4. Facilitator Manuals for Counselors and Trainers	Retail Rate
5. Consulting and Business Plan Coaching	Hourly and Daily Rates

Assess Your Product or Service

Here are a number of questions to help with assessing a product or service:

1. **Is it simple?**

   Complexity repels customers. Even if something is complex, it must be presented to the customer in a simple form.

2. **Is it a building block?**

   Larger complex projects or products should be broken down into smaller building blocks.

3. **Is it profitable?**

   Is the product or service profitable at lower and higher levels of production?

4. **Is it scaleable?**

   Can you increase production or sales incrementally while maintaining efficiency and profitablilty?

5. **Can it be sold effectively through the Internet?**

   Is the product digital or can distribution channels be arranged to fulfill orders efficiently?

6. **Is it free from glue?**

   Is the product or service mired in government regulations, politics or bureaucratic processes?

7. **Is it a one-person purchase?**

   Whenever a buying decision must go through one or more committees, the sales process is more cumbersome and therefore more expensive.

8. **Is it within your timelines?**

   Are the business timelines consistent with your personal goals?

9. **Is it controllable?**

   There are many threats to project or product control. Understanding these threats entails industry savvy and market research. Examples of threats are existing or new government regulations, supplier power or changes, natural disasters, industry trends.

10. **Can you afford it?**

   This information can only be obtained through a detailed financial plan.

Tip: The more widespread any particular problem is, the larger the potential market or number of customers for the solution.

Selling the Benefits

As a business owner, one of the greatest skills you can cultivate is to be able to understand how your customer thinks in order to see what he or she needs and wants. This skill will enable you to identify what the benefits are to your customers.

Sell the benefits, or as someone said, "Sell the sizzle, not the steak." This works for a number of different business and personal situations, the most obvious being the selling of your products or services. Selling the benefits also works for negotiating, be it for employee contracts, serving customers, writing proposals, creating business plans, dealing with family members or mapping out our own life goals.

It is important to understand the difference between features and benefits. Features are about the product or service, whereas benefits are about what the product or service will do for the customer.

Turning Problems into Features and Benefits

Businesses solve problems for customers. The nature of the problem determines the features, and therefore the benefits, to customers. For example, most of my work involves my computer; I travel a great deal and need ready access to my computer files and I also need to be able to work while away from my office. The problem: my old PC was not transportable. Other people had this problem as well. The more people that have a common problem or need, the larger the potential market for the solution to the problem. Along came the laptop computer, solving the problem for me and many other customers. My laptop computer is lightweight and easy to carry wherever I go, making it possible for me to have my office and personal information with me wherever I am. The features = benefits.

How do you turn features into benefits? The real key is to listen to your customers first, to ensure you are solving real problems and meeting real needs. Once you clearly understand your customers' needs you can then design the features and communicate the benefits.

The following table shows the Macrolink products and services, features, benefits and the competitive advantage for each.

Example: Competitive Advantage

PRODUCT / SERVICE	FEATURES	BENEFITS	COMPETITIVE ADVANTAGE
1. Books for Business Planners · Business Plan or BUST! · The RoadMap™ · The Forecaster's Handbook	· Comprehensive · Organized into logical steps · Competitively priced · Created for the novice · Integrated system	· You can trust it · You can manage it · You save time & money · You can do it yourself · You build a complete understanding of your business	A system that works for entrepreneurs who want or need to develop their own business plans.
2. Digital Tools for Business Planners · Biz4Caster™ · RiskBuster™ Business Planner	· Competitively priced · Comprehensive · Simplified input tasks · Web supported · Complex tasks are automated · Integrated system	· You save money · You won't miss critical points · You can do it step by step · You can email for help · You save time and energy · You prove your business case	Transforms your business planning experience into a safe and fun learning adventure!
3. Workshops for Business Planners and Trainers · Half Day · One Day · Two Day	· Interactive, hands-on · Create parts of your plan · Creative learning activities · 99-step business planning process	· You learn while you plan · You build confidence · You feel safe to experiment · You are organized & thorough	A practical, interactive way to explore entrepren-eurship.
4. Facilitator Manuals For Counselors and Trainers	· Comprehensive · Modularized · Easy to use · Ready to deliver · Proven training techniques · Portable · Fully integrated system	· You adapt to learner needs · You provide variety · You save preparation time · You earn money instantly · You deliver with confidence · You take training to clients · You save development time	A fully integrated, ready to use business planning system for counselors and trainers.
5. Consulting and Coaching Service · Hourly	· Affordable · Effective · Efficient	· You get results · You save time · You save money	A seasoned entrepreneur in your corner.

Macrolink Action Plans Inc. Holds Copyright For All Of The Products And Materials Listed Above.

Tip: *The Forecaster's Handbook is a step-by-step process for forecasting financial scenarios, included as part of the RiskBuster™ CD.*

The manufacturer or service provider defines the features and we the customers define the benefits. The manufacturer did their homework before, during and after creating my laptop, ensuring that they met my needs, therefore benefiting me (the customer) in the end.

Here is what you are faced with at the beginning of the business process. You need to somehow get into the customer's head and determine what the benefits are so you can then ensure that your product or service meets the customer needs. How? Simply talk to your prospective customers. Describe what you wish to create for them; you will likely describe your product according to features. Ask your customers what they need and listen to their answers.

Task List

1. Use the *Products and Services Worksheet* below or another suitable method and list your products and services.

2. Using the *Competitive Advantage Worksheet* on the following page, develop a list of the main features, benefits and competitive advantage for each product and for each service.

3. Copy your list of products and services directly into the Products and Services Element of your business plan.

4. If you think it appropriate, copy the list of features and benefits into your business plan.

You need to somehow get into the customer's head and determine what the benefits are so you can then ensure that your product or service meets the customer needs.

WORKSHEET: PRODUCTS AND SERVICES	
PRODUCT OR SERVICE	UNITS
1.	
2.	
3.	
4.	
5.	
6.	
7.	
8.	
9.	
10.	
11.	
12.	

Tip: To convert features into benefits, ask yourself what the feature will do for the customer. One way to do this is to use the statement, "What this means to you (the customer) is..." For example, if your car gets more miles per gallon of gasoline, you save money. Your car gets more miles per gallon (feature). What this means to you is you save money (benefit).

WORSHEET: COMPETITIVE ADVANTAGE			
PRODUCT / SERVICE	FEATURES	BENEFITS	COMPETITIVE ADVANTAGE
1.			
2.			
3.			
4.			
5.			
6.			
7.			
8.			
9.			
10.			
11.			
12.			

Tip: For any product or service, the competitive advantage must answer the question, "Why will the customer buy this product of service from you instead of the competition?"

Describe Your Industry

This is a snapshot of the industry or industries in which your business will compete.

MUST HAVE
RECOMMENDED
NICE TO HAVE

Example: Description of the Industry

Macrolink sells its products and services to entrepreneurs in virtually all sectors and industries, primarily in Canada and the United States. For taxation purposes, the business is classified in the Independent Artists, Writers and Performers Industry. From a practical standpoint, the business is providing its products and services to anyone considering, starting or growing a business.

The Macrolink business case is built on providing practical and affordable business planning solutions to entrepreneurs who need to develop their own business plans. The owner conservatively estimates the potential market in Canada and the United States to be more than $110 million each year.

The outlook for the sale of business books is strong and positive. According to industry authorities, business books are a hot market and tend to pick up sales momentum as time passes. Books about small business are especially hot and have excellent backlist potential.

The Macrolink business case is based on the following industry trends and factors:

1. It is generally getting more complex to start and operate a business, making it more important than ever for entrepreneurs to develop business plans.

2. In British Columbia in 2004, 98% or 337,400 of businesses were small businesses; 83% were micro-businesses with fewer than 5 employees; 54% were single owners with no paid help. In 2004, three quarters of all businesses in British Columbia were in the service sector.

3. "How-to" e-books are the fastest growing area of the book publishing industry.

4. In the United States, 10 million adults are engaged in trying to start new firms at any time.

5. Entrepreneurship involves adults of all ages, except people over 65.

6. Young men aged 25-34 are the most active group involved in starting businesses, followed by women in the same age group.

7. Globally, the market for business planning products is huge. The GEM 2003 study showed that more than 300 million people of the 2.4 billion labor force in the 40 countries analyzed, are entrepreneurs involved in new business formation.

The main barriers to selling business planning products and services are: standing out from the many similar products and services, gaining brand recognition and getting distribution.

The Opportunity

For most people considering starting a business, the realization that they need a business plan is like hitting a wall. This generates a great deal of frustration and causes many potential business owners to either give up on their business idea or push ahead into business without a business plan. The current situation allows room in the market for practical and affordable products that make the task of business planning manageable for entrepreneurs who realize they need to build their own business plans.

Tip: Nobody expects you to become an economist in order to start your small or micro business. Your most important goal with this Element is to clarify that you understand the industry your business is in. Unless you have the background to enable you to create a highly technical description of your industry, keep this Element simple and practical.

Tip: Ride on the shoulders of giants. Adapt existing information from other sources to shape your industry Element. You don't have time to dig deep enough to build your Industry Element from the bottom up.

Task List

To complete this Element you must first do your secondary market research and then develop your list of key information in Step 18. By now you will also have completed some or all of your primary market research and added useful local information to your library of information about your business. Using all the information gathered, write a description of your industry or industries, including the following points:

Tip: If you've been working in your industry for a number of years you probably know the answers to most of the questions to the right. But it can still be a challenge to get the information out of your head and onto the page. Try having someone ask you the questions and write your answers for you while you talk.

1. Tell which industry or industries your business is in.
2. Describe the quantity and value of goods sold.
3. Describe the industry outlook and growth potential.
4. List the past, present and future industry trends.
5. Explain any key points about your industry that help support your business case.
6. Chart or describe relevant population shifts and/or consumer trends.
7. Describe the main challenges faced by the industry.
8. Describe any barriers or incentives to entry by new businesses.
9. Describe any new developments in the industry.
10. Describe the size of the total market and your local market area.
11. Describe the opportunity or gap your business will serve.

Write Your Biography

Introduce yourself and any other owners of the business.

Many people find it difficult to write about themselves. This is an opportunity to toot your horn. In this Element you must step forward and display your achievements in a positive way, without bragging.

Step 34

MUST HAVE
RECOMMENDED
NICE TO HAVE

Example: The Owner

> Dan Boudreau is the sole owner, President and CEO for the business:
>
> - Involved in small business development since 1980, as owner, coach, trainer and consultant.
> - Worked in community economic development for 15 years.
> - Served ten years on Finance and Lending Committee for a $5 million loan fund for entrepreneurs.
> - Manages a $15 million fund that provides grants for economic development projects.
> - Nominated twice as Entrepreneur of the Year – 1997 and 1999.
> - Develops and delivers workshops for entrepreneurs (Business Planning, Train the Trainer).
> - Published *Dream Catcher Business Planning Toolkit* and *Scratchpad* (since 1995).
> - Published *Business on a Shoe String* e-zine – 1999 to 2003.
>
> Boudreau's resumé is in Appendix A and a list of references is in Appendix B.

Tip: This Element works well as a bulleted list.

Task List

To complete this Element you will need to gather information about yourself that is relevant to the business you are starting and then:

1. Provide a brief snapshot of yourself, including any relevant educational or business achievements.
2. Briefly outline your work experience and training as it relates to the specific business you plan to start.
3. List your strengths and what you feel you will contribute to the business to make it successful.
4. List your relevant achievements and successes.
5. Note that your detailed resumé in the Appendices will support this Element.

Develop Your Strategic Plan and Goals

Step 35

Build your strategic plan and short-term business goals.

Example: Strategic Plan and Goals

Macrolink strategies include:

1. Effective financial management.
2. Effective marketing strategy for positive organizational growth.
3. Continuous research, development and innovation.
4. Advancement of service and product quality.
5. Effective communication with all stakeholders.
6. Team members have the skills, knowledge and systems to serve customers.

The short-term business goals are:

GOALS	TIMELINES
1. To publish the books – hard copy and digital (e-book).	March 2006
2. To secure trademark / intangible property protection on all brands.	May 2006
3. To complete development of the RiskBuster™ CD and download.	June 2006
4. To create a website with shopping cart and e-commerce capabilities.	Aug. 2006
5. To launch the website, book and digital products.	Sept. 2006
6. To achieve gross revenues of $128,242 for year one.	Sept. 2007
7. To retain net income before taxes of $12,061 for year one.	Sept. 2007
8. To sell a minimum of 1,330 books and 419 CDs.	Sept. 2007

Task List

To complete this Element you will need to have completed most of your primary and secondary market research and then do the following.

1. Using your mission and vision statements as a base, develop three to six strategic objectives for your business. Strategic objectives are broad in scope and more general, less specific than goals.

2. Set goals for year one. Some areas to consider setting short-term goals are: gross revenues, net profits, the number of units to be sold, the number of employees, location, new marketing, franchising, new products and/or services, diversification, quality, customers, growth, return on investment, training and professional development. You don't need goals for every one of these topics; set goals only for the ones that are most important to you.

3. Prioritize your goals and determine who will perform each.
4. Set deadlines for completion (if applicable).
5. Copy the appropriate information from this segment into the Strategic Plan and Goals Element of the business plan.

WORKSHEET: STRATEGIC PLAN	
OBJECTIVE	
1.	
2.	
3.	
4.	
5.	
6.	
7.	
8.	

Tip: Unless there is an advantage for doing so, it can be problematic to put goals with deadlines into this Element of your business plan. This is because the plan quickly becomes outdated, necessitating continuous updating to remain accurate. Although you will need timelines for internal planning purposes, it can be simpler to leave the dates out of this Element.

WORKSHEET: GOALS AND TIMELINES	
GOAL	**TIMELINES**
1.	
2.	
3.	
4.	
5.	
6.	
7.	
8.	

Tip: Ensure the business will support your personal financial goal. If you state you hope to earn a certain amount from your business, it is important that this be consistent with your short-term business goals.

MAP YOUR MARKETING SECTION

The purpose of this Section is to plan and describe how you will get your goods into the hands of paying customers.

Here are the ten business plan Elements in this Section and the corresponding RoadMap™ steps:

BUSINESS PLAN ELEMENT	ROADMAP™ STEPS
Market Area	36
Location: Marketing	37
Profile of the Customers	38
Competition and Differentiation	39
Sales and Distribution	40
Servicing and Guarantees	41
Image	42
Advertising and Promotion	43
Pricing Strategy	44
Marketing Action Plan	45

Here is a brief description of each of the Elements of the Marketing Section.

BRIEF INTRODUCTION TO THE MARKETING ELEMENTS	
ELEMENT	DESCRIPTION
Market Area	The purpose of this Element is to define the geographic area in which your business will operate. *Key points:* geographical area; a definite area that can be marked on a map; can be a building or neighborhood, a city, a community, a region, a province, an industry, a type of business, government.
Location: Marketing	The purpose of this Element is to describe where your business is located in terms of customers and sales. You will need to consider things like communicating to your customers and getting your products or services to customers. *Key points:* home-based or office. Does the business require walk-in traffic? Where does your business need to be to access raw materials? Is the necessary transportation infrastructure in place? Where are similar businesses located?
Profile of the Customers	The purpose of this Element is to develop a profile of your customers using primary and secondary sources to identify the key information. *Key points:* gathering information; primary and secondary sources; demographics; psychographics. What are the principle buying motives? Who influences the buying decisions? How much will they pay? How much will your average sale be? Who are your target customers? What product or service features are most important to your customers? How sensitive are the buyers to pricing differences?
Competition and Differentiation	The purpose of this Element is to develop a profile of your competitors. To differentiate your business from the competitors you must understand their strengths and weaknesses. *Key points:* sources of information; names and locations of firms; appearance of business sites; layout of operation; history; similarities in source, features, and price; related products or services; number of employees; sales; put any detailed comparisons or test results in the appendices.

Sales and Distribution	The purpose of this Element is to determine which sales activities will best reach your customers. The methods you choose will be determined in part by your product, your customer and the methods used by your competition. **Key points:** direct mail, email, door-to-door, mail order, fax, sales representatives, shows and fairs, conventions and conferences; indirect - telemarketing, toll-free numbers, retail, national retail chains, regional chains, independent distributors, joint marketing relationships, outside marketing company. How can your products or services be distributed? How can you best reach the customer?
Servicing and Guarantees	The purpose of this Element is to clarify the level of service you will offer and what promises or guarantees you will make for those who purchase your products or services. This Element consists of promises that a business person must live up to. **Key points:** consider what your guarantees might cost and build costs into price; never promise more than you can deliver, always deliver more than you promise.
Image	The purpose of this Element is to create an effective image for your business. How do you want your business to appear in the mind of your customers? **Key points:** your personal style; business graphics; methods of sales; telephone use; service; physical surroundings.
Advertising and Promotion	The purpose of this Element is to determine the most effective approaches, tools and methods to increase your customers' awareness of your products and services. **Key points:** advertising - display ads in newspapers, trade journals, classified ads, direct mail, shoppers and flyers, yellow pages and other directories; promotion - specialty advertising, trade shows, samples, coupons and premiums, contests, and demonstrations. What amount of time and money can you afford? How will you inform, persuade and influence your customers? How will you stimulate interest in your product or service?
Pricing Strategy	The purpose of this Element is to set prices for your products and services. To set prices you must first be clear about costs. **Key points:** What are your costs? How much will the customer pay? What are the competitors' prices? What is the relationship of supply to demand? What are the consumer buying trends? What reductions will be required by distributors? What is your level of risk? What is your desired profit margin?
Marketing Action Plan	The purpose of this Element is to create an action plan for marketing your products and services. **Key points:** type of marketing; consider the sales and distribution methods and how to best communicate with your customers. Will you build a website? Do you need written communications, brochures, flyers, posters? Set timelines and estimate the costs for each major milestone.

Tip: The business of getting to know your customer is achieved through your market research. If you are finding this Section difficult, it may be that you have not yet done enough market research.

Task List

1. Read the Marketing Section of the business plan in Chapter 6 to get a sense of what you are trying to achieve in this Section.

Describe Your Market Area

Step 36

efine the geographic area in which your business will operate.

Market area can be defined a number of different ways. It can be a geographical area, a definite area that can be marked on a map. It might also be a building, a neighborhood, a city, a reserve, a region, a tribal council jurisdiction, a province, a country or global.

Example: Market Area

Macrolink will offer its hard copy business planning solutions to clients throughout North America and its digital products to customers who can access the Internet.

Task List

To complete this Element you will need to have completed most of your primary and secondary market research and then:

1. Write a description of the geographic area in which your business will operate.

Tip: This Element can be text but a small map or picture might make it more effective.

WORKSHEET: DESCRIBE YOUR MARKET AREA

Describe Your Location

Determine where to locate your business in terms of customers, marketing and sales.

This Element requires that you think about the issues of communicating and getting your products or services to your customers. Further, it pushes you to make some fundamental decisions. Questions to consider:

- Will your business be home-based or storefront?
- Does the business require walk-in traffic?
- Where should you be located relative to your supply or raw materials?
- If you're shipping goods, do you need to be located near major transportation arteries such as rail, road, water or airports?
- If you're serving businesses, will some locations be advantageous over others?
- Do you or will you need electrical, telephone or Internet access?
- Where and how are similar businesses set-up?

Example: Location Marketing

From a marketing perspective, Macrolink is located in the city of Prince George in North Central British Columbia. The city has the necessary infrastructure to enable Macrolink to operate globally through the use of its technology. The highway and air transportation infrastructures support travel to and from most of the major cities, making it easy to ship products and attend events.

Task List

To complete this Element you will need to:

1. Determine the best location for your business in relation to your customers.
2. Decide whether the business will be home-based, commercial, retail, urban or rural.
3. Research where similar businesses are located and identify the reasons why.
4. Describe how the chosen location will help facilitate communication with, and sales to, your customers.

Step 37

MUST HAVE
RECOMMENDED
NICE TO HAVE

Tip: In describing this Element, consider using a mixture of text, pictures, a map, or all three.

Describe Your Customers

Step 38

Develop a market profile using primary and secondary sources to identify the key information.

In the process of researching your market you should have written a draft description of your customers in Step 20 and then fine-tuned it in Step 29. If you're keeping pace, it should already be in the working copy of your business plan.

Example: Profile of Customers

Macrolink's primary customers will be entrepreneurs in Canada and the United States. In the 25 to 54 age group, Canada hosts 13,440,355 and the United States 122,718,203, totaling more than 136 million people in the ideal business planning age group. If only 12% of this group were involved in entrepreneurial activity, this would be a potential market of more 16 million. In a 1999 Yankelovich poll, over one-third of Americans predicted they would own their own business within a decade.

Characteristics of this client group are: shortage of time, scarcity of money, lack of business planning skills, limited understanding of market research, and a desire or need to be involved in entrepreneurial activity. Ideally, customers will own computers and have access to the Internet; however, the books are equally effective using only a pencil and calculator. To entice this customer to purchase, Macrolink will need to provide affordable, upbeat and safe ways for each individual to participate in the business planning process with different options available for them to advance at their own pace.

Macrolink's primary customers will include the one million Canadians and ten million American entrepreneurs striving to start businesses at any given time. Marketing efforts will be focused on the <u>eleven million North American entrepreneurs</u> engaged in starting businesses.

The following table shows various customer groups:

TOP PRIORITY	SECOND PRIORITY	THIRD PRIORITY
1 Million Workforce Age People Starting Businesses in Canada Male and Female	Economic and Enterprise Development Agencies In Canada and the US	18 Million Non-Employer Business Owners in Canada and the US
10 Million Workforce Age People Starting Businesses in the US Male and Female	Independent Distributors Bookstores, Colleges, Libraries, Chains that Sell Books	Workforce Age People Starting Businesses in Countries Other Than Canada and the US

Task List

1. Revisit your Profile of the Customers Element and fine-tune it, with attention to the following questions:

    - Who influences the buying decisions?

    - How much will customers pay for your products and services?

    - What will your average sale be?

    - How are the key competitors positioned in the mind of the customers?

    - How sensitive are the buyers to pricing differences?

    - What motivates customers to buy your products and services?

Tip: This Element can be more effective with the addition of tables.

WORKSHEET: PROFILE OF CUSTOMERS

The following table shows the various customer groups:

TOP PRIORITY	SECOND PRIORITY	THIRD PRIORITY

Affirmation

I am privileged to serve customers. When customers come to me, I put my heart into serving them what they need and want. I always provide my very best service for customers. In my mind, I see them telling others of the great service they received. This leads to more and more customers for my service and business prospers.

Analyze Your Competitors and Differentiate

Step 39

Develop a profile of your competitors and differentiate your business from them. In order to differentiate your business from the competitors you must understand their strengths and weaknesses.

Example: Competition and Differentiation

Entrepreneurs currently address their business planning requirements in a variety of ways, from ignoring the need and starting their enterprise without a business plan to hiring a consultant to create the plan for them. Starting a business without a plan is like trying to fly a jet without first taking the time to learn how to fly. For the typical owner/operator of a small or micro-business, hiring a consultant to develop one's business plan makes about as much sense as paying someone else to take flying lessons. In order to understand their business, most entrepreneurs should develop their own business plans.

The following options currently dominate the market: books, digital products, workshops, consulting services and business counseling services.

Books: There are a variety of publications in the market that are available through bookstores and the Internet. Analysis shows prices from a low of $14.95 to a high of $69.95, with the majority of books competing in the $20 to $40 range. Also available are a number of free publications offered by all or most financial institutions and government agencies. In the course of researching to write the Business Planner's Toolkit, Boudreau purchased 24 books and gathered a number of free publications from a variety of sources. The problem with most of the available systems and materials is that they do not adequately prepare the novice to complete his or her business plan. Many books offer the reader opportunities to learn <u>about</u> various aspects of business planning, but do not show the user <u>how to navigate</u> the market research and business planning processes. More importantly, most books present pieces of the puzzle but do not effectively blend the market researching and business planning processes or lead the user from idea to implementation.

Digital Products: There are a number of digital business planning products available, ranging from free to over $500. There are two that currently seem to dominate the market, Business Plan Pro and Bizplan Builder, both currently selling at approximately $115 ($99USD). The writer has purchased and tested nine different software options and found that most do not successfully deal with both the narrative and the financial portions of the business plan. Business planning software products are either beyond the capacity of the novice or are so streamlined they enable the user to fabricate a relatively slick business plan without actually having to learn about their business. In the interest of making it easy for the end user, software options typically neglect the most important benefit of business planning, which is to gain confidence through learning about one's business by researching the market.

Workshops: Most communities have local facilitators who provide business planning workshops at prices ranging from $350 to $1,000 per day, however, not many have specialized in business planning. Most often they are either experienced facilitators offering business planning as one of many topics, or consultants with knowledge but limited facilitation skills. During the past 15 years Boudreau has attended business planning workshops by 27 different facilitators, a number of which have never actually developed their own business plan. With the RoadMap™ as a foundation, Macrolink workshops not only teach the participant <u>about</u> business planning, they also equip the user with an organized approach so that he or she knows <u>how to navigate</u> the market research and business planning processes.

Consulting Services: It will typically cost between $30 and $100 per hour to have a consultant write a business plan for you. It can cost from $2,000 to $30,000 or more to have a consultant develop a business plan, which is simply not viable for most small or micro-businesses. Macrolink will differentiate from consultants by positioning as a business planning coach for customers who wish to develop their own business plans. Macrolink will not develop business plans <u>for</u> customers.

Business Counseling Services: Many economic and enterprise development agencies provide free counseling services for business planners. For example, most of the Community Futures Development Corporations in rural communities across Canada employ Business Analysts and sometimes Self-Employment Benefits (SEB) Coordinators, whose job is to assist entrepreneurs with business planning. Most of these competitors differ from Macrolink's coaching services in that they are usually gatekeepers for either loan funds or the SEB Program. Boudreau's marketing strategy will include inviting and encouraging counselors to become customers by using the Macrolink Business Planning System and where possible, distributing the books and digital products to their clients.

The majority of people who need business plans face the following challenges:

1. They are unfamiliar and uncomfortable with business forecasting, planning and writing.

2. They tend to be intimidated by gatekeepers (bankers, advisors, analysts).

3. They are unsure which of the confusing array of business planning formats to use.

4. They do not have access to a clear, effective, step-by-step business planning process.

Macrolink business planning solutions will be differentiated in the following ways:

1. The RoadMap™ will dovetail the market research and business planning processes, enabling the user to navigate from the business idea to implementation step by step.

2. They will transform the business planning process into a safe, manageable, learning adventure.

3. Books will be positioned in the medium to high price range and in the high quality category.

4. CDs and digital downloads will be positioned in the lower price and high quality category.

5. Macrolink Action Plans Inc. will serve ordinary, down-to-earth entrepreneurs who will develop their own business plans. The service will not include developing business plans for customers.

Macrolink Business Planning System empowers the novice with a viable proposal to prove his or her business case and create a meaningful business plan.

Task List

1. Review the market research and results from Step 22.

2. List the names and locations of the major competitors.

3. Compare the various competitors on the basis of appearance of their business sites, the layout of their operations, how many employees, and how long they have been in business.

4. Compare products and services between the different businesses.

5. Note similarities and differences in brand, features, benefits and prices.

Tip: Do not bad-mouth your competitors. It is far better to promote your strengths and benefits than to say negative things about your competitors.

6. Estimate the sales or market share for each competitor.

7. Compare all competitor strengths and weaknesses.

8. Determine why customers buy from your competitors.

9. Differentiate your business from the competitors and clarify why the customer will buy from your business.

10. Develop this Element and enter it into the working copy of your business plan.

11. Save any important comparisons, survey and test results in the Appendices.

12. Tables can be used to demonstrate the similarities and differences between competitors.

Describe How You Will Sell Your Products and Services

D etermine which sales activities will best reach your customers. The methods you choose will be determined in part by your product, by your customer and by the methods used by your competitors. This step leads to writing the Sales and Distribution Element in the Operations Section of your business plan.

Step 40

MUST HAVE
RECOMMENDED
NICE TO HAVE

Example: Sales and Distribution

The main objective of Macrolink's marketing strategy is to get distribution. During the first three years of business, the owner will self-distribute the books and digital products as well as promoting and selling through the shopping cart at the Trafford Publishing website. Trafford will do some marketing of the book via the Internet, as well as publishing the books on demand – this will eliminate the need to publish or stock large inventories of books until orders are in place.

Once the Macrolink website is established the owner will approach bookstores, economic development agencies, associations and organizations in the economic development field. Boudreau will actively promote himself as a speaker and facilitator at strategic conferences – for example, Western Canadian Community Futures Development Corporations will schedule a training session during spring 2006.

Macrolink will sell its products and services through the following methods:

· Digital and hard copy products via a website shopping cart at www.riskbuster.com.

· Books sold by Trafford Publishing through its website bookstore at www.trafford.com.

· Facilitator manuals and business planning products sold directly to trainers.

· Facilitators will receive a discount on hard copy and digital learner materials.

· Boudreau will sell products directly to book stores, retailers and distributors.

· Co-op promotion agreements established with software and business development organizations.

· Boudreau will offer affordable three-hour seminars to generate book and CD sales.

· Boudreau will sell books and CDs at trade shows.

Boudreau will be the salesperson for the first three years of the business.

Tip: This Element is probably best as text or a bulleted list.

Task List

To complete this Element you will need to complete your analysis of the various competitors and then:

1. Identify which sales methods are being used most successfully by the competition.

2. Determine the industry standard for getting products and services to the customers.

3. Choose which sales methods will best work for you, with careful consideration to the amount of available time, energy and money.

Clarify Your Servicing and Guarantees

Step 41

Clarify the level of service you will offer and what you will promise to replace or repair. This Element consists of promises that a business person must live up to.

Example: Servicing and Guarantees

> Macrolink offers the following guarantee:
>
> Your success is our success. We stand behind the quality of our products and services. If for any reason you are not completely satisfied, return all materials to us within 15 days of purchase to receive a full refund. This policy does not apply to digital products downloaded from our website; however, we will replace any defective digital products within 15 days of purchase.
>
> **The guarantee will be posted at the Macrolink website and in promotional materials.**

Task List

To complete this Element you will need to complete your analysis of the various competitors and then:

Tip: Never promise more than you can deliver, always deliver a little more than your customer expects.

1. Identify any guarantees your competitors offer with their products and services.
2. Clarify and write your customer service philosophy.
3. Describe your servicing and guarantee strategy.
4. Estimate any related costs and build them into your prices.

Craft Your Business Image

Create an effective corporate image.

Step 42

Example: Image

> Macrolink is in business to serve entrepreneurs. Its products and services are practical, affordable and professional. To maintain a consistently professional image, all communications, materials and printed products will maintain a professional quality and tone. Customers who purchase products and services from Macrolink will receive excellent value for their investment. As the logo portrays, Macrolink is a responsible corporation that respects the environment and empowers ordinary people through learning. By year four, assuming continued and growing profitability, the business will begin contributing 5% of pre-tax profits to assist micro-entrepreneurs with business plan development and start-up capital. These monies will be vetted through existing not-for-profit enterprise development agencies.

Task List

Tip: This Element will require some text - consider using pictures or graphics.

To complete this Element you will need to complete your analysis of the various competitors and then:

1. Decide what kind of image your business will project.

2. Review your customer profile, paying attention to likes and dislikes, needs and what's important to them.

3. Consider your likes and dislikes and how you wish your business to be perceived in the marketplace.

4. How will your business put back? In other words, what will your business contribute to the community(s) it serves? Consider whether your business will share a portion of the wealth it generates and if so, which cause you will dedicate the funds to.

5. Write a description of your business image.

6. Define as many Elements of your marketing package as you are able to, with attention to your business graphics, logo design, business cards, letterhead, packaging, signs, advertising style, methods of sales, telephone use, service, how interruptions are managed and physical surroundings.

Affirmation

I surround myself with positive pictures, healthy plants, interesting objects, upbeat sounds, pleasant odors, inspirational writings, motivating posters and images. My work area is a lively, fun place to create solutions for myself and my customers.

Develop Your Advertising and Promotion Plan

Step 43

MUST HAVE
RECOMMENDED
NICE TO HAVE

Determine the most effective approaches, tools and methods to increase your customers' awareness of your products and services.

Knowing that I am solely responsible for marketing and selling my products and services, I considered the various methods in the following table. I know my strategy will operate on a limited budget.

ADVERTISING AND PROMOTION PLAN			
Ad Specialties	Coupons	Lighting	Sandwich Signs
Advertising Services	Courses	Letters (Personalized)	Seminars
Answering Machine	Customer Appreciation Day	Listings	Shelf Merchandising
Articles	Décor	Magazine Ads	Signs
Audiocassettes	Demonstrations	Matchbooks	Special Events
Balloons	Direct Mail	Name Tags	Sponsorships
Billboards (Bus, Highway, Bench)	Directories	Movie Theater Ads	Statement Stuffers
Birthday Cards	Distributors	News Releases	Surveys
Books	Donations	Newsletters	T-shirt Ads
Booths (Displays)	Door Hangers	Newspaper Ads	"Take Ones"
Brochures	Electronic Bulletin Boards	Parking Meter Ads	Telemarketing – Inbound
Bulletin Boards	Exhibits	Party Plan	Telemarketing – Outbound
Business Cards	Fairs	Per Inquiry Ads	Television
Business Card Ads	Fax Broadcast	Personal Contact	Trade Shows
Calendar Listings	Feature Stories	Placemats	TV Guides
Canvassing	Fixtures	Point of Purchase	Uniforms
Car Cards	Fliers	Postcards	Vanity Radio
Card Decks	Frequent Purchase Program	Posters	Videocassette Box Ads
Catalogs	Fund Raisers	Premiums	Vehicle Ads
Celebrities	Gift Certificates	Public Speaking	Videotapes
Centers of Influence	Gifts	Publicity	Word-of-mouth
Clinics	Greeting Cards	Radio Spots	Workshops
Co-op Mailings / Ads	Group Mailings	Recorded Phone Messages	www / Internet Home Page
Color Schemes	Info-Lines	Reports	Yellow Pages
Columns	Inserts	Restroom Ads	Toll-Free Number
Contests		Sales Reps	

Example: Advertising and Promotion

As a part of the package price for publishing the book, Trafford will offer the book for sale at its website at www.trafford.com. Trafford's "Best Seller" package also includes notifying Amazon.com, Borders.com, Barnes & Noble, Chapters.Indigo, Baker & Taylor distributors, Bowker's Books-in-Print, BookData UK and PubStock.

In addition to the Trafford marketing, the owner will actively market and promote Macrolink products and services. Each product or service will include ads or coupons for other Macrolink products and services. In this way, the marketing will be fully integrated, creating opportunities for existing customers to purchase other products and services from Macrolink. All materials will advertise the website.

The business will convey a consistent message and build a high profile by:

· Producing quality marketing materials for products and services (business cards, brochures, postcards and posters) that drive traffic to the website.

· Providing affordable business planning workshops and seminars.

· Hosting websites at various strategic domains currently held by Macrolink - **www. riskbuster.com** – **www.Biz4Caster.com** – **www.riskbuster.com** – **www.bp99.com**.

· Placing advertisements for specific products and services in strategic publications.

· Publishing and delivering a free, opt-in monthly e-zine for entrepreneurs.

· Writing articles on business planning and related topics for e-zines and magazines.

· Maintaining a professional image on all communications, products and documents.

· Hosting display booths at key tradeshows in the target industry sectors.

Word-of-mouth will account for a portion of sales as customers succeed by using Macrolink products and services. The owner will publish success stories at the website and in strategic publications.

Tip: This Element can be effective as text, bulleted or numbered lists and tables.

Task List

To complete this Element you will need to complete your analysis of various competitors and then:

1. Determine what the industry standard is as to the percentage of revenue put towards advertising and marketing.

2. Establish which methods within your means will enable you to achieve your goals.

3. Develop a detailed 12-month advertising and promotion plan and budget using the worksheet.

4. Brainstorm how your business can get free publicity or how you can partner with other businesses or agencies to conserve costs.

5. Include the detailed budget in the Appendices Section of your business plan.

6. Identify areas needing further market research and set goals to carry it out.

7. Develop a summary of your advertising, promotion and publicity plan for this Element.

Present Your Prices and Pricing Strategy

Step 44

Set prices for your products and services. In order to set prices you must first be clear about costs.

There are at least three ways to set your prices. To establish prices for your products and services, you will likely employ all three methods: pricing to market, pricing to cost and break-even pricing.

1. Pricing To Market

Pricing to market means setting your prices according to the competitive market prices. Using this method will restrict you to finding your profit through efficiencies and savings on your costs. Some types of business will compel you to set your prices to market.

2. Pricing To Cost

Pricing to cost means determining your cost to make your product or service and adding your desired profit margin in order to arrive at your price. Another way to state this is determine your cost of goods sold, identify the industry standard mark-up for the product or service, then add the two together to create your price.

3. Break-Even Pricing

Break-even pricing means determining how much you need for your business to break-even overall and then setting your product and service prices to break even and earn you a profit.

Things to Consider when Setting Prices for Your Products and Services

1. How price sensitive are your customers?
2. Do your customers decide to buy based on price or on other characteristics such as quality, location or convenience?
3. What is the cost of producing your products or services?
4. What are your competitors' prices for similar products or services?
5. How many units do you have to sell to break-even or profit?
6. What are the industry standard mark-ups or margins for your product or service?
7. What discount rates will you offer for bulk purchases?
8. How much can the customer afford to pay for your product or service?
9. How much will your customer pay for your product or service?
10. What is the relationship of supply to demand?
11. What are the consumer buying trends?

12. What is your level of risk?

13. What is your desired profit margin?

14. What are your personal and corporate financial goals?

Establishing Your Pricing Strategy

Most likely your first concern will be to determine whether your product or service can live in the market place. In other words, can you hope to sell it for enough to pay your bills, survive and earn a small profit? Unless you are already financially independent and are starting your business for purely altruistic reasons, your first priority should be to ensure the numbers work.

Beyond the first priority of establishing viability, there are a number of other concerns that enable you to chart your course with regard to setting pricing objectives. Here are a few considerations to help you get started.

1. What are your desired timelines to become established in the market?

2. Do you wish to sell more products or services for lower profits or fewer products or services for higher profits?

3. Will you initiate price wars by selling at prices lower than your competitors?

4. Do you have the resources to survive a prolonged price war or do your competitors have deeper pockets?

5. Do you have control over or flexibility with your product and service costs?

6. Do you have control over or flexibility with your prices to customers?

7. Are there existing industry standard mark-up percentages you must adhere to?

8. What levels of the distribution will you occupy and which will you target as customers?

9. What image will your price create with your customers?

Example: Pricing Strategy

Macrolink pricing strategy is to offer clients *practical and affordable business planning solutions*.

Since 2001, the owner has surveyed more than 500 entrepreneurs. Those surveyed include individual male and female adults from 20 to 54 years old, with a demonstrated interest in starting a business. Feedback indicates that 90% of those surveyed will pay between $29 and $99CAD for business planning solutions. The list below shows the 12 units and prices used to forecast sales for the first three years of operation for the business.

PRODUCT OR SERVICE UNIT	COST OF GOODS SOLD	CUSTOMER UNIT PRICE
1. Books - Trafford - Retail	14.63	36.58
2. Books - Trafford - Bookstores	14.63	21.95
3. Books - Trafford - Distributors	14.63	18.29
4. Books - Owner - Retail	14.19	36.58
5. RiskBuster™ CD - Retail	5.00	29.50
6. RiskBuster™ CD - Distributors	5.00	29.50
7. Digital Downloads Retail	5.00	29.50
8. Half-Day Workshops		350.00
9. Full-Day Workshops		495.00
10. Seminars to Individuals		49.00
11. Facilitator Manuals	50.00	99.95
12. Consulting and Coaching Hours		40.00

Book Discount Rates

· 15% to libraries & college bookstores

· 25% to publishers

· 40% to bookstores

· 50% to distributors

Notes to Pricing

1. All prices are in Canadian dollars.

2. Cost of Goods Sold (COGS) is estimated at the highest rate (retail, one book on demand) for all book sales.

3. COGS are entered at the highest cost of production ($5 per CD), although prices will be less for volume purchases.

4. The COGS for digital downloaded products is estimated at the same as the CD even though the actual cost is lower.

5. Unit 8 and 9 – Sales are projected using the lowest rates for repeat deliveries of workshops. Not included in the projections are the "one-off" or custom workshops and conference engagements, which will be billed at $995 per day.

Task List

To complete this Element you will need to complete your analysis of competitor prices, gather all information related to your costs and then:

1. Familiarize yourself with the three methods of pricing, including pricing to market, pricing to costs and break-even pricing. Take all three methods into consideration in order to determine where to position your product or service.

2. You can begin the process by setting your prices to market, but it is important to understand that you must confirm viability by completing the Financial Section and comparing the other two methods; pricing to your costs and pricing to your break-even. You can only truly determine whether or not your pricing strategy works by completing your financial projections. You will then be able to see the overall impact on the bottom line in your projected income statement.

3. Using the information gathered for your competitive analysis, develop a grid or table to compare the various competitor prices.

4. Create a bottom-up or cost-based price for each product or service. You can use the worksheet following this list or the pricing worksheet in the Biz4Caster™.

5. Write a summary of your pricing strategy in this Element and include relevant detail in the Appendices.

6. Use pricing notes to clarify any potentially confusing points for your reader. Make notes of any assumptions or key information on which you have based your estimates.

WORKSHEET: PRICING					
PRODUCT & SERVICE UNITS	SUPPLIER COST (COGS)*	PRICE TO CUSTOMER INPUT	CUSTOMER OR UNIT PRICE	YEAR 2 GROWTH %	YEAR 3 GROWTH %
1.					
2.					
3.					
4.					
5.					
6.					
7.					
8.					
9.					
10.					
11.					
12.					

Tip: In situations where your service will include product, keep them as separate units. For example, my training service might be accompanied by the sale of books and CDs as separate units. Keeping each unit separate offers more flexibility in forecasting, in marketing and in selling your products and services.

* Note: Products will always have a Cost of Goods Sold, while services typically do not UNLESS they are subcontracted.

Develop Your Marketing Action Plan

Step 45

Plan a strategy for marketing your products and services.

Example: Marketing Action Plan

Tip: After a few days, re-read your Marketing Action Plan with attention to its practicality. Is it logical? Can you realistically carry out the objectives and goals with the available time and money? Are your marketing costs reflected in your Financial Section? Have you done the research to know your costs?

OBJECTIVES AND GOALS	WHO	BUDGET
1. Build a website at www.macrolink.ca · Create website with shopping cart capabilities	Owner Sys Admin	$5,000
2. Secure legal rights and develop logos for domains and names · Brand Biz4Caster.com and riskbuster.com	Owner Sys Admin	2,000
3. Publish book · Establish marketing, schedule and organize book launch	Owner Publisher	2,000
4. Develop, schedule and organize business planning seminars · Organize seminars for areas demonstrating demand	Owner	1,000
5. Proactively seek publicity · Develop press releases, email & fax to selected media · Write & submit business planning articles to target media	Owner	100
6. Design integrated materials that drive traffic to the website(s) · Build marketing copy into each product package · Design & publish brochures, posters, business cards	Owner Designer	2,500
7. Design and place product ads in strategic publications · Identify various target publications, research costs, run tests	Owner	2,000
8. Market owner & author as speaker/facilitator for conferences · Develop marketing materials & copy · Actively seek engagements by contacting conference organizers	Owner	4,400
9. Post content, free products and functions that draw traffic to the website, including: · A free e-zine for entrepreneurs · Archived articles on business planning related topics · A searchable glossary of business terms · Free downloadable Business Planning Shell™ · Sample business plans · Downloadable movie "how-to" clips (e.g. how to do a cash flow)	Owner	1,000
Total Marketing Budget		**$20,000**

Task List

1. Review your market research and identify any information that you consider to be helpful in creating your Marketing Action Plan.

2. Copy the Advertising and Promotion Element into a separate file and use it as a benchmark from which to build your Marketing Action Plan.

3. Build your list of Marketing Objectives and arrange them chronologically, that is in the order they are likely to unfold.

4. Develop a brief list of action goals for each objective.

5. Estimate a budget for each of the components of your marketing action plan. This can be done in a spreadsheet either in the cash flow projection or separately; ultimately these costs must be put into your cash flow projection.

6. Option – go back and reorganize your Advertising and Promotion Element to be more consistent with your Marketing Action Plan.

Tip: If you are outsourcing your marketing tasks, the estimated budget figures may be directly transferable into your cash flow worksheet. If you're doing part of the work yourself you will need to subtract your labor from the amounts to avoid doubling this expense in your cash flow.

WORSHEET: MARKETING ACTION PLAN		
OBJECTIVES AND GOALS	WHO	BUDGET
1.		
2.		
3.		
4.		
5.		
6.		
7.		
8.		
Total Marketing Budget		

Tip: Unless there is an advantage for doing so, it can be problematic to put goals with deadlines into your Marketing Action Plan. This is because the plan quickly becomes outdated, necessitating continuous updating to remain accurate. Although you will need timelines for internal planning purposes, it can be less complicated to leave the timelines out of this Element.

ORGANIZE YOUR OPERATIONS SECTION

Provide your reader with an understanding of how your operations will run.

Here are the business plan Elements in this Section and the corresponding RoadMap™ steps:

BUSINESS PLAN ELEMENT	ROADMAP™ STEPS
Description of the Operation	46
Equipment and Methods	47
Materials and Supplies	48
Risk and Mitigation	49
Management	50
Professional Services	51
Employees and Contractors	52
Operational Action Plan	53

Here is a brief description of each of the Elements of the Operations Section.

BRIEF INTRODUCTION TO THE OPERATIONS ELEMENTS	
ELEMENT	DESCRIPTION
Description of the Operation	The purpose of this Element is to clarify where and how your business will operate. *Key Points:* zoning and other bylaws; building regulations and codes; agreements with owners; legal aspects; business license; health inspection and permit. How convenient is the location for delivery of materials, or for customer traffic? Will customers be comfortable? What image does the location present? Do you need more than one location?
Equipment and Methods	The purpose of this Element is to determine your equipment needs and methods for meeting those needs. *Key points:* office equipment; business equipment; determine whether to buy, lease, or rent. How much can you afford? Consider the financial implications of introducing costly equipment items at different times.
Materials and Supplies	The purpose of this Element is to determine what materials and supplies you will require to create your products or services, and to identify sources for each. This information will be necessary in order for you to complete your financial projections. *Key points:* determine where to find suppliers; research how the suppliers manage credit, compare different sources, identify suppliers terms of sale.
Risk and Mitigation	The purpose of this Element is to assess threats to your business and determine how you will manage risk. *Key points:* employee or contractor disputes, health and safety, personal safety, lawsuits or fines, fire and emergency, facilities and equipment, technology, intangible properties, sales shortfall, product or service quality, supply, competitor reaction, politics, legal and regulatory, cash flow shortfall, bad debts. What are your risks? What can you afford to lose? What types of insurance do your competitors carry? How much insurance can you afford to carry or not carry?

Management	The purpose of this Element is to describe your management team. This is one of the most important parts of your business plan from a lender's perspective. Whether you're working with a team or alone, the success of your business rides on the quality of the management. ***Key points:*** skills, experience, capacity, expertise; salary or wage rates; responsibilities and training requirements.
Professional Services	The purpose of this Element is to identify and choose your professional advisory team. One approach is to choose your advisors early and include them in the business planning process. ***Key points:*** lawyer, accountant, bookkeeper, industry expert, business advisor, designer. Do you feel comfortable with the individual? What are their rates?
Employees and Contractors	The purpose of this Element is to describe the number and type of employees and subcontractors you will need for your first year in business. ***Key points:*** identify the desired skills and knowledge; determine how much product or service you can deliver; identify where help is needed; develop roles and responsibilities; decide whether to hire employees or contractors; clarify pay rates; consider recognition, on-the-job training, apprenticeships, mentor-learner relationships; workshops, seminars; books, videos.
Operational Action Plan	The purpose of this Element is to develop an action plan to implement your short and long-term operational goals. ***Key points:*** set up of premises and facilities; purchase of major equipment; purchase of materials and supplies; mitigation of risks; engagement of employees or contractors; set timelines and estimate the costs for each major milestone

Tip: *This Section must be practical. Have you visited the operations of similar businesses to learn how they work? When you get this Section to draft stage, consider having someone read through it. Encourage them to ask questions about anything they don't understand; their questions will alert you to potential areas of confusion.*

Task List

1. Read the Operations Section of the business plan in Chapter 6 to get a sense of what you are trying to achieve.

2. Go on to the next step.

The next few steps will enable you to build a practical Operations Section.

Tip: *If your business is a single owner home-based business, this Section will be fairly brief.*

Describe Your Operation

Step 46

MUST HAVE
RECOMMENDED
NICE TO HAVE

*Less important
for some service
businesses.*

C larify how and where your business will operate.

Example: Description of the Operation

Macrolink is a home-based company licensed in the city of Prince George, British Columbia. The owner outsources the core functions of bookkeeping, technical services and product production. No walk-in traffic is necessary as all products and services are produced and provided off-site.

Products and services will be provided as follows:

· Books will be published on-demand at Trafford's location in Victoria, BC. Boudreau will have the option of purchasing higher volumes at discounted rates. Storage facilities will be rented as-needed to house products.

· CD production will be outsourced. Storage space will be rented as-needed, keeping overhead low.

· Facilitator manuals are anticipated to be much lower volume and will initially be produced by the owner. If demand increases beyond the capacity of the home office, the owner will either outsource the production of the manuals to a local print shop or publish them through Trafford.

· Workshops, seminars and consulting services will either be provided at the customer's location or other suitable facilities, to be rented as needed to provide these services.

The Owner uses a portable notebook computer and is able to work from anywhere with an Internet connection.

*Tip: Beware of locking
into long term leases with
percentage of sales clauses.
Huge success in your business
can trigger massive lease
payments.*

Task List

When making decisions about your business location, consider cost, customer convenience and your needs and capabilities.

To complete this Element you will need to complete your analysis of competitor locations, gather all information related to your business location and then:

1. Decide whether to rent or lease office space or to operate from your home.

2. Check out all legal aspects related to the chosen location, including zoning, bylaws, building regulations, building codes, agreements with owners, health and fire inspections and permits.

*Tip: This Element can be
effective as text - pictures can
bring it to life. In fact, pictures
are essential if your operation
is complex or unfamiliar to the
readers of your business plan.*

Determine Your Equipment Requirements and Methods

D etermine your equipment needs and methods for meeting those needs.

Step 47

| MUST HAVE |
| RECOMMENDED |
| NICE TO HAVE |

Importance depends on the amount of equipment.

Example: Equipment and Methods

The Macrolink home office is equipped with enough office furniture to meet the business' needs for the first few years of operation. Research and development costs for writing the books and creating the digital products, estimated to be in excess of $40,000, are not included in the opening balance sheet.

EQUIPMENT LIST			
ITEM	SOURCE	CREDIT DETAILS	COST
Satellite Notebook	Future Shop	Owner Contribution	$1,800
HP Inkjet 2200	Boudreau	Owner Contribution	$200
Brother IntelliFAX 2800	Boudreau	Owner Contribution	$100
Jeep Cherokee 2000	Boudreau	$1,000 equity/ $14,000 debt	$15,000
Satellite 330 laptop	Boudreau	Owner Contribution	$300
M3 Presenter	Boudreau	Owner Contribution	$200
TOTAL			**$17,600**

Task List

1. To complete this Element you will need to gather information related to all equipment needed to operate as well as the costs and the methods used to acquire the items (purchase, rent, or lease).

2. Determine your operational methods, equipment requirements and costs. For example: manufacturing machinery, sewing machines, delivery vehicles, trade tools, etc.

3. Determine your office systems, equipment requirements and costs. For example: filing cabinets, in-out file baskets or trays, desks, lamps, chairs, shelving or bookcases, staplers, paper punches, file folders, dividers, labels, paper clips, binders, invoice and receipt forms, pens, pencils, paper, telephone message forms, magazine storage boxes, etc. Consider also: telephones (office, cell), answering machine, personal computers, notebooks, modems, printers, fax machine, photocopier, etc.

WORSHEET: EQUIPMENT LIST			
ITEM	SOURCE	CREDIT DETAILS	COST
TOTAL			

Tip: A table or a bulleted or numbered list may be the most effective method for this Element.

Source Your Materials and Supplies

Determine what supplies and materials you will require to create your product or service and sources for each. This will be a critical step toward completing the Financial Section of your business plan.

MUST HAVE

RECOMMENDED

NICE TO HAVE

Critical for product businesses, less important where you provide a service.

Example: Materials and Supplies

The publisher provides a detailed list of costs for books, based on the number of pages and the quantities purchased. To limit the risk and control overhead, the owner will purchase higher quantities of books only as the demand dictates.

CDs will be created by an established replication service from the Vancouver area.

For all training and trainer resources, supplies and materials will be purchased from local office suppliers. All bulk photocopying is done at highly competitive rates by a local provider near the Macrolink office.

Task List

To complete this Element you will need to gather all information from different suppliers and compare their literature and terms, then:

1. Consider your financial ability and how it fits with the supplier terms.

2. Ensure that you can meet your customer obligations and stay on top of inventory costs.

3. In the case of human resource suppliers, consider subcontracting and establishing a 15- or 30-day payment policy to give yourself room to collect from clients before having to pay your contractors.

4. Decide which suppliers you will use and if possible get a letter of commitment from them or complete their credit application and open an account.

5. Make a list of your materials, supplies and sources.

WORKSHEET: MATERIALS AND SUPPLIES			
SUPPLIER	AVAILABILITY	CREDIT TERMS	POLICIES

Tip: A bulleted or numbered list can also be effective for this Element.

Identify Your Risks and How You Will Control Them

Step 49

Assess threats to your business and determine how you will manage risk.

I stated earlier that you are surrounded by 360 degrees of risk from the first moment you step into business. As you researched to get to this stage, you have undoubtedly become more aware of the risks inherent to your business. Now is the time to take an open-minded look at which threats you might encounter and to develop your strategies for mitigating risk. Business and life are risky, there's no getting away from that. Your goal with this Element is to chart a path that you can live with. Here are some of the demons you might face and things to consider — feel free to add a few of your own.

POTENTIAL THREATS AND MITIGATION STRATEGIES	
THREATS	POSSIBLE MITIGATION
Employee or Contractor Disputes	Do your due diligence before hiring or signing contracts. Develop clear agreements and ensure you live up to your end of those agreements.
Health and Safety	Know the regulations, be vigilant for liabilities, create and distribute policies and procedures, buy the appropriate insurance for workers.
Personal Safety	Be aware of areas within your operations where personal safety could become an issue — for example, parking lots. Provide ongoing education for your employees about risky areas and suggest safe practices. Develop and publicize standards and policies for all nature of harassment. Make it part of your mission to create a working environment free from discomfort, intimidation or offensive acts of any kind.
Fatigue and Burnout	I hope you enter a type of business that you enjoy and one that doesn't keep you stressed and fatigued. Youthful vigour has pulled me through many 20-hour days, and too many 100+ hour work weeks. Being committed to your business is a good thing until it begins to take a toll on your health. Often it's when the business gets into trouble that an owner finds himself or herself slugging it out for long hours, days or weeks on end. The scariest thing about burnout is that it creeps up on you. In my case, it wasn't until long after the business crises that I fully realized how thoroughly drained I was. Stay fit, exercise regularly, eat well, get an appropriate amount of sleep and play. Learn and pay attention to the signs of burnout and make adjustments when it hits.
Lawsuits or Fines	Operate in a spirit of fairness, document everything, develop and use procedures for documenting and dealing with critical incidents.
Fire and Emergency	Create escape procedures, place them in visible locations, research the relevant regulations, train staff and contractors, buy insurance.
Facilities and Equipment	Facilities bring with them a host of threats, from fire and theft to health and safety issues. The insurance industry provides coverage for just about every occasion. It is possible to spend all of your would be profits on insurance. You must determine your level of risk and purchase the right amount of insurance.
Computers, Website and Technology	Today's workplace is highly dependant on technology. For the most part, if our computer, email, website or file server misses a beat, we cannot work. This means taking safety and security seriously from the ground up. Use quality equipment and back-up everything regularly. Use a reputable Internet Service Provider and a level of technical support appropriate to your need.
Product or Service Quality	When it comes to dealing with customers, a business owner is fully responsible to maintain product or service quality. There may be many others in the supply line who have control over aspects of the quality, but you are accountable to your customer. Develop a quality statement and live up to it. Your customers will thank you by referring other customers to your business.

Intangible Properties, Copyright and Trademark Protection	The world of intangible properties is undergoing dramatic changes as businesses and governments struggle to embrace issues globally. This area, as witnessed by the music industry, is a hotbed of theft, wrongdoing and litigation. Your best path for mitigation is to engage a competent Intellectual Property lawyer and play by the rules for each jurisdiction in which you operate. Recognize there are areas in the world where your copyright and trademark protection have barely enough substance to serve as toilet paper.
Sales Shortfall	Your business plan is only as strong as your confidence in your sales projections. If you are not confident in your ability to meet the sales projected in your business plan, redo the projections until you are. New business start-ups tend to be too optimistic in projecting sales. Keep your projections as comfortably low as you can. If possible, it is healthy to have a certain amount of money set aside (contingency) to see you through if sales fall short.
Supply	A number of factors can create interruptions in your goods or services supply. It is important that you assess these factors and prepare alternate plans to provide your product or service. The entire world runs on supply and demand. If your supply chain is rife with threats, perhaps you need to consider alternates. The dynamics are very different for a simple service business where you, the owner, provide the service. Any supply problems are then directly related to your ability to provide the service.
Competitor Reaction	How will your competitors react to your entry into business? If you anticipate a competitor will lower prices, can you withstand a protracted price war? Sometimes an industry is large enough, or a business differentiated enough, that competition is not a big concern. Other situations require going head-to-head with existing businesses. Whatever the situation, the onus will be on you to stay ahead of your competitors.
Politics	Ah, politics; the oldest prostitution! You will not escape politics; they are pervasive, ever-changing and powerful. The time to assess and understand the politics affecting your business is during the start-up stage. How is your crystal ball working? Educate yourself on the politics of your business, determine the level of risk and then decide whether you can live comfortably with those risks. Once you are in business, stay involved; keep a thumb on the pulse of your industry and your business.
Legal and Regulatory	The onus is on you to know the laws and regulations affecting your business. Ignorance is not a viable defense. As with politics, pre-start-up is the time to assess and determine whether you can live with the laws and regulations governing your business. Know the rules and stay on top of changes.
Cash Flow Shortfall	Cash flow is the lifeblood of your business. Stop the cash flow and your business quickly dies. From opening day onward you are responsible for orchestrating a balance between revenues and expenses. This will entail making sales, collecting receivables, purchasing supplies, maintaining equipment, paying expenses and hopefully paying yourself. There are a few things you can do to stack the cards in your favor. Foster a positive credit rating, develop a solid relationship with your banker, maintain access to an operating loan, keep headroom on your credit cards, pay expenses promptly to avoid interest charges, open and use trade accounts where appropriate and regularly save money to build up a contingency fund.
Bad Debts	Some types of business require that you extend credit to customers. For example, many government contracts tend to pay two to three months after a service is provided. If it's the industry standard, you will likely have to conform in order to remain competitive. If the industry standard is to be paid cash, stick to it. If there is no compelling reason to extend credit, don't. Limit the amount of credit you extend to customers and stay on top of your receivables. If you detect a customer slipping away on you, communicate directly with him or her.

Your goal with this Element is to chart a path that you can live comfortably with. Here are some of the demons you might face and things to consider — feel free to add a few of your own.

WORSHEET: THREATS AND MITIGATION	
THREATS	POSSIBLE MITIGATION
Employee or Contractor Disputes	
Health and Safety	
Personal Safety	
Fatigue and Burnout	
Lawsuits or Fines	
Fire and Emergency	
Facilities and Equipment	
Computers, Website and Technology	
Product or Service Quality	
Intangible Properties	
Sales Shortfall	
Supply	
Competitor Reaction	
Politics	
Legal and Regulatory	
Cash flow Shortfall	
Bad Debts	

Tip: Research local insurance agents. If possible, get name referrals from your network. Select two or three agents and invite them for a coffee to discuss your needs. Choose an insurance agent you trust and then view everything with a jaundiced eye; scrutinize every piece of paper he or she puts in front of you. Purchase only the amount of insurance you need. Review your insurance strategy often, certainly every time you have a major shift in your business. Shop around; insurance is a competitive business.

Task List

To complete this Element you will need to determine your facility, equipment and liability risk, then:

1. Review your market research with an eye to threats to your business.

2. Brainstorm and prioritize a list of risks to your business.

3. List your strategies to mitigate each risk or threat. Do more research, if necessary.

4. Contact a trusted or referred insurance agent to determine your insurance needs.

5. Consider your level of comfort with risk and your pocketbook when determining how much insurance you purchase.

6. Keep the appropriate insurance documentation in your Appendices Section.

Some of your threats will require insurance. The list of different types of insurance is endless. A few types of insurance you may want to consider: house or business premises, vehicle, liability, inventory, business interruption, disability, partnership and loan insurance.

Some things to consider:

• What are your risks?

• What can you afford to lose?

• What types of insurance do your competitors carry?

• How much insurance can you afford to carry or not carry?

• Which types of insurance are you required to carry by lenders, suppliers or clients?

Describe Your Management Team

Determine who will manage your business and describe your Management Team.

Because management is such a critical aspect of any business, you will want to put careful thought into this Element. If you are hiring a manager you will need to consider a number of key points within your business planning process:

- Establish job descriptions and hiring criteria.
- Identify the Manager's roles and responsibilities.
- Determine what training you will provide for a Manager.
- Assess industry standards and establish a budget for salary and training.
- Consider what rewards and recognition you will establish for employees.

In my case, this was an easy Element because I am the chief cook and bottle washer – end of story. My biography already exists in the Owner Element of the Business Concept Section. There is nothing to be gained by replicating what has been written there, so I chose to elaborate on my history as a business manager.

Tip: If you are the only person working in the business and you have already provided your background information in The Applicant Element, you need only to focus here on your training needs and strengths that were not highlighted there.

Example: Management Team

Dan Boudreau, owner, will manage the business. Boudreau has owned and managed five small businesses in the past 24 years. He will manage the company until it grows to the point that it can sustain an Office or Operations Manager, at which time job descriptions and hiring criteria will be developed. Management salary will be set at $180 per day until the business can sustain a higher rate. More information on the owner is in Appendix 6.1.

Task List

To complete this Element you will need to identify your own strengths and weaknesses, then:

1. Determine whether or not you will manage the business yourself.
2. Identify what training you or your manager will require.
3. Forecast all management related salaries and training costs.

Research and Select Your Professional Services

Research and select your professional service providers and describe your Professional Services.

At a minimum you will want to consider the following professionals for your team: lawyer, accountant, bookkeeper, industry expert, business advisor and graphics designer.

Step 51

Definitely do, not necessarily in the business plan.

Selecting Your Professionals

Take some time to research and select your professional team. You may be getting married for a long time, assuming your business will be successful. Changing professionals can be disruptive and costly. You are the customer and as such you have every right to expect service and value for your money.

Questions to Ask Your Banker

1. What services do you provide for small business?
2. Under what circumstances would you lend money to a new business?
3. What interest rate and what fees would I pay on a term loan or an operating loan?
4. What are your policies with regard to security / collateral?
5. When lending to a small business, what do you consider to be the minimum and ideal percentage of owner equity or investment?
6. What is your experience or impression of the business (restaurants, tourism, service, etc)?
7. What size of loans do you make the decisions for before having to refer the package to a higher authority?
8. Who would you recommend as an accountant for a business like mine?
9. Who would you recommend as a lawyer for a business like mine?

Tip: Professionals often specialize in different disciplines. Be sure to find professionals that understand your business.

Questions to Ask Your Accountant

1. Describe your services for small business.
2. What are your rates for accounting? What are your rates for bookkeeping?
3. For a business of my type and size, what are the annual accounting and bookkeeping costs?
4. Can you tell me how much it would cost to set up my chart of accounts?
5. If necessary, would you be able to prepare financial projections for my business?
6. What accounting software do you use? Do you use email?
7. What are your payment terms?

8. Who would you recommend as a banker for a business like mine?

9. Who would you recommend as a lawyer for a business like mine?

Questions to Ask Your Lawyer

1. Please describe your services for small business.

2. Can you tell me what area of law you focus on (experience with corporate and contract law).

3. What are your hourly rates?

4. Can you tell how much it will cost to set up my proprietorship, corporation, etc.?

5. What word processing software do you use?

6. If necessary, can I communicate with you via email?

7. What are your payment terms?

8. Who would you recommend as an accountant for a business like mine?

9. Who would you recommend as a banker for a business like mine?

Questions to Ask Your Bookkeeper

1. Please describe your services for small business.

2. Do you have the ability to provide monthly draft financial statements?

3. How many and what types of small businesses do you currently provide bookkeeping services for? Can you provide me with three references?

4. What training/educational background do you have as a bookkeeper?

5. How many years experience do you have providing bookkeeping services?

6. What equipment do you currently have in your office and what accounting software do you use?

7. If necessary, can I communicate with you via email?

8. What are your hourly rates?

9. What are your payment terms?

Example: Professional Services

Accounting, legal and insurance will be outsourced from established businesses.

Task List

To complete this Element you will need to ask around to get some name referrals and then:

1. Prepare in advance by determining what you wish to learn from each professional.
2. Within the business network in your area, ask for names of recommended professionals.
3. Contact the professionals you wish to consider and arrange a meeting to discuss your needs.
4. Decide which advisors you will engage and enter their information in the table below.

WORKSHEET: PROFESSIONAL SERVICES			
SPECIALTY	NAME	COMPANY	TEL/FAX/EMAIL
Accountant			
Lawyer			
Insurance			

Tip: There is one practice you will want to follow when dealing with professionals: always prepare yourself by clarifying, in advance, what you want them to do for you. The more you can organize your thoughts prior to meeting with a lawyer, a banker or an accountant, the less time it will take for him or her to understand and carry out your requests. More importantly, it will cost you less. An ounce of preparation is worth a pound of profit.

Tip: One approach is to choose your advisors early and include them in the business planning process.

Determine Your Employee and Contractor Requirements

Step 52

Only important if you will have employees or contractors.

Tip: Your labor requirements, whether employee or contract, are driven by the amount of product or service you provide to your customers. It is critical that you compare this to your projected sales to ensure consistency with the fluctuations in your sales forecast. For example, it seems logical that your labor projections would increase commensurate with a growth in sales. If for some reason this is not the case, you should provide an explanation for your reader.

Tip: This Element may be easier to envision and create once you have forecasted your sales. At a minimum, it must be developed in conjunction with your sales projection. Don't be surprised or concerned if you find yourself bouncing back and forth between these two Elements a few times before you become confident in your projection.

P lan and describe how many employees and contractors you will need for your first year in business.

In completing this process you will want to consider the following:

• Your skills and the skills required for your business

• Your experience and credibility for the products or services you plan to provide

• Whether to employ or subcontract – consider the industry standard

• How many employees or contractors you will engage and what rates you will pay them

Example: Employees and Contractors

> The owner will do all the operations work until demand for products and services increase to the point that extra help is required. Staff will be engaged as needed. Initially, the organization will contract with a part-time systems administrator and a part-time bookkeeper.

Task List

To complete this Element you will need to determine how much of the required work you will perform yourself, then:

1. Determine the amount of product or service you can create and/or deliver by yourself.

2. Identify areas of knowledge or skill you require (i.e. bookkeeping).

3. Determine whether you will employ or subcontract the additional help.

4. Research and clarify hourly or day rates for each position and ensure the availability of each type of worker.

5. Use the Labor Projections Worksheet on the following page to develop a one year projection of work days for each employee and/or subcontractor. Note each row is split horizontally to allow for entry of the number of hours in the top half and the total cost in the bottom half. If you will be using a spreadsheet program or the Biz4Caster™, you only need calculate the hours in this table. Either way, this is the preparation work necessary in order for you to complete your Labor Projections Element in the Financial Section of your business plan.

6. Summarize your labor requirements in the business plan and keep the detail for the Appendices.

WORKSHEET: LABOR PROJECTIONS

POSITION	Unit Rate	1	2	3	4	5	6	7	8	9	10	11	12	TOTAL

TOTALS

Tip: To complete this worksheet, enter the name of the person or the job position and the amount the position will pay per unit (hour, day, month). In the upper half of each split row, forecast the number of units per month and in the lower half calculate the amount to be paid for each month

Tip: If you decide to subcontract instead of employ, be aware the tax authorities prefer to collect their pound of flesh from one employer rather than several subcontractors. For this reason there are a number of "tests" to determine whether the relationship is one or the other. The "tests" ensure most will be employees. For more information visit the relevant tax authority's website.

Develop Your Operational Action Plan

Step 53

Not necessary for small service businesses.

Develop an action plan to achieve your short and long-range operational goals.

In some cases it is difficult to determine whether a goal should fall into this Element or the Marketing Action Plan in the Marketing Section of your business plan. In my case for example, which Element should house a task such as "building a website" or "providing a seminar"? I decided to leave the website production in the Marketing Section and to include the production of the seminar here. The key is to compare the two action plans in order to avoid duplication or repetitiveness.

Example: Operational Action Plan

> The main actions required are:
> · Complete and publish the books by March 2006
> · Complete development of the digital products by June 2006
> · Establish a website with a shopping cart by August 2006

Tip: Unless there is an advantage for doing so, it can be problematic to put goals with deadlines into your Operational Action Plan. This is because the plan quickly becomes outdated, necessitating continuous change to remain accurate. Although you will need timelines for internal planning purposes, it can be less complicated to leave the timelines out of this Element.

Task List

To prepare yourself to complete this Element, first go back and review your Strategic Plan and Goals in the Business Concept Section, your Marketing Action Plan in the Marketing Section and all Elements of this, the Operations Section - then develop your Operational Action Plan with attention to the following categories:

1. Set up of your premises and facilities.
2. Purchase and set up of equipment.
3. Purchase of materials and supplies.
4. Steps required for mitigating potential risks.
5. Engagement of management, professionals, employees or contractors.

Tip: You can let your imagination soar, but be very careful not to scare off your reader by dwelling on wildly unrealistic long range plans.

WORKSHEET: OPERATIONAL ACTION PLAN	
GOAL	TIMELINES
1.	
2.	
3.	
4.	
5.	
6.	
7.	
8.	

FORECAST YOUR FINANCIAL SECTION

The purpose of this Section is to determine if your business will make money.

Here are the business plan Elements in this Section and the corresponding RoadMap™ steps:

BUSINESS PLAN ELEMENT	ROADMAP™ STEPS
Sales Forecast	54
Explanation of Projections	55
Market Share	56
Cost of Goods Sold	57
Labor Projections	58
Cash Flow Forecast	59
Projected Income Statement	60
Break-even Analysis	61
Pro Forma Balance Sheet	62
Start-up Expenses	63
Uses and Sources of Funds	64

A 20 Minute Introduction to the Financial Section

It is important to understand that the Financial Section of your business plan is not just for the gatekeeper, it's also for you. Its most important function is that it helps you to understand your business. The process of completing your financial projections, although at times stressful, causes you to ask and answer a number of critical questions and make several decisions about your business. It is an opportunity to learn how money flows in and out of your business.

Here is a brief description of each of the Elements of the Financial Section.

BRIEF INTRODUCTION TO THE FINANCIAL ELEMENTS	
FINANCIAL ELEMENT	DESCRIPTION
Sales Forecast	A first year, 12-month projection of the number of units and the values for each product or service you will sell. This Element shows slower times, busier times and growth or shrinkage – it is the basic building block that enables you to determine whether or not the business will meet your financial expectations.
Explanation of Projections	Explanations of anything that might be confusing to the reader.
Market Share	This Element shows the total potential market value and what portion of that market your business will capture.
Cost of Goods Sold (COGS)	This is the cost to purchase or produce your product or service. All products will have a COGS. Services provided by an owner do not have a COGS, while if you contract labor to provide the services that labor cost becomes the COGS for those services.

Labor Projections	A first year, 12-month projection of the value of all wages or salaries that will paid to the owner, employees and subcontractors.
Cash Flow Forecast	This Element shows the flow of cash into and out of your business. This is the lifeline of your business. It will enable you to clarify how much money you will require to operate each month.
Operating Expenses	A 12-month projection of all operating expenses for the first year of business. This shows how much it will cost to operate your business, even if you make no sales.
Projected or Pro Forma Income Statement	In its most simplistic form, the income statement is sales minus expenses and what's left over is income. The income statement tells us whether or not the business is actually earning or losing money.
Break-even Analysis	The break-even chart identifies that point in the year when operating expenses are paid and the business begins to profit. This Element tells how much product and/or service your business will have to sell before it begins to profit.
Pro Forma Balance Sheet	The balance sheet is a financial snapshot in time that shows everything the business owns and all that it owes. Your business' net worth is what's left over after all liabilities are subtracted from the value of all assets. Pro Forma means the balance sheet is projected for some point in the future.
Start-up Expenses	This is a listing of all expenses required to get the business to opening day. Start-up expenses may include some of the first few months operating costs, depending on the financial requirements of the business during that time.
Uses & Sources of Funds	This is a snapshot, usually created in conjunction with your analyst or banker, that show all funds needed at the point of borrowing money and what those funds will be used for.

A Briefing on Forecasting

As mentioned at the beginning of this 99-step process, your business plan is comprised of three main parts: narrative, financial and supporting information.

In building your Financial Section it's critical you understand you are forecasting, not accounting. The difference between forecasting and accounting is illustrated in the following table:

THE DIFFERENCE BETWEEN FORECASTING AND ACCOUNTING	
FORECASTING	ACCOUNTING
· Is an educated guess at future scenarios	· Is a detailed compilation of past transactions
· Happens before the period of business	· Happens after the period of business
· Provides an approximate picture of the future	· Provides an accurate record of business past
· Relies on assumptions and unknowns	· Relies on precise records and receipts
· Is best done by you	· Is best done by an accountant

Each of the Elements in this Section presents the reader with a different view of the financials for the business. The combination of the various Elements or views provides the reader with a complete picture of the financial state of the business. Each view tells us a part of the story about the business.

The 12 Elements in this Section are necessary for you to complete your financials. Depending on what you're using the plan for, you may not have to include all of the Elements in your completed plan. For example, all lenders will want to see your cash flow forecast, many will want to see your projected income statement and break-even analysis. As a lender, my preference is to see all of the Elements because that is the only way to get a complete financial picture.

Task List

1. Read the Financial Section of the sample business plan in Chapter 6 to get a sense of what you are trying to achieve.

2. The Biz4Caster™ will slash many hours and a lot of the stress from the task of projecting and building your Financial Section. If you haven't been introduced to the Biz4Caster™ yet, visit **www.Biz4Caster.com**.

Forecast Your Sales

Step 54

E stimate the sales or revenue your business will capture.

Forecasting for Businesses with Numerous Products

Here are a few suggestions to help you create a reliable sales forecast.

1. You can project sales by groups of products or by product lines to reduce the number of line items in your sales forecast.

2. You can get away from projecting by product by using the average sale as your unit. For example, if your market research reveals that three out of every ten visitors to your business will spend an average of $50 on your products or services, you can use this as your unit and project sales based on the expected number of visitors.

3. You can base your sales projection on the average sales per day. For example, $500 per day x 6 days per week x 52 weeks will give you a forecast for one year. Don't forget to adjust for holidays and special occasions.

Example: Sales Forecast Summary

UNITS	PRICES	YEAR 1 UNITS	YEAR 1 SALES	YEAR 2 SALES	YEAR 3 SALES
1. Books - Trafford - Retail	$36.58	385	$14,083	$16,900	$21,970
2. Books - Trafford - Bookstores	21.95	260	5,707	6,848	8,903
3. Books - Trafford - Distributors	18.29	140	2,561	3,073	3,995
4. Books - Owner - Retail	36.59	545	19,942	23,930	31,109
5. RiskBuster™ CD - Retail	29.50	159	4,691	5,629	7,317
6. RiskBuster™ CD - Distributors	29.50	180	5,310	6,372	8,284
7. Digital Downloads Retail	29.50	260	7,670	9,204	11,965
8. Half-Day Workshops	350.00	6	2,100	2,310	2,541
9. Full-Day Workshops	495.00	24	11,880	13,068	14,375
10. Seminars to Individuals	49.00	100	4,900	5,880	7,644
11. Facilitator Manuals	99.95	14	1,399	1,679	2,183
12. Consulting / Coaching Hours	40.00	1200	48,000	50,400	55,440
Total Sales			**$128,242**	**$145,293**	**$175,725**
Gross Profit Margin Percentage			**82.13%**	**81.07%**	**79.66%**
COGS Percentage			**17.87%**	**18.93%**	**20.34%**

Note: For a 12-month sales forecast refer to Appendix C of the Macrolink Action Plans Inc. business plan in Chapter 6.

Task List

To complete this Element you will need to have completed most of your primary and secondary market research. Your basic blocks for building your sales forecast (created in Step 44) are your product and service units and the corresponding unit prices.

If you are using the Biz4Caster™, the directions within the template will guide you through preparing your entire Financial Section. If you do not have Biz4Caster™, you can either use the form following this list or create a spreadsheet. Whether you are using a pencil and calculator or a sophisticated spreadsheet program, your process will be as follows:

1. Decide which will be your first month in operation and enter the month at the top of each of the twelve columns for your first twelve months of business.

2. Down the left-hand column, enter the name of each unit, using the units developed in Step 44.

3. In column two, enter your unit price for each of the units entered in the first column.

4. For each unit, forecast the number of units you will sell for each month.

5. For each month, multiply the projected number of units times the unit price.

6. Total the sales dollars forecasted in each column to arrive at the total sales for each month.

7. Total the sales dollars forecasted in each row to arrive at the total sales for each individual unit for your first year.

8. Total the entire sales across the bottom row or down the right hand column to arrive at the total sales for your first year.

9. Repeat steps one to eight as necessary, until you have a conservative achievable sales forecast.

10. Once you are satisfied with your first year forecast, estimate your growth for year two.

11. Once you are satisfied with your second year forecast, estimate your growth for year three.

12. Enter your sales for year one, two and three into a summary table in your business plan.

Use the following Sales Forecast form for forecasting your units and dollar amounts for each month in detail for the first 12 months of your business.

Tip: Forecast your sales conservatively. Avoid pie-in-the-sky projections. Forecasting your sales at a lower rate than you think possible will enable you to have more confidence in your projections.

Tip: If your forecast makes you uncomfortable, imagine how your banker will feel about it. Adjust your estimates until you are comfortable with them.

WORSHEET: SALES FORECAST

Tip: Once you have built a draft sales forecast you can begin to test different scenarios. For example, what if you achieve only 50% or 80% of the sales you forecast?

UNIT NAME	Unit Price	1	2	3	4	5	6	7	8	9	10	11	12	TOTAL

TOTAL SALES

After working through the monthly sales in detail, you might wish to create a sales summary to go into your business plan.

WORKSHEET: SALES FORECAST SUMMARY					
UNITS	**UNIT PRICE**	**YEAR 1 # UNITS**	**YEAR 1 SALES**	**YEAR 2 SALES**	**YEAR 3 SALES**
1.					
2.					
3.					
4.					
5.					
6.					
7.					
8.					
9.					
10.					
11.					
12.					
TOTAL SALES					
GROSS PROFIT MARGIN PERCENTAGE					
COGS PERCENTAGE					

Tip: Part of the confidence in your sales forecast will come from proving portions of your sales. As an example, three line items in my forecast are pre-sold with contracts in place. Back this up with contracts or letters of intent in your Appendix and you are on your way.

Explain Your Projections

Step 55

Clarify any points in your projections that might be confusing to the reader.

In building your financial scenario, it is generally accepted that you need to base your projections on certain assumptions. For example, you might have to assume certain currency rates, the interest rate for a bank loan or seasonal adjustments to the amount of sales for products or services. While these rationales might make perfect sense to you, they may be confusing to your reader. Worse, unexplained points can undermine your efforts to convince the reader of your business' viability.

Example: Explanation of Projections

These financial projections are based on the following assumptions and key points:

1. Year one is from September 1, 2006 to August 31, 2007.

2. E-book sales are expected, but not included in these projections because test marketing is not yet complete.

3. Book and CD projections are based on the assumption that roughly 220 units of each will be sold at distributor rates.

4. Unit nine projections are based on the assumption that all 24 units will be sold.

5. Unit twelve projections are based on the assumption that the current contract will continue through the forecasted period.

6. Based on #3, #4 and #5 above, a total of $66,040 of the year one revenue is reasonably certain.

7. All unit prices are purposely estimated at conservative rates while the cost of goods sold calculations are on the high side, making the overall projections very conservative and quite attainable.

Task List

Here are the steps to complete this Element:

1. As you work through the financial worksheets and tables, keep a list of any points that might be confusing to your reader.

2. By the time you have completed your Financial Elements to draft stage you should have a healthy list of explanations. If you find it helpful, print a copy of your Financial Elements to study your projections. It can be very effective to have someone read through your projections. Their questions may alert you to points that need clarification.

3. Using the *Explaining Your Projections Worksheet*, create a list of your assumptions and any notes you believe will help the reader to understand how you arrived at your financial calculations.

WORSHEET: EXPLAINING YOUR PROJECTIONS	
Bank Loan – Estimated Interest Rate	
Bank Loan – Estimated Term of Loan	
Owner #1 – Monthly Salary	
Owner #2 – Monthly Salary	
Percentage of Your Sales that Will Be Paid in less than 30 Days	
Percentage of Your Sales that Will Be Paid in 30 to 60 Days	
Percentage of Your Sales that Will Be Paid in 60 to 90 Days	
Percentage of Your Sales that Will Be Paid in 90 to 120 Days	
Your WCB Rate Expressed as a Percentage of Payroll	
Your Employer Payroll Burden Expressed as a Percentage of Payroll	
Your Tax Percentage For Year One	
Your Tax Percentage For Year Two	
Your Tax Percentage For Year Three	
The Amount of Your Own Money You Will Invest In Your Business at Start-up	
The Amount of Your Own Non-Cash Equity You Will Invest In Your Business at Start-up	
The Amount of Fixed Assets You Will Invest In Your Business at Start-up	
Your Anticipated Depreciation Percentage	

Tip: *One way to extract the necessary explanations for this Element is to put the sales forecast in front of your spouse, friend or business planning team. The questions they ask may alert you to points that need clarification in this Element.*

Tip: *The purpose of this Element is to clarify potentially confusing points for your reader. Instead of doing this as a separate Element you can opt to embed your clarification in the other Elements and eliminate this Element entirely. For example, you can provide clarification of the sales forecast right in the Sales Forecast Element, etc.*

Tip: *Key points are easy to read as bulleted or numbered lists.*

Estimate Your Market Share

MUST HAVE
RECOMMENDED
NICE TO HAVE

Can be confusing to novices.

Determine your share of the potential sales volume within the market area. A market area and your target market within it will support a certain level of sales of a given product or service. To sell your product or service you need to understand how the market is divided and what portion you might obtain.

Example: Market Share

	YEAR 1 SALES	YEAR 2 SALES	YEAR 3 SALES
Estimated Number of Customers	2,200,000	2,200,000	2,200,000
Average Expenditure per Customer	$50	$50	$50
Total Potential Market	$110,000,000	$110,000,000	$110,000,000
Total Projected Sales	$128,242	$145,293	$175,725
Market Share	0.12%	0.13%	0.16%

Task List

Tip: This Element can be text, tables or charts to show the different competitors' shares. It works very well as a pie chart.

To complete this Element you will need to have completed your primary and secondary market research and your sales forecast, then:

1. Describe how you estimated your market share.

2. Using the summary table below, estimate and enter your total market for years 1, 2, and 3.

3. Determine the average expenditure per customer for year 1, 2 and 3.

4. For each year, multiply the number of customers times the average sale to arrive at the Total Potential Market.

5. Enter your Total Projected Sales for years 1, 2 and 3 (from your sales forecast).

6. For each year, divide your Total Projected Sales by the Total Potential Market to arrive at your market share percentage.

7. Add any necessary clarifying points to help your reader understand how you arrived at your conclusions.

WORKSHEET: MARKET SHARE			
	YEAR 1 SALES	YEAR 2 SALES	YEAR 3 SALES
Estimated Number of Customers			
Average Expenditure per Customer			
Total Potential Market			
Total Projected Sales			
Market Share			

Present Your Cost of Goods Sold

Determine what your products and services will cost and develop your Cost of Goods Sold (COGS) Element.

MUST HAVE
RECOMMENDED
NICE TO HAVE

Recommended for all businesses with COGS, not necessary for service businesses with no COGS.

Example: Cost of Goods Sold

UNITS	COGS % OF SALES	YEAR 1 COGS	YEAR 2 COGS	YEAR 3 COGS
1. Books - Trafford - Retail	40.00%	$5,633	$6,760	$8,788
2. Books - Trafford - Bookstores	66.67%	3,805	4,566	5,935
3. Books - Trafford - Distributors	80.00%	2,048	2,458	3,196
4. Books - Owner - Retail	38.79%	7,735	9,282	12,067
5. RiskBuster™ CD - Retail	16.95%	795	954	1,240
6. RiskBuster™ CD - Distributors	16.95%	900	1,080	1,404
7. Digital Downloads Retail	16.95%	1,300	1,560	2,028
8. Half-Day Workshops	0.00%			
9. Full-Day Workshops	0.00%			
10. Seminars to Individuals	0.00%			
11. Facilitator Manuals	50.03%	700	840	1,092
12. Consulting Hours	0.00%			
Total COGS		$22,917	$27,500	$35,750

Tip: If you typically provide the services and the business pays your salary there are no COGS. However, if you hire a subcontractor to provide your service you will want to add the subcontractor's cost to your price, even though your price will likely not change. The subcontractor's fee becomes your Cost of Goods Sold.

Task List

To complete this Element you will need to have completed your Sales Forecast and have revisited your Pricing and Pricing Strategy Element and the table of costs, prices, mark-ups and COGS percentages. Using your sales projections and the COGS for each unit you then:

1. Work with each unit individually to calculate the COGS for month one by multiplying the number of units forecasted by the COGS percentage.

2. Repeat task one for each unit for the first twelve months of business.

3. Total the COGS for all units at the bottom of your table.

4. Transfer the total COGS figures to the COGS line in both your Cash Flow Forecast and in your Projected Income Statement.

Tip: When in doubt, calculate your COGS a bit high rather than low. Like all other expenses, build projections that show your business can survive.

WORKSHEET: COST OF GOODS SOLD				
UNITS	COGS % OF SALES	YEAR 1 COGS	YEAR 2 COGS	YEAR 3 COGS
1.				
2.				
3.				
4.				
5.				
6.				
7.				
8.				
9.				
10.				
11.				
12.				
Total COGS				

Tip: This Element can be text or a table, or a combination of both.

Tip: With some costs, such as shipping, it can be unclear whether or not to categorize the cost as an operating expense or include it as part of your Cost of Goods Sold (COGS). Generally, costs that vary (increase or decrease) with the amount of product or service purchased should be included in your COGS. Be sure the cost is in one place or the other, but not in both.

Summarize Your Labor Projections

Estimate how much your business will spend on labor for the first twelve months of operation and develop your Labor Projections Element.

Step 58

	MUST HAVE
	RECOMMENDED
	NICE TO HAVE

Example: Projected Labor Summary

	YEAR 1	YEAR 2	YEAR 3
Management Salaries	$43,200	$43,200	$43,200
Wages & Subcontractor Fees	7,200	7,200	7,200
Employer Wage Burden	5,040	5,040	5,040
Workers' Compensation	161	161	161
Total Projected Labor	**$55,601**	**$55,601**	**$55,601**

Task List

Review your Labor Requirements Worksheet that were calculated in Step 52 and summarize the requirements for this Element.

1. Determine what you will use as a unit of pay for employees (monthly, daily, hourly, etc.).

2. Calculate how much you will pay each employee per unit, not including the employer wage burden (Pension Plan, Employment Insurance, Holiday Pay and Workers' Compensation).

3. Estimate the number of units each person will work for each of the first twelve months of business operation.

4. Multiply the number of units each month times the unit rate to arrive at the total labor projection for each worker for each month.

5. If desired, you can use the table below to enter your labor projections into your business plan. Unless your situation is complex, your reader should get the information he or she needs from the cash flow projection.

WORKSHEET: PROJECTED LABOR SUMMARY			
	YEAR 1 PAYROLL	YEAR 2 PAYROLL	YEAR 3 PAYROLL
Management Salaries			
Wages & Subcontractor Fees			
Employer Wage Burden			
Workers' Compensation			
Total Projected Labor			

Tip: Proprietors can choose not to pay themselves a wage or salary (in the Management Salaries row). From a taxation perspective this is technically correct because as a proprietor, you are taxed on all earnings after expenses. This will only be accurate if you actually do not take any payment from your business until the end of the year. However, if you plan to take a salary or owner's drawings, I recommend that you project the amounts as Management Salaries. This should be done monthly for the first year in business and annually for year two and three. Projecting the drawings when they actually come out of your bank account will do two important things for your business plan:

· it will make your cash flow projection more accurate, and

· it will enable the reader of your business plan to see how much money you plan to extract from your business.

Develop Your Cash Flow Forecast

Step 59

Determine the flow of cash into and out of your business. This is the lifeline of your business. It will enable you to clarify how much money you will require to operate each month.

The secret to completing a meaningful cash flow is research. The cash flow is an opportunity to build tremendous confidence in your business. That confidence arises from knowing your business and basing your estimates on well researched assumptions and facts. If you have done your homework, your cash flow will be easy to project.

A solid Cash Flow Forecast will include detailed inflow (cash in) and outflow (cash out) of monies from your business for year one. Year one is typically forecasted in detail, month by month while year two and three are usually projected as a percentage increase over the previous year. Typically only yearly totals are provided beyond year one.

Key points to remember about completing your cash flow:

- Project your sales conservatively.
- Allow more than you think you will need for expenses.
- Cash in items are entered into a cash flow <u>during the month they enter your bank account</u> and cash out items are entered <u>during the month they exit your bank account</u>.
- Your cash flow is the snapshot you and your banker need in order to determine how much you need for an operating loan.
- Business analysts and bankers will use your cash flow as a measure of whether or not you know your business.

(Note: The Example and Worksheet for this step follow the Task List.)

Task List

There are at least a couple of approaches to completing your cash flow. One is to do one month or column at a time, from top to bottom. The other is to complete each line item or row from left to right. Use the method that works best for you.

1. At the top of your Cash Flow Worksheet, enter the names of your first 12 months of operation. If you are using the Biz4Caster™, this will already be done for you.

2. From your Sales Forecast, enter all sales in the months during which the cash actually enters your bank account.

3. Enter all other sources of cash entering your bank account during the month they enter your bank account. Include sources of cash other than sales, such as loans or grants.

4. Calculate the total cash-in amounts for each month and enter the totals into the Total Cash In row.

5. In the cash-out section, calculate and enter your total Cost of Goods Sold into each month in the Purchases (COGS) row.

6. In the cash-out section, project your expenses for each of the first 12 months and enter them into the month during which the expense will be paid.

7. Enter your management salaries and wages for each of the first 12 months.

8. Calculate and enter the employer wage burden and workers' compensation amounts.

9. Enter any loan payments, usually separating the interest from the principle. This is because the interest is an expense to your business while the principle is not.

10. Calculate the total cash-out amounts for each month and enter the totals into the Total Cash Out row.

11. In the Cash Flow Summary, enter zero as your opening balance for the first month.

    a. For the first month of operation, enter the total cash-in and the total cash-out.

    b. Beginning with the opening balance, add the cash-in and then subtract the cash-out. The result is your closing cash balance.

    c. Carry the closing cash balance for month one to become the opening balance for month two.

    d. Repeat this process until you have completed all of the first 12 months of operation.

12. Calculate the first year totals for all cash-in and all cash-out line items.

13. For year two and three, estimate total amounts for all cash-in and all cash-out line items. Most businesses will project a modest increase in sales for year two, which will necessitate increases for some but not all expenses.

14. Clarify and write any assumptions on which you have based your estimates (interest rates, growth percentages, etc.).

Tip: The Financial Section must convey that you understand the financial workings of your business. The financial information must be consistent with the text portion of your plan. For example, if you state in your Marketing Section that you will have monthly advertisements in your local newspaper, your Cash Flow Forecast must reflect that monthly expense.

Tip: Project Owner's Drawings conservatively. Unless your business can truly sustain higher Owner's Drawings, keep them low. If you are planning to borrow money or access a government grant, paying yourself a conservative rate shows diligence and commitment.

Tip: Most simple business plans do not account for inflation. I recommend you only include calculations for inflation if it is a significant expense to your business.

Example: Cash Flow Forecast

	Sept.	Oct.	Nov.	Dec.	Jan.
Total Sales Forecast	**$7,699**	**$9,147**	**$11,044**	**$13,080**	**$8,851**
Cash Receipts (Cash In)					
Cash Sales	6,929	8,232	9,939	11,772	7,966
Accounts Receivable		385	842	1,010	1,206
Owner Capital & Non-Cash Equity	20,000				
Loan Proceeds	10,850				
Other Cash Received (Grants)					
Total Cash In	**$37,779**	**$8,617**	**$10,781**	**$12,782**	**$9,172**
Cash Disbursements (Cash out)					
Purchases (Cost of Goods Sold)	1,027	1,533	2,115	3,138	1,285
Advertising	600	600	600	600	600
Auto (Includes Repairs & Insurance)	554	554	554	554	554
Interest, Bank Charges	83	83	83	83	83
Insurance, Licenses, Fees	1,700				
Professional (Accounting, Legal)	125	125	125	125	125
Rent (Equipment)					
Rent (Premises)	200	200	200	200	200
Office Supplies & Expenses	200	200	200	200	200
Business Licenses & Permits				130	
Telephone	150	150	150	150	150
Utilities					
Repairs & Maintenance					
Travel & Promotion		400	400	400	400
Owner Equity & Fixed Asset Purchase	20,000				
Supplies & Small Tools					
Processing, Legal, Broker Fees	850				
Auto (Gas, Oil)	250	250	250	250	250
Security deposit, last month's rent					
Management Salaries	3,600	3,600	3,600	3,600	3,600
Wages & Subcontractor Fees	600	600	600	600	600
Employer Wage Burden	420	420	420	420	420
Workers' Compensation	13	13	13	13	13
Loan Payments - Principal		418	421	424	427
Loan Payments - Interest		72	70	67	64
Total Cash Out	**$30,373**	**$9,219**	**$9,801**	**$10,954**	**$8,972**
Cash Flow Summary					
Opening Balance		7,406	6,803	7,783	9,611
Add: Cash In	37,779	8,617	10,781	12,782	9,172
Subtract: Cash Out	30,373	9,219	9,801	10,954	8,972
Monthly Cash Inflow (Outflow)	7,406	(603)	980	1,828	201
Less: Taxes Payable Previous Year					
Add: Opening Accounts Receivable					
Add: Ending Accounts Payable					
Less: Opening Accounts Payable					
Closing Cash Balance	**$7,406**	**$6,803**	**$7,783**	**$9,611**	**$9,812**

Tip: Start-up expenses are usually put into the first month of your cash flow forecast.

Tip: Take off your rose-colored glasses and create a worst-case financial scenario. Forecast your sales as low are possible, while projecting expenses a little higher than expected. What you want to be able to do is project sales low and expenses high, and still demonstrate that your business will survive (and pay off any loans).

Feb.	March	April	May	June	July	Aug.	Year 1
$9,247	**$9,600**	**$12,730**	**$11,012**	**$11,012**	**$11,012**	**$13,810**	**$128,242**
8,322	8,640	11,457	9,911	9,911	9,911	12,429	115,418
1,097	905	942	1,117	1,187	1,101	1,101	10,893
							20,000
							10,850
$9,418	**$9,545**	**$12,400**	**$11,027**	**$11,098**	**$11,012**	**$13,530**	**$157,161**
1,583	1,749	1,845	2,129	2,129	2,129	2,254	22,917
600	600	600	600	600	600	600	7,200
554	554	554	554	554	554	554	6,648
83	83	83	83	83	83	83	996
							1,700
125	125	125	125	125	125	125	1,500
200	200	200	200	200	200	200	2,400
200	200	200	200	200	200	200	2,400
							130
150	150	150	150	150	150	150	1,800
400	400	400	400	400	400	400	4,400
							20,000
							850
250	250	250	250	250	250	250	3,000
3,600	3,600	3,600	3,600	3,600	3,600	3,600	43,200
600	600	600	600	600	600	600	7,200
420	420	420	420	420	420	420	5,040
13	13	13	13	13	13	13	161
430	433	435	438	441	444	447	4,759
61	58	55	52	49	47	44	639
$9,269	**$9,435**	**$9,531**	**$9,815**	**$9,815**	**$9,815**	**$9,940**	**$136,940**
9,812	9,961	10,070	12,939	14,151	15,434	16,631	
9,418	9,545	12,400	11,027	11,098	11,012	13,530	157,161
9,269	9,435	9,531	9,815	9,815	9,815	9,940	136,940
149	109	2,868	1,212	1,283	1,197	3,590	20,221
							1,988
$9,961	**$10,070**	**$12,939**	**$14,151**	**$15,434**	**$16,631**	**$20,221**	**$22,209**

Tip: Be sure to pay yourself enough from the business to cover your personal expenses. This will usually be shown in the "Management Salaries (Drawings)" line of your Cash Flow Forecast. To determine your personal expenses use the Owner's Drawings Worksheet on page 35, also downloadable from www.riskbuster.com.

WORSHEET: CASH FLOW FORECAST					
	1	2	3	4	5
Cash Receipts (Cash In)					
Cash Sales					
Accounts Receivable					
Owner's Capital					
Loan Proceeds					
Other Income Received (Grants)					
Total Cash In					
Cash Disbursements (Cash out)					
Purchases (Cost of Goods Sold)					
Advertising					
Auto (Includes Repairs & Insurance)					
Interest, Bank Charges					
Insurance, Licenses, Fees					
Professional (Accounting, Legal)					
Rent (Equipment)					
Rent (Premises)					
Office Supplies & Expenses					
Business Licenses & Permits					
Telephone					
Utilities					
Repairs & Maintenance					
Travel & Promotion					
Purchase Fixed Assets					
Purchase Other Assets					
Processing, Legal, Broker Fees					
Auto (Gas, Oil)					
Management Salaries (Drawings)					
Wages & Subcontractor Fees					
Employer Wage Burden					
Workers' Compensation					
Loan Payments - Principal					
Loan Payments - Interest					
Total Cash Out					
Cash Flow Summary					
Opening Balance					
Add: Cash In					
Subtract: Cash Out					
Monthly Cash Inflow (Outflow)					
Less: Taxes Payable Previous Year					
Add: Opening Accounts Receivable					
Add: Ending Accounts Payable					
Less: Opening Accounts Payable					
Closing Cash Balance					

6	7	8	9	10	11	12	YR 1 TOTALS

Identify Your Operating Expenses

Step 60

Not necessary if you include a full income statement in your business plan.

Tip: *You want to review all the expense categories in the Operating Expenses Worksheet to make sure you aren't missing any. Use the blank rows at the bottom to add those expenses not already listed.*

Summarize your operating expenses for year one, two and three. These are the expenses that will be incurred whether or not you make any sales.

Example: Operating Expenses

	YEAR 1	YEAR 2	YEAR 3
Advertising	$7,200	$7,200	$7,200
Auto (Includes Repairs & Insurance)	6,648	6,648	6,648
Interest, Bank Charges	996	996	996
Insurance, Licenses, Fees	1,700	1,700	1,700
Professional (Accounting, Legal)	1,500	1,500	1,500
Rent (Equipment)			
Rent (Premises)	2,400	2,400	2,400
Office Supplies & Expenses	2,400	2,400	2,400
Business Licenses & Permits	130	130	130
Telephone	1,800	1,800	1,800
Utilities			
Repairs & Maintenance			
Travel & Promotion	4,400	4,400	4,400
Supplies and Small Tools		1,000	1,000
Processing, Legal, Broker Fees	850	850	850
Auto (Gas, Oil)	3,000	3,000	3,000
Management Salaries	43,200	43,200	43,200
Wages & Subcontractor Fees	7,200	7,200	7,200
Employer Wage Burden	5,040	5,040	5,040
Workers' Compensation	161	161	161
Loan Payments - Interest	639	285	3
Total Operating Expenses	**$89,264**	**$89,910**	**$89,629**

Task List

To complete this step you will need to complete your cash flow forecast, then:

1. Enter all year one, two and three totals into the table below.
2. Check each expense thoroughly to ensure it is accurate and realistic.
3. If changes are needed, go back to the cash flow worksheet and enter them there.

Note: If you have completed the Cash Flow Projection in Step 59, you will already have the total operating expenses for years 1, 2 and 3.

WORSHEET: OPERATING EXPENSES			
	YEAR 1	YEAR 2	YEAR 3
Advertising			
Auto (Includes Repairs & Insurance)			
Interest, Bank Charges			
Insurance, Licenses, Fees			
Professional (Accounting & Legal)			
Rent (Equipment)			
Rent (Premises)			
Office Supplies & Expenses			
Business Licenses & Permits			
Telephone			
Utilities			
Repairs & Maintenance			
Travel & Promotion			
Purchase Other Assets			
Processing, Legal & Broker Fees			
Auto (Gas, Oil)			
Management Salaries			
Wages & Subcontractor Fees			
Employer Wage Burden			
Workers' Compensation			
Loan Payments - Interest			
Total Operating Expenses			

Tip: *Once you have calculated your expenses, build in a contingency. That is, include in your forecast a little extra money for unexpected costs. The amount of contingency will be relative to the degree of risk. For example, the higher the risks, the larger you will want your rainy day fund to be. For most new businesses you will want to add at least 3 to 5%. If it doesn't get used it becomes profit at the end of the year; if you need it during the year you will be thankful you included it in your forecasts.*

Develop Your Projected Income Statement

Step 61

MUST HAVE
RECOMMENDED
NICE TO HAVE

You will want this for yourself, ask your gatekeeper if he or she wants it included.

etermine your profit or loss for each of the first three years.

The Income Statement, also referred to as the Profit and Loss Statement, tells you whether your business is earning or losing money. Do not confuse this with the financial view presented in the Cash Flow Forecast, which tells you how much money is remaining in your bank account at the beginning and end of each month. Contrary to what is believed by many new business owners, the cash flow projection does not tell how much a business is earning. If you find this confusing, I recommend you re-read this paragraph until you understand it — it's important.

The formula for the income statement is:

Sales – Cost of Goods Sold = Gross Profit Margin

Gross Profit Margin – Total Operating Expenses – Depreciation = Net Income (Or Loss) Before Tax

Task List

If you are using Biz4Caster™, your income statement will be done automatically.

To complete this Element you will first need to complete the Elements called Sales Forecast, Labor Projections, and Cash Flow Forecast, and then:

1. If you are using the income statement form that follows, the process still applies except you will need to complete your calculations manually.

2. Enter the total Revenue/Sales for Year 1.

3. Enter the total Cost of Goods Sold (COGS) for Year 1.

4. Calculate the Gross Profit Margin by subtracting COGS from Revenue/Sales and enter the amount in the Summary.

5. Enter all Operating Expenses for Year 1 – these amounts will come from the totals column in the Cash Flow Forecast.

6. Total the Operating Expenses column and enter the amount in the Summary.

7. Calculate depreciation for Year 1 for all equipment over $250 in value. This may require that you use a separate worksheet. Enter the total amount.

8. In the Summary, use this formula to calculate the Net Income: Gross Profit Margin minus Total Operating Expenses plus Depreciation equals Net Income before Tax.

9. Determine what percentage your sales will increase for Year 2 and Year 3, and repeat the process above, with careful consideration to any potential changes to each cost.

Example: Projected Income Statement

	YEAR 1	YEAR 2	YEAR 3
Sales Forecast	$128,242	$145,293	$175,725
Minus: Cost of Goods Sold (COGS)	22,917	27,500	35,750
Gross Profit Margin	**$105,326**	**$117,793**	**$139,975**
Gross Profit Margin Percentage	82.13%	81.07%	79.66%
Other Cash Received (Grants)	$0.00	$0.00	$0.00
Operating Expenses			
Advertising	$7,200	$7,200	$7,200
Auto (Includes Reparis & Insurance)	6,648	6,648	6,648
Interest, Bank Charges	996	996	996
Insurance, Licenses, Fees	1,700	1,700	1,700
Professional (Accounting, Legal)	1,500	1,500	1,500
Rent (Equipment)	0	0	0
Rent (Premises)	2,400	2,400	2,400
Office Supplies & Expenses	2,400	2,400	2,400
Business Licenses & Permits	130	130	130
Telephone	1,800	1,800	1,800
Utilities	0	0	0
Repairs & Maintenance	0	0	0
Travel & Promotion	4,400	4,400	4,400
Processing, Legal, Broker Fees	850	850	850
Auto (Gas, Oil)	3,000	3,000	3,000
Management Salaries	43,200	43,200	43,200
Wages & Subcontractor Fees	7,200	7,200	7,200
Employer Wage Burden	5,040	5,040	5,040
Workers' Compensation	161	161	161
Interest on Long-term Debt	639	285	3
Supplies and Small Tools	0	1,000	1,000
Total Operating Expenses	**$89,264**	**$89,910**	**$89,629**
Summary	YEAR 1	YEAR 2	YEAR 3
Gross Profit and Other Income	$105,326	$117,793	$139,975
Total Operating Expenses	89,264	89,910	89,629
Subtract: Depreciation	4,000	4,800	5,600
Net Income Before Tax	**$12,061**	**$23,083**	**$44,746**
Income Tax	2,125	4,067	7,884
Net Income After Tax	**$9,936**	**$19,015**	**$36,862**

Tip: There is no benefit
to using all three tables
(Operating Expenses,
Projected Income Statement
and Projected Income
Summary) in your business
plan. If you use the Projected
Income Statement, you can
dispense with the other two
tables, or vice versa.

WORKSHEET: PROJECTED INCOME STATEMENT	YEAR 1	YEAR 2	YEAR 3
Sales Forecast			
Less: Cost of Goods Sold			
Gross Profit Margin			
Gross Profit Margin Percentage			
Other Income Received (Grants)			
Operating Expenses			
Advertising			
Auto (Includes Repairs & Insurance)			
Interest, Bank Charges			
Insurance, Licenses, Fees			
Professional (Accounting, Legal)			
Rent (Equipment)			
Rent (Premises)			
Office Supplies & Expenses			
Business Licenses & Permits			
Telephone			
Utilities			
Repairs & Maintenance			
Travel & Promotion			
Processing, Legal, Broker Fees			
Auto (Gas, Oil)			
Management Salaries			
Wages & Subcontractor Fees			
Employer Wage Burden			
Workers' Compensation			
Interest on Long-term Debt			
Purchase Other Assets			
Prepaid Expenses			
Total Operating Expenses			
Summary	YEAR 1	YEAR 2	YEAR 3
Gross Profit Margin			
Total Operating Expenses			
Subtract: Depreciation			
Net Income Before Tax			
Income Tax			
Net Income After Tax			

Example: Projected Income Summary

	YEAR 1	YEAR 2	YEAR 3
Sales Forecast	$128,242	$145,293	$175,725
Minus Cost of Goods Sold	22,917	27,500	35,750
Equals Gross Profit Margin	$105,326	$117,793	$139,975
Subtract Total Operating Expenses	89,264	89,910	89,629
Subtract Depreciation	4,000	4,800	5,600
Equals Net Income Before Tax	$12,061	$23,083	$44,746

WORKSHEET: PROJECTED INCOME SUMMARY			
	YEAR 1	YEAR 2	YEAR 3
Sales Forecast			
Minus Cost of Goods Sold			
Equals Gross Profit Margin			
Subtract Total Operating Expenses			
Subtract Depreciation			
Equals Net Income Before Tax			

Determine What Level of Sales You Will Need to Break-Even

Step 62

D etermine the point in the year when your business will *break-even* or begin to earn a profit from sales.

Example: Break-Even Analysis

	YEAR 1	YEAR 2	YEAR 3
Total Sales	$128,242	$145,293	$175,725
Total Cost of Goods Sold	22,917	27,500	35,750
Equals: Gross Profit Margin	105,326	117,793	139,975
Gross Profit Margin Percentage	82.13%	81.07%	79.66%
Total Operating Expenses	89,264	89,910	89,629
Break-Even Point	**$112,181**	**$117,410**	**$125,379**

Tip: Some products or services have higher profit margins than others, which means each will contribute a different amount to the overall break-even for a business. For example, the labor to fix a vehicle might bring a higher profit margin or percentage per unit than the parts required for the repairs. The break-even point is the result of the combination of all of your products and services. You can impact your break-even by adding products or services with higher profit margins per unit.

Task List

To complete this Element you will need to have completed the first edition of all or most of the other Financial Elements to enable you to calculate different scenarios, then:

1. Calculate your Total Sales for Year 1
2. Calculate your Total Cost Of Goods Sold for Year 1
3. Calculate your Total Gross Margin for Year 1 (#1 Minus #2)
4. Calculate your Gross Margin Percentage for Year 1 (#3 Divided By #1)
5. Calculate your Total Operating Expenses for Year 1
6. Determine your Break-Even Point for Year 1 (#2 Plus #5)
7. Repeat steps one to six for Year 2 and Year 3

Tip: Break-even is the point in a year when a business begins to profit; it is a powerful risk assessment tool. The break-even point enables you (and your gatekeeper) to assess whether or not your sales projections are realistic. Can you do the amount of work necessary to make enough sales to reach break-even?

WORKSHEET: BREAK-EVEN ANALYSIS			
	YEAR 1	YEAR 2	YEAR 3
1. Total Sales			
2. Total Cost of Goods Sold			
3. Equals: Gross Profit Margin			
4. Gross Profit Margin Percentage			
5. Total Operating Expenses			
6. Break-Even Point			

Note: This method of calculating break-even will be accurate for the product or service mix you have forecasted for any particular scenario. If you sell more or less of any given unit the ratios can change, which may also change the break-even point.

Develop Your Pro Forma Balance Sheet

Determine the net worth of your business. It is a snapshot of your business at a specific time. If it is developed for some point in the future it is referred to as a *Pro Forma* Balance Sheet.

When doing this Element it is important to keep in mind that you are forecasting, not accounting, therefore you are estimating.

Step 63

MUST HAVE
RECOMMENDED
NICE TO HAVE

You will want this for yourself, ask your gatekeeper if he or she wants it included.

Example: Pro Forma Balance Sheet

	START-UP	YEAR 1	YEAR 2	YEAR 3
ASSETS				
CURRENT ASSETS				
Cash and Bank Accounts	$10,850	$22,209	$35,961	$75,336
Accounts Receivable		1,932	2,188	2,647
Inventory				
Prepaid Rent				
TOTAL CURRENT ASSETS	10,850	24,140	38,150	77,983
FIXED AND OTHER ASSETS				
Fixed Assets	20,000	20,000	24,000	28,000
Other Assets				
Accumulated depreciation		(4,000)	(8,800)	(14,400)
TOTAL FIXED & OTHER ASSETS	20,000	16,000	15,200	13,600
TOTAL ASSETS	$30,850	$40,140	$53,350	$91,583
LIABILITIES				
CURRENT LIABILITIES				
Accounts Payable		$1,988	$1,844	$1,885
Corporate Income Taxes Payable		2,125	4,067	7,884
Current Portion of Long-term Debt		5,604	487	
TOTAL CURRENT LIABILITIES		9,717	6,399	9,770
LONG-TERM DEBT				
Mortgages and Liens Payable	10,850	487		
Shareholder's Loan	20,000	20,000	18,000	16,000
TOTAL LONG-TERM DEBT	30,850	20,487	18,000	16,000
TOTAL LIABILITIES	$30,850	$30,204	$24,399	$25,770
OWNERS' EQUITY				
Retained Earnings		9,936	28,951	65,813
TOTAL EQUITY & LIABILITIES	**$30,850**	**$40,140**	**$53,350**	**$91,583**

Task List

Tip: This Element may be entirely optional for a start-up business. Depending what the purpose of your business plan is, you might choose to eliminate this Element altogether. If the plan is for yourself it will depend on your preference; if the plan is targeted for a bank or other lending agency, ask whether they expect to see this Element as part of your plan.

1. To determine the net worth of your business, subtract liabilities from assets. The equation for this is: assets minus liabilities equal net worth.

2. Estimate your total current assets. This will include all cash, inventory, prepaid expenses and accounts receivable.

3. Estimate your total fixed assets. This might include investments and capital equipment.

4. Determine the current liabilities. This might include financial obligations, taxes owed, accounts payable and unpaid bills.

5. Calculate your long-term liabilities such as mortgages, bank loans and/or equipment leases.

6. Subtract your total liabilities from your total assets to determine your owners' equity (retained earnings). This is the equity or money you have invested in your business.

Tip: This Element is called a Balance Sheet because it must balance. "Total Assets" must equal "Total Equity plus Liabilities."

WORKSHEET: PRO FORMA BALANCE SHEET				
	START-UP	YEAR 1	YEAR 2	YEAR 3
ASSETS				
CURRENT ASSETS				
Cash and Bank Accounts				
Accounts Receivable				
Inventory				
Prepaid Rent				
TOTAL CURRENT ASSETS				
FIXED AND OTHER ASSETS				
Fixed Assets				
Other Assets				
Accumulated depreciation				
TOTAL FIXED & OTHER ASSETS				
TOTAL ASSETS				
LIABILITIES				
CURRENT LIABILITIES				
Accounts Payable				
Bank loans				
Corporate Income Taxes Payable				
Current Portion of Long-term Debt				
TOTAL CURRENT LIABILITIES				
LONG-TERM DEBT				
Mortgages and Liens Payable				
Shareholder's Loan				
TOTAL LONG-TERM DEBT				
TOTAL LIABILITIES				
OWNERS' EQUITY				
Retained Earnings				
TOTAL EQUITY & LIABILITIES				

Identify and Calculate Your Start-Up Expenses

Determine your start-up expenses. These are all the costs related to getting your business up and running.

It's important to understand that you have some discretion as to which costs get included in start-up. Some analysts will include all the costs for months prior to the opening day and reflect this in the business plan by including a 15-month rather than a 12-month cash flow projection. I prefer to use a 12-month cash flow projection with the start-up costs slotted into the first month.

Another issue that can generate confusion is the difference between a start-up loan, an operating loan, capital equipment loan and inventory loan. You do not need to get tangled up with the labels, as your banker or lending agency will slot the amounts into the appropriate categories.

Practically speaking, you need enough money at start-up to get you successfully to the operating stage.

Step 64

MUST HAVE
RECOMMENDED
NICE TO HAVE

Example: Start-up Expenses

	TOTALS
Start-up Inventory	$1,500
Advertising	800
Auto (Includes Repairs & Insurance)	554
Interest, Bank Charges	83
Insurance, Licenses, Fees	1,700
Office Supplies & Expenses	200
Business Licenses & Permits	130
Telephone	150
Owner's Non-cash Equity & Purchase Fixed Assets	20,000
Purchase Other Assets	
Processing, Legal, Broker Fees	850
Auto (Gas, Oil)	250
Management Salaries	3,600
Wages & Subcontractor Fees	600
Employer Wage Burden (CPP, IE, Holiday Pay)	420
Workers' Compensation	13
Total Start-up Expenses	**$30,850**

Tip: When seeking to borrow money for your business start-up be conservative but realistic. Be sure to ask for enough money to succeed in your efforts. The reader will want to see that you have thought your plan through.

Tip: Include the equity you bring to the business in your start-up calculations. For example, if you own tools and equipment that you will roll into the business, show the value of the items as owner equity at start-up. This will strengthen your business proposal. If you include any equipment, such as a vehicle, with loans outstanding, be sure to include both the asset and the liability (your equity and the amount owing on the loan).

Tip: Most new entrepreneurs underestimate the amount of money they will need to get their business into operation.

Tip: If you have the security of ongoing sales you can relax a little on the amount of contingency funds because your risk is lowered due to the certainty of those sales.

Task List

To complete this Element you will need to determine what you must have in place to begin conducting business and you must have researched the related costs, then:

1. Enter all amounts you will need in place to begin doing business.

2. In listing your start-up expenses, note that the cash flow forecast includes all costs for the twelve months following the start-up. Be sure that you do not duplicate expenses by including them in both start-up and in your operating expenses.

WORKSHEET: START-UP EXPENSES	
START-UP EXPENSES	**TOTALS**
Start-up Inventory	
Advertising	
Auto (Includes Repairs & Insurance)	
Interest, Bank Charges	
Insurance, Licenses, Fees	
Professional (Accounting, Legal)	
Rent (Equipment)	
Rent (Premises)	
Office Supplies & Expenses	
Business Licenses & Permits	
Telephone	
Utilities	
Repairs & Maintenance	
Travel & Promotion	
Purchase Fixed Assets	
Purchase Other Assets	
Processing, Legal, Broker Fees	
Auto (Gas, Oil)	
Management Salaries	
Wages & Subcontractor Fees	
Employer Wage Burden	
Workers' Compensation	
Loan Payments - Interest	
Total Start-up Expenses	

Clarify Your Sources and Uses of Funds at Start-Up

List all sources and uses of funds at start-up. This Element is very much tied to the Start-up Expenses Element in that your use of funds is a summary of the start-up expenses.

Step 65

MUST HAVE
RECOMMENDED
NICE TO HAVE

May not need to do this table if you're not borrowing money at start-up.

Example: Use and Source of Funds

USE OF FUNDS		SOURCE OF FUNDS	
Operating Expenses	**Amount**	**Owner Investment**	**Amount**
Start-up Expenses	$10,850	Owner of Business: Cash	$10,000
Other Operating Needs		Owner of Business: Equity	10,000
Owner Equipment Equity	10,000	**Debt Sources**	
Other		Family	
		Friends	10,850
Capital Purchases		Community Futures	
		Chartered Banks	
Purchase of Fixed Assets	10,000	Credit Union	
Purchase of Other Assets		Angel	
Total Funding Needed	**$30,850**	**Total Funding Sourced**	**$30,850**

Task List

To complete this Element you will need to have completed the start-up calculations, then:

1. Working from the Start-up Expenses table, calculate and enter the dollar amounts in the appropriate cells in the following table for uses (what the money will pay for) and for sources (where the money will come from).

2. This Element will help you clarify whether you need financing and if so, how much you need.

3. The table communicates to the reader how much you are personally investing and how much you are requesting from other sources.

4. The totals at the bottom of the sources column must equal the total at the bottom of the uses column.

WORSHEET: USE AND SOURCE OF FUNDS			
USE OF FUNDS		**SOURCE OF FUNDS**	
Operating Expenses	**Amount**	**Owner Investment**	**Amount**
Start-up Expenses		Owner of Business: Cash	
Other Operating Needs		Owner of Business: Equity	
Owner Equipment Equity		**Debt Sources**	
Other		Family	
		Friends	
Capital Purchases		Community Futures	
		Chartered Banks	
Purchase of Fixed Assets		Credit Union	
Purchase of Other Assets		Angel	
Total Funding Needed		**Total Funding Sourced**	

Tip: With the exception of unusual circumstances, you must come to the table with equity – the more equity the stronger your proposal. Unless you're dealing with a development lender or have access to a strong co-signer, the owner must have a minimum of 10% equity or investment in a loan package, but a 20% investment by the owner makes a stronger case. Each lending agency or bank will have its policy or preference on how much and what type of equity or investment the owner(s) must provide. Research your target lender to determine what his or her requirements are.

ASSEMBLE YOUR APPENDICES

The purpose of this Section is to provide all additional information that supports the objectives of the plan. The contents of this Section will vary according to the requirements of the lender or investor. I recommend that you prepare the Elements of this Section for your own benefit and that they be provided with the business plan as required by the target audience or readers.

Here is an example of an Appendices Goal Worksheet for Macrolink Action Plans Inc.

Example: Appendices Goal

APPENDICES ELEMENT	STEP #	NEED TO DO / PROOF
1. Resumés	66	Update
2. Personal Net Worth Statement(s)	67	Will use Royal Bank form
3. Certificates and Accreditation	68	N/A
4. Historical Financial Statements	69	Produce 3-year summary on one page
5. Organizational Charts	70	N/A
6. Board or Band Council Resolution	71	N/A
7. List of References	72	Update and include a brief, relevant list
8. Letters of Reference	73	Will include brief testimonials with list of references
9. Letters of Intent	74	N/A
10. Contracts or Offers	75	If appropriate, I will make contracts available on request
11. Partnership Agreement	76	N/A
12. Lease Agreement	77	N/A
13. Insurance Documents	78	N/A
14. Price Lists	79	N/A
15. Price Quotes	80	N/A, although at some point could have one for the book
16. Appraisals	81	N/A
17. Market Survey Results	82	Will provide only on request
18. Map of Area	83	N/A
19. Environmental Information	84	N/A
20. Publicity	85	Am collecting and will use where appropriate
21. Promotional Material	86	Will not be ready initially, could include later
22. Product Literature	87	May develop one-page descriptions
23. Technical Specifications	88	N/A
24. Glossary of Terms	89	N/A

Task List

Hopefully you will have dealt with setting up your Appendices files and folders back in Step 11. To avoid duplication, you should probably go back and review what you did then.

1. Identify what you need to do to for each of the Appendices you have chosen to use.

WORSHEET: APPENDICES GOALS		
APPENDICES ELEMENT	STEP #	NEED TO DO / PROOF
1. Resumés	66	
2. Personal Net Worth Statement(s)	67	
3. Certificates and Accreditation	68	
4. Historical Financial Statements	69	
5. Organizational Charts	70	
6. Board or Band Council Resolution	71	
7. List of References	72	
8. Letters of Reference	73	
9. Letters of Intent	74	
10. Contracts or Offers	75	
11. Partnership Agreement	76	
12. Lease Agreement	77	
13. Insurance Documents	78	
14. Price Lists	79	
15. Price Quotes	80	
16. Appraisals	81	
17. Market Survey Results	82	
18. Map of Area	83	
19. Environmental Information	84	
20. Publicity	85	
21. Promotional Material	86	
22. Product Literature	87	
23. Technical Specifications	88	
24. Glossary of Terms	89	

Build a Resumé

Create a resumé that demonstrates why you are qualified to operate your business.

A resumé is a concise inventory of your personal experiences, your educational background and any job-related personal traits. Job seekers prepare resumés to submit to prospective employers, while entrepreneurs use their resumé to support their business plan and proposals. Your resumé outlines what you personally offer to make your business successful. A strong resumé helps you make a good impression and in some cases is the only means of securing a loan or a client; prepare it carefully.

In making their decisions, lenders and investors place the highest importance on the quality of the manager or management team. A poorly written resumé can be detrimental even though your business plan excels in every other way.

Taking the time to prepare a professional looking resumé will give you a definite edge over your competitors. It indicates a businesslike approach and shows motivation and initiative.

MUST HAVE
RECOMMENDED
NICE TO HAVE

Action Words to Use

Consider the following words when preparing your resumé or completing your application. They will help you make a positive, favorable impression.

Tip: Choose the resumé style that will present your experience in the best possible way.

ACTION WORDS CHECKLIST			
☐ Competent	☐ Stable	☐ Established	☐ Initiated
☐ Successful	☐ Well educated	☐ Communicated	☐ Created
☐ Capable	☐ Varied background	☐ Processed	☐ Organized
☐ Resourceful	☐ Equipped	☐ Participated	☐ Trained
☐ Qualified	☐ Accomplished	☐ Sold	☐ Worked
☐ Versatile	☐ Profitable	☐ Engineered	☐ Led
☐ Proficient	☐ Positive	☐ Implemented	☐ Coordinated
☐ Efficient	☐ Completed	☐ Controlled	☐ Analyzed
☐ Knowledgeable	☐ Investigated	☐ Guided	☐ Improved
☐ Consistent	☐ Designed	☐ Administered	☐ Repaired
☐ Experienced	☐ Developed	☐ Managed	☐ Employed
☐ Productive	☐ Maintained	☐ Directed	☐ Expanded
☐ Effective	☐ Built	☐ Supervised	☐ Achieved
☐ Specialized			

Tip: Your resumé must be perfect. Poor grammar and misspelled words will erode the credibility you are working to build.

Parts of a Combination Resumé

Personal Information

- Includes: Name, Address, Telephone Numbers, Fax Number, Email Address, Website Address

---

Objective

- Tells the gatekeeper your business intensions
- Other titles: Job Objective, Career Objective, Summary, Profile, Career Field, Areas of Contribution

---

Key Strengths

- Points of primary interest to the gatekeeper
- Other titles: Skills Summary, Assets, Highlights of Qualifications, Professional Qualifications

---

Accomplishments

- Optional
- Summarizes areas of expertise with brief facts
- Other titles: Relevant Experience, Professional Experience

Work History

- In reverse chronological order
  1. Dates (or number of years at job)
  2. Name, area of company
  3. Job Title
  4. Skills and accomplishments not given above, give description of duties performed

---

Education

- Shows training related to the business
- Put this Section near the top if it is more important to the gatekeeper

---

Interests

- Optional - keep brief. Indicates fitness, community involvement, volunteer work, hobbies

---

References

- Option - have separate reference sheet.
- Use only references that are current and confirmed
- Ensure the contact information for each reference is accurate

Tip: Spacing is important in creating an impression of neatness and orderliness. It is better to reduce the amount of information on the page than to crowd it with too many details. Glancing at your finished copy, it should look neat, clean and easy to read. Limit your resumé to one or two pages.

WORKSHEET: RESUMÉ FOR ENTREPRENEURS		
Name:	Email address:	
Address:		
City:	Province:	Postal Code:
Phone (Home):	Phone (Bus):	Fax:

BUSINESS OBJECTIVE

STRENGTHS

ACCOMPLISHMENTS

Tip: Give careful consideration as to whether to include both the Owner Element and your Resumé. If only one is necessary for your business plan, decide which one to include.

WORKSHEET: RESUMÉ FOR ENTREPRENEURS Continued

WORK HISTORY

Title	Company	Date

EDUCATION & TRAINING

INTERESTS

Tip: If you have a long work history, consider eliminating anything beyond twenty years, as well as short-term positions that may not be significant.

Example: Resume

DANIEL BOUDREAU
Box 101, Station "A", Prince George, BC V2L 4R9

Business Telephone: (250) 612-9161   Residence Telephone: (250) 555-9161

CAREER HISTORY

Key Strengths	**Tenacious Project Builder**	**Proficient at Due Diligence**
	Skillful Use of Computer & Technology	**Effective Proposal Developer**
	Positive, Dynamic Facilitator	**Competent Business Planner**

07 2004 to Present   **NECHAKO-KITAMAAT DEVELOPMENT FUND SOCIETY**
NKDF Investment Area (Vanderhoof to Kitamaat Village)
Manager

Activities:
- providing secretariat services for the society
- overseeing all of the society's operations
- review & due diligence on all proposals and business plans
- management of approximately 30 ongoing projects in rural communities, from Vanderhoof to Kitamaat Village
- bookkeeping, accounting, investment tracking & financial reporting
- budget management, business planning & annual reporting
- communications leading up to & resulting from board meetings
- management of website

07 2003 to 06 2004   **COMMUNITY FUTURES DEVELOPMENT CORPORATION**
Fraser Fort George Region & Stuart Nechako Region
Community Outreach Officer, SICEAI
Softwood Industry Community Economic Adjustment Initiative

Activities:
- reviewed and performed due diligence on proposals & business plans
- interaction & communications with SICEAI personnel & applicants
- community networking to identify SICEAI clients
- communication & information dissemination for applicants
- consultation with First Nations & Metis groups
- administration & file management

03 1987 to Present   **MACROLINK ACTION PLANS INC.,** Prince George, BC
President & CEO

Activities:
- business planning coach
- deliver business planning, marketing, *Train the Trainer* workshops
- assist clients with business plan & proposal development
- supervised up to nine training coordinators, 50 trainers & 22 staff
- managed & co-ordinated government projects to $350,000
- proficient in use of MS Word, Excel, PowerPoint, ACCPAK Simply Accounting, Internet

Daniel Boudreau (Continued)   Page 2

<u>12 1991 to 10 1996</u>   **P G NATIVE FRIENDSHIP CENTRE,** Prince George, BC
Small Business Advisor & Coordinator, *Native Entrepreneurial Training*

Activities:
- designed, developed, & delivered *Native Entrepreneurial Training*
- business counselling & advisory services
- information dissemination for entrepreneurs
- coordinated various speakers, trainers & activities
- assisted clients with business planning, budgeting & proposal development
- increased the profile of Aboriginal businesses in the Prince George area
- developed & coordinated the *Prince George Area Aboriginal Lending Circles*
- managed program budgeting & forecasting
- recruited & selected personnel & program participants
- delivered workshops on a variety of business related topics
- advertised & marketed the program & the business advisory services

<u>04 1979 to 01 1988</u>   **SUNDANCE REFORESTATION LTD.,** Prince George, BC
President/Owner

Activities:
- founded & grew the business to $1,600,000 revenue within three years
- trained field personnel, supervisors & project managers
- *managed up to 150 forestry field workers, up to 25 project & crew supervisors, & up to five clerical & office staff*

EDUCATION & TRAINING

1996	• Human Resource Management For Non-Profit Organizations (SFU)
1995	• Native Adult Instructor Diploma (NAID) Program
1994	• Financial Management For Non-Profit Organizations (SFU)
1994	• How Adults Learn II - Curriculum Development (John Baker)
1990	• The Excellence Series (Context Associated)
1978	• Completed Carpentry Apprenticeship - Inter-Provincial Journeyman Ticket
	• Class 4, British Columbia Driver's Licence

INTERESTS

- Volunteered more than ten years on the Finance & Lending Committee for Community Future Development Corporation of Fraser Ft George
- Past Member & Executive for Toastmaster's Clubs
- Developed the *Dream Catcher Business Planning System* & Biz4Caster
- Kayaking, Writing, Snowboarding, Travelling, Music

Task List

This task list can be carried out using a pencil and the Resumé Worksheet for Entrepreneurs in the Appendices, or by loading the information directly into your word processing program.

1. Gather and organize your personal and business contact information, such as your name, address, telephone numbers, fax number, email address and website address.

2. List and prioritize your key strengths according to their importance to the person or team who will receive your resumé. Use the list of positive words under *Action Words to Use* to help you arrive at a dynamic list of key strengths that sell you, but don't overdo it.

3. Compile a list of your accomplishments. This is optional, as you may choose to simply list your accomplishments under each segment of your work history. Once you have listed your achievements, prioritize them according to their importance to the reader of your resumé or business plan.

4. Make a list your of past jobs or business experiences, beginning with the most recent and working your way backwards in time. For each listing, include dates or number of years of the engagement, name of the organization, your job title, and a list of the most relevant skills, accomplishments and/or duties. You can pick and choose the parts of your work history that are most relevant to your business.

5. List your educational and training achievements, beginning with the most recent and working your way back in time. If this segment is more important to the reader of your resumé feel free to place it before the work history.

6. Briefly list your interests. Your objective with this is to reflect that you have a life, but not so much of a life that you're too busy to work. Use this segment to reflect aspects of your life or personality that are not obvious in other parts of your resumé. For example, fitness, community involvement, volunteering, hobbies, etc. This segment is optional.

7. Compile a list of references and either include them at the end of your resumé. In all cases be sure to ask permission of anyone you intend to use as a reference and ensure that you provide accurate, up-to-date contact information for the reference. Use only those who will provide positive references.

Tip: If you have already developed the Owner Element, review it to ensure it is consistent with your resumé.

Tip: If you are unable to fit your resumé on two full pages, you're likely being too detailed or too wordy. Keep sifting until you are able to fit the required information on two pages or less while still maintaining adequate white space. The amount of time you invest in building a succinct document will be appreciated by the reader of your resumé. I am aware of many professionals with hiring responsibilities who simply toss longer resumés in the round file, never to be read.

Develop Your Personal Net Worth Statement

Step 67

Will need this if
you're borrowing
money.

P rovide a potential lender with a clear snapshot of your current financial situation. You want to provide enough information for the lender to make an informed decision as to whether or not to invest in your business venture.

WORKSHEET: PERSONAL NET WORTH STATEMENT

Property

Own ☐ Rent ☐ Board ☐	If you rent or board, the monthly rate: $

Purchase Price: $	Yr bought:	Assessment Value: $	Year:

Mortgage (1st): (name & address)			
Orig. Amount: $	Rate %	Monthly Pymts: $	Balance: $
Mortgage (2nd): (name & address)			
Orig. Amount: $	Rate %	Monthly Pymts: $	Balance: $
Value today: $	Total Owing: $		Equity: $

Other Debts

Owing To:	Monthly Pymt	Balance Owing	Security
TOTAL DEBTS	$	$	

Asset / Liability Summary

ASSETS		LIABILITIES	
Cash / Savings Accounts	$		$
Stocks / Bonds	$		$
RRSPs	$		$
Real Estate	$		$
Automobiles	$	1st Mortgage	$
Furniture	$	2nd Mortgage	$
Other: (specify)	$	Other Debts: (specify)	$
TOTAL ASSETS	$		$

Life Insurance Held:
Details on Contingent Liabilities:
(lease payments, support/alimony payments, co-signed debts, guarantees)

X	X
Applicant Date: (_____ / _____ / 20_____) day month year	Applicant's spouse Date: (_____ / _____ / 20_____) day month year

NOTE: By signing, you are giving permission to the lending party to do credit & reference checks.

Tip: Do not inflate the value of your assets. Inflating the value of assets tends to deflate your credibility. If you are seeking to borrow money your task is to build credibility with the lending agency. Consider having a third party provide a valuation of certain assets, real estate, equipment, etc.

Tip: Your personal net worth tells a story about how you manage money in your personal life and reflects how you will manage money in your business. Use this worksheet to advantage by identifying financial issues you can tidy up **before** approaching a lending agency. For example, can you consolidate debts or sell any toys (boats, campers, bikes, Ski-doos or Sea-doos) to reduce or eliminate unnecessary debt? If you view your own personal net worth statement as though you are the lender, would you lend your money to anyone else with this financial picture? When you can realistically answer yes to that question, you may be in a position to convince someone else to invest.

Organize Your Certificates and Accreditation

Provide evidence of certification and accreditation that will build your credibility.

Provide only the certificates that are relevant to this business. Do not overdo it. Your purpose here is to build your credibility, not pass a paperweight test.

Here are some points to consider in gathering documents for this Element:

- Is the document relevant to this business?
- Is the achievement related to the type of work you will do in the business?
- Is the certificate from a recognized institution?
- How credible is the organization to the reader(s) of your business plan?
- Is the organization still in existence?
- Is the document clean and professional looking?
- Does the document add credibility to your business plan?

Task List

1. Gather any relevant certificates or documentation that will add credibility to your business plan.
2. Make copies of your documents and keep originals in a safe place.

WORKSHEET: LIST OF CERTIFICATES AND DOCUMENTS

Step 68

MUST HAVE
RECOMMENDED
NICE TO HAVE

Tip: If you have a few documents for this Element, consider scanning or copying them at a reduced size in order to get more than one per page. A small investment in this may provide you with an efficient and professional tool to be reused many times in the future.

Tip: If any of your documents include telephone numbers or other contact information, confirm the accuracy of the information and update it where necessary.

Produce Your
Historical Financial Statements

Step 69

Not relevant for
new businesses.

Tip: When buying a business, if
the seller offers any resistance
to providing you with historical
financial statements, you
should probably not pursue
the deal any further.

Tip: When providing you with
historical financial statements,
it is entirely reasonable for
the seller to require you to
sign a confidentiality or non-
disclosure agreement. Be sure
the agreement permits you
to share the information with
your accountant, lawyer and
potential bankers or lenders.

Tip: Unless the business is
less than three years old, you
can expect to show the past
three years historical financial
statements, including income
statements and balance
sheets for all three years.

P rovide any historical financial statements for existing businesses.

This step is for existing businesses only, and will likely be most applicable for those aspiring to buy an existing business.

If You're Buying a Business

When purchasing an existing business, historical financial statements are of critical importance. You will want them first for yourself, to clarify what you are buying and validate the seller's claims of vast profits and no problems forever. If you are planning to borrow money to complete the purchase, your lender will not even begin the dialogue without financial statements for the past three years of operation.

Example: Historical Financial Summary

	2004	2005	2006
Net Annual Sales	$552,155	$796,045	$912,158
Income Before Taxes	(28,086)	46,482	81,601
Income After Taxes	(21,658)	36,294	63,706
Current Assets	112,882	131,653	293,333
Total Assets	138,749	161,164	348,975
Current Liabilities	144,928	128,381	180,154
Net Owners' Equity	$(6,179)	$30,115	$93,821

Task List

1. Gather and include copies of historical financial statements in this Appendix.
   - At a minimum, include income statements and balance sheets from the last three years.
   - Consider including documentation proving the taxes have been paid.

Create Your Organizational Chart

Make it easy for your reader to understand how the human resource part of your business is organized.

If you are a single owner-operator you need not build an organizational chart... unless you have several personalities with complex lines of reporting to each other!

Here is a sample organizational chart:

Step 70

MUST HAVE
RECOMMENDED
NICE TO HAVE

No need for chart if single owner/ operator.

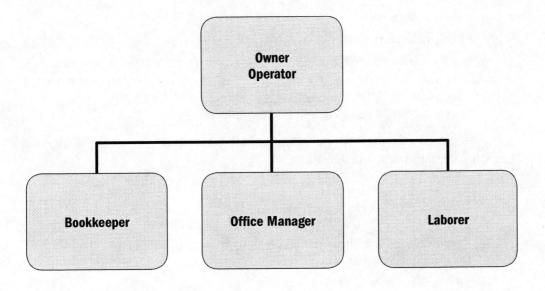

Task List

1. If appropriate, create an organizational chart to include either in this Appendix or in the body of your business plan.

Get the Approval of Your Board

Step 71

Only relevant where needed.

Tip: *If you must get the permission of a Board of Directors for your business idea, you may have to complete your business plan first. Your business plan then becomes the communication tool you use to get the permission of the Board.*

Provide documentation to prove that your business plan is supported by the legal decision makers for the organization.

You may require this type of documentation if your business:

• Is a not-for-profit or government owned organization.

• Requires the support of a political body such as a First Nations government.

• Has a Board of Directors.

• Is a publicly held corporation.

No example is provided here because each Board of Directors will have a standard format used for such purposes. For example, First Nations will usually use a Band Council Resolution (BCR), whereas a Board of Directors for a non-profit organization might provide a copy of the approved Board motion.

If you do not serve or need the permission of a Board of Directors, skip this step and drop this Element from your Appendices.

Task List

1. Determine the best time to submit your request to the Board, including meeting times and deadlines for submissions.

2. Prepare a letter or written request for the approval you seek.

3. Submit your request within the appropriate timelines, attaching your business plan or summary.

4. Prior to the Board meeting or deadline, follow-up to ensure everything is in order.

5. After the Board meeting, follow-up to learn the Board's decision.

Build Your List of References

Provide your reader with a clear path to research you and your business plan by communicating with key references.

Here are some tips on building a list of references:

- Call them and ask their permission to use their name.
- Confirm that you have accurate contact information for each reference.
- Ask permission to use contact information and only use contact information with permission.
- Cut any negative, dated or uncertain references from your list.
- Use only the references most relevant to your reader.

Step 72

MUST HAVE
RECOMMENDED
NICE TO HAVE

Example: List of References

NAME & TITLE	ORGANIZATION	LOCATION	WORK PHONE	HOME PHONE	EMAIL
Jerry Rockford Manager	JR Packing Plant	Rock Creek, BC	(250) 555-2468	(250) 555-2469	jerry@example.com
Donna Wood	Wood Delivery Inc	Rock Creek, BC	(250) 555-1179		dw@example.com

Tip: Make it easy for your reader to do his or her due diligence. Provide accurate and current names, titles, addresses, organizations, telephone numbers and email addresses. Be sure to obtain current permission from your references. A valued reference that has time to prepare is more likely to think of nice things to say about you – a surprised reference is not always your best reference!

Task List

1. Determine which people and organizations will be the strongest, most relevant references for your application.

2. Gather the pertinent contact information for each reference, including name, title, organization, addresses, phone numbers, email addresses and websites.

3. Call each reference and ask his or her permission to use them as a reference. Confirm the accuracy of all contact information and whether you may use it (for example, home numbers may be off limits).

4. Be prepared to clarify what you will be using the reference for – this will help the person focus on providing you their best reference.

WORKSHEET: LIST OF REFERENCES					
NAME & TITLE	ORGANIZATION	LOCATION	WORK PHONE	HOME PHONE	EMAIL

Request and Include Letters of Reference

MUST HAVE
RECOMMENDED
NICE TO HAVE

*Determine if
appropriate for
your type of
business and
situation.*

The challenge with letters of reference is that they quickly become outdated. Nonetheless, a glowing letter of reference is a strong marketing tool to help support your business plan.

Unfortunately, you will not have a lot of control over the quality of reference letters, which will be mostly determined by the skill level of the writer. It is not cool to provide a sample or to suggest what should go into a reference letter, unless specifically requested by the person you approach. In most cases a savvy ex-boss will ask what the reference letter will be used for – this creates an opening for you to explain the purpose of the letter and mention the important attributes the recipient might be looking for in your application. Here are some things to keep in mind about letters of reference:

- The appearance of the letter is important. The letter will be more credible if it is typewritten and on the writer's letterhead.

- The letter should be dated and fairly current.

- The letter should include reference to your relationship with the writer. For example, was he or she your supervisor, accountant or contract manager? If this information is not included in the reference, ensure that you provide it some other way.

- Your reference letters will be stronger if they come from an individual or organization the reader can relate to. If you are submitting your business plan for the purpose of obtaining a loan, your strongest reference letters might be from current customers and trade accounts where you have a track record for paying your bills on time.

Example: Letter of Reference

Macrolink Action Plans Inc
Box 101, Prince George, BC V2L 4R9

January 3, 2006

To Whom It May Concern:
I have known Theresa Williams since the early 1990s where she contracted on a few occasions with my business to provide safety related workshops to our clients.
Theresa's responsibilities included traveling to remote locations, setting up the facilities at the client's location, greeting the participants as they arrived, providing the training and all administrative duties, including reporting, grading participant's exams and evaluation of the workshops.
Theresa has shown the kind of initiative which is necessary to be successful in the training business. She has excellent organizational and presentation skills, and is clearly focused on the needs of the client. She is a self-starter, a conscientious worker and has an excellent work ethic.
I recommend Theresa to you as a competent trainer and facilitator. If you have any further questions, please feel free to call me at 250-612-9161.
Sincerely,

Dan Boudreau
President & CEO

Gather and Include Letters of Intent

Letters of intent are statements written by individuals or organizations declaring their intention to commit to something, typically to use or purchase a product or service, but also for other things.

A letter of intent can be appropriate for situations where you are not able to produce a contract. It can add valuable strength and credibility to your claims in the business plan. For example, you might build a sales forecast on the assumption that certain key clients will make regular purchases, even though no contract exists; a clear letter of intent from one or more key clients or customers will help you build your business case.

Unlike a letter of reference, it is acceptable to provide a template or suggested wording for the writer of your letter of intent. Everyone you approach is likely to be busy – unless the person has written a letter of intent they are unlikely to know exactly what you are looking for. I suggest you put together a generic letter of intent to provide to those who commit to doing one for you.

Here are some key points to know about letters of intent. An effective letter of intent:

- Must include the date it was written and it should be fairly current.
- Will appear more credible if it is written on the writer's letterhead.
- Must come from a credible decision maker or person with the authority to honor promises made in the letter.
- Will be stronger if more specific, weaker if more general. In other words, it will help your business case if the writer states he or she will purchase an amount of goods or services within a specific time period. A general or vaguely written letter of intent doesn't provide a banker with a strong foundation on which to base his or her decision.

Step 74

MUST HAVE
RECOMMENDED
NICE TO HAVE

Not appropriate for all situations, but very helpful where possible.

Unlike a letter of reference, it is acceptable to provide a template or suggested wording for the writer of your letter of intent. I suggest you put together a generic letter of intent to provide to those who commit to doing one for you.

Example: Letter of Intent

ABC Business Development Center
Box 1000, Prince George, BC V2L 4J3

January 3, 2006

To Whom It May Concern:
The purpose of this letter is to express our intention to purchase products and services from Macrolink Action Plans Inc.
In the 12 months beginning September 2006, I will contract the services of Mr. Boudreau a minimum of 5 days each month at a rate of $495 per day.
If you have any questions, please feel free to call me at 250-612-1234.
Sincerely,

John Williams
Executive Director

Copy and Include Signed Contracts or Offers

Step 75

MUST HAVE
RECOMMENDED
NICE TO HAVE

Where applicable.

There is nothing quite as strong as a signed contract to substantiate your assumption or claim that a customer will buy your product or service. A written offer is almost as strong in terms of credibility, certainly as strong as a contract.

No example is provided here because the nature and type of contracts varies so widely. The important thing is that you research your particular industry and get to know what the industry standard is for contracts for your business.

If you are bidding or responding to calls for proposals for government or industry contracts, the buyer will usually dictate and provide the contract. Most government agencies work from boilerplate contract templates that they adapt to your specific situation. In these instances, your only real control lies with how you write your proposal and how thoroughly you proof the draft contract before signing it.

If you are not experienced at writing and reading contracts, I strongly recommend that you engage a competent lawyer to assist you. A good lawyer, in spite of all those bad lawyer jokes, will save you money.

Tip: If your contract is too lengthy to include, consider including only the pertinent pages from the contract. This might be the first or cover page, signature page and possibly specific financial or deliverables pages. If you choose this path, be sure to state that the full document(s) are available upon request.

Task List

1. Determine whether or not a contract should be in your business plan and include it or the appropriate portions in this Appendix.

Create a Partnership Agreement

Over the years I have been involved in four different partnerships and while they haven't all been beds of roses, I firmly believe in the value of partnerships for the right situations. Of the four partnerships, three have worked out fine and one was a disaster. In my view, the success or failure of the partnership is directly related to the quality of the people involved. A partnership is a marriage, and as such, demands the same degree of care and attention required to nurture and grow a successful marriage. As with a marriage, you are well advised to get to know who you're setting up shop with before signing the agreement.

Partnerships are not appropriate for every situation. The first rule of partnering – if you don't need a partner, don't have one. However, there are a number of good reasons for getting into a partnership, such as:

- To attract someone with skills or knowledge you don't already have
- To bring more money to the table
- To handle a job or business that is too large for you to manage alone
- To keep a great person on your team by sharing responsibilities and profits

A Few of the Common Causes of Partnership Breakdown or Failure

- Lack of communication
- Unclear role definition
- Differing visions or desires for the business
- Different values
- Personality conflicts
- Business can't afford all or both partners
- Greed or unrealistic expectations of the business or each other
- One of the partners does all the work
- Dishonesty on the part of one or more partners
- Lack of trust

Common Misunderstandings about Partnerships

- That you don't have to work at keeping the relationship healthy
- That you don't need a signed partnership agreement
- That a partnership lightens the workload — fact is, with more mouths to feed you might have to work harder (at a minimum, you will have to invest more time communicating)

Step 76

MUST HAVE
RECOMMENDED
NICE TO HAVE

Only needed if you have partners.

Partnerships are not appropriate for every situation. The first rule of partnering – if you don't need a partner, don't have one.

Key Points about Partnerships

- Partner with someone who complements your skill set or who has skills that you don't. Clarify both or all of your roles.
- Negotiate and sign a partnership agreement — have a lawyer draw it up.
- Assume nothing — communicate often, honestly and openly.
- Define your vision for the business together and make any changes to the vision together.
- Before getting into business together get to know any potential partner well enough to know whether you have compatible values.
- Prior to signing an agreement ensure that you and any potential partners can effectively resolve conflicts.
- Discuss your expectations for and from each other and the business.
- Ensure the business can afford all the partners.
- Just as you would before hiring an employee, research your potential partner's work and/or investment history to know his or her track record. If he or she has sued half a dozen previous employers for wrongful dismissal, you probably have a fairly clear indication of where you will find yourself if the partnership goes sideways.
- Exit of one or more partners can cause business disruption — be sure to include a shotgun or exit clause in your partnership agreement.

If you are considering a partnership, tread softly and carry a bullet-proof partnership agreement. Treat your partner with respect, communicate openly, keep your expectations realistic and be loyal to each other. These things will go a long way to fostering a long-term, successful partnership.

Task List

1. Determine whether or not you need a partner.
2. Identify and select the right person to be your partner.
3. Discuss all aspects of the partnership agreement with your partner, making notes.
4. Use the services of a competent lawyer to write a partnership agreement. If appropriate, use separate lawyers for each partner.

Copy and Include Lease Agreement(s)

When getting into business, it takes either deep pockets or a lot of guts to sign a lease.

Take a long, hard look at the downside risk before locking yourself into any business related lease. I have observed too many bailout applications from failing businesses rife with costly long-term leases. When my own business went down in flames in 1986, I was the proud signatory on iron-clad leases for a few brand spitting new 4x4 trucks. If the hair doesn't stand up on the back of your neck when considering a lease, you are either really confident in your business or not paying attention. Signer beware!

Heads-up for anyone considering locking into a lease for the early stages of business:

1. Lease agreements are typically for a longer period of time than a rental agreement.

2. Leases typically offer lower rates in return for locking you in for a longer period of time.

3. Lease agreements are often easy to get into and very difficult, if not impossible to get out of.

4. Even when you think you can get out of a lease, there are clauses that seem to pop out of the paperwork.

5. Lease agreements are usually created by and for the lessor rather than the lessee (that would be you).

6. Be wary of commercial leases which provide the lessor with the option to increase your lease commensurate with your revenue or profit. I recall looking with shock at a case involving a small shop whose lease payments had increased from a couple of thousand dollars per month to more than $8,000 due to such a clause.

Task List

1. Include a copy of the lease agreement or the relevant portions in this Appendix.

Step 77

MUST HAVE
RECOMMENDED
NICE TO HAVE

Where applicable.

Tip: *The time to get advice from your lawyer and accountant is before you sign a lease, not after.*

Tip: *Prior to signing your lease, be clear as to whether you can make leasehold improvements and who owns them once they are made.*

Tip: *For a new business, given a choice between a shorter or longer lease, it's usually wiser to take the shorter option should business be slow and you have to make changes. Keep as much flexibility as you can.*

Tip: *If your lease agreement is long, consider providing only the cover and signature page and state that the full document is available upon request.*

Copy and Include Insurance Documents

Step 78

| MUST HAVE |
| RECOMMENDED |
| NICE TO HAVE |

Where applicable.

Y ou don't need to include entire contracts or policies, only proof of purchase. For example, my liability insurance policy has one page that proves that I am insured and provides enough information to satisfy the business plan reader.

Task List

1. Secure a copy of the appropriate insurance documentation and include it in this Appendix.

INSURANCE CHECKLIST	
Research Insurance Needs	
General Liability Insurance	
Product Liability Insurance	
Errors & Omissions Liability Insurance	
Malpractice Liability Insurance	
Automobile Liability Insurance	
Fire & Theft Insurance	
Business Interruption Insurance	
Overhead Expense Insurance	
Personal Disability Insurance	
Key-Person Insurance	
Shareholders' Or Partners' Insurance	
Business Loan Insurance	
Term Life Insurance	
Medical Insurance	
Group Insurance	

Tip: Keep your original documents and include copies in your Appendix; readers may not return the originals.

Tip: In the relevant parts of the body of your business plan, refer your reader to this Element.

Develop Your Price List(s)

I nclude your list of prices for your products and or services.

If your business sells very few products or services (12 or less), include your price list in the body of your business plan. If you are selling a broad range of products or services you may opt to include your price list here.

Prices are also referred to as unit prices.

Step 79

MUST HAVE
RECOMMENDED
NICE TO HAVE

Businesses with only a few products or services won't need this. Info can be included in the body of the business plan.

Example: Price List

PRODUCT OR SERVICE	RETAIL	LIBRARY	PUBLISHER	BOOKSTORE	DISTRIBUTOR
DISCOUNT		15%	25%	40%	50%
Books	$36.58	$31.09	$27.44	$21.95	$18.29
CDs and Downloads	$29.95	$25.46	$22.46	$17.97	$14.98

Task List

1. Create your price list.
2. Include your price list in this Appendix.

Tip: Consider using a table that includes your competitor prices and provides a clear view of how you are differentiated from your competition.

WORKSHEET: PRICE LIST					
PRODUCT/SERVICE					

Gather and Include Written Price Quotes

Any documentation you gather for this Section will protect you later – for example, it is a healthy thing to get quotes from suppliers in order to keep straight what was said, when it was said and by whom. There's nothing quite as strong as the written word to quash any discrepancies or arguments that might arise later.

Items which require price quotes might include:

- Product or service suppliers
- Proposed equipment purchases
- Property
- Leases

Task List

1. Get written price quotes from as many sources as is appropriate, usually at least three. It is appropriate to have just one quote if there is only one supplier available.

2. Include only the best source in this Appendix, unless you feel strongly that one or more of the others proves a point.

Tip: A written quote is worth a thousand words; a verbal quote is only as strong as the combination of your credibility and the credibility of the person that made the quote.

Tip: Demonstrate wise buying practices by shopping around — if possible, get quotes from at least three different sources.

Tip: Be sure the quotes are dated.

Build Credibility with Written Appraisals and Estimates

O btain independent appraisals or estimates of the value of any large ticket items in your business plan.

Lenders will always view your self-appraisals with a jaundiced eye; it is far more credible to include a written appraisal or estimate from a third party, such as a professional appraiser or some other highly credible firm.

There are a number of situations that might benefit by including an appraisal or estimate, such as:

1. Real estate (the most common example).
2. When seeking a loan to purchase equipment, it will strengthen your case to include a written estimate from someone known for his or her knowledge about the item.
3. When you aspire to use tools and/or equipment which you already owned as owner's equity or security on a sought after loan.

Task List

1. Review your assets, capital purchases and any items you are offering to provide for security.
2. Determine whether the value of any of the items is likely to be challenged by the lenders or potential investors.
3. Determine which individual or organization could provide the most credible appraisal, valuation or assessment.
4. Have the individual or organization do the appraisal, valuation or assessment.
5. Include the appropriate documentation in this Appendix.

MUST HAVE
RECOMMENDED
NICE TO HAVE

Only necessary for certain situations.

Tip: Lenders will always place their own value on items in spite of your efforts, but appraisals and estimates provide a stronger benchmark to work forward from.

Tip: Beware of the negative impact of inflated values. There is a tendency to want to present overoptimistic values for items we own; the danger is that it tends to undermine one's credibility and could cause the reader to question other parts of the business plan.

Tip: Consider providing the reader with two value estimates, one realistic and one fire sale value. Fire sale value is the amount a seller might expect if the goods had to be sold in a hurry.

Provide the Right Amount of Market Survey Information

Step 82

Keep any important market surveys in this Appendix. Rarely will you be asked to include copies of your market surveys in your business plan, but you will want to store them somewhere for future reference.

If you're uncertain whether or not to include copies of actual surveys, ask the person who will receive your business plan. In most cases, a summary of your survey information will be sufficient.

Task List

1. Summarize your market survey information and include it in this Appendix.

Caution: You will not impress anyone by dumping a disorganized pile of paper in this Element. Summaries, tables and graphics are more effective methods for getting your point across.

Tip: Refer your reader to this Element in the appropriate places in the body of your business plan.

Create a Map of Your Market Area

S ometimes a simple map can help the reader locate your business in their mind.

Step 83

Task List

1. Source and include a map of your market area in this Appendix.

Caution: Don't include a map just because there is an Appendix for it — determine for yourself whether or not it will enhance the communication process. Leave it out if it's unnecessary.

Tip: Ensure that the document at least matches the level of professionalism represented in the rest of your business plan — for example, clean up any poor quality photocopies.

Tip: If your map can be portrayed in an uncomplicated way on less than half a page, consider placing it directly into the body of your business plan.

Gather and Include Environmental Information

Step 84

MUST HAVE
RECOMMENDED
NICE TO HAVE

Where relevant.

If you are opening a gas station, for example, you may be scrutinized and regulated by certain government agencies. If your business will impact the environment you may risk attracting negative publicity from environmental groups or concerned neighbors. For example, if you wish to access funding from government sources, you will be required to complete or have an expert complete an Environmental Assessment Impact or similar form. Contracts or loans from government will likely require that you carry out a formal environmental impact assessment or study.

Whatever your business, you must have one eye on the environment and make every effort to protect and/or manage it in the course of your business. In spite of my disdain for government forms and processes, I would hope you would want to do this anyway — it's just good business.

Readers of your business plan will want to know that you have educated yourself on any environmental issues and that you have taken every precaution to manage environmental risks.

Task List

Tip: For lengthy documents, summarize the key points and state that the full document is available upon request.

1. Gather and store pertinent environmental information in this Appendix and refer your reader to it in the relevant parts of the body of your business plan.

Build Credibility with Free Publicity

This Appendix is most relevant for existing businesses. Although it's not always practical, you can sometimes create publicity as you work toward starting your business.

Task List

1. Gather and include published articles or promotional pieces that have been written about you, your business, your products or your services.

Tip: For articles of more than two pages, consider capturing the highlights and quality quotes — state that the full article is available upon request.

Create Dynamic Promotional Materials

Step 86

No matter what type of business you choose, at some point you will need to create promotional materials.

Promotional materials can include brochures, flyers, business cards, posters and various digital outputs. If you have the equipment you might decide to produce your promotional materials yourself; if not, you will need to choose a professional to do it for you. Whether or not you use a professional, you should maintain responsibility for the set up, decision making and quality control. After all, you are the boss.

The following Section is adapted from a workshop developed by Carmen Brown for Macrolink.

First Considerations

When starting down the path of designing your own promotional materials, ask yourself:

- What do you want to achieve?
- Who is the message aimed at?
- What needs to be said?
- How will you convey this message?

Tip: If you've done a thorough job of developing your business plan, you will have created the raw data for building your promotional materials. For example, The Business and the Products and Services Elements will have the raw material needed for a brochure.

Use the AIDA Format for Creating Promotional Materials

The **AIDA** format is helpful in creating your marketing material, whether it is a brochure, a poster or flyer. The four elements of **AIDA** are:

A — Attention (grabber)
How does this flyer capture the consumer's attention?
Example: African Monkey successfully forecasts financials with Macrolink's Biz4Caster™!
Picture of an ecstatic looking monkey using a computer.

I — Interest (highlights features)
What keeps the consumer interested in reading?
Example: CD houses ready-to-use business plan and financial templates
Don't have to think about the technical; let's you focus on your business.

D — Desire (describes benefits)
What's in it for the consumer?
Example: Start your dream business today with confidence!
Saves you valuable time, energy and money!

A — Action (call to do something)
What is the call to action?
Example: Sale ends Tuesday. Call us while supplies last, at 250-612-9161.

Some Budget Considerations

Listed below are a number of factors that affect the cost of promotional materials. You can use several variables from the information below to keep within your budget.

THINGS TO CONSIDER WHEN DEVELOPING PROMOTIONAL MATERIALS		
	LEAST EXPENSIVE	MOST EXPENSIVE
Paper weight	20lb bond white	80lb cover stock colored
Paper color	White	Colored
Paper finish	Linen (checker finish) cheapest Laid (line finish) 2nd cheapest	Smooth (cover stock) most expensive
Paper size	8.5" X 11"	17.5" X 23.5" standard size Die cut/odd shape paper
Ink colors	One color	Four colors
Number of brochures	More = cheaper per copy at a print shop Less = cheaper to print on your home computer	Small number runs - set up fees are the same for large runs or small at print shops
Layout and design	Created by self and supplied in a compatible format to printer	Set up time at print shop
Proofing .	Ensuring text and layout are correct and confirming with printer all the specifics prior to printing	Reprinting entire run after errors are discovered
Photographs	Provide photographs yourself	Hire a professional for top quality photographs

Be careful not to fall into the trap of assuming that your marketing is finished once you produce promotional materials. Your work is actually just beginning at that point.

Pitfalls to Avoid When Creating Promotional Materials

Your promotional material are your face in the marketplace. You will want to avoid these common pitfalls:

- Blurry logos, print or photographs
- Incorrect website address such as .com instead of .net
- Spelling or grammatical errors
- Color doesn't match up to your other marketing materials
- Folding is sloppy or inaccurate
- Cost is much higher than anticipated, mostly due to added setup costs

Be careful not to fall into the trap of assuming that your marketing is finished once you produce promotional materials. Your work is actually just beginning at that point. Professional marketing materials supplement, not replace your marketing efforts. Your strongest marketing technique is getting yourself out into your market and interacting with your customers.

Questions to Ask When Choosing a Print Shop

If you have decided to use a print shop, the following questions will help you to choose the best shop to meet your needs:

1. Can you look at samples of work the printer has produced?
2. What page sizes and volume can they handle?
3. Can they do full color? What method is used?
4. Are they knowledgeable about paper selection?
5. Do they prefer camera-ready artwork, negatives, or electronic files?
6. If you supply the electronic files, what format do the files have to be in?
7. Do they have a graphic designer you can work with on the set up?
8. Do they display cleanliness, good customer service, and knowledge?
9. Are they patient in answering your questions?
10. How long have they been in business?
11. How long will the job take?
12. Will they give you a written estimate? How long is it valid?
13. What are the terms of payment?
14. What are your responsibilities? What are their responsibilities?
15. Who is responsible for mistakes?
16. Will they provide you with samples of paper?

Tips for Choosing a Print Shop

- Get estimates in writing from at least three printers for each job.
- Determine costs for set-up, costs for first printing and costs for additional printing.
- Decide if you need quantity, quality or a combination.
- Choose a printer that you can work with on a long term basis.
- Read the fine print before signing a contract and make sure you understand the lingo.
- Never assume anything – check twice, print once – make sure your product is perfect.

How to Evaluate a Print Shop Job

Check for:

1. Overall quality
2. Even ink coverage
3. Quality of photographs
4. Color quality
5. Fold and trim quality
6. Correct quantity received

Add a Pinch of Product
or Service Literature

When you are selling a product or service provided by a third party or supplier, you should be able to obtain their literature, preferably at no cost.

If you are creating your product or service for sale, you will need to create your own literature.

This Element can be a simple printed document or a more expensive output, such as a glossy color brochure printed by professionals.

Product or service literature is intended to help the reader visualize what you are selling.

Task List

1. Gather or create any product or service literature and put it into this Element.

Step 87

Where detail is
needed for clarity.

Tip: Go easy on the eye candy! Promotional materials can be pretty, but the real meat of your business plan will be of more interest to most readers.

Add a Titch of Technical Information

Step 88

Where detail is needed for clarity.

Technical information is most useful when you have a product or service that is complex or not easily understood by your reader. It is preferable to include detailed information such as this in the Appendices, rather than in the body of your business plan. Some will read it, others won't.

One of the advantages of this type of information is that it can often be gathered from those who supply your products or services. If you are creating your own product or service you will need to create your own technical information.

Although Technical Information is similar to Product or Service Literature, it is likely to be written for technicians and have less of a marketing angle. If technicians are your target customers these two Elements might be the same.

Tip: Don't overdo it! If your technical information outweighs the body of your plan, you're probably getting a tad carried away. Technical information should supplement your plan, not tilt it toward the garbage bin.

Tip: You can use far more detail and jargon in the material in this Element than is possible in the body of your business plan. The body of your plan must communicate to a more general audience, while this Element can talk techie.

Task List

1. Gather or create any technical detail your more pedantic reader is likely to hunger for and put it into this Element.

Explain Any Confusing Terms

E ach business has its jargon. Jargon is typically a language that is used within an industry or business type. One characteristic of jargon is that it may not not be understood by those outside the industry or business, thereby requiring clarification. Only use this Element if absolutely necessary.

Task List

Create a Glossary of Terms for your reader.

1. Reread your business plan.
2. Identify any words that may be confusing to your reader.
3. Make a list of the terms along with explanations or definitions.
4. Place your Glossary of Terms as the last Appendix in your business plan.

Tip: When you discover you have used jargon or a confusing term, search for another way to say the same thing as often there are many ways to communicate thoughts and ideas.

Tip: If your business plan contains very few confusing words or terms, provide your explanations in the body of your plan or as footnotes.

CRAFT YOUR INTRODUCTION AND FINAL PRESENTATION

The purpose of this Section is to create the introductory part of your business plan.

Here are the four Elements in this Section and the corresponding RoadMap™ steps:

BUSINESS PLAN ELEMENT	ROADMAP™ STEPS
Title Page	90
Executive Summary	91
Table of Contents	92
Confidentiality and Copyright	93

If you're using a computer and working with the Biz4Caster™ template, your Title Page, Table of Contents and Confidentiality Statement will already be substantially finished.

Here is a brief snapshot of the Introductory Elements.

BRIEF INTRODUCTION TO THE MARKETING ELEMENTS	
ELEMENT	EXPLANATION
Title Page	The purpose of this Element is to provide a face, or cover, for your business plan. **Key points:** legal name of the company, date, contact name, address, telephone numbers, prepared by:, confidential.
Executive Summary	The purpose of this Element is to provide a short introduction to your business plan, and highlight the important points. It is your "grabber" and usually the first part of the plan to get read by an investor or banker. If this Element is weak or poorly written, it is unlikely the rest of the plan will get read. **Key points:** Identity Statement, Mission Statement, Vision Statement, description of products and/or services, trends and gaps, objectives, competition and advantages, financial requirements, and security.
Table of Contents	The purpose of this Element is to provide direction to the various parts of the plan and to make it easy for the reader to locate the information they are looking for.
Confidentiality and Copyright	The purpose of this Element is to clarify ownership of the business plan, protect the rights of the owner, and prohibit the reader from wrongful use of the plan.

Create Your Title Page

T**he purpose of this Element is to build the cover for your business plan.**

The cover page is one of the finishing touches to your business plan. It should include your company name and logo, it should be identified as a business plan and include the date, your name, mailing address, phone number and email address — similar to the example in the next chapter.

A few things to note about the cover page:

• Your cover page should look professional.

• It is OK to use graphics, but too many tend to detract from a professional appearance.

• Use a font that is clear and easy to read.

• Include your contact information and business name.

• You might consider adding the name of the agency you are submitting the plan to; for example, add "Prepared For" or "Submitted To."

Task List

1. Create your title page, including:
   • the legal name of your business
   • the publishing date of your business plan
   • your name
   • your address
   • your telephone numbers
   • your email and website addresses; and
   • write "Confidential" somewhere on the page.

Step 90

MUST HAVE
RECOMMENDED
NICE TO HAVE

Tip: If you're using The Shell™, the Title Page is already set-up for you.

Write Your Executive Summary

Step 91

MUST HAVE
RECOMMENDED
NICE TO HAVE

*Mini or smaller
business plans
may not need this.*

The purpose of the Executive Summary is to provide the reader with a brief introduction to you, your business, your plan and your request. This Element will highlight the important points contained in the business plan. It is your "grabber" and usually the first part of the plan to be read by an investor or banker. If the Executive Summary is poorly written, the reader may likely not read the remainder of the business plan.

The Executive Summary is usually the first Element your reader will read and it is the last Element you will write. It is mainly comprised of small segments copied or adapted from the main body of your business plan. However, if you wrote your Business Vision in Step 9, and if it was relatively accurate, you may have already completed the bulk of your Executive Summary. If your concept has changed significantly from when you wrote the Business Vision, you may find it easier to use the process in the task list to pull together your Executive Summary.

Example: Executive Summary

Identity Statement

Macrolink Action Plans Inc. (Macrolink) is a privately held corporation headquartered in Prince George and registered in the Province of British Columbia. Founded in 1987, the business has focused mainly on delivery of training throughout northern BC. This business plan is the owner's RoadMap™ to reconfigure the business and implement a new marketing strategy for growth. The owner and principal shareholder is Dan Boudreau.

Mission and Vision

Macrolink provides practical, affordable business planning solutions for do-it-yourself entrepreneurs. The vision is to be the resource of choice for entrepreneurs, ensuring customer satisfaction every time.

Description of Products and Services

Each year millions of people get involved in starting businesses. Most of those who successfully navigate the start-up phase will need a business plan. While it may be realistic for well educated and adequately funded entrepreneurs to create a business, many do not have MBAs or deep pockets. Most are taken aback to learn they must build a business plan and traumatized by the realization that they will likely have to do it themselves. Tragically, many give up in frustration instead of starting their dream business. Macrolink business planning products and services empower the novice, having a viable proposal, to prove his or her business case and create a meaningful business plan. Macrolink offers the following products and services:

1. Books for Business Planners
2. Digital Tools for Business Planners
3. Workshops for Business Planners
4. Facilitator Manuals for Business Plan Counselors and Trainers
5. Consulting and Business Plan Coaching

Trends and Objectives

This business plan is built on the following trends and key points:

- It has become more complex to start and operate a business in the past 20 years.
- The book publishing industry is growing; it has become easier for individuals to participate.
- E-books are the fastest growing area of the book publishing industry, particularly how-to books.
- The fastest growing types of businesses are non-employer service businesses.
- 300 million or 12.5% of the workforce in 40 countries are involved in entrepreneurial activity.
- In Canada and the United States alone, more than 11 million people are trying to start a business at any given time. The writer estimates 20% will invest a minimum of $50 on business planning products, creating a potential market of $110 million for business planning products.

The main objectives of this business plan are to create a marketing strategy to penetrate the market for business planning products and to demonstrate sustainability achieving modest sales targets in a market with huge upside potential.

Competition and Advantages

There are a number of business planning books and digital products already available in the marketplace, ranging from free to very expensive. Macrolink's success rides on the following competitive advantages:

1. The 99-step RoadMap™ makes business planning manageable for ordinary people.
2. The digital products transform business planning into a safe, fun learning adventure.
3. The workshops offer learners a practical, interactive way to explore entrepreneurship.
4. The facilitator manuals and materials offer counselors and trainers a fully integrated, ready to use business planning and training system.
5. The consulting and coaching services are affordable, effective and efficient.

Keys to Success

The keys to Macrolink's success in the marketplace are:

- Successfully penetrating the market by reaching individual entrepreneurs.
- Providing consistently high quality products and services at affordable prices.
- Achieving brand recognition in the minds of the target customers.
- Developing co-marketing alliances with strategic organizations.
- Within three years, attracting a major publisher or distributor.
- Keeping overhead to a minimum.

Qualifications

Dan Boudreau, President and CEO, has been involved, both as a decision maker and an analyst in projects and business proposals ranging as high as $16 million. As a business owner since 1979, Boudreau has a first-hand understanding of the challenges faced by business owners. Since 1990 he has coached thousands of entrepreneurs through the business planning hurdle. For more than 10 years Boudreau has served on the Finance and Lending Committee for Community Futures Development Corporation of Fraser Fort George. This has equipped Boudreau with knowledge and insight into a broad range of small and micro-businesses.

> **Purpose of this Business Plan**
>
> This business plan has been created to:
>
> · Serve as the blueprint for Macrolink Action Plans Inc.
> · Serve as a tool for communicating the Macrolink vision to others.
> · Provide benchmarks for evaluating Macrolink's success in the future.
> · Provide a *real* business plan for trainers and coaches to use as a teaching aid.
>
> This business plan is scheduled for implementation beginning September 2006, with first year sales forecasted at $128,242, a little over 1% of the total potential market.
>
> The owner is not currently seeking any financing.

Task List

1. Either work from the Business Vision you completed in Step 9, or gather the relevant information from the various Elements of your completed business plan to build your Executive Summary.

Here is a list of the key topics and a process for creating your Executive Summary:

Tip: The Executive Summary is the last Element the writer will write and the first Element the reader will read.

PROCESS FOR CREATING YOUR EXECUTIVE SUMMARY	
Identity Statement	Copy your Identity Statement from Step 31.
Mission Statement	Copy your Mission Statement from Step 31.
Vision Statement	Copy your Vision Statement from Step 31.
Brief Description of Products and Services	Copy or rewrite your summary of the products and services from Step 32 or from your business plan Products and Services Element. Keep it short.
Trends and Gap	From your business plan reread The Industry Element, developed in Step 33. From this Element write a summary of the industry trends and the product or service gap your business will serve.
Objectives	From the Strategic Plan and Goals Element, capture the three most important objectives. This Element of your business plan was developed in Step 35.
Customers	From the Profile of the Customers Element copy the summary of your customers. This Element was developed in Step 38.
Competition and Advantages	From the Competition and Differentiation Element, create a brief paragraph that describes your competitors overall and explains clearly why customers will buy from your business. This Element was developed in Step 39.
Qualifications	From the The Owner Element, create one brief paragraph about each owner. Explain why the owner(s) is/are qualified to make this business a success. This Element was developed in Step 34.
Financial Request or Requirements	If applicable, review Section 5 of your business plan and create a paragraph explaining how much and what type of loan or loans you are asking to borrow.
Security	If applicable, describe what you are prepared to offer the lender for security on your loan.

Once you have completed the tasks in the table above, invest the necessary time to craft your Executive Summary to communicate effectively to your reader.

WORKSHEET: EXECUTIVE SUMMARY	
TOPIC	NARRATIVE — NOTES
Identity Statement	
Mission Statement	
Vision Statement	
Brief Description of Products and Services	
Trends and Gap	

Tip: The Executive Summary is a summary of your business plan. For a shorter business plan (10 to 15 pages) it should be no more than one page; for a longer plan (20 pages or more) it should be no more than two pages in length. A business plan less than 10 pages probably won't need an Executive Summary.

Objectives	
Customers	
Competition and Advantages	
Qualifications	
Financial Request or Requirements	
Security	

Develop Your Table of Contents

This Element of the business plan provides an easy way for the reader to quickly locate the various Elements. Set up should be similar to the sample business plan in Chapter 6 of this book and contain accurate headings, sub-headings and page numbers. Word processing programs have automatic table of contents functions that ensure accurate page numbering.

Step 92

MUST HAVE
RECOMMENDED
NICE TO HAVE

Task List

This process is for setting up a table of contents using Microsoft Word:

1. Ensure that all headers within the document are the same formats (example, Header 1, Header 2, etc.).

2. Place your cursor at the place where you want to insert the table of contents.

3. On the Insert menu, point to Reference, and click Index and Tables.

4. Click the Table of Contents tab and choose a design by selecting one in the Formats box.

Tip: If you're using The Shell™, the Table of Contents is already set-up for you.

Write Your Confidentiality and Copyright Statements

Step 93

Here is a sample to use as a format.

Example: Confidentiality Statement

> The reader acknowledges that the information provided by Macrolink Action Plans Inc. in this business plan is confidential, therefore readers agree not to disclose it without the express written permission of the writer. Other than information that is in the public domain any disclosure or use of the information by the reader may cause harm or serious damage to Macrolink Action Plans Inc. Upon request this document is to be returned promptly to Dan Boudreau.

Example: Copyright Statement

> Copyright © Macrolink Action Plans Inc. 2005
>
> All rights reserved.
>
> No part of this document may be reproduced or transmitted in any form or by any means now known or to be invented, electronic or mechanical, including photocopying, recording or other information storage or retrieval system without written permission from Macrolink Action Plans Inc.
>
> Created by: Macrolink Action Plans Inc.
>
> Box 101, Prince George, BC V2L 4R9

Tip: If you're using The Shell™, this Element is already set-up for you.

Task List

1. Create your confidentiality and copyright statements. If they work for you, borrow from my examples above. If you are engaging legal assistance, have them review your legal statements and follow their advice.

Evaluate Your Business Plan

L et's assume you have written a draft of your business plan. You can now evaluate it yourself or have others evaluate it. The following table is an evaluation tool to help you focus on different aspects of the business plan.

Go through and rate each item from 1 to 5 (1 is low and 5 is high). Naturally, the lower numbers may mean you have some work to do.

Step 94

MUST HAVE
RECOMMENDED
NICE TO HAVE

WORSHEET: BUSINESS PLAN EVALUATION					
QUESTION	L 1	2	3	4	H 5
1. Do you have experience relevant to the industry and the business?					
2. Are you clear as to which products or services the business will sell?					
3. Have you confirmed a reliable supply of materials, products and services?					
4. Have you surveyed potential customers to confirm demand?					
5. Have you confirmed the number of customers and the size of the market?					
6. Are you clear as to why a customer would buy the product or service from this business rather than from the competition?					
7. Are there credible pro forma financial projections and do they show enough headroom (gross profit margin) for the business to survive, pay the bills and profit?					
8. Have you communicated a clear understanding of the industry?					
9. Have you created a credible marketing plan to get the goods to the customers?					
10. Have you carried out both primary and secondary market research?					
11. Has the product or service been tested or proven by you or others?					
12. Are all product and service prices realistic and competitive?					
13. Do you have a clear understanding of your competitors?					
14. Have you researched and engaged an accountant, a lawyer, a bookkeeper?					
15. Do you understand the major risks or threats to the business?					
16. Have you identified the number and type of staff required?					
17. Do you have the knowledge and skills to operate the business?					
18. Do the credit checks reveal a positive history for managing finances?					
19. Have you completed a detailed cash flow projection for the first 12 months?					
20. Have you indicated a reasonable rate of growth is projected for year 2 & 3?					
21. In your mind, have you proved the business case?					
22. Does the plan show that you can access enough money to make the business work?					
23. Do the financials show that the business can repay any borrowed monies?					
24. Are you committing enough personal investment to the business?					
25. Is the available security sufficient to attract the amount of funding requested?					
26. Have you stated credible sources for the factual and numerical information?					
27. Do you or your team have enough capacity to implement this business plan?					
28. Would you invest your money in this business?					
29. After reading this business plan, is your confidence in it high or low?					
30. Would you, or someone you know, purchase these products or services?					

Have Your Business Plan Critiqued by Others

Step 95

A lthough this step is parked at the tail end of the RoadMap™, critiquing can begin much earlier in the process. You can do some of your own critiquing, but it is important to have others read and provide feedback.

Task List

1. Develop your business plan to draft stage and have at least one person proof read it and make suggestions.

2. Select three to five willing people to participate in a buzz session.

3. Make copies and distribute them to each person. Ask them to read, make notes and provide feedback.

4. After an appropriate amount of time, meet with each person or the group to debrief.

5. Incorporate all valuable or useful feedback into your business plan.

Tip: If you have been working with a team throughout the business planning process you will have had many opportunities to review and evaluate your business plan.

Revise and Rewrite Your Business Plan

The time you invest in revising your document will make the difference between clear and unclear writing.

Allow a couple of days to distance yourself from your writing to help you look at it more objectively. Read the draft as a reader, rather than as the writer. Be eager to find mistakes and correct them. Give yourself plenty of time to read the document several times. Use the list below as a guide to focus yourself on the kinds of problems that may need work. This entails rereading your entire plan at least ten times! Never try to look for all potential problems in one go-through — this process takes time and concentration.

Step 96

MUST HAVE
RECOMMENDED
NICE TO HAVE

Tip: Each ounce of energy you invest in revision will save your reader a pound of effort in attempting to understand your message!

BUSINESS PLAN REVISIONS CHECKLIST	
ITEM	CHECKED
Write in the third person.	
Lead reader from general to specific.	
Be thorough.	
Maintain accuracy.	
Be consistent with names and terminology.	
Use an active voice.	
Write positively.	
Minimize jargon, abbreviations, acronyms.	
Be concise.	
Avoid clichés, superlatives.	
Choose the right words.	
Eliminate awkwardness.	
Correct all typos and grammatical errors.	
Create a visual format that is easy to read.	
Use appropriate pictures and diagrams.	
Include your sources for key information.	
Include important detail in the Appendices.	
Refer the reader to related information.	
Ensure numerical information matches text statements.	
Build a complete, cohesive communication package.	

Complete Your Application for Financing

Step 97

Only relevant if you're applying for a loan.

A sample Application is provided here for your convenience. However, lending agencies will have their version and I recommend using theirs.

Name of Applicant(s):	
Name of Company: (incorporated companies only)	
Trade Name / Type of Company:	
Mailing Address:	Postal Code:
Street Address:	Postal Code:
Home: Work:	Fax:
Amount Of Loan Requested: $	Over How Many Years:
Funds Needed For:	
# of Existing Jobs: FT PT	# of Expected Jobs: FT PT

Personal Information

Surname:	First:	Middle:
Social Insurance Number:	Birthdate: (D/M/Y)	Home Phone:
Current Address:		Years there:
Previous Address:		Years there:
Current/Last Employer:		Occupation:
Phone:	Years there:	Annual Income: $
Prev. Employer:		Occupation:
Phone:	Years there:	Annual Income: $
Marital Status: ☐ Single ☐ Separated	☐ Married ☐ Divorced	☐ C/L ☐ Widowed	# of Dependants: (excluding spouse)

Spousal Information (if applicable)

Surname:	First:	Middle:
Social Insurance Number:	Birthday (D/M/Y)	Home Phone:
Current Address:		Years there:
Previous Address:		Years there:
Current/Last Employer:		Occupation:
Phone:	Years there:	Annual Income: $
Prev. Employer:		Occupation:
Phone:	Years there:	Annual Income: $

References (customers / previous employers only - NOT family or friends)

Name:	Relationship:
Company:	Phone:
Name:	Relationship:
Company:	Phone:
Name:	Relationship:
Company:	Phone:

Tip: If you're planning to borrow money from an agency, find out if they have a standard or preferred Application for Financing form and use it.

Write Your Cover Letter

Your business plan is complete and ready to go to the reader! It's time to write your cover letter.

If you have not already done so, research the organization(s) you will provide your business plan to and get the accurate names, titles and addresses of the person(s) to whom you will send copies of your business plan.

The purpose of your cover letter is to introduce you and your business plan to the reader. A healthy cover letter should be no more than four paragraphs, including: an introduction to the business plan, an introduction to yourself, a brief confidentiality and directive paragraph and a polite conclusion. It should be approximately half a page; almost no circumstances call for more than one page. Your goal is to have the reader quickly set the cover aside and be mentally ready and eager to read your business plan.

Paragraph One: Introduction to your business plan

- Introduce business plan, name of business
- Brief (one or two sentences) description of the business
- Explain why the reader is receiving the plan (i.e. to consider for a loan or grant)

The purpose of your cover letter is to introduce you and your business plan to the reader

Paragraph Two: Introduction of yourself

- Introduce yourself
- Brief (one or two sentences) about yourself
- Tell how your expertise or background qualifies you for the business

Paragraph Three: Confidentiality and direction

- Explain the purpose of providing the business plan to the reader
- Ask that the reader respect confidentiality. Authorize appropriate sharing of the plan
- If appropriate, request the business plan be returned using self-addressed stamped envelope

Paragraph Four: Conclusion

- If you have deadlines, time restrictions or expectations, briefly state what they are
- Thank your reader and optimistically close the letter

Cover Letter Pitfalls

- Too wordy
- Too vague
- Tone – crisp or cold
- Too much hype
- Too many fonts or graphics
- Typos, misspelled words, poor grammar
- Too clever

Cover Letter Must-do's

- Be professional, business-like
- Be brief
- Include a self-addressed, stamped envelope (if you want it returned)
- Be neat, clean, and no-nonsense
- Proof for typos, spelling and grammar
- Be optimistic
- Sell your strengths

Example: Cover Letter

Mr. Terry Scrooge
Economic Development Officer
Business Development Corporation
PO Box 1743
Opportunity City, BC
V2L 3R9

<date>

Dear Mr. Scrooge:

Attached please find a copy of a business plan for Macrolink Action Plans Inc. The document has been prepared to prove the business case for a home-based micro-business in Prince George, BC. The business will provide practical & affordable business planning solutions for do-it-yourself entrepreneurs. The financial projections cover a three-year period beginning in September 2005.

I have completed the market research and developed this business plan myself. For the past 15 years I have been coaching entrepreneurs to develop their own business plans. Over the past 10 years I have served as a member of the Community Futures Development Corporation Finance and Lending Committee, which provides loans to new and existing businesses in the Prince George area. My background in community economic development and small and micro-business lending qualifies me to create the business plan and positions me to operate the business described herein.

The Macrolink business plan is a confidential document provided as a part of my application to obtain a loan from your organization. I encourage you to share it with any professionals you consider vital to the decision making process. Once you have finished with it, I ask that you please return the business plan to me using the enclosed self-addressed, stamped envelope.

Thank you for taking the time to review my business plan.

I look forward to hearing from you soon.

Sincerely,
Macrolink Action Plans Inc

Dan Boudreau
President and CEO

Task List

1. Determine to whom you will provide your business plan.
2. Obtain accurate name, title, organization and address.
3. Ask how many copies of the plan your reader requires.
4. Write your cover letter; proof it several times.
5. Determine the cost to mail your package and put together a self-addressed, stamped envelope.

Put It All Together

MUST HAVE
RECOMMENDED
NICE TO HAVE

O nce you know the purpose of your plan and the target reader, you are in a position to determine what form it will take.

When it comes to professionalism, don't worry about overdoing it — go the extra mile. In other words, if you're wondering whether or not to include a cover letter, include it. If you're wondering whether to include color pictures or not, include them with the package. If you are unsure whether you should include telephones numbers for your references, put them in. Once you have gone to all the effort to build your business plan, why would you scrimp on the quality of the final package?

It is also advisable to go the distance with communications when submitting your business plan. For example, you might call the recipient to ask when would be a good time to drop off your plan, and then deliver it personally, if possible.

If your business plan is due by a deadline, be sure to get it to the receiver prior to the deadline, then call to confirm it was received. If possible, allow yourself enough time to resubmit if the first copy was not received.

> *When it comes to professionalism, don't worry about overdoing it — go the extra mile.*

Pay attention to detail. Did the bank or institution request more than one copy? In addition to the hard copy(s), did the receiver request a digital copy on disk or via email? What supporting material was requested? If the recipient is a government organization did they request that you include a "Signature Page," a page stating that you are who you are and that you are the one submitting the plan on a certain date?

Follow-up to ensure the recipient received your package. Assure them that you are available to answer questions, clarify any unclear points or retrieve further information. Thank the receiver for the opportunity to present your plan.

Business Plan for You — The First Customer

The business plan you create for yourself will be the longest version. It will include an Executive Summary, all of the narrative and Financial Elements you've created and all of the supporting documents in the relevant Appendices. Create one cohesive, bound document that can be easily replicated. Ideally, weave the entire business plan into one digital file as well. This might entail scanning some of the stray supporting documents in order to insert them into your main business plan file. My preferred process is to use Adobe Acrobat to create a pdf file, which makes it easy to print, email and/or publish at internal or external websites. The idea is to make it easy for the reader to receive, to navigate and to reproduce for committee members.

> *Once you've created your full business plan, you have the raw material to easily create different presentations for a variety of applications.*

Once you've created your full business plan, you have the raw material to easily create different presentations for a variety of applications. For some situations it may be appropriate to use the full business plan while for others it will suffice to use only the Executive Summary or certain Elements of your plan. Although most of your modifications will be in the Cover Letter and the Executive Summary, here are some tips for presenting your business plan to different audiences:

Business Plan for Business Analysts and Other Gatekeepers

Business analysts and other gatekeepers will most likely want a copy of your completed business plan. If you've been effective at distilling vast quantities of market research to succinct narrative Elements in the body of your business plan, it should meet the needs of most gatekeepers. The key to creating an effective presentation for this audience is to ask which Elements they want included. As an analyst, I prefer to receive both a hard copy and a digital copy of the business plan. The digital file enables me to copy and paste to create my presentation to the decision makers.

Business Plan for Your Banker

Bankers are financial people. The presentation you create for your banker might include the Executive Summary, Assumptions, Sales Forecast, Cash Flow Forecast, Projected Income Statement and Pro Forma Balance Sheet. An option is to attach your full business plan as an Appendix to your presentation, that way your banker will have the option of digging deeper where desired.

Business Plan for Your Employees or Customers

The scope of the business plan you present for employees will be in part guided by your philosophy on how much employees should know about the inner workings of your business. To present to employees in the past I have used the narrative portion of the business plan plus the 3-year sales forecast, but excluded the entire Financial Section, Historical Financial Statements and Appendices.

Business Plan for Investors

In developing your presentation for investors, keep in mind what is most important to the reader. Investors will need to know whether you are seeking debt or equity financing and items such as the potential return on their investment, risk and mitigation, security and exit strategies.

Sample Business Plan

Table of Contents

BUSINESS PLAN 2006

CONFIDENTIAL

"When I began to investigate starting my own home-based business, I wanted to maximize my chances of success by doing appropriate research and using effective business planning tools. Having reviewed a fairly wide array of materials, programs and services, I highly recommend the products produced by Macrolink Action Plans Inc. – namely, the Roadmap, the Biz4Caster and the RiskBuster. As I work on my business plan, I am finding that these tools are comprehensive, user-friendly, and very effective at providing me with a complete view of my business planning needs. The practical, step-by-step guide to producing a business plan is very valuable – the best I've seen. I expect to produce an excellent business plan, and my confidence in securing a successful business is greatly increased."
 - **David Leman, Consultant, Internet Mapping and Land Use Planning**

Name	**Dan Boudreau**
Address	**Box 101, Station A,**
	Prince George, BC V2L 4R9
Phone Number	**1-250-612-9161**
Email Address	**danb@macrolink.bc.ca**
Website	**http://www.macrolink.bc.ca**
Date	**September 1, 2006**

EXECUTIVE SUMMARY

Identity Statement

Macrolink Action Plans Inc. (Macrolink) is a privately held corporation headquartered in Prince George and registered in the Province of British Columbia. Founded in 1987, the business has focused mainly on delivery of training throughout northern BC. This business plan is the owner's RoadMap to reconfigure the business and implement a new marketing strategy for growth. The owner and principal shareholder is Dan Boudreau.

Mission and Vision

Macrolink provides practical, affordable business planning solutions for do-it-yourself entrepreneurs. The vision is to be *the resource of choice for entrepreneurs, ensuring customer satisfaction every time.*

Description of Products and Services

Each year millions of people get involved in starting businesses. Most of those who successfully navigate the start-up phase will need a business plan. While it may be realistic for well educated and adequately funded entrepreneurs to create a business, many do not have MBAs or deep pockets. Most are taken aback to learn they must build a business plan and are traumatized by the realization that they will likely have to do it themselves. Tragically, many give up in frustration instead of starting their dream business. Macrolink business planning products and services empower the novice with a viable proposal to prove his or her business case and create a meaningful business plan. Macrolink offers the following products and services:

1. Books for Business Planners
2. Digital Tools for Business Planners
3. Workshops for Business Planners
4. Facilitator Manuals for Business Plan Counsellors and Trainers
5. Consulting and Business Plan Coaching

Trends and Objectives

This business plan is built on the following trends and key points:

- It has become more complex to start and operate a business in the past 20 years.
- The book publishing industry is growing; it has become easier for individuals to participate.
- E-books are the fastest growing area of the book publishing industry, particularly *how-to* books.
- The fastest growing types of businesses are non-employer service businesses.
- 300 million or 12.5% of the workforce in 40 countries are involved in entrepreneurial activity.
- In Canada and the United States more than 11 million people are trying to start a business at any given time. The writer estimates 20% will invest a minimum of $50 on business planning products, creating a potential market of $110 million per year for business planning products.

The main objectives of this business plan are to create a marketing strategy to penetrate the market for business planning products and to demonstrate sustainability achieving modest sales targets in a market with huge upside potential.

Competition and Advantages

There are a number of business planning books and digital products already available in the marketplace, ranging from free to very expensive. Macrolink's success rides on the following competitive advantages:

1. The 99-step RoadMap makes business planning manageable for ordinary people.
2. The digital products transform business planning into a safe and fun learning adventure.
3. The workshops offer learners with a practical, interactive way to explore entrepreneurship.
4. The facilitator manuals and materials offer counsellors and trainers a fully integrated, ready to use business planning and training system.
5. The consulting and coaching services are affordable, effective and efficient.

Keys to Success

The keys to Macrolink's success in the marketplace are:

- Successfully penetrating the market by reaching individual entrepreneurs.
- Providing consistently high quality products and services at affordable prices.
- Achieving brand recognition in the minds of the target customers.
- Developing co-marketing alliances with strategic organizations.
- Within three years, attracting a major publisher or distributor.
- Keeping overhead to a minimum.

Qualifications

Dan Boudreau, President and CEO, has been involved, as a decision maker and an analyst in projects and business proposals ranging as high as $16 million. As a business owner since 1979, Boudreau has a first-hand understanding of the challenges faced by business owners. Since 1990 he has coached thousands of entrepreneurs through the business planning hurdle. For more than 10 years Boudreau has served on the Finance and Lending Committee for Community Futures Development Corporation of Fraser Fort George. This has equipped Boudreau with knowledge and insight into a broad range of small and micro-businesses.

Purpose of this Business Plan

This business plan has been created to:

- Serve as the blueprint for Macrolink Action Plans Inc.
- Serve as a tool for communicating the Macrolink vision to others.
- Provide benchmarks for evaluating Macrolink's success in the future.
- Provide a *real* business plan for trainers and coaches to use as a teaching aid.

This business plan is scheduled for implementation beginning September 2006, with first year sales forecasted at $128,242, a little over 1% of the total potential market.

The owner is not currently seeking any financing.

Table of Contents

2 BUSINESS CONCEPT

2.1   The Business

~ *"Practical & Affordable Business Planning Solutions for Do-It-Yourself Entrepreneurs"* ~

Macrolink Action Plans Inc. is a privately held corporation headquartered in Prince George and registered in the Province of British Columbia. Founded in 1987, the business has focused mainly on the delivery of training throughout Northern BC. This business plan is the owner's blueprint to reconfigure the business and implement a new marketing strategy for growth. The owner and principal shareholder is Dan Boudreau.

The Macrolink vision is to become the resource of choice for entrepreneurs, ensuring customer satisfaction every time.

Customers are entrepreneurs, business counsellors and trainers. This includes clients from many areas of the globe, encompassing all range of start-ups, new firms, economic development organizations and business financing agencies. The primary market will be entrepreneurs from Canada and the US.

Macrolink is a home-based business, with the majority of client interactions taking place either at the customer's location, by telephone or via email and the Internet.

Macrolink's mailing address is Box 101, Prince George, BC V2L 4R9. The phone number is 250-612-9161. The company hosts a website at www.macrolink.bc.ca. Boudreau can be reached via email at danb@macrolink.bc.ca.

2.2   Products and Services

Macrolink offers the following products and services:

PRODUCT OR SERVICE[1]	UNITS[2]
1. Books for Business Planners[3]	Retail, Bookstore, and Distributor Rates
2. Digital Tools for Business Planners[4]	CD and Downloadable from Website
3. Workshops for Business Planners	Day Rate, Half-day Rate, Individual Seat
4. Facilitator Manuals for Counsellors and Trainers	Retail Rate
5. Consulting and Business Plan Coaching	Hourly and Daily Rates

At the core of Macrolink service is an enduring commitment to excellence. The business creates learning programs and business planning tools that customers quickly come to view as indispensable. Macrolink products and services are practical, usable by most people regardless of educational or technical background. Because of this, clients who use Macrolink products and services are able to successfully develop their own business plans.

---

[1] All products and workshops are Copyright © Macrolink Action Plans Inc.
[2] Units are the basic building blocks for pricing (page 13) and forecasting sales (page 17 and Appendix C).
[3] Business Plan or BUST! (soft cover), The Business Planner's RoadMap (soft cover & e-book).
[4] RiskBuster Business Planner & Biz4Caster (CD ROM & Digital Download).

Macrolink products and services offer the following features, benefits and competitive advantages:

PRODUCT / SERVICE	FEATURES	BENEFITS	COMPETITIVE ADVANTAGE
1. Books for Business Planners • Business Plan or BUST![5] • The RoadMap[6] • The Forecaster's Handbook[7]	• Comprehensive • Organized into logical steps • Competitively priced • Created for the novice • Integrated system	• You can trust it • You can manage it • You save time & money • You can do it yourself! • You build a complete understanding of your business	A system that works for entrepreneurs who want or need to develop their own business plans.
2. Digital Tools for Business Planners • Biz4Caster[8] • RiskBuster[9]	• Competitively priced Comprehensive • Simplified input tasks • Web supported • Complex tasks are automated • Integrated system	• You save money • You won't miss critical points • You can do it step by step • You can email for help • You save time & energy • You prove your business case	Transforms your business planning experience into a safe & fun learning adventure.
3. Workshops for Business Planners & Trainers[10] • Half Day • One Day • Two Day	• Interactive, hands-on • Create parts of your plan • Creative learning activities • 99-step business planning process	• You learn while you plan • You build confidence • You feel safe to experiment • You are organized & thorough	A practical, interactive way to explore entrepreneurship.
4. Facilitator Manuals For Counsellors & Trainers[11]	• Comprehensive • Modularized • Easy to use • Ready to deliver • Proven training techniques • Portable • Fully integrated system	• You adapt to learner needs • You provide variety • You save preparation time • You earn money instantly • You deliver with confidence! • You take training to clients • You save development time	A fully integrated, ready to use business planning system for counsellors & trainers.
5. Consulting & Coaching Service • Hourly	• Affordable • Effective • Efficient	• You get results • You save time • You save money	A seasoned entrepreneur in your corner.
Macrolink Action Plans Inc. Holds Copyright For All Of The Products And Materials Listed Above.			

[5] Business Plan or BUST! is a 400 page soft cover book – includes the Business Planner's Primer and the RoadMap.
[6] The RoadMap is a 99-step process for completing market research and a business plan –both soft cover and as an e-book.
[7] The Forecaster's Handbook is a step-by-step process for forecasting financial scenarios.
[8] The Biz4Caster is a digital forecasting tool – produced on CD and also downloadable from website.
[9] RiskBuster is a business planning CD – includes Business Plan Shell, Biz4Caster, Sample Plans, Financial Scenarios.
[10] Inc.ludes business planning and forecasting workshops ranging from three hours to twelve hours in duration, as well as a comprehensive Train-the-Trainer modules from one to five days in length. Read what Macrolink Train-the-Trainer graduates have to say at www.macrolink.bc.ca/trainer/TTTquotes.html.
[11] The Facilitator Manuals enable the user to step easily into the role of business planning coach or trainer – experiential training activities are designed around the RoadMap, which can be used as a learner handout.

2.3 The Industry

Macrolink sells its products and services to entrepreneurs in virtually all sectors and industries, primarily in Canada and the United States. For taxation purposes, the business is classified in the Independent Artists, Writers and Performers Industry. From a practical standpoint, the business is providing its products and services to anyone considering, starting or growing a business.

The Macrolink business case is built on providing practical and affordable business planning solutions to entrepreneurs who need to develop their own business plans. The owner conservatively estimates the potential market in Canada and the United States to be more than $110 million each year.

The outlook for the sale of business books is strong and positive. According to industry authorities, business books are a hot market and tend to pick up sales momentum as time passes. Books about small business are especially hot and have excellent backlist potential.

The Macrolink business case is based on the following industry trends and factors:

1. It is generally getting more complex to start and operate a business, making it more important than ever for entrepreneurs to develop business plans.

2. In British Columbia in 2004, 98% or 337,400 of businesses were small businesses; 83% were micro-businesses with fewer than 5 employees; 54% were single owners with no paid help. In 2004, three quarters of all businesses in British Columbia were in the service sector. [12]

3. "How-to" e-books are the fastest growing area of the book publishing industry. [13]

4. In the United States, 10 million adults are engaged in trying to start new firms at any time. [14]

5. Entrepreneurship involves adults at all ages, except people over 65 years old.

6. Young men aged 25-34 are the most active group involved in starting businesses, followed by women in the same age group. [15]

7. Globally, the market for business planning products is huge. The GEM 2003 study showed that *more than 300 million people of the 2.4 billion labor force in the 40 countries analyzed, are entrepreneurs involved in new business formation.* [16]

The main barriers to selling business planning products and services are standing out from the many similar products and services, gaining brand recognition and getting distribution.

The Opportunity

For most people considering starting a business, the realization that they need a business plan is like hitting a wall. This generates a great deal of frustration and causes many potential business owners to either give up on their business idea or push ahead into business without a business plan. The current situation allows room in the market for *practical and affordable products* that make the task of business planning manageable for entrepreneurs who realize they need to build their own business plans.

---

[12] BC Stats 2004.
[13] 1000 Ways to Market Your Books – John Kremer.
[14] The Entrepreneur Next Door – Ewing Marion Kauffman Foundation (www.kauffman.org).
[15] Global Entrepreneurship Monitor 2003, Ewing Marion Kauffman Foundation (www.kauffman.org).
[16] "Nascent entrepreneurs" are defined as those involved in starting businesses or owning new firms less than 42 months old. Global Entrepreneurship Monitor 2003, Ewing Marion Kauffman Foundation (www.kauffman.org).

2.4 The Owner

Dan Boudreau is the sole owner, President and CEO for the business:

- Involved in small business development since 1980, as owner, coach, trainer and consultant.
- Worked in community economic development for 15 years.
- Served 10 years on Finance and Lending Committee for a $5 million loan fund for entrepreneurs.
- Manages a $15 million fund that provides grants for economic development projects.
- Nominated twice as *Entrepreneur of the Year* – 1997 and 1999.[17]
- Develops and delivers workshops for entrepreneurs (Business Planning, Train the Trainer).[18]
- Published *Dream Catcher Business Planning Toolkit* and *Scratchpad* (since 1995).[19]
- Published *Business on a Shoe String* e-zine – 1999 to 2003.[20]

Boudreau's resumé is in Appendix A and a list of references is in Appendix B.

2.5 Strategic Plan and Goals

Macrolink strategies include:

1. Effective financial management.
2. Effective marketing strategy for positive organizational growth.
3. Continuous research, development and innovation.
4. Advancement of service and product quality.
5. Effective communication with all stakeholders.
6. Team members have the skills, knowledge and systems to serve customers.

The short-term business goals are:

GOAL	TIMELINES
1. To publish the books – hard copy and digital (e-book).	March 2006
2. To secure trademark / intangible property protection on all brands.	May 2006
3. To complete development of the RiskBuster CD and download.	June 2006
4. To create a website with shopping cart and e-commerce capabilities.	August 2006
5. To launch the website, book and digital products.	September 2006
6. To achieve gross revenues of $128,242 for year one.	September 2007
7. To retain net income before taxes of $12,061 for year one.	September 2007
8. To sell a minimum of 1,330 books and 419 CDs.	September 2007

---

[17] Ernst & Young (www.ey.com) recognizes the most successful and innovative entrepreneurial business leaders in more than 30 countries around the globe.
[18] Workshop descriptions can be viewed at www.macrolink.bc.ca/trainer and www.macrolink.bc.ca/training.
[19] Dream Catcher Materials can be viewed at http://www.macrolink.bc.ca/dreamcatcher.
[20] E-zine article archives can be viewed at www.macrolink.bc.ca/e-zines/capacity/index.html.

3   MARKETING

3.1   Market Area

Macrolink will offer its hard copy business planning solutions to clients throughout North America and its digital products to customers who can access the Internet.

3.2   Location: Marketing

From a marketing perspective, Macrolink is located in the city of Prince George in North Central British Columbia. The city has the necessary infrastructure to enable Macrolink to operate globally through the use of its technology. The highway and air transportation infrastructures support travel to and from most of the major cities, making it easy to ship products and attend events.

3.3   Profile of the Customers

Macrolink's primary customers will be entrepreneurs in Canada and the United States. In the 25 to 54 age group, Canada hosts 13,440,355 and the United States 122,718,203, totaling more than 136 million people in the ideal business planning age group.[21] If only 12% of this group were involved in entrepreneurial activity, this would be a potential market of more than 16 million. In a 1999 Yankelovich poll, over one-third of Americans predicted they would own their own business within a decade.[22]

Characteristics of this client group are: shortage of time, scarcity of money, lack of business planning skills, limited understanding of market research, and a desire or need to be involved in entrepreneurial activity. Ideally, customers will own computers and have access to the Internet; however, the books are equally effective using only a pencil and calculator. To entice this customer to purchase, Macrolink will need to provide affordable, upbeat and safe ways for each individual to participate in the business planning process with different options available for them to advance at their own pace.

Macrolink's primary customers will include the one million Canadians and ten million American entrepreneurs striving to start businesses at any given time. Marketing efforts will be focused on the *eleven million North American entrepreneurs* engaged in starting businesses.[23]

The following table shows the various customer groups:

TOP PRIORITY	SECOND PRIORITY	THIRD PRIORITY
1 Million Workforce Age People Starting Businesses in Canada Male and Female	**Economic and Enterprise Development Agencies In Canada and the US**	**18 Million Non-Employer Business Owners in Canada and the US**
10 Million Workforce Age People Starting Businesses in the US Male and Female	**Independent Distributors Bookstores, Colleges and Libraries Chains That Sell Books**	**Workforce Age People Starting Businesses in Countries Other Than Canada and the US**

---

[21] Statistics Canada (www.statcan.ca) and US Census Bureau (www.census.gov).
[22] A poll conducted by Yankelovich Partners in 1999 (www.yankelovich.com).
[23] The Entrepreneur Next Door – Ewing Marion Kauffman Foundation (www.kauffman.org).

3.4 Competition and Differentiation

Entrepreneurs currently address their business planning requirements in a variety of ways, from ignoring the need and starting their enterprise without a business plan to hiring a consultant to create the plan for them. Starting a business without a plan is like trying to fly a jet without first taking the time to learn how to fly. For the typical owner/operator of a small or micro-business, hiring a consultant to develop their business plan makes about as much sense as paying someone else to take flying lessons. In order to understand their business, most entrepreneurs should develop their own business plans.

The following options currently dominate the market: books, digital products, workshops, consulting services and business counselling services.

Books: There are a variety of publications that are available through bookstores and the Internet. Analysis shows prices from a low of $14.95 to a high of $69.95, with the majority of books competing in the $20 to $40 range. Also available are a number of free publications offered by all or most financial institutions and government agencies. In the course of researching to write *Business Plan or BUST!*, Boudreau purchased 24 books and gathered a number of free publications from a variety of sources. The problem with most of the available systems and materials is that they *do not adequately prepare the novice to complete his or her business plan*. Many books offer the reader opportunities to learn *about* various aspects of business planning, but do not show the user *how to navigate* the market research and business planning processes. More importantly, most books present pieces of the puzzle but do not effectively blend the market researching and business planning processes or lead the user from idea to implementation.

Digital Products: There are a number of digital business planning products available, ranging from free to over $500. There are two that currently seem to dominate the market: *Business Plan Pro* and *Bizplan Builder* (both currently selling at approximately $99US.[24]). The writer has purchased and tested nine different software options and found that most do not successfully deal with both the narrative and the financial portions of the business plan. Business planning software products are either beyond the capacity of the novice or are so streamlined they enable the user to fabricate a relatively slick business plan without actually having to learn about their business. In the interest of making it easy for the end user, software options typically neglect the most important benefit of business planning, which is to gain confidence by learning about the business by researching the market.

Workshops: Most communities have local facilitators who provide business planning workshops at prices ranging from $350 to $1,000 per day, however, not many have specialized in business planning. Most often they are either experienced facilitators offering business planning as one of many topics, or consultants with knowledge but limited facilitation skills. During the past 15 years Boudreau has attended business planning workshops by 27 different facilitators, a number of which have never actually developed their own business plan. With the RoadMap as a foundation, Macrolink workshops not only teach the participant *about* business planning, they also equip the user with an organized approach so that he or she knows *how to navigate* the market research and business planning processes.

Consulting Services: It will typically cost between $30 and $100 per hour to have a consultant write a business plan for you. It can cost from $2,000 to $30,000 or more to have a consultant develop a business plan, which is simply not viable for most small or micro-businesses. Macrolink will differentiate from consultants by positioning as a business planning coach for customers who wish to develop their own business plans. Macrolink will not develop business plans *for* customers.

---

[24] *Business Plan Pro* (www.paloalto.com) and *BizPlan Builder* (www.jian.com).

Business Counselling Services: Many economic and enterprise development agencies provide free counselling services for business planners. For example, most of the Community Futures Development Corporations in rural communities across Canada employ Business Analysts and sometimes Self-Employment Benefits (SEB) Coordinators, whose job is to assist entrepreneurs with business planning. Most of these competitors differ from Macrolink's coaching services in that they are usually gatekeepers for either loan funds or the SEB Program. Boudreau's marketing strategy will include inviting and encouraging counsellors to become customers by using the *RiskBuster Business Planning System*, and where possible, distributing the books and digital products to their clients.

The majority of people who need business plans face the following challenges:

1. They are unfamiliar and uncomfortable with business forecasting, planning and writing.
2. They tend to be intimidated by gatekeepers (bankers, advisors, analysts).
3. They are unsure which of the confusing array of business planning formats to use.
4. They do not have access to a clear, effective, step-by-step business planning process.

Macrolink business planning solutions will be differentiated in the following ways:

1. The RoadMap will dovetail the market research and business planning processes, enabling the user to navigate from the business idea to implementation step by step.
2. They will transform the business planning process into a safe, manageable, learning adventure.
3. Books will be positioned in the medium to high price range and in the high quality category.
4. CDs and digital downloads will be positioned in the lower price and high quality category.
5. Macrolink Action Plans Inc. will serve ordinary, down-to-earth entrepreneurs who will develop their own business plans. The service will not include developing business plans for customers.

> *Macrolink Business Planning System empowers the novice with a viable proposal to prove his or her business case and create a meaningful business plan.*

3.5 Sales and Distribution

The main objective of Macrolink's marketing strategy is to get distribution. During the first three years of business, the owner will self-distribute the books and digital products as well as promoting and selling through the shopping cart at the Trafford Publishing website. Trafford will do some marketing of the book via the Internet, as well as publishing the books on demand – this will eliminate the need to publish or stock large inventories of books until orders are in place.

Once the Macrolink website is established the owner will approach bookstores, economic development agencies, associations and organizations in the economic development field. Boudreau will actively promote himself as a speaker and facilitator at strategic conferences.

Macrolink will sell its products and services through the following methods:

- Digital and hard copy products via a website shopping cart at www.macrolink.bc.ca.
- Books sold by Trafford Publishing through its website bookstore at www.trafford.com.
- Facilitator manuals and business planning products sold directly to trainers.
- Facilitators will receive a discount on hard copy and digital learner materials.
- Boudreau will sell products directly to book stores, retailers and distributors.
- Co-op promotion agreements established with software and business development organizations.
- Boudreau will offer affordable three-hour seminars to generate book and CD sales.
- Boudreau will sell books and CDs at trade shows.

Boudreau will be the salesperson for the first three years of the business.

3.6   Servicing and Guarantees

Macrolink offers the following guarantee:

"Your success is our success. We stand behind the quality of our products and services. If for any reason you are not completely satisfied, return all materials to us within 15 days of purchase to receive a full refund. This policy does not apply to digital products downloaded from our website; however, we will replace any defective digital products within 15 days of purchase."

The guarantee will be posted at the Macrolink website and in promotional materials.

3.7   Image

Macrolink is in business to serve entrepreneurs. Its products and services are practical, affordable and professional. To maintain a consistently professional image, all communications, materials and printed products will maintain a professional quality and tone. Customers who purchase products and services from Macrolink will receive excellent value for their investment. As the logo portrays, Macrolink is a responsible corporation that respects the environment and empowers ordinary people through learning. By year four, assuming continued and growing profitability, the business will begin contributing 5% of pre-tax profits to assist micro-entrepreneurs with business plan development and start-up capital. These monies will be vetted through existing not-for-profit enterprise development agencies.

3.8   Advertising and Promotion

As a part of the package price for publishing the book, Trafford will offer the book for sale at its website at www.trafford.com. Trafford's "Best Seller" package also includes notifying Amazon.com, Borders.com, Barnes & Noble, Chapters.Indigo, Baker & Taylor distributors, Bowker's Books-in-Print, BookData UK and PubStock.[25]

In addition to the Trafford marketing, the owner will actively market and promote Macrolink products and services. Each product or service will include ads or coupons for other Macrolink products and services. In this way, the marketing will be fully integrated, creating opportunities for existing customers to purchase other products and services from Macrolink. All materials will advertise the website.

The business will convey a consistent message and build a high profile by:

- Producing quality marketing materials for products and services (business cards, brochures, postcards and posters) that drive traffic to the website.

---

[25] Trafford's Best Seller Package can be viewed at www.trafford.com.

- Providing affordable business planning workshops and seminars.
- Hosting websites at various strategic domains currently held by Macrolink – www.macrolink.bc.ca – www.biz4caster.com – www.riskbuster.com – www.bp99.com.
- Placing advertisements for specific products and services in strategic publications.
- Publishing and delivering a free, opt-in monthly e-zine for entrepreneurs.
- Writing articles on business planning and related topics for e-zines and magazines.
- Maintaining a professional image on all communications, products and documents.
- Hosting display booths at key tradeshows in the target industry sectors.

Word-of-mouth will account for a portion of sales as customers succeed by using Macrolink products and services. The owner will publish success stories at the website and in strategic publications.

3.9 Pricing Strategy and Positioning

Macrolink pricing strategy is to offer clients *practical and affordable business planning solutions.*

Since 2001, the owner has surveyed more than 500 entrepreneurs. Those surveyed include individual male and female adults from 20 to 54 years old, with a demonstrated interest in starting a business. Feedback indicates that 90% of those surveyed will pay between $29 and $99CA for business planning solutions. The list below shows the 12 units and prices used to forecast sales for the first three years of operation for the business.

PRODUCT OR SERVICE UNIT	COST OF GOODS SOLD	CUSTOMER UNIT PRICE
1. Books - Trafford - Retail	$14.63	$36.58
2. Books - Trafford - Bookstores	14.63	21.95
3. Books - Trafford - Distributors	14.63	18.29
4. Books - Owner - Retail	14.19	36.58
5. RiskBuster CD - Retail	5.00	29.50
6. RiskBuster CD - Distributors	5.00	29.50
7. Digital Downloads Retail	5.00	29.50
8. Half-Day Workshops		350.00
9. Full-Day Workshops		495.00
10. Seminars to Individuals		49.00
11. Facilitator Manuals	50.00	99.95
12. Consulting & Coaching		$40.00

Book Discount Rates

- 15% to libraries & college bookstores
- 25% to publishers
- 40% to bookstores
- 50% to distributors

Notes to Pricing

1. All prices are in Canadian dollars.
2. Cost of Goods Sold (COGS) is estimated at the highest rate (retail, one book on demand) for all book sales.
3. COGS are entered at the highest cost of production ($5 per CD), although prices will be less for volume purchases.
4. The COGS for digital downloaded products is estimated at the same as the CD even though the actual cost is lower.
5. Unit 8 and 9 – Sales are projected using the lowest rates for repeat deliveries of workshops. Not included in the projections are the "one-off" or custom workshops and conference engagements, which will be billed at $995 per day.

3.10 Marketing Action Plan

OBJECTIVES AND GOALS	WHOM	BUDGET
1. Build a website at www.macrolink.ca[26]	Owner	
• Create website with shopping cart capabilities	Sys Admin	$5,000
2. Secure legal rights and develop logos for domains and names	Owner	
• Brand biz4caster.com and riskbuster.com	Sys Admin	2,000
3. Publish book	Owner	
• Establish marketing, schedule and organize book launch	Publisher	2,000
4. Develop, schedule and organize business planning seminars[27]		
• Organize seminars for areas demonstrating demand	Owner	1,000
5. Proactively seek publicity		
• Develop press releases, email & fax to selected media	Owner	100
• Write & submit business planning articles to target media		
6. Design integrated materials that drive traffic to the website(s)	Owner	
• Build marketing copy into each product package	Designer	2,500
• Design & publish brochures, posters, business cards		
7. Design and place product ads in strategic publications		
• Identify various target publications, research costs, run tests	Owner	2,000
8. Market owner & author as speaker/facilitator for conferences[28]		
• Develop marketing materials & copy	Owner	4,400
• Actively seek engagements by contacting conference organizers[29]		
9. Post content, free products and functions that draw traffic to the website, including:	Owner	1,000
• A free e-zine for entrepreneurs		
• Archived articles on business planning related topics		
• A searchable glossary of business terms		
• Free downloadable Business Plan Shell		
• Sample business plans		
• Downloadable movie "how-to" clips (e.g. how to do a cash flow)[30]		
Total Marketing Budget		**$20,000**

Notes: All of the costs in the above table are incorporated into the Cash Flow Forecast – see footnotes below for details.

---

[26] Line items #1, 2 and 3 ($9,000) are entered as Fixed Asset Purchases in the Cash Flow Forecast.
[27] Line items #4, 5, 6, 7 and 9 ($6,600) form part of the Advertising budget in the Cash Flow Forecast.
[28] Line item #8 ($4,400) is included in the Travel and Promotion in the Cash Flow Forecast.
[29] Because this revenue source will take time to develop, no sales have been projected in the first three years.
[30] No cost is allocated for these items because they either already exist or will be created by the owner.

4 OPERATIONS

4.1 Description of the Operation

Macrolink is a home-based company licensed in the city of Prince George, British Columbia. The owner outsources the core functions of bookkeeping, technical services and product production. No walk-in traffic is necessary as all products and services are produced and provided off-site.

Products and services will be provided as follows:

- Books will be published on-demand at Trafford's location in Victoria, BC.[31] Boudreau will have the option of purchasing higher volumes at discounted rates. Storage facilities will be rented as-needed to house products.

- CD production will be outsourced. Storage space will be rented as-needed, keeping overhead low.

- Facilitator manuals are anticipated to be much lower volume and will initially be produced by the owner. If demand increases beyond the capacity of the home office, the owner will either outsource the production of the manuals to a local print shop or publish them through Trafford.

- Workshops, seminars and consulting services will either be provided at the customer's location or other suitable facilities, to be rented as needed to provide these services.

The Owner uses a portable notebook computer and is able to work from anywhere with an Internet connection.

4.2 Equipment and Methods

The Macrolink home office is equipped with enough office furniture to meet the business' needs for the first few years of operation. Research and development costs for writing the books and creating the digital products, estimated to be in excess of $40,000, are not included in the opening balance sheet.

4.3 Materials and Supplies

The publisher provides a detailed list of costs for books, based on the number of pages and the quantities purchased. To limit the risk and control overhead, the owner will purchase higher quantities of books only as the demand dictates.

CDs will be created by an established replication service from the Vancouver area.[32]

For all training and trainer resources, supplies and materials will be purchased from local office suppliers. All bulk photocopying is done at highly competitive rates by a local provider near the Macrolink office.

---

[31] Trafford Publishing, Victoria, British Columbia (www.trafford.com).
[32] Sonrise in Richmond, British Columbia (www.sonriseonline.com).

4.4 Risk and Mitigation

The publishing industry is not without its challenges. The two main barriers to a new independent writer entering the industry are the *building of credibility and brand recognition* and the *high cost of penetrating the market*. The owner has identified the following risks and mitigation strategies:

THREAT	MITIGATION STRATEGY
Cash Flow Shortfall	• maintain a high level of consulting work until product sales increase • maintain positive relations with bank
Lack Of Book Sales	• self-publish for a few months to get input from existing clients • adapt as necessary to build the customer base and positive feedback • owner will continue consulting until book and CD sales increase
Government And Other Regulatory Barriers, Trans-Border or Jurisdiction Issues	• ensure that outsourced work goes to businesses that work within the bounds of the pertinent regulatory issues and controls • keep current with similar businesses by maintaining memberships with associations • research local governments and test each new area before launching a full marketing strategy • build relationships with international distributors, associations and corporations
Competitor Retaliation	• the biggest threat might be governments offering free materials to entrepreneurs – will endeavor to convert some of the agencies into customers • market is huge, there is room for all, minimal competitor reaction anticipated

4.5 Professional Services

Accounting, legal and insurance will be outsourced from established businesses.

4.6 Employees and Contractors

The owner will do all the operations work until demand for products and services increase to the point that extra help is required. Staff will be engaged as needed. Initially, the organization will contract with:

- A part-time Systems Administrator
- A part-time Bookkeeper

4.7 Operational Action Plan

The main actions required are:

- Complete and publish the books by March 2006
- Complete development of the digital products by June 2006
- Establish a website with a shopping cart by August 2006

> "Without the Biz4Caster it would have taken me hours and hours longer to complete my financial projections." – **Charlene Cruezot, CJ Accounting**.

5 FINANCIAL

5.1 Sales Forecast[33]

UNITS	PRICES	YEAR 1 UNITS	YEAR 1 SALES	YEAR 2 SALES	YEAR 3 SALES
1. Books - Trafford - Retail	$36.58	385	$14,083	$16,900	$21,970
2. Books - Trafford - Bookstores	21.95	260	5,707	6,848	8,903
3. Books - Trafford - Distributors	18.29	140	2,561	3,073	3,995
4. Books - Owner - Retail	36.59	545	19,942	23,930	31,109
5. RiskBuster CD - Retail	29.50	159	4,691	5,629	7,317
6. RiskBuster CD - Distributors	29.50	180	5,310	6,372	8,284
7. Digital Downloads Retail	29.50	260	7,670	9,204	11,965
8. Half-Day Workshops	350.00	6	2,100	2,310	2,541
9. Full-Day Workshops	495.00	24	11,880	13,068	14,375
10. Seminars to Individuals	49.00	100	4,900	5,880	7,644
11. Facilitator Manuals	99.95	14	1,399	1,679	2,183
12. Consulting / Coaching Hours	40.00	1200	48,000	50,400	55,440
Total Sales			**$128,242**	**$145,293**	**$175,725**
Gross Profit Margin Percentage			82.13%	81.07%	79.66%
COGS Percentage			17.87%	18.93%	20.34%

Although sales have been forecasted conservatively, there is considerable upside potential for the sale of books and digital products. The writer feels it important to demonstrate viability showing minimal revenues even though sales could very likely be higher than projected.

5.2 Explanation of Projections

These financial projections are based on the following assumptions and key points:

1. Year one is from September 1, 2006 to August 31, 2007.

2. E-book sales are expected, but not included in these projections because test marketing in not yet complete.

3. Book and CD projections are based on the assumption that roughly 220 units of each will be sold to Community Futures Development Corporation of Fraser Fort George at distributor rates.

4. Unit nine projections are based on the assumption that all 24 units will be sold to CFDC of FFG.

5. Unit twelve projections are based on the assumption that the current contract with Nechako-Kitamaat Development Fund Society will continue through the forecasted period.

6. Based on #3, #4 and #5 above, a total of $66,040 of the year one revenue is reasonably certain.

7. All unit prices are purposely estimated at conservative rates while the cost of goods sold calculations are on the high side, making the overall projections very conservative and quite attainable.

---

[33] See Appendix C for a detailed 12-month forecast for year one.

5.3 *Cash Flow Forecast*

	September	October	November	December	January
Total Sales Forecast	**$7,699**	**$9,147**	**$11,044**	**$13,080**	**$8,851**
Cash Receipts (Cash In)					
Cash Sales	6,929	8,232	9,939	11,772	7,966
Accounts Receivable		385	842	1,010	1,206
Owner Capital & Non-Cash Equity	20,000				
Loan Proceeds	10,850				
Other Cash Received (Grants)					
Total Cash In	**$37,779**	**$8,617**	**$10,781**	**$12,782**	**$9,172**
Cash Disbursements (Cash out)					
Purchases (Cost of Goods Sold)	1,027	1,533	2,115	3,138	1,285
Advertising	600	600	600	600	600
Auto (Includes Repairs, Insurance)	554	554	554	554	554
Interest & Bank Charges	83	83	83	83	83
Insurance, Licenses, Fees	1,700				
Professional (Accounting, Legal)	125	125	125	125	125
Rent (Equipment)					
Rent (Premises)	200	200	200	200	200
Office Supplies & Expenses	200	200	200	200	200
Business Licenses & Permits				130	
Telephone	150	150	150	150	150
Utilities					
Repairs & Maintenance					
Travel & Promotion		400	400	400	400
Owner Equity & Fixed Asset Purchase	20,000				
Supplies & Small Tools					
Processing, Legal, Broker Fees	850				
Auto (Gas, Oil)	250	250	250	250	250
Security Deposit & Last Month's Rent					
Management Salaries	3,600	3,600	3,600	3,600	3,600
Wages & Subcontractor Fees	600	600	600	600	600
Employer Wage Burden	420	420	420	420	420
Workers' Compensation	13	13	13	13	13
Loan Payments - Principal		418	421	424	427
Loan Payments - Interest		72	70	67	64
Total Cash Out	**$30,373**	**$9,219**	**$9,801**	**$10,954**	**$8,972**
Cash Flow Summary					
Opening Balance		7,406	6,803	7,783	9,611
Add: Cash In	37,779	8,617	10,781	12,782	9,172
Subtract: Cash Out	30,373	9,219	9,801	10,954	8,972
Monthly Cash Inflow (Outflow)	7,406	(603)	980	1,828	201
Less: Taxes Payable Previous Year					
Add: Opening Accounts Receivable					
Add: Ending Accounts Payable					
Less: Opening Accounts Payable					
Closing Cash Balance	**$7,406**	**$6,803**	**$7,783**	**$9,611**	**$9,812**

February	March	April	May	June	July	August	Year 1
$9,247	**$9,600**	**$12,730**	**$11,012**	**$11,012**	**$11,012**	**$13,810**	**$128,242**
8,322	8,640	11,457	9,911	9,911	9,911	12,429	**115,418**
1,097	905	942	1,117	1,187	1,101	1,101	**10,893**
							20,000
							10,850
$9,418	**$9,545**	**$12,400**	**$11,027**	**$11,098**	**$11,012**	**$13,530**	**$157,161**
1,583	1,749	1,845	2,129	2,129	2,129	2,254	**22,917**
600	600	600	600	600	600	600	**7,200**
554	554	554	554	554	554	554	**6,648**
83	83	83	83	83	83	83	**996**
							1,700
125	125	125	125	125	125	125	**1,500**
200	200	200	200	200	200	200	**2,400**
200	200	200	200	200	200	200	**2,400**
							130
150	150	150	150	150	150	150	**1,800**
400	400	400	400	400	400	400	**4,400**
							20,000
							850
250	250	250	250	250	250	250	**3,000**
3,600	3,600	3,600	3,600	3,600	3,600	3,600	**43,200**
600	600	600	600	600	600	600	**7,200**
420	420	420	420	420	420	420	**5,040**
13	13	13	13	13	13	13	**161**
430	433	435	438	441	444	447	**4,759**
61	58	55	52	49	47	44	**639**
$9,269	**$9,435**	**$9,531**	**$9,815**	**$9,815**	**$9,815**	**$9,940**	**$136,940**
9,812	9,961	10,070	12,939	14,151	15,434	16,631	
9,418	9,545	12,400	11,027	11,098	11,012	13,530	**157,161**
9,269	9,435	9,531	9,815	9,815	9,815	9,940	**136,940**
149	109	2,868	1,212	1,283	1,197	3,590	**20,221**
							1,988
$9,961	**$10,070**	**$12,939**	**$14,151**	**$15,434**	**$16,631**	**$20,221**	**$22,209**

5.4 Projected Inc.ome Statement

	YEAR 1	YEAR 2	YEAR 3
Sales Forecast	$128,242	$145,293	$175,725
Minus Cost of Goods Sold	22,917	27,500	35,750
Equals Gross Profit Margin	105,326	117,793	139,975
Subtract Total Operating Expenses[34]	89,264	89,910	89,629
Subtract Depreciation	4,000	4,800	5,600
Equals Net Inc.ome Before Tax[35]	$12,061	$23,083	$44,746

5.5 Break-even Analysis

	YEAR 1	YEAR 2	YEAR 3
Total Sales	$128,242	$145,293	$175,725
Total Cost of Goods Sold	22,917	27,500	35,750
Equals: Gross Profit Margin	105,326	117,793	139,975
Gross Profit Margin Percentage	82.13%	81.07%	79.66%
Total Operating Expenses	89,264	89,910	89,629
Break-even Point	$112,181	$117,410	$125,379

5.6 Start-up Expenses

	TOTALS
Start-up Inventory	$1,500
Advertising	800
Auto (Includes Repairs, Insurance)	554
Interest & Bank Charges	83
Insurance & Licenses & Fees	1,700
Office Supplies & Expenses	200
Business Licenses & Permits	130
Telephone	150
Owner's Non-cash Equity & Purchase Fixed Assets[36]	20,000
Purchase Other Assets	
Processing, Legal, Broker Fees	850
Auto (Gas, Oil)	250
Management Salaries	3,600
Wages & Subcontractor Fees	600
Employer Wage Burden (CPP, IE, Holiday Pay)	420
Workers' Compensation	13
Total Start-up Expenses	**$30,850**

[34] Total Operating Expenses include loan interest (not principle) and a $1,000 allowance for purchase of "Supplies and Small Tools" for each of year 2 and 3.

[35] As a corporation, Macrolink will be taxed at a rate of 17.62% on all pre-tax income.

[36] This figure includes the owner's non-cash (equipment) equity contribution of $10,000 plus purchase of fixed assets in the amount of $10,000. The total of $20,000 is reflected in both the "Cash In" and the "Cash Out" segments of the Cash Flow Forecast.

5.7 Pro Forma Balance Sheet

	START-UP	YEAR 1	YEAR 2	YEAR 3
ASSETS[37]				
CURRENT ASSETS				
Cash & Bank Accounts	$10,850	$22,209	$35,961	$75,336
Accounts Receivable		1,932	2,188	2,647
Inventory				
Prepaid Rent				
TOTAL CURRENT ASSETS	10,850	24,140	38,150	77,983
FIXED AND OTHER ASSETS				
Fixed Assets[38]	20,000	20,000	24,000	28,000
Other Assets				
Accumulated depreciation		(4,000)	(8,800)	(14,400)
TOTAL FIXED & OTHER ASSETS	20,000	16,000	15,200	13,600
TOTAL ASSETS	$30,850	$40,140	$53,350	$91,583
LIABILITIES				
CURRENT LIABILITIES				
Accounts Payable		$1,988	$1,844	$1,885
Corporate Inc.ome Taxes Payable		2,125	4,067	7,884
Current Portion of Long-term Debt		5,604	487	
TOTAL CURRENT LIABILITIES		9,717	6,399	9,770
LONG-TERM DEBT				
Mortgages & Liens Payable	10,850	487		
Shareholder's Loan[39]	20,000	20,000	18,000	16,000
TOTAL LONG-TERM DEBT	30,850	20,487	18,000	16,000
TOTAL LIABILITIES	$30,850	$30,204	$24,399	$25,770
OWNERS' EQUITY				
Retained Earnings		9,936	28,951	65,813
TOTAL EQUITY & LIABILITIES	$30,850	$40,140	$53,350	$91,583

"After working through the Roadmap with the help of the Risk Buster CD I completed my business plan much sooner than I had originally anticipated. There was still a great deal of work to be done but these tools made the work much more focused and easily completed. I have since used my business plan to secure funding and to have a viable plan for my business's future. I would highly recommend any or all of these tools to anyone who is serious about getting into business for him or herself. Thanks Dan."
  - Brad J. Grantham, B.Sc., Practical Tactical & Martial Arts Supply, Prince George, BC

---

[37] Research and development costs for writing the books and creating the digital products, estimated to be in excess of $40,000, are not included in the opening balance.
[38] The $20,000 in the start-up balance sheet includes $10,000 owner's equipment contribution plus $10,000 in fixed assets purchased at start-up.
[39] This figure includes $10,000 owner's cash contribution and $10,000 owner's equipment contribution.

6 Appendices

6.1 *Appendix A: Resume for Dan Boudreau*

Business Telephone: (250) 612-9161   Residence Telephone: (250) 555-9161

<u>**CAREER HISTORY**</u>

<u>Key Strengths</u>	**Tenacious Project Builder**	**Proficient at Due Diligence**
	Skillful Use of Computer & Technology	**Effective Proposal Developer**
	Positive, Dynamic Facilitator	**Competent Business Planner**

<u>07 2004 to Present</u>   **NECHAKO-KITAMAAT DEVELOPMENT FUND SOCIETY**
NKDF Investment Area (Vanderhoof to Kitamaat Village)
Manager

Activities:
- providing secretariat services for the society
- overseeing all of the society's operations
- review & due diligence on all proposals and business plans
- management of approximately 30 ongoing projects in rural communities, from Vanderhoof to Kitamaat Village
- bookkeeping, accounting, investment tracking & financial reporting
- budget management, business planning & annual reporting
- communications leading up to & resulting from board meetings
- management of website

<u>07 2003 to 06 2004</u>   **COMMUNITY FUTURES DEVELOPMENT CORPORATION**
Fraser Fort George Region & Stuart Nechako Region
Community Outreach Officer, SICEAI
Softwood Industry Community Economic Adjustment Initiative

Activities:
- reviewed and performed due diligence on proposals & business plans
- interaction & communications with SICEAI personnel & applicants
- community networking to identify SICEAI clients
- communication & information dissemination for applicants
- consultation with First Nations & Metis groups
- administration & file management

<u>03 1987 to Present</u>   **MACROLINK ACTION PLANS INC.,** Prince George, BC
President & CEO

Activities:
- business planning coach
- deliver business planning, marketing, *Train the Trainer* workshops
- assist clients with business plan & proposal development
- supervised up to nine training coordinators, 50 trainers & 22 staff
- managed & co-ordinated government projects to $350,000
- proficient in use of MS Word, Excel, PowerPoint, ACCPAK Simply Accounting, Internet

Daniel Boudreau (Continued)   Page 2

<u>12 1991 to 10 1996</u>   **P G NATIVE FRIENDSHIP CENTRE,** Prince George, BC
                             Small Business Advisor & Coordinator, *Native Entrepreneurial Training*

Activities:
- designed, developed, & delivered *Native Entrepreneurial Training*
- business counselling & advisory services
- information dissemination for entrepreneurs
- coordinated various speakers, trainers & activities
- assisted clients with business planning, budgeting & proposal development
- increased the profile of Aboriginal businesses in the Prince George area
- developed & coordinated the *Prince George Area Aboriginal Lending Circles*
- managed program budgeting & forecasting
- recruited & selected personnel & program participants
- delivered workshops on a variety of business related topics
- advertised & marketed the program & the business advisory services

<u>04 1979 to 01 1988</u>   **SUNDANCE REFORESTATION LTD.,** Prince George, BC
                             President/Owner

Activities:
- founded & grew the business to $1,600,000 revenue within three years
- trained field personnel, supervisors & project managers
- managed up to 150 forestry field workers, up to 25 project & crew supervisors, & up to five clerical & office staff

EDUCATION & TRAINING

1996	Human Resource Management For Non-Profit Organizations (SFU)
1995	Native Adult Instructor Diploma (NAID) Program
1994	Financial Management For Non-Profit Organizations (SFU)
1994	How Adults Learn II - Curriculum Development (John Baker)
1990	The Excellence Series (Context Associated)
1978	Completed Carpentry Apprenticeship - Inter-Provincial Journeyman Ticket
	Class 4, British Columbia Driver's Licence

INTERESTS

- Volunteered more than ten years on the Finance & Lending Committee for Community Future Development Corporation of Fraser Ft George
- Past Member & Executive for Toastmaster's Clubs
- Developed *Dream Catcher Business Planning System* & Biz4Caster
- Kayaking, Writing, Snowboarding, Travelling, Music

6.2 Appendix B: References

Mr. Mike Robertson, Chair[40] Nechako-Kitamaat Development Fund Society[41] Box 909, Burns Lake, BC V0J 1E0	Work 250.694.3334 Home 250.694.3603 cheslattanation@yahoo.com
Mr. Don Zurowski, General Manager[42] Community Futures Development Corporation of Fraser Fort George 1566 Seventh Avenue, Prince George, BC, V2L 3P4	Work 250.562.9622 Cell 250.613.5622 donz@cfdc.bc.ca
Mr. Keith Federink, General Manager[43] Community Futures Development Corporation of Stuart Nechako 2750 Burrard Avenue, Vanderhoof, BC V0J 3A0	Work 250.567.5219 Home 250.567.5023 cfdcsn@telus.net
Ms. Laurie Gowans, Senior Advisor, Aboriginal Directorate[44] Ministry of Community, Aboriginal and Women's Services 3rd Floor, 800 Johnson Street, Victoria, BC V8W 9R1 (Formerly with Ministry of Small Business (YouBET!))	Work 250.387.2179 Cell 250.418.1252
Mr. Norman Dale, Project Manager, Wood-bee Business Planning Team[45] Northern John Howard Society 1150 4th Avenue, Prince George, BC V2L 3J3	Work 250.561.0510 Cell 250.613.5280 n.dale@shaw.ca

"All team members came to this project with very limited experience with the ideas and vocabulary of business planning. The RoadMap is quite simply the most well-written, clear nearly fool-proof guide that we have seen for the novice business planner. By breaking the tasks down into so many small steps and providing good summaries of how these are to be done, Mr. Boudreau has made the whole process less intimidating and yet comprehensive. Many other books and publicly available resources we have looked at seemed either too simplistic or hard to understand. It's obviously quite a feat to accomplish both full coverage and transparency.

Once we began to generate data we came to rely on the Biz4Caster as a way to organize and understand our potential and limitations. Again, the model appears to cover all the possible combinations of factors and really draws one's attention to the most critical data gaps and substantive weaknesses in one's concept. We used Biz4Caster to generate a first cut overview of cash flow and then built on the results, drilling down on the factors to which our future success seemed to most depend. This actually forced us to rethink some of our planned product lines and cost items leading to an outcome that we believe will be sustainable."
– **Norman Dale, Project Manager, Wood-bee Business Planning Team.**

---

[40] Boudreau is currently serving as contract manager for NKDFS, 1200 hrs per year.
[41] Nechako-Kitamaat Development Fund Society provides grants for economic development projects in the communities from Vanderhoof to Kitamaat Village (www.nkdf.org).
[42] Boudreau serves CFDC of Fraser Fort George in two ways – as contract business planning trainer and as a volunteer member of the Finance and Lending Committee.
[43] Boudreau served CFDC of Stuart Nechako during 2004 as a contract Outreach Officer for the Softwood Industry Community Economic Adjustment Initiative.
[44] Boudreau provided business planning workshops in the northern half of the Province for the Youth Entrepreneurship Business & Entrepreneurial Training (YouBET! 1997 – 2001).
[45] Norman Dale and the Wood-bee Business Planning Team used Macrolink products during the latter half of 2005 to research and develop a business plan for a small wood manufacturing business.

6.3 Appendix C: Year 1 – 12-Month Sales Forecast

Units	Price	Sept	Oct	Nov	Dec	Jan	Feb	Mar	April	May	June	July	Aug	Year 1
1. Books - Trafford	$36.58	20 $732	25 $915	50 $1,829	50 $1,829	30 $1,097	30 $1,097	30 $1,097	30 $1,097	30 $1,097	30 $1,097	30 $1,097	30 $1,097	385 $14,083
2. Books - Bookstores	$21.95	$0	20 $439	30 $659	50 $1,098	20 $439	20 $439	20 $439	20 $439	20 $439	20 $439	20 $439	20 $439	260 $5,707
3. Books - Distributors	$18.29	$0	$0	$0	$0	$0	20 $366	20 $366	20 $366	20 $366	20 $366	20 $366	20 $366	140 $2,561
4. Books - Owner	$36.59	50 $1,830	50 $1,830	50 $1,830	100 $3,659	20 $732	20 $732	25 $915	30 $1,098	50 $1,830	50 $1,830	50 $1,830	50 $1,830	545 $19,942
5. CD's - Retail	$29.50	$0	5 $148	7 $207	8 $236	9 $266	10 $295	15 $443	20 $590	20 $590	20 $590	20 $590	25 $738	159 $4,691
6. CD's - Distributors	$29.50	$0	18 $531	20 $590	18 $531	20 $590	20 $590	14 $413	14 $413	14 $413	14 $413	14 $413	14 $413	180 $5,310
7. Downloads - Retail	$29.50	5 $148	10 $295	20 $590	25 $738	25 $738	25 $738	25 $738	25 $738	25 $738	25 $738	25 $738	25 $738	260 $7,670
8. Workshop - 1/2 Day	$350	$0	$0	1 $350	$0	$0	$0	$0	1 $350	1 $350	1 $350	1 $350	1 $350	6 $2,100
9. Workshop - 1 Day	$495	2 $990	2 $990	2 $990	2 $990	2 $990	2 $990	2 $990	2 $990	2 $990	2 $990	2 $990	2 $990	24 $11,880
10. Seminar - Seats	$49	$0					$0	$0	50 $2,450	$0	$0	$0	50 $2,450	100 $4,900
11. Facilitator - Manuals	$99.95	$0	$0	$0	$0	$0	2 $200	2 $200	2 $200	2 $200	2 $200	2 $200	4 $400	14 $1,399
12. Consulting	$40	100 $4,000	100 $4,000	100 $4,000	100 $4,000	100 $4,000	100 $4,000	100 $4,000	100 $4,000	100 $4,000	100 $4,000	100 $4,000	100 $4,000	1,200 $48,000
Total Sales		$7,699	$9,147	$11,044	$13,080	$8,851	$9,247	$9,600	$12,730	$11,012	$11,012	$11,012	$13,810	$128,242

MACROLINK ACTION PLANS INC. 25

Chapter 7

The Fast Track Business Plan

Table of Contents

When to Fast Track Your Business Plan

Most people wish business planning was easier. Some situations demand and warrant a faster planning process. For example, if you're already in business and successful, it's inlikely you will need to prove your business case from the bottom up. If the model is successful and the business is meeting your financial goals, your proof is as simple as providing a list of customers and financial statements.

The Fast Track Business Plan may be suitable for you if:

- Your existing business is successful and you need to borrow money or communicate with potential investors.

- You are getting into a business you fully understand and don't need to borrow money.

- You are starting a business using only your own money and have no concerns about the risk.

- You are updating an existing business plan.

- You are selling an existing successful business.

One caution — if you have bypassed the RoadMap™ and find the fast track isn't working, you may have to go back and do all or some of the RoadMap™ steps. If the Fast Track doesn't meet your goals, roll up your sleeves, go back to the RoadMap™, and do the foundation work required to ensure your business plan meets your needs.

The following is an example Fast Track Business Plan for Macrolink Action Plans Inc. for your reference. There is no new information in the Fast Track Business Plan; it all comes from the complete version of the business plan. If the attachments were included this business plan would be 10 to 12 pages.

Macrolink Action Plans Inc.

Description of the Business

~ *"Practical & Affordable Business Planning Solutions for Do-It-Yourself Entrepreneurs"*

Macrolink Action Plans Inc. is a privately held corporation headquartered in Prince George and registered in the Province of British Columbia. Founded in 1987, the business has focused mainly on the delivery of training throughout Northern BC. This business plan is the owner's blueprint to reconfigure the business and implement a new marketing strategy for growth. The owner and principal shareholder is Dan Boudreau.

The Macrolink vision is to become the resource of choice for entrepreneurs, ensuring customer satisfaction every time.

Customers are entrepreneurs, business counsellors and trainers. This includes clients from many areas of the globe, encompassing all range of start-ups, new firms, economic development organizations and business financing agencies. The primary market will be entrepreneurs from Canada and the US.

Macrolink is a home-based business, with the majority of client interactions taking place either at the customer's location, by telephone or via email and the Internet.

Macrolink's mailing address is Box 101, Prince George, BC V2L 4R9. The phone number is 250-612-9161. The company hosts a website at www.macrolink.bc.ca. Boudreau can be reached via email at danb@macrolink.bc.ca.

Products and Services

Each year millions of people get involved in starting businesses. Most of those who successfully navigate the start-up phase will need a business plan. While it may be realistic for well educated and adequately funded entrepreneurs to create a business, many do not have MBAs or deep pockets. Most are taken aback to learn they must build a business plan and traumatized by the realization that they will likely have to do it themselves. Tragically, many give up in frustration instead of starting their dream business. Macrolink business planning products and services empower the novice with a viable proposal to prove his or her business case and create a meaningful business plan. Macrolink offers the following products and services:

1. Books for Business Planners
2. Digital Tools for Business Planners
3. Workshops for Business Planners
4. Facilitator Manuals for Business Plan Counsellors and Trainers
5. Consulting and Business Plan Coaching

Macrolink holds copyright on all of the above products.

Trends and Opportunities

The Macrolink business case is built on providing practical and affordable business planning solutions to entrepreneurs who need to develop their own business plans. The owner conservatively estimates the potential market in Canada and the United States to be more than $110 million.

The outlook for the sale of business books is strong and positive. According to industry authorities, business books are a hot market and tend to pick up sales momentum as time passes. Books about small business are especially hot and have excellent backlist potential.

The Macrolink business case is based on the following industry trends and factors:

1. It is generally getting more complex to start and operate a business, making it more important than ever for entrepreneurs to develop business plans.
2. In British Columbia in 2004, 98% or 337,400 of businesses were small businesses; 83% were micro businesses with fewer than 5 employees; 54% were single owners with no paid help. In 2004, three quarters of all businesses in British Columbia were in the service sector.
3. "How-to" e-books are the fastest growing area of the book publishing industry.
4. In the United States, 10 million adults are engaged in trying to start new firms at any time.
5. Entrepreneurship involves adults at all ages, except people over 65 years old.
6. Young men aged 25-34 are the most active group involved in starting businesses, followed by women in the same age group.
7. Globally, the market for business planning products is huge. The Global Entrepreneurship Monitor 2003 study showed that *more than 300 million people of the 2.4 billion labor force in the 40 countries analyzed, are entrepreneurs involved in new business formation.*

The main barriers to selling business planning products and services are: standing out from the many similar products and services; gaining brand recognition, and; getting distribution.

For most people considering starting a business, the realization that they need a business plan is like hitting a wall. This generates a great deal of frustration and causes many potential business owners to either give up on their business idea or push ahead into business without a business plan. The current situation allows room in the market for *practical and affordable products* that make the task of business planning manageable for entrepreneurs who realize they need to build their own business plans. This is the niche served by Macrolink.

Business Goals

GOAL	TIMELINES
1. To publish the books – hard copy and digital (e-book).	March 2006
2. To secure trademark / intangible property protection on all brands.	May 2006
3. To complete development of the RiskBuster CD and download.	June 2006
4. To create a website with shopping cart and e-commerce capabilities.	August 2006
5. To launch the website, book and digital products.	September 2006
6. To achieve year 1 gross revenues of $128,242 and net income of $12,061	September 2007
7. To sell a minimum of 1,330 books and 419 CDs.	September 2007

Profile of the Customers

Macrolink's primary customers are entrepreneurs in Canada and the United States. In the 25 to 54 age group, Canada hosts 13,440,355 and the United States 122,718,203, totaling more than 136 million people in the ideal business planning age group. If only 12% of this group were involved in entrepreneurial activity, this would be a potential market of more than 16 million. In a 1999 Yankelovich poll, over 30% of Americans predicted they would own their own business within a decade.

Characteristics of this client group are: shortage of time, scarcity of money, lack of business planning skills, limited understanding of market research, and a desire or need to be involved in entrepreneurial activity. Ideally, customers will own computers and have access to the Internet, however, the books are equally effective using only a pencil and calculator. To entice this customer to purchase, Macrolink provides affordable, upbeat and safe ways for each individual to participate in the business planning process with different options available for them to advance at their own pace.

Macrolink's primary customers include the one million Canadians and ten million American entrepreneurs striving to start businesses at any given time. Marketing efforts are focused on the *eleven million North American entrepreneurs* engaged in starting businesses.

The following table shows the various customer groups:

TOP PRIORITY	SECOND PRIORITY	THIRD PRIORITY
1 Million Workforce Age People Starting Businesses in Canada Male and Female	**Economic and Enterprise Development Agencies In Canada and the US**	**18 Million Non-Employer Business Owners in Canada and the US**
10 Million Workforce Age People Starting Businesses in the US Male and Female	**Independent Distributors Bookstores, Colleges and Libraries Chains That Sell Books**	**Workforce Age People Starting Businesses in Countries Other Than Canada and the US**

Competition and Differentiation

Entrepreneurs currently address their business planning requirements in a variety of ways, from ignoring the need and starting their enterprise without a business plan to hiring a consultant to create the plan for them. Starting a business without a plan is like trying to fly a jet without first taking the time to learn how to fly. For the typical owner/operator of a small or micro-business, hiring a consultant to develop their business plan makes about as much sense as paying someone else to take flying lessons. In order to understand their business, *most entrepreneurs should develop their own business plans.*

The following options currently dominate the market: books, digital products, workshops, consulting services and business counselling services.

Books: There are a variety of publications available through bookstores and the Internet. Analysis shows prices from a low of $14.95 to a high of $69.95, with the majority of books competing in the $20 to $40 range. Also available are a number of free publications offered by all or most financial institutions and government agencies. In the course of researching to write the *Business Plan or BUST!*, Boudreau purchased 24 books and gathered a number of free publications from a variety of sources. The problem with most of the available systems and materials is that they *do not adequately prepare the novice to complete his or her business plan*. Many books offer the reader opportunities to learn *about* various aspects of business planning, but do not show the user *how to navigate* the market research and business planning processes. More importantly, most books present pieces of the puzzle but do not effectively blend the market researching and business planning processes or lead the user from idea to implementation.

Digital Products: There are a number of digital business planning products available, ranging from free to over $500. There are two that currently seem to dominate the market, *Business Plan Pro* and *Bizplan Builder*, both currently selling at approximately $115 ($99US). The writer has purchased and tested nine different software options and found that most do not successfully deal with both the narrative and the financial portions of the business plan. Business planning software products are either beyond the capacity of the novice or are so streamlined they enable the user to fabricate a relatively slick business plan without actually having to learn about their business. In the interest of making it easy for the end user, software options typically neglect the most important benefit of business planning, which is to gain confidence through learning about the business by researching the market.

Workshops: Most communities have local facilitators who provide business planning workshops at prices ranging from $350 to $1,000 per day, however, not many have specialized in business planning. Most often they are either experienced facilitators offering business planning as one of many topics, or consultants with knowledge but limited facilitation skills. During the past 15 years Boudreau has attended business planning workshops by 27 different facilitators, a number of which have never actually developed their own business plan. With the RoadMap as a foundation, Macrolink workshops not only teach the participant about business planning, they also equip the user with an organized approach so that he or she knows *how to navigate* the market research and business planning processes.

Consulting Services: It typically costs between $30 and $100 per hour to have a consultant write a business plan for you. It can cost from $2,000 to $30,000 or more to have a consultant develop a business plan, which is simply not viable for most small or micro-businesses. Macrolink differentiates from consultants by positioning as a business planning coach for customers who wish to develop their own business plans. Macrolink does not develop business plans *for* customers.

Business Counselling Services: Many economic and enterprise development agencies provide free counselling services for business planners. For example, most of the Community Futures Development Corporations in rural communities across Canada employ Business Analysts and sometimes Self-Employment Benefits (SEB) Coordinators, whose job is to assist entrepreneurs with business planning. Most of these competitors differ from Macrolink's coaching services in that they are usually gatekeepers for either loan funds or the SEB Program. Boudreau's marketing strategy includes inviting and encouraging counsellors to become customers by using the *RiskBuster Business Planning System*, and where possible, distributing the books and digital products to their clients.

The majority of people who need business plans face the following challenges:

1. They are unfamiliar and uncomfortable with business forecasting, planning and writing.
2. They tend to be intimidated by gatekeepers (bankers, advisors, analysts).
3. They are unsure which of the confusing array of business planning formats to use.
4. They do not have access to a clear, effective, step-by-step business planning process.

Macrolink business planning solutions are differentiated in the following ways:

1. The RoadMap dovetails the market research and business planning processes, enabling the user to navigate from the business idea to implementation step by step.
2. Products and services transform the business planning process into a safe and manageable learning adventure.
3. Books are positioned in the medium to high price range and in the high quality category.
4. CDs and digital downloads are positioned in the lower price and high quality category.
5. Macrolink Action Plans.serves ordinary, down-to-earth entrepreneurs who develop their own business plans. The services do not include developing business plans for customers.

> *Macrolink Business Planning System*
> *empowers the novice with a viable proposal*
> *to prove his or her business case*
> *and create a meaningful business plan.*

Keys to Success

The keys to Macrolink's success in the marketplace are:

- Successfully penetrating the market by reaching individual entrepreneurs.
- Providing consistently high quality products and services at affordable prices.
- Achieving brand recognition in the minds of target customers.
- Developing co-marketing alliances with strategic organizations.
- Within three years, attracting a major publisher or distributor.
- Keeping overhead to a minimum.

Pricing Strategy and Positioning

Macrolink pricing strategy is to offer clients *practical and affordable business planning solutions.*

Since 2001, the owner has surveyed more than 500 entrepreneurs. Those surveyed include individual male and female adults from 20 to 54 years old with a demonstrated interest in starting a business. Feedback indicates that 90% of those surveyed will pay between $29 and $99CA for business planning solutions. The list below shows the 12 units and prices used to forecast sales for the first three years of operation for the business.

PRODUCT OR SERVICE UNIT	COST OF GOODS SOLD	CUSTOMER UNIT PRICE
1. Books - Trafford - Retail	$14.63	$36.58
2. Books - Trafford - Bookstores	14.63	21.95
3. Books - Trafford - Distributors	14.63	18.29
4. Books - Owner - Retail	14.19	36.58
5. RiskBuster CD - Retail	5.00	29.50
6. RiskBuster CD - Distributors	5.00	29.50
7. Digital Downloads Retail	5.00	29.50
8. Half-Day Workshops		350.00
9. Full-Day Workshops		495.00
10. Seminars to Individuals		49.00
11. Facilitator Manuals	50.00	99.95
12. Consulting and Coaching		$40.00

Book Discount Rates

- 15% to libraries & college bookstores
- 25% to publishers
- 40% to bookstores
- 50% to distributors

Qualifications

Dan Boudreau is the sole owner, President and CEO for the business:

- Involved in small business development since 1980 as owner, coach, trainer and consultant.
- Worked in community economic development for 15 years.
- Served 10 years on Finance and Lending Committee for a $5 million loan fund for entrepreneurs.
- Manages a $15 million fund that provides grants for economic development projects.
- Nominated twice as *Entrepreneur of the Year* – 1997 and 1999.
- Develops and delivers workshops for entrepreneurs (Business Planning, Train the Trainer).
- Published *Dream Catcher Business Planning Toolkit* and *Scratchpad* (since 1995).
- Published *Business on a Shoe String* e-zine – 1999 to 2003.

Boudreau's resumé will be provided upon request.

Purpose of this Business Plan

This business plan has been created to:

- Serve as the blueprint for Macrolink Action Plans Inc.
- Serve as a tool for communicating the Macrolink vision to others.
- Provide benchmarks for evaluating Macrolink's success in the future.
- Provide a *real* business plan for trainers and coaches to use as a teaching aid.

This business plan is scheduled for implementation beginning September 2006, with first year sales forecasted at $128,242, a little over 1% of the total potential market.

The owner is not currently seeking any financing.

Appendices

3-Year Sales Forecast
3-Year Cash Flow Forecast
3-Year Income Statement
3-Year Pro Forma Balance Sheet
List of Key Customers
3-Year Historical Financial Statements
Personal Financial Statement

Creating Your Fast Track Business Plan

The Fast Track Business Plan is a solution that should not take more than a couple of evenings. Depending how well you know your business, it may actually take much less time.

If you have already worked through the RoadMap™, this exercise can be achieved by copying and pasting from various Elements of your business plan. Alternatively, providing answers to the following questions will result in a 6 to 12 page plan.

Holes-lead-to-goals; have a piece of paper handy to write a list of "things to research" for any information you are missing.

Description of the Business (One half page)

Reference: RoadMap™ Step 31

1. Describe your business.
2. What is the name of your company?
3. What is the legal form or structure of your business?
4. Where is the business headquartered, licensed, registered?
5. When did or when will your business start?
6. What is the nature of your business (home-based, retail, services or products)?
7. What is the scope of your business (local, regional, national, international or global)?
8. Who are your customers?
9. What industry is your business in?
10. What is your competitive advantage?
11. What is your business vision?

Products and Services (One to two paragraphs)

Reference: RoadMap™ Step 32

1. List your products and services.
2. What proprietary features (patents or trademarks) do you hold for your products and services?
3. What are some innovative characteristics of your products and services?
4. What are the benefits and features of your products and services?

Trends and Opportunities (One to four paragraphs)

Reference: RoadMap™ Step 33

1. Describe your industry trends and the opportunities your business takes advantage of.
2. What size is your industry in terms of quantity and value of goods sold?
3. Is your industry static, shrinking or growing?
4. What are the main challenges currently faced by your industry?
5. What are the most prominent new developments in your industry?
6. What are the major trends affecting your industry?
7. What gap or niche does your business serve?

Business Goals (Maximum seven main points)

Reference: RoadMap™ Step 35

1. List your most important short-term business goals.
2. What are your sales projections for year one, two and three of your plan?
3. How many workers will you employ in year one, two and three of your plan?
4. What major achievements will you accomplish in year one?

Tip: The Fast Track Business Plan may be suitable for seasoned owners of existing businesses, but start-ups should go through the RoadMap™ first and then scale down a shorter business plan. This is because the main benefit of doing the business plan is to learn your business and build confidence.

Profile of the Customers (One-half to one page)

Reference: RoadMap™ Step 38

1. Describe your customers.
2. What are your customers' age, gender, and family status?
3. What best describes the area where your customers live?
4. How many customers are there?
5. If your customers are businesses, describe their size and type, their numbers of employees and their locations.

Competition and Differentiation (One paragraph or table)

Reference: RoadMap™ Step 39

1. Describe the competing products and services.
2. Who are your main competitors and how many are there?
3. What key product or service characteristics motivate your customers to buy?
4. What are your advantages over the competition?
5. Explain how your products and services are different from the competitors' offerings.

Keys to Success (A brief bulleted list)

Reference: RoadMap™ Step 93

1. Describe the main keys to the success of your business.

2. What are the main barriers to the success of your business?

Pricing Strategy and Positioning (A paragraph, a table or both)

Reference: RoadMap™ Step 44

1. Provide a rationale or reason for your pricing.

2. List prices for your products and services.

3. Explain any price breaks or reductions for quantity purchases.

Qualifications (A paragraph or bulleted list)

Reference: RoadMap™ Step 34

1. Explain why you and/or your team are qualified to operate your business.

2. Who owns and/or manages your company?

3. What related business, education or experience qualifies you or your team to operate this business?

4. How and why are you qualified to operate this business?

5. If there are weaknesses, how will you compensate for them?

Tip: The trick to knowing which attachments to include is to approach the receiver of your business plan and ask which items he or she wishes to see.

Purpose of the Business Plan (A paragraph or bulleted list or combination)

Reference: RoadMap™ Step 93

1. Explain the purpose of your business plan and outline your financial requirements.

2. List the main reasons for creating your business plan.

3. Will you finance your start-up or growth yourself or will you need to borrow money?

4. How much money do you need?

5. When do you need the money?

6. If you are approaching other organizations for financing, what type of loan or grant are you seeking?

7. What terms are you requesting or offering?

8. What can you offer to your lender or financial institution to reduce their risk?

9. How much will you invest in your business and what form will your investment be?

Appendices (Two to six pages)

Reference: RoadMap™ Steps 54 to 89

1. Attach the most important elements of proof that support your business case.

2. Provide a 1-year sales forecast or summary (recommended).

3. Provide a 3-year cash flow forecast (recommended).

4. Provide a 3-year income statement (recommended).

5. Provide a 3-year pro forma balance sheet (on request).

6. List your key customers (recommended).

7. Present your historical financial statements (necessary for existing businesses only).

8. Provide your personal net worth statement (necessary for most small or new businesses).

Glossary of Terms

Access Provider: A business that provides connectivity to the Internet.

Accountant: One who is skilled at keeping business financial records.

Accounting Period: The period of time for which a financial statement is produced.

Accounts Payable: Money owed by a business to its suppliers and other creditors, accounts to be paid, usually has a due date. Also referred to as a current liability.

Accounts Receivable: Money owed to a business by clients or customers. Also referred to as a current asset.

Accrual Accounting or Reporting: One of two methods of bookkeeping where income and expenses are recorded in the period when they occurred, regardless of when actually received or paid. This method includes changes to inventory, accounts receivable and accounts payable. (See also Cash Accounting or Reporting)

Accrued Expenses: Expenses incurred but not paid.

Advertising: Techniques and activities involved in conveying information about a product or service to persuade people to buy.

Agent: A person authorized to act for another person – a principal – in dealing with a third party.

Amortization: The systematic reduction of an account balance by means of regular payments sufficient to meet current interest and to be paid out by maturity, most often used for long-term liability; i.e., a mortgage.

Angel: Private individuals with money to invest in business ventures.

Annual Report: A report made at the end of the fiscal year that presents financial transactions of the past year and their results.

Application Service Provider: Hosting services that will operate, support, manage and maintain your application for a fee.

Appreciate: To increase in value.

Arbitration: The resolution of a dispute between two parties by an impartial third party.

Arrears: Payments that are overdue.

Assessment: The setting of value of land, buildings and other assets for tax purposes.

Assets: Items of value owned by a business; e.g., cash and cash equivalents, receivables, equipment, land, inventory (stock). (See also Capital or Fixed Assets, Current Assets, Tangible Assets, Intangible Assets, Liquid Assets, and Long-term Assets)

Asymmetrical Digital Subscriber Line (ADSL): Provides high-bandwidth connections to the Internet using regular phone lines.

Audit: Verification of financial records and accounting procedures generally conducted by an accountant.

Authentication: The process which verifies the identity of a user logging onto a network.

Bad Debts: Money owed that cannot be collected.

Bait and Switch: An illegal selling technique, where a special is advertised, but is sold out when the customer arrives. The customer is expected to purchase something else.

Balance Sheet: A financial report showing the status of assets, liabilities and owner's equity of the business on the last day of the reporting period. Assets should equal Liabilities and the Owner's Equity.

Balloon Payment: A lump sum paid on a loan. For example, some loans require interest-only payments for a term, followed by a lump sum paid on the principle.

Bandwidth: Describes the amount of data that can travel through the Internet or communications network in a specific period of time, usually measured in seconds.

Bank Rate: Rate of interest charged by the Bank of Canada to chartered banks and financial institutions. (Also Prime Rate)

Bankruptcy: Financial and legal position of a person or corporation unable to pay debts.

Basis for Competing: A differential advantage and any strengths held over competitors.

Beginning Statement of Assets, Liabilities and Owner's Equity: A statement that documents the assets, the liabilities and the owner's equity at the beginning of the planning period.

Benefit Segmentation: The division of a market according to the benefits consumers want from the product.

Berg, Iceberg: The many layers of complexity that live beneath a perceived problem or task.

Bindery: How the pages in a document are held together.

Bleed: Graphic accent that extends beyond the normal margins of a page to the edge. Bleeds increase costs but can be an extremely powerful design tool.

Body Copy: The text portion of a brochure, advertisement or other document.

Bond: A third-party obligation to pay if the borrower fails to fulfill obligations under a contract. Types of bonds include License, Performance, Bid, Indemnity and Payment.

Bookmark: Provides the user with the ability to make their favorite pages and web sites for quick retrieval.

Brainstorming: An approach to problem solving or discussion that consists of gathering ideas without setting limits or boundaries - all ideas are valid.

Branding: A marketing method involving creating a name, symbol or design that identifies or differentiates a product or service from others.

Break-even Analysis: Method used to determine the point when the business would neither make a profit nor incur a loss.

Break-even Point: The point when sales equal total costs, expressed as either the total revenue exactly offset by total expenses; or as total production costs which exactly equals the income derived by their sale.

Bricks and Mortar: Physical buildings and assets as in a "facility"; usually the fixed assets of a business as opposed to the systems and intangible properties.

Browser: Software applications, such as Netscape Communicator, Mozilla or Microsoft Internet Explorer, which interpret HTML and web documents.

BTW: By the way (cyber)

Budgeting: Basic tool of financial planning that shows revenues vs. expenses that are planned for the coming period.

Bullet: A symbol used at the beginning of a list. The text is indented and there is one bullet for each different point in the list.

Bulletin Board System (BBS): Allows users to read, comment and electronically post new messages to an interest group on the Internet.

Business: Production of goods or services for profit.

Business Concept: A basic idea around which a business is built. Also the part of a business plan which describes or explains a business.

Business Expense: Cost of producing and selling a product, which can be deducted from gross income to arrive at net income for taxation purposes.

Business Plan: A written summary of the business; including strengths, weaknesses, needs and plans; to provide focus and direction to achieve goals.

Business to Business (B2B): The marketing, sale and support of goods and services to businesses on the Internet.

Business to Consumer (B2C): The marketing, sale and support of goods and services to consumers on the Internet.

Camera Ready: A document that is ready to print as-is.

Capital: Total assets owned or used in a business.

Capital Assets or Fixed Assets: Assets that represent long-term investments, usually involved in the production of goods and services. These assets are not readily convertible into cash; i.e., land, buildings and equipment.

Capital Costs: Costs involved in the acquisition of fixed assets.

Capital Equipment: Equipment used in the business and not intended to be sold for profit.

Capital Gain: Used for income tax purposes, the profit obtained when an asset is disposed of for more than the original cost.

Capital Lease: A lease that transfers all risks and benefits of ownership of the asset to the lessee (user); e.g., vehicle lease. This type of lease is usually longer than a year and may provide for transfer of ownership at the end of the term.

Capital Loss: The loss which occurs when a long-term asset is disposed of for less than its original cost.

Capital Requirement: The amount of money needed to get a business established.

Capital Sales and Purchases, Planned: Summary statement of planned purchases and sales, showing trade-in value, purchase price, cash down and financing. Details include amount of financing, interest rate, payment frequency, amount of annual payment, principal and interest.

Capital Stock: The money invested in a business by stockholders who purchase part of the owner's equity in the form of shares.

Caption: A title, heading, subheading or explanation accompanying a picture.

Cash Accounting or Reporting: One of two methods of bookkeeping where income and expenses are recorded only when payment is received or paid, regardless of when the agreement to sell or purchase occurred. Considered the simplest method and does not include changes to inventory, accounts receivable or accounts payable. (See also Accrual Accounting or Reporting)

Cash Conversion Cycle: The amount of time it takes to convert your cash outlays to income.

Cash Discount: Incentive provided by vendors of merchandise and services to speed up collection of accounts receivable.

Cash Flow: The cash receipts or disbursements that the business has. Receipts are from customers, loans and grants received, owner investments, etc. Disbursements include payments to suppliers, employees, loan repayments, finance expenses, and dividends paid to owners, etc.

Cash Flow Forecast, Projection or Statement: A summary, usually monthly projections, showing revenue or sales, how much and when, and expenses that will occur within the same time frame as the revenue or sales. Some expenses occur monthly even when there may be no revenue; the cash flow statement identifies cash needed to meet projected monthly expenses.

Cash Poor: Situation where a profitable business runs out of cash, usually because it is growing at a rate that cannot be supported by profit alone.

Casualty Insurance: Insurance other than accident and life insurance; i.e., fire, theft, general liability.

Caveat Emptor: A caution, warning. "Let the Buyer Beware"

CD-ROM: Consumer Device, Rendered Obsolete in Months.

Certified Cheque: Cheque bearing a guarantee from the signer's bank that funds have been reserved to cover it.

Change in Inventory: On the Income Statement, describes the adjustment to inventory of goods. This adjustment is eventually reflected on the Balance Sheet showing either increase or decrease from one reporting period to another.

Chat: Systems that enable users of networks and the Internet to communicate in real time.

Clip Art: Computer graphics that can be inserted into documents.

Cluster: A small group of businesses with similarities or characteristics that make them distinct from the larger industry.

CMYK: A color mode made up of cyan (C), magenta (M), yellow (Y), and black (K). In the CMYK color mode, color values are expressed as percentages, so a value of 100 for an ink means that it is applied at full saturation. CMYK is used in most full-color commercial printing.

Cold Sales Calls: Direct contact of a potential customer by a salesperson without leads or established previous contact.

Collateral: Assets that can be sold for cash and which can be used to secure or guarantee a loan.

Color Key Proof: A proof of a document printed in true color. It will look exactly like the documents that will come off the printing press.

Color Laser Proof: A proof of a document printed in color on a laser printer from a print shop to check accuracy. It is not a true color proof (the colors will not be the same as when it is printed on the printing press).

Color Separation: The process by which an image is separated into two or more plates for printing - one for each color.

Color Wheel: A graphic consisting of twelve color segments (along with their tints and shades) arranged in an orderly progression allowing the user to visualize the sequence of color balance and harmony.

Commissions: Payments to salespeople, distributors and agents for sales generated, usually calculated as a percentage of the sales volume.

Committee: A body that keeps minutes and wastes hours.

Company-owned Unit: An outlet owned and operated by a parent company.

Competition: A market in which rival sellers are trying to gain extra business at another's expense and thus are forced both to be as efficient as possible and to hold prices down.

Competitive Advantage: Factors that make your product, service or business more desirable to the purchaser over other offerings (lower price, easier to use, higher quality, more durable, etc.).

Complimentary Colors: A color scheme using colors directly opposite on the color wheel.

Compound Interest: Interest earned or previously accumulated interest plus the original principal.

Confidentiality: Keeping ideas or inventions private to ensure no copying occurs.

Confidentiality Agreement: A written promise not to disclose information about ideas or inventions.

Concentration Strategy: A process by which a business directs its marketing effort towards a single market segment through one marketing mix.

Consignment: Sale of goods through a third party whereby ownership of the goods remains in the name of the supplier until the goods have been sold, at which time the seller is indebted to the supplier.

Consortium: A group of companies involved in a joint venture to the benefit of all.

Consumer Market: Purchasers or individuals in their households who personally consume or benefit from the purchased products and do not buy products primarily to make a profit.

Content: Actual material, graphics, text and other multi-media that make up a website.

Contingent Liability: Potential liability; e.g., loan guarantee; that is subject to the results of a future event (i.e., failure of the borrower to repay the debt).

Contract: A formal agreement between two or more to do or to deliver something. Contracts can be complex and should always be reviewed by an attorney. A contract may not be binding if not correctly drafted and executed.

Contrast: The usage of varied colors, shapes, etc. to heighten the effect of a composition.

Contribution Margin: Direct income minus directly related variable expenses. The difference between income from sale of a product and the direct costs of producing that product. The contribution margin is then applied to the indirect costs of running the business.

Cookie: A text file that gathers and stores your personal preference information during the time you visit a website.

Co-op Promotion: Arrangements between two or more businesses to cross promote their products or services to customers.

Copyright: Protection of creative works from theft or copying; includes writing, music, videos and computer software.

Corporate Identity: The consistent image created by a business' print communications by using consistent and limited number of typefaces, type sizes, colors and logos. These elements typically appear in the same position at the same size on each type of document.

Corporate Tax: The tax owed by the company according to the tax regulations and its net profit before tax.

Corporation: A business organization that may have many owners, each liable only for the amount of his investment in the business.

Cost: The amount paid for goods and services used to run the business. See also Fixed Cost and Variable Cost.

Cost of Goods Sold (COGS): The cost of production or purchases of all products and services that are sold in the reporting period. Calculated either by multiplying the cost of each product or service by the quantity sold or by calculating the open inventory plus purchases during the period less the closing inventory.

Cover Stock: Super heavyweight paper available in a variety of colors.

CPM: Cost per thousand.

Credit Report: A listing of an individual or business financial history of repaying past loans and other liabilities.

Creditor: One to whom money is owed.

Crop Marks: Marks that indicate how the image area should be placed on the printed page.

Current Assets: Assets which are readily convertible into cash without substantial loss; i.e., cash, investments, receivables, prepaid expenses, and inventory.

Current Debt: Any debt or partial debt that is due to be paid within the current business year or operating cycle.

Current Liabilities: Financial obligations that will be paid out of business earnings within a year or within the normal operating cycle. They include accounts payable, bank overdrafts, short-term loans, etc.

Current Ratio: The ratio of current assets to current liabilities, indicating the ability to pay (the short-range liquidity and stability of the business).

Customer Profile: A description of the key characteristics of the people who buy your products and services.

Customs Invoice: Prepared by the exporter or forwarder, this is a copy of the seller's commercial invoice, describing the goods bought.

Cyan: Blue ink.

Cyberspace: Describes where people interact, communicate and exchange information using the Internet.

Dealer: A person or business that markets a product within a defined area.

Debit: Entry on the left side of a balance sheet, indicating an asset or prepaid expense.

Debt: Money that must be paid back to someone else, usually with interest.

Debt Capital, Debt Capital Financing, Debt Financing: Loan, usually long-term, used to establish, expand or run a business.

Debt-to-Equity Ratio: The ratio of long-term debt to owner's equity. Measures overall profitability.

Debt-to-Worth Ratio: The ratio of total liabilities to net worth of a business.

Deferred Income Taxes: A Revenue Canada provision whereby a portion of income taxes due may be deferred. Consult your accountant.

Defrag: To reorganize (a computer file, a business process) to eliminate fragmentation.

Demand: The combined desire, ability, and willingness on the part of the consumer to buy goods or service. Demand is determined by income and by price, which is, in part, determined by supply.

Demand Loan: A debt for which the lender may demand payment-in-full at any time upon notification to the borrower under the terms of the contract.

Demographics: Statistics based on population-related factors

Depreciation: The reduction in value of a fixed asset through use, obsolescence, inadequacy, or other physical or functional cause. The periodic amount allows the cost to be distributed over its useful life and is a tax-deductible expense.

Descriptor: Variables used to profile or build a fuller picture of target segments.

Dial-Up Networking: Allows a computer to dial into its server and connect to the Internet.

Differential Advantage: An attribute of a product or a business that is not currently matched by rival companies or products and which is highly desired by the target market's customers.

Distribution Channel: A method of providing goods or services to customers, such as on-line malls, portals, retail outlets or distributors.

Distributor: The agent or business that provides goods to retail dealers or companies; i.e., middle person, wholesaler.

Dividends: The proportion of net earnings declared by a corporation for distribution to shareholders in proportion to quantity of shares owned.

Domain Name: A unique name that is used to identify a website (www.riskbuster.com).

Domino Effect, Ripple Effect: Any action or series of actions that occur as a result of another action.

Downrules: Vertical rules added between columns to prevent readers from reading across the space between columns.

Drop Cap: The first letter of the first word cut into the paragraph it introduces - usually dropping down three lines in height. It may be the same font or it may be a fancier font for a more dramatic effect.

Drop Shipment: Shipped directly from the manufacturer to the consumer.

Due Diligence: Actions investors should do to confirm the value of an investment.

Dust: Mud with the juice squeezed out.

EBIT: Earnings before interest and taxes.

EBITDA: Earnings before interest, taxes, depreciation and amortization.

E-Business: Doing business on the Internet.

Electronic Commerce: Selling products and services via the Internet. Commonly referred to e-commerce.

Electronic Data Interchange or EDI: When manufacturers and retailers link their computer to each other for the purpose of ordering and inventory processing.

Email: Service allowing a computer user to send and receive written messages through electronic communications.

Employed Capital: The capital that is required to run the business in the long range including the total liabilities and equity of the business less the short-term liabilities.

Employee Stock Ownership Plan - ESOP: A plan where employees have vested interest in the company; stock ownership.

Employment Standards: The provincial or federal labor laws which establish minimum wages, hours, overtime pay, parental leave, paid vacation, etc.

Ending Statement of Assets, Liabilities and Owner's Equity: A statement that documents the assets, the liabilities and the owner's equity at the end of the planning period.

Entrepreneur: One who will work 14-hour days at $5 per hour to avoid a regular job paying $20 per hour. One who assumes the risk and responsibility for initiating, organizing and operating a business venture.

Equity: The difference between the assets and liabilities of a company. Often referred to as net worth.

Equity Capital: The owner's portion of the assets of a business, calculated as the difference between the value of the assets and the amount of liabilities.

Equity Financing: Money invested in a business in return for part ownership; shares.

Escrow: Temporary monetary deposit with an independent third party by agreement between two parties and held until agreed conditions have been met.

E-tailing: Selling retail goods online.

Excise Tax: A tax on specific goods or service, such as alcohol or tobacco.

Executive Summary: A summary of a business plan, usually the first part read by the reader.

Expense: Any identifiable cost relating to a business operation during a given financial period.

Extensible Markup Language (XML): A language for the web, more powerful than HTML.

Extranet: Private wide area networks that run on public protocols for the purpose of sharing information between organizations.

E-zine: Newsletters or magazines published electronically or online.

Factoring: The buying and selling of a company's invoices or accounts receivables at less than full paper value. The purchasing firm is called a factor, and makes its profits by collecting at full value.

Failure: Going out of business because the business cannot be run at a profit. Not always equivalent to bankruptcy.

Fair Market Value: The price a commodity can command on a free market.

Feasibility Study: The study of a project to see if it is technically possible and commercially profitable.

Fiduciary: A person or company entrusted with assets owned by another party and responsible for investing the assets until they are turned over to the owner (beneficiary).

File Server: A computer that stores and makes available data and programs to other computer on a network.

File Transfer Protocol (FTP): A protocol used on the Internet to transfer many different types of information in the form of files and data.

Fill: Adding color to a graphic or document.

Finance Expenses / Income: Finance expenses include interest payments to banks and other financial organizations for the capital and loans provided to the business, and commissions paid to banks for operations, credit lines, etc. Finance income includes income that the company earns from funds loaned to other businesses and organizations or from deposits and stocks the company holds.

Finances: Money.

Financial Accounting: Formalized accounting methods, within "generally established accounting principles", which are used to establish the financial position of a business within a given period of time.

Financial Leverage: The ratio of equity to external liabilities, which indicates the business's long-range stability and its ability to raise external financing.

Financial Statements: Documents that show your financial situation. Two major statements are needed to cover the information necessary to run a business and get financing.

Financing: Obtaining money resources.

Firecracker: Identifies a personality type or an approach to life and problem solving. One who creates idea explosions by connecting seemingly unrelated thoughts and activities with no visible focus or boundary.

Firewall: A software/hardware combination that separates an internal local area network from the external Intranet for security purposes.

First Refusal: The right of a party to have the first option to buy shares or property, usually has a specific time period attached to it.

Fiscal Year: The 12-month period used by a business to prepare financial statements.

Fixed Assets: Assets that may be realized in the long term; e.g., plant, equipment, land, and investments in subsidiaries.

Fixed Costs or Expenses: Costs that remain relatively unchanged regardless of volume of production or sales.

Flip: Shuffling information as one would a deck of cards. This can be very positive for thinking outside the box, but tends to be confusing, frustrating and costly when applied to budgets.

Foldout: An over-sized document that has a section that folds out for added information.

Font: A particular style of a letter, number, punctuation mark or character used in printing. All fonts are a variation of three basic types: serif, sans serif and script.

Footer: Text and graphic elements automatically repeated at the bottom of each page.

Foreclose: Sale of a property when the owner fails to meet mortgage, tax, or other debt payment on it. Must be approved by the courts.

Franchise: A form of business licensing requiring a franchise fee, a common trade name and a continuous relationship with a parent company.

Free Along Side - FAS: Price of goods to delivery on the docks during loading. The buyer becomes responsible for the goods once they are on the docks alongside the ship.

Free on Board - FOB: Price of goods on board a vessel at a port of shipment. From this point all transportation, insurance, and other charges are payable by the customer.

Free-forming: The spontaneous discussion of ideas by spring-boarding or pinging off each other's ideas and comments without boundaries or limitations.

Frequently Asked Questions (FAQ): A list of regularly asked questions placed where a user, visitor or customer can easily review them.

Friendly Market: A market that wants your products and services and attracts rather than repels.

FWIW: For what it's worth (cyber).

FYI: For your information.

Gain: An increase in equity which does not result from income or a direct contribution to equity; i.e., an item is sold for more than its "book value".

Gateway: A software or hardware component that links two otherwise incompatible applications or networks.

Gator: A particularly malicious and dangerous berg with teeth, recognisable only by a beady eyeball above the surface and which can swallow you whole if you get too close.

General & Administration Expenses (G&A): Operational expenses of the business, which include salaries of management and administration, rent and office expenses, telephone, postage, electricity and water, legal expenses, accountants and bookkeepers, consultants, etc.

Glue: Ongoing royalties or any form of rent-seeking, sometimes visible and agreed to and other times unsolicited, less obvious and extracted by force as with post-contract administration that accompanies government contracts.

Goal: A short-term detailed target with a clear and measurable deadline.

Going Concern: The idea that a company will continue to operate indefinitely, and will not go out of business and liquidate its assets. The value of the assets is assessed differently from the current market value.

Good Faith: Unspoken attitude of honesty and serious intention between two or more parties.

Goodwill: An intangible asset generated through high community standing, strategic location, superior management, etc. The financial value, once established is added to the fair market value of a business based on the tangible assets.

Gopher: A navigational tool that finds resources and information on the Internet by using a multi-level menu system.

Grace Period: Time allowed to a debtor before legal action is taken by a creditor to collect late payments.

Gradient: Background fill characterized by a smooth transition from one color to another.

Grant: Money provided by a government or public fund for a specific purpose. Repayment is usually not required, provided that the rules and conditions of the grant are followed.

Grid: A series of non-printing horizontal and vertical rules used to align page elements.

Gross: Total amount before deductions.

Gross Margin or Gross Profit or Gross Profit Margin: Income less the cost of goods sold. Reflects profit before operating, financing, tax and other expenses.

Guarantee: A written commitment by an individual or authorized legal entity to pay back a loan if the borrower is unable to do so.

Guaranteed or Insured Loan: Program whereby the federal government will indemnify a lender against part or all of any defaults by those responsible for repayment of the loan.

Guarantor: Person or company that guarantees to pay the financial obligations of a business or contract.

Gutter: Horizontal space between columns and between the right margin of a left page and the left margin of the right page.

Hacking: Gaining illegal or unauthorized access to a file or network.

Hardware: Computer components.

Header: Text and graphic elements automatically repeated at the top of each page.

Heterogeneous Market: A market in which all customers have different requirements.

Hijacking: Hacking into a domain name database and making the necessary changes to effectively "steal" the domain name from the owner.

Home Page: The first page a user sees after entering a URL for a website.

Homogeneous Market: To define an entire market as the target market for a particular product or service, usually including a single market mix for the entire market.

Hyperlink: An electronic link that can be programmed so that it is possible to make a jump from one document or web page to another.

Hypertext Markup Language (HTML): The language used to create a webpage.

Hypertext Transfer Protocol (HTTP): A protocol used to transfer information within the World Wide Web.

Hypothecate: To pledge a security without transferring title to the creditor.

Icon: Graphic element used in place of something else, typically words or commands.

Identity Statement: A simple, factual description of an organization, usually including basic information such as the businesses name, the form or structure, where it's located, when it started, the nature and scope of the business and what industry it is a part of.

Impressions: The number of times part of a page has been viewed by an individual browser.

Income: Money or revenue earned or received by a business.

Income Statement: Summary of income earned from the sale of goods and services, including expenses incurred to earn the income for a given period.

Income/Receipts: Cash income received by the business from customers, combined with receivables in a given period.

Indemnity: Insurance against or compensation for loss or damage.

Industrial Design Protection: Protection against copy of the shape and appearance of an invention.

Industry Ratios: Financial ratios established by comparing many businesses in an industry, generally accepted as a norm against which businesses can be measured.

Inflation: Cutting money in half without damaging the paper.

Initial Cap: Oversize letter used to introduce the first paragraph of a story or to break up long text columns. Initial caps can be dropped or raised.

Innovation: Use of a new idea, material or technology by an industry to change either the goods or services produced or the way in which the goods or services are produced or distributed.

Inserts: Flyers that are inserted into newspapers.

Intangible Assets: Assets that add value or benefit to the business, but cannot be seen or touched; e.g., goodwill, experience, brand equity, trademarks, leaseholds, mineral rights and quotas.

Intaxication: A euphoric state experienced by one receiving a tax refund, which lasts until you realize it was your money in the first place.

Integrated: Built to work together, as with spreadsheets that are linked together.

Intellectual Property: Knowledge and information which can be legally owned, as defined by laws governing copyright, trademarks, patents, royalty obligations, etc.

Interest: A fee charged on borrowed money.

Internal Rate of Return: The discount rate that will bring the net present value calculation to zero. When compared to the alternative interest rate in the financial market, it indicates the business's profitability and the level of risk involved.

Internet: Worldwide network of computers that use the TCP/IP network protocols to facilitate data transmission and exchange (syn: cyberspace)

Internet Protocol (IP): Software that divides information into packets and transmits it via the Internet.

Internet Service Provider (ISP): Provide web hosting, email and other services to individuals and organizations on the Internet.

Intranet: A private, secure Internet-based network used by a specific group of computers, such as by all employees and/or associates of a business.

Internic: Governing body that issues and controls Internet domains and addresses.

Integrated Services Digital Network (ISDN): Enables telephone lines to transmit digital signals, permitting faster dial up and transmission speeds.

Invention: A new product or process. To be eligible for patent, the invention must be new, useful and not obvious beforehand.

Inventory: Items for sale by the business, also including items that may be used in the production of goods for sale.

Inventory Days or Turnover: The inventory level relative to the cost of goods sold, which indicates the efficiency of the inventory holding. Inventory days of 30 days means that the average inventory level is sufficient for one month.

Invest: Put money into an enterprise with the expectation of earning a profit.

Investment Capital: Money set aside for starting a business.

IRC, Internet Relay Chat: Enables users to chat on the Internet.

ISP: See Internet Service Provider.

IT: Abbreviation for Information Technology.

Italics: Text that slants to the right.

Java: A programming language created in 1995 by Sun Microsystems; it allows content and software to be distributed through the Internet.

Job Sharing: An arrangement that allows the responsibilities and hours of one job position to be carried out by two people.

Joint and Several Liability: Legal term meaning that each (general) partner is fully liable for all the debts of the partnership and his personal assets may be required to pay off debts incurred by another partner.

Joint Venture: Business partnership formed for the sake of a specific project.

Justify: Aligns or justifies text at both the left and right margins or paragraph indents.

Kaizen: A Japanese term meaning continuous improvement.

Kerning: Increasing or decreasing spacing between specified pairs of letters.

LAN: See Local Area Network.

Laser: Identifies a personality type or an approach to life and problem solving. One who applies a concentrated, far-reaching beam of thought or action.

Launch: To initiate action.

Leading: Increasing or decreasing spacing between lines of text.

Leads: Names and contact information of potential customers.

Lease: An agreement in which the owner (lessor) of an asset conveys the right to use the asset to another (lessee) for a specified period of time in return for some consideration, usually monetary. (See also Capital Lease and Operating Lease)

Leasehold Improvements: Renovation and other improvements made to the business premises. These become the property of the landlord.

Leverage: The relationship or ratio between the total liabilities and the equity of a business. The higher the ratio of debt to equity, the greater the leverage.

Liabilities: Obligations of the business resulting from transactions made in the past for payment in the future. (See also Current Liabilities and Long-term Liabilities)

Lien: The legal right to retain possession of someone else's property until a debt is paid, or to have it sold or applied in payment of a claim.

Lifestyle Entrepreneur: An entrepreneur who starts or owns a business more for the lifestyle it affords than for other reasons, such as making money.

Limited Company: Separate legal entity that is owned by shareholders for the purpose of carrying on business. Assets and liabilities of owners are separate from the company. Also called incorporated company or corporation or limited liability corporation.

Limited Liability: Legal protection accorded shareholders of an incorporated company whereby the owner's financial liability is limited to the amount of his share ownership.

Limited Partnership: Legal partnership where certain owners assume responsibility only up to the amount of their investment.

Line of Credit: An agreement between a lender and a borrower in which a maximum is established and which the borrower may draw as needed.

Linking: Referencing a graphic instead of importing it into a document, reducing the file size. Double-clicking the image in the document loads the source file so you can edit it. If the source file is edited the linked image is automatically updated.

Liquid Assets: Those assets, generally current assets, which may quickly be turned into cash without disrupting normal business operations.

Liquidation: Sale of the assets of a business to pay off debts.

Liquidation Value: The estimated value of a business after its operations are ceased, its assets are sold, and its liabilities are paid.

Liquidity: Solvency of the business; readiness to convert assets to cash to meet short-term liabilities and other commitments.

Loan: Money lent at interest for a fixed period of time. (See Demand Loan and Operating Loan)

Local Area Network (LAN): A group of computers connected together in one location.

Logistics: Moving objects, such as products from one location to another.

Logo: A business or product name set in type in a distinctive way, often accompanied by a graphic.

LOL: Laughing out loud (cyber).

Long-term Assets: Assets which have a useful life greater than one year.

Long-term Liabilities: Financial obligations that may be paid out in a period longer than a year or beyond the normal operating cycle, excluding any portion of the debt principal that must be paid within the year.

Loss Leader: Item sold at a loss to attract buyers who will then buy other items as well.

Mainframe: Computer with a large central processing unit and huge memory.

Management: The administration and policy makers of a business; those responsible for planning of goals and objectives.

Manufacturer: A person or business that produces or manufactures goods on a large scale.

Margin: The space between text columns or visuals and the physical edge of a page.

Marginal Cost: Additional cost associated with producing one more unit of output.

Market: A number of people or organizations, who have a need for certain products or services and the ability, willingness and authority to purchase those products or services.

Market Economy: An economy where the setting of prices and allocating of resources are determined largely by the forces of supply and demand.

Market Niche: Special advantage in the marketplace where a business places itself.

Market Research: The collection of information about potential buyers or customers and about the competition from whom they currently buy.

Also see 'primary market research' and 'secondary market research'.

Market Segmentation: The identification of target customer groups in which customers are grouped according to their similar requirements and buying characteristics.

Market Share: Amount of a company's sales for a particular product as a percentage of total industry sales for that product.

Market Survey: An analysis of a particular market or of a particular aspect of a market.

Market Value: Value of an asset based on reasonable expectations of what a willing buyer would pay a willing seller.

Marketing: The process of advertising and selling goods and services.

Marketing Plan: Marketing program that outlines what you want to accomplish and how you propose to achieve these goals.

Markup: The amount a seller adds to the purchase price of a product or service. Markup usually covers operating expenses and profit.

Maximum Exposure: Indicates the maximum loss that might occur if the business terminates at the most critical moment, after all investments in fixed assets and working capital have been committed and before the business provides any earnings. It is calculated based on the lowest values of the accumulated profit (loss) plus fixed assets and inventory that occurs during the analyzed period.

Merchandise: Goods bought and sold in a business, a part of inventory.

Middle Person: A person or business specializing in the purchase and sale of goods.

Minicomputer: Midsize computer, falling between a mainframe and a micro in cost, memory and speed.

Minimum Turnover Method: Technique for deciding on how much to buy based on maintaining a certain level of inventory turnover for a certain item.

Minority Businesses: Businesses owned by people who are socially and economically disadvantaged.

Misleading Advertising: Advertising that deceives, implicitly or explicitly, about the price, quality, or use of a product.

Mission Statement: A succinct statement which describes what a business does, its product(s) or service(s), its customers and its competitive advantage.

Modem: Device that enables computers to communicate and transmit information over telephone lines.

Monopoly: Domination of the entire market for a product by one supplier.

Morph, Morphing: The act of going through one or more changes; reinventing or reshaping your business. Ability to dramatically change with relative ease, greatly adaptable, usually in a computer-related way.

Mortgage: An agreement to convey the legal interest of property, which is held as security for payment of a debt or discharge of an obli-gation, until the debt is paid or the obligation discharged.

Multi-level Marketing: A method of selling goods and services through distributors. Distributors receive commissions for their sales and for the sales of those new distributors they have recruited. Plans that offer to pay commissions for recruiting new distributors are called "pyramids" and are illegal.

Multimedia: The term used to describe many forms of media, such as graphics, animation, audio and video.

Negotiating: Act of reaching an agreement through bargaining.

Net: Internet.

Net Assets: Fixed assets combined with working capital. Net assets should equal the employed capital.

Net Book Value: The value of an asset calculated as the difference between the accumulated depreciation and the historical cost of the asset.

Net Cash Flow: The sum of all the cash transactions that were received or paid by the business.

Net Income: The excess of revenue over expenses for a specified period of time.

Net Lease: Signifies a property lease where a lessee is responsible for all costs such as taxes, heat, light, power, insurance, and maintenance.

Net Loss: The excess of expenses over revenue for a specified period of time.

Net Present Value (NPV): A formula that calculates the present value (at any given time) of future cash transactions. The result is related to the discount rate and the timing of future transactions.

Net Profit: Reflects profit for a reporting period after all expenses (including finance expenses, taxes and other expenses) have been accounted for.

Net Value: Amount that remains from a gross amount after expenses or debts have been deducted.

Net Worth: The difference between the market value of assets and the market value of liabilities. Net worth represents an estimate of how much cash would be received if all assets were disposed of and all liabilities discharged.

Net Worth Statement: A summary of the net worth of an individual and his business. Assets are estimated at fair market value, liabilities are subtracted from the assets and the result is the estimate of net worth.

Newsgroups: Electronic discussion groups where users can login and take part in a discussion with other users. Newsgroups exist for a variety of topics.

Newsreader: Software program that enables a user to subscribe to newsgroups.

Node: An addressable point on a network, such as a server, a printer or an individual computer.

Note Payable: Term used to distinguish a liability in the form of a promissory note from other liabilities such as Accounts Payable.

Note Receivable: Term used to distinguish an asset in the form of a promissory note from other assets such as Accounts Receivable.

Nutritional Requisition Registrar: Waiter or waitress.

Objectives: A broad, usually long-term target to aim for. The essential starting point for any planning process.

On Consignment: Goods shipped or turned over to an agent for sale, with payment to the shipper to follow sale, or products given to a retail outlet with payment to follow retail sale.

Operating Costs: Expenditures arising out of current business activities.

Operating Lease: A lease in which the lessor (owner) retains almost all risks and benefits of ownership of the asset.

Operating Loan: Cash advanced to a business to pay for operating costs, usually repaid within one year of the normal operating cycle.

Operational Cash Flow: The sum of cash transactions that come from the business operations; i.e., receipts from customers and payments to suppliers and employees. Not included are financial transactions such as loans and owner's equity.

Operational Profit: Presented in the profit and loss report and reflects the profit before finance expenses/income, taxes and other expenses. It is calculated based on the gross profit less operating expenses such as marketing expenses, general administrative, etc.

Operator: The owner or manager of a business or an enterprise.

Outsourcing: Obtaining products or services from outside a business rather than creating them internally.

Overdraft: A debt to the bank incurred by withdrawing more money from an account than it holds.

Overhead or Overhead Expenses: Business expenses not directly related to the goods and services produced; e.g., utilities.

Owner Manager: One who owns and operates a business.

Owner's Equity: The owner's investment in the business.

Packaging: The wrapping for a product.

Palette: A limited number of colors that project a unified image yet contain enough variety for both background and foreground colors.

Pancake: A problem that rapidly increases in size, scope and speed, involving more and more people; an explosion of confusion into the workplace. Usually results from not knowing who to ask for assistance.

Partnership: Two or more persons associated to pursue a business for profit.

Patent: The legal right to own an invention in Canada, on which royalties can be charged. A patent provides protection against others making, using or selling an invention without permission.

Patient Capital: Money that doesn't need to paid back right away. Also see Love Money.

Payable Days: Represents the amount due to payables relative to purchases/ expenses amount and indicates the effective terms of payment that the company gets from its suppliers.

Payables: Trade or other liabilities that are due.

Payback Period: The time in which investment in the business is covered by the net income. After payback in achieved, the business's accumulated profit becomes positive.

Payments: Cash payments that were made in a given period to suppliers, payables and employees.

Peripherals: Devices such as printers or disk drives that are added to the basic hardware to perform specific functions; the computer's input and output devices.

Piecework: Money paid based on quantity of work produced, rather than by hours worked.

Ping, Pinging: Bouncing ideas off other people; useful for market research or for fine-tuning a product or service by "pinging" off potential clients.A request to a machine to reply; used to verify that the machine exists and is functioning correctly.

Plug-ins: Extend the capability of a web browser to enable it to run other programs and multimedia applications.

Point: The standard unit for measuring type size, equal to 0.33mm (1/72 inch) or 72 points equal 1".

Point of Presence (POP): The location of an Internet server.

Positioning: Refers to a product, a service or a business in terms of its position in the marketplace. For example, largest, smallest, fastest, most competitive. The process of creating an image for a product in the minds of target customers.

Positioning Statement: A brief, believable, memorable written statement of a product or brand's desired stature, including the main target customer, what the business sells, and the main benefit the product or service brings to the customer.

Posting: Act of making an entry in a ledger account.

Power of Attorney: The legal authority to act for another person; the document conferring that authority.

Preferred: Debtors that come ahead of subordinated debtors. Preferred debtors are paid first, before subordinated debtors.

Prepaid Expense: An operating expense, other than for inventory, that will benefit the business in the future. The amount is carried on the balance sheet as an asset to be charged to expenses when used.

Pre-press: Anything the print shop has to do to a document, or file, in order to ready it for printing.

Price Fixing: Collusion among competitive businesses to keep prices up.

Price Skimming: Charging a high price for a new product for which there is no competition, to take advantage of a demand that cannot be met elsewhere.

Price-earnings Ratio: The ratio of the price of a share to the profit per share, which indicates the number of years that it will take the share buyer to cover the share price. It indicates how attractive shares bought and sold in the financial markets are.

Primary Market Research: Research information gathered first-hand through observation, personal interviews, focus groups, formal surveys, mail surveys and/or telephone surveys.

Principal: Property or capital assets as opposed to income. Also, one who is directly concerned in a business enterprise, such as the owner or a shareholder.

Print Run: Each time a job is printed on the printing press it is considered one run. If you had the same document printed a second time from the same print shop it would be considered the second run and may be cheaper because the pre-press set up would already be done and paid for on the first run.

Printing Press: Used for mass printing. Plates are made for each color.

Pro Forma: A projection or estimate of future results from actions in the present. A pro forma financial statement shows how the actual operation of the business will turn out if certain assumptions are realized.

Process Colors: Colors created by mixing the four basic ink colors on a page (cyan, yellow, magenta and black).

Product Positioning: Relates a product to its competition in the market, based on several criteria such as quality, price, image, etc.

Profiling: Building up a fuller picture of a target segment of a market.

Profit: The excess of the selling price over all costs and expenses incurred in making the sale.

Profit and Loss Statement: (See Income Statement)

Profit Margin: Difference between selling price and costs.

Projected Cash Flow Statement: Statement showing expected future sources of cash and how the cash will be used for business expenses, loan payments, capital purchases, and owner withdrawals from the business.

Promissory Note: A formal written promise to pay a stated sum of money to a particular person on a specified date, or on demand.

Prompt Payment Act: A federal law that requires federal agencies to pay interest to companies on bills not paid within 30 days of invoice or completion of work.

Proprietorship: See Sole Proprietorship.

Protected Territory: Exclusive territory granted to an operator by a parent company in which to sell goods or services.

Prototype: An early working model of an idea or invention which is tested so that the design may be changed if necessary.

Psychographics: Classifying customers according to their activities, interests and opinions.

Pull Quote: Short, significant phrase often set in a different typeface and larger size that summarizes material in adjacent columns of text. They provide readers an opportunity to become interested enough to start reading the article.

Quick Ratio: The ratio of current assets to the current liabilities, which indicates the business's stability and ability to liquidate in the very short term. Also acid test ratio.

Rack Jobber: A wholesaler serving retail stores, who sells primarily on consignment basis; although often on other terms.

Rate of Return: The amount an investor will earn, usually expressed as an annual percentage.

Readability: A measure of how easily readers can comfortably comprehend extended text passages.

Read Only Memory (ROM): A memory chip that stores data at the time of manufacturing that cannot be easily changed.

Receivable: An asset in the form of an amount due from a borrower or purchaser.

Receivable Days: Represents the amount owed by receivables relative to the sales volume and indicates the effective terms of payment that the company gives to its customers.

Receivership: Control of a business and its assets by a Receiver, usually a Chartered Accountant. Appointed by the creditor under the terms of a debenture, this person remains in control until debts are paid or business or assets are sold.

Registration Marks: Marks that help the print shop align each layer (or page) on the printing press.

Rent Seeker: The label applied to people and organizations that strive to collect residual benefits off others, usually for little or no investment or effort.

Research & Development (R&D) Expenses : Part of operational expenses and includes all expenses that are spent on developing new products, services or technologies. Included are related salaries, tools and materials used in product development, purchase of know-how and technologies, payments to sub-contractors, etc.

Resolution: A measure of sharpness with which pages are created. Increased resolution creates sharper images and smoother graduated background fills. Measured in dpi (dots per inch).

Retail: The sale of goods individually or in small quantities to the public, or dealing with the final consumer of goods and services.

Retained Earnings: The accumulated net profit of the business during its period of activity in the past and in the reporting period. Dividends paid to the owners are deducted from the retained earnings.

Return on Assets (ROA): The net profit divided by the business's assets. This indicates the profitability of the business and the efficiency in using its assets.

Return on Equity (ROE): The net profit divided by the owner's equity including retained earnings. This indicates the profitability for the owners and the efficiency of the equity employed.

Return on Investment (ROI): An indicator that measures how attractive the investment is for the investors. It is calculated based on the net profit divided by the required investment.

Return on Sales (ROS): The profit divided by sales revenues is the return on sales. This indicates profitability and the operational efficiency of the business. A decline in ROS indicates higher levels of expenses or a decline in sales.

Revenue: Income.

Rich Text Format or RTF: A standard word-processing format that can be used by most word processors.

Ripples: The effects of actions. Example: a change in the price of a product could create ripples with customers.

Rivers: Visual distraction in page layout typically caused by spaces inside consecutive lines of text that line up with each other. Often found in narrow columns of justified text where two spaces follow each period.

ROM: See Read Only Memory.

Rough: A draft copy of a brochure or other document. No detailed text is added. It is a layout and design technique to quickly try several different layouts in order to decide on the best one.

Royalties: Percentage of the revenue from the sale of a book, performance of a work, use of a patented invention or of land, paid to the author, inventor or owner.

Rules: Graphic accents created with a program's line-drawing tool. Rules can be used as borders, between columns, to emphasize text or to indicate the end of one text element and the beginning of a new element.

Sales and Marketing Expenses: Business expenditures for sales and marketing purposes. Include related salaries, advertising, public relations, exhibitions, commissions paid to sales people, agents, etc.

Sans Serif: A typeface design lacking the small finishing strokes that provides letter-to-letter transitions. (i.e., Arial)

Saturation: A measure of the strength of color. colors can be printed at 100% strength or printed as tints such as 10%, 30%, 50%, 80%, etc.

Scalability: How well a solution to some problem will work when the size of the problem increases. For example, a product that is easily replicated for a large number of customers is scalable.

Scale: Increasing or reducing the size of a text or graphic element while retaining the proportion (height to width ratio) of the original.

Scan: Converts a photograph or image into a digital file.

Screen: Converts a continuous tone into a series of dots that can be reproduced as a half tone. Most software enables you to specify screens in 10% increments.

Search Engine: Enables users to search the World Wide Web, Usenet newsgroups and other Internet resources, using descriptive words.

Secondary Market Research: Research information gathered from secondary sources, such as Statistics Canada, US Census Bureau, reports, articles in trade or consumer magazines and the Internet.

Security: Something given or pledged to guarantee payment of a loan; collateral.

Segmentation Variables: The characteristics or dimensions of individuals, groups or businesses that are used for dividing a total market into segments.

Serif: A typeface design with the small finishing strokes that provide letter-to-letter transitions. Serifs enhance readability by guiding the reader's eyes from one letter to the next. (i.e., Times New Roman)

Server: A term used to describe both the hardware and the software that provides information or executes functions for computers attached to a network.

Share Capital: The ownership interest in an incorporated company, represented by the shares of that company.

Shareholders' Equity: The excess of the net book value of the assets of an incorporated company over the value of its liabilities.

Shareware: Software that is made available to users by the developers at no cost.

Simple Interest: Interest calculated only on the principal of the loan.

Simplification: The act of making a business or function easier, faster, less problematic.

Single Variable Segmentation: Using only one variable to segment the market. This is the simplest type of segmentation.

Snip, Snippage: Commonly used terms within email to indicate that portions of an original message have been removed. Snip is used when one section is removed; snippage is used when multiple sections have been removed.

Software: Programmed instructions that tell the computer what to do. There are two types: operating system software and applications software.

Sole Proprietorship: Ownership by one person of the business is the simplest form of business organization. The owner has complete control and is personally liable for all debts of the business.

Spam, UBE, UCE: Spam is a generic term to describe unwanted email messages (email that is forced upon you, electronic junk mail). UBE — Unsolicited Bulk Email; UCE — Unsolicited Commercial Email

Spider: Software programs that browse the Internet for information to add to a search tool's database.

Spoofing: Impersonating someone on the Internet.

Spotcolor: Two or morecolors that are mixed in advance and applied in one pass.

Spread: View of a publication showing both left and right pages together, as readers will encounter them.

Stake a Claim: To raise your flag on new cyberspace territory, to register a domain name.

Statement of Changes in Financial Position: A statement that shows sources of cash from business operations, sales of assets, owner's contributions and borrowings for the past financial year. It also shows cash use for business operations, loan payments, assets purchased and owner withdrawals from the business.

Statement of Income: (See Income Statement)

Stickiness : A term used to describe the characteristics of a website that attract and keep users.

Streaming Video: Using a plug-in to watch a video in real time as it is downloaded, as opposed to storing it as file.

Style Sheet: A collection of styles that work together to govern the appearance of a drawing. You can choose a pre-set template or create your own template.

Styles: Time saving feature that allows you to save the typographic formatting choices contained in a file as a template or style sheet.

Subhead: Typographic device used to divide long articles into manageable, bite-sized chunks.

Subordinated: Debtors that come behind preferred debtors. Preferred debtors are paid first, before subordinated debtors.

Supplier Discounts: Price reductions given by suppliers based on the kind of customer or the size of orders, or to encourage prompt payment, etc.

Sweat Equity: The investment in time and effort by the owner into a new business.

Symmetry: Design term used to describe individual pages or two-page spreads characterized by left-right balance.

Table: Design technique that organizes complicated information in row and column format.

Takeover: Acquisition of one company by another.

Tangible Assets: The physical assets such as equipment, cash, buildings, inventory, etc.

Targeting: The act of deciding which market segment(s) to prioritize for sales and marketing efforts.

Target Market: The specific individuals, distinguished by socio-economic, demographic and interest characteristics who are most likely potential customers for the goods and services of a business.

Tariffs: Foreign government taxes levied on exports.

Template: A read-only file containing the formatting information necessary to create a finished document.

Term Loan: A medium or long-term loan, usually extended to purchase fixed assets (land, buildings, equipment, leasehold improvements, etc.)

Terms of Sale: Conditions concerning payment for a purchase.

Tint: The addition of white to a color.

Tracking: Increasing or decreasing letter spacing uniformly throughout a headline or column of text to improve the appearance of the text.

Trade Credit: Credit terms offered by one business to another. Example, a building supply vendor might extend credit to a trusted renovator.

Trademark: Name, symbol or other mark that identifies a product to customers, and is legally owned by its manufacturer or inventor.

Trend Analysis: Analysis of a business's financial ratios over a period of time, to determine whether its financial situation has improved or deteriorated.

Trial Balance: Result of adding all credits and all debits to check that the two sums are equal.

Trimming: Cutting off edges of the paper. Usually done in conjunction with a bleed.

True Type: A typeface promoted by Apple and Microsoft. True type fonts often print faster on laser printers than competing typeface formats.

TTFN: Ta, Ta for now (cyber)

TTYL: Talk to you later (cyber)

Tunneling: A secure mechanism which permits transmission of data across points of access on the Internet.

Turn Key Operation: Project, such as setting up a business or an office, where all the work is done by a contractor and handed over in working order to the owner. The owner will then just "turn the key".

Turnaround: The act of taking a company from a downward path to a prosperous one.

Turnover: Number of times per year that a product is sold and reordered.

Type 1: Adobe's universally accepted typeface format characterized by the largest selection of typefaces and the easiest acceptance by service bureaus such as print shops.

Typeface: Variations of font characters.

UBE: See Spam

UCE: See Spam

Undifferentiated Or Total Market Approach: An approach that assumes that all customers have similar wants and needs and they can be served with a single marketing mix.

Uniform Resource Locators (URL): The standard address format for the World Wide Web, including domain name, IP address and protocol type.

Unique Selling Proposition: The reason a product or service is different and better than the competitors' products or services.

Unit: Any item or group of items considered as one for sale by the business; e.g., one wooden item for a craftsperson, one hour for a researcher.

Unlimited Liability: Fully responsible for all debts of a business; i.e., personal assets can be required to pay off the business debt.

Unreasonable: Not governed by reason; ignoring what appears to be reasonable in order to create outcomes that appear to be impossible. A forceful and visionary approach to solving a problem or changing a paradigm.

Variable Cost or Expense: Costs which may vary according to the amount of production or sales activity.

Venture Capital: Funding provided to new or existing businesses that exhibit potential for above-average growth, used to support new or unusual undertakings; equity, risk or speculative investment capital.

Venture Capitalist: An investor or organization that invests in businesses with a considerable level of risk and is willing to invest in a medium-to high-risk business in exchange for a very high level of return.

VERONICA: Acronym for Very Easy Rodent Oriented Netwide Index, a network utility that enables a user to search thousands of Gopher servers throughout the world.

Vision Statement: A brief statement that describes what a business wants to be, how it wishes to be viewed by its customers, and how it will treat its internal and external customers.

Virtual Private Network (VPN): A Wide Area Network (WAN) formed by connecting two or more Local Area Networks (LANs) securely through the Internet.

Virus: A program developed to attack computer systems and create problems.

Visualization: The creative act of conceiving how you want the project to look when finished and printed.

Warranty: Promise to the buyer that the product sold is of good quality and that, if not, certain repairs and replacements will be made.

Web: The sub-section of the Internet that can be browsed (i.e., with a "web browser").

Web Server: A computer containing World Wide Web documents, connected to the Internet.

Weight: Typeface with different strokes of thickness ranging from light to heavy, permitting you to add visual interest and voice to your text without choosing a different typeface.

White Space: A page layout term referring to areas of rest and quiet on a page. White space is free from text, visuals or graphic elements, providing the contrast necessary to frame text and visuals.

Wholesaler: A middle person who sells to retailers and to other merchants, or to industrial, institutional and commercial users; not usually to the end consumers.

Wide Area Network (WAN): Two or more local networks connected together via high-speed telephone lines.

Winding Up: Legal procedures of closing down a limited company.

Working Capital: The capital that is required for the current operations of the business including credit extended to customers less credit received from suppliers for inventory, etc.

World Wide Web (www): A collection of standards and protocols that make it possible to view and retrieve information from the Internet.

Wrinkles: Something other people have. You have character lines.

Write-off: Removal of a worthless asset from the company's books.

WYSIWYG: Acronym for What You See Is What You Get. Text and graphics that print in the same format as is visible on the computer screen.

XML: See Extensible Markup Language.

Zone Pricing: Setting the price of an item according to where it is sold, to allow for extra shipping charges or other costs that vary from region to region.

Appendix

Table of Contents

RoadMap™ Checklist #1

Get Equipped For Your Business Planning Adventure	1__	Welcome to the Macrolink Business Planner's RoadMap™
	2__	Prepare to Embark on Your Journey
	3__	Chart Your Path
	4__	Organize Your Work Space
	5__	Establish Your Timelines
	6__	Create Your Action Plan
	7__	Wade Into Your Industry
	8__	Start Your Research Scrapbook
	9__	Write Your Business Vision in an Hour
	10__	Set Out to Prove Your Business Case
Embrace Your Market Research: Become the Expert	11__	Set Up Your List of Appendices
	12__	Brainstorm Your Products and Services
	13__	Prioritize and Select Your Products and Services
	14__	Discover and List Your Assumptions
	15__	Identify Market Research Issues and Strategic Objectives
	16__	Clarify and Write Your Market Research Questions
	17__	Prove or Disprove Your Assumptions
	18__	List the Important Information about Your Industry
	19__	Segment Your Market
	20__	Write a Draft Description of Your Customers
	21__	Assess What You Are Learning About Your Business
	22__	Identify and Research Your Competitors
	23__	Prioritize and Target Your Customers
	24__	Clarify and Write Your Primary Market Research Questions
	25__	Determine the Best Method to Gather Primary Research
	26__	Create Your Market Survey Questionnaire
	27__	Survey Your Customers
	28__	Compile and Analyze Your Market Survey Information
	29__	Rewrite Your Description of Your Customers
	30__	Make a Go / No-Go Decision
Build Your Business Concept Section	31__	Describe Your Business
	32__	List Your Products and Services
	33__	Describe Your Industry
	34__	Write Your Biography
	35__	Develop Your Strategic Plan and Goals

Map Your Marketing Section	36__	Describe Your Market Area
	37__	Describe Your Location
	38__	Describe Your Customers
	39__	Analyze Your Competitors and Differentiate
	40__	Describe How You Will Sell Your Products and Services
	41__	Clarify Your Servicing and Guarantees
	42__	Craft Your Business Image
	43__	Develop Your Advertising and Promotion Plan
	44__	Present Your Prices and Pricing Strategy
	45__	Develop Your Marketing Action Plan
Organize Your Operations Section	46__	Describe Your Operation
	47__	Determine Your Equipment Requirements and Methods
	48__	Source Your Materials and Supplies
	49__	Identify Your Risks and How You Will Control Them
	50__	Describe Your Management Team
	51__	Research and Select Your Professional Services
	52__	Determine Your Employee and Contractor Requirements
	53__	Develop Your Operational Action Plan
Forecast Your Financial Section	54__	Forecast Your Sales
	55__	Explain Your Projections
	56__	Estimate Your Market Share
	57__	Present Your Cost of Goods Sold
	58__	Summarize Your Labor Projections
	59__	Develop Your Cash Flow Forecast
	60__	Identify Your Operating Expenses
	61__	Develop Your Projected Income Statement
	62__	Determine What Level of Sales You Will Need to Break-even
	63__	Develop Your Pro Forma Balance Sheet
	64__	Identify and Calculate Your Start-up Expenses
	65__	Clarify Your Sources and Uses of Funds at Start-up

	66__	Build a Resumé
	67__	Develop Your Personal Net Worth Statement
	68__	Organize Your Certificates and Accreditation
	69__	Produce Your Historical Financial Statements
	70__	Create Your Organizational Charts
	71__	Get the Approval of Your Board
	72__	Build Your List of References
	73__	Request and Include Letters of Reference
	74__	Gather and Include Letters of Intent
	75__	Copy and Include Signed Contracts or Offers
	76__	Create a Partnership Agreement
Assemble Your Appendices	77__	Copy and Include Lease Agreement(s)
	78__	Copy and Include Insurance Documents
	79__	Develop Your Price List(s)
	80__	Gather and Include Written Price Quotes
	81__	Build Credibility with Written Appraisals and Estimates
	82__	Provide the Right Amount of Market Survey Information
	83__	Create a Map of Your Market Area
	84__	Gather and Include Environmental Information
	85__	Build Credibility with Free Publicity
	86__	Create Dynamic Promotional Materials
	87__	Add a Pinch of Product or Service Literature
	88__	Add a Titch of Technical Information
	89__	Explain any Confusing Terms
	90__	Create Your Title Page
	91__	Write Your Executive Summary
	92__	Develop Your Table of Contents
	93__	Write Your Confidentiality and Copyright Statements
Incorporate Your Introductory Section	94__	Evaluate Your Business Plan
	95__	Have Your Business Plan Critiqued by Others
	96__	Revise and Rewrite Your Business Plan
	97__	Complete Your Application for Financing
	98__	Write Your Cover Letter
	99__	Put It All Together

RoadMap™ Checklist #2: 4-Week

Timeline	Week 1 - Steps 1-19			Complete by:						
	Week 2 - Steps 20-30			Complete by:						
	Week 3 - Steps 31-53			Complete by:						
	Week 4 - Steps 54-99			Complete by:						
Week 1 **Steps 1-19**	1__	2__	3__	4__	5__	6__	7__	8__	9__	10__
	11__	12__	13__	14__	15__	16__	17__	18__	19__	
Week 2 **Steps 20-30**	20__	21__	22__	23__	24__	25__	26__	27__	28__	29__
	30__									
Week 3 **Steps 31-53**	31__	32__	33__	34__	35__	36__	37__	38__	39__	40__
	41__	42__	43__	44__	45__	46__	47__	48__	49__	50__
	51__	52__	53__							
Week 4 **Steps 54-99**	54__	55__	56__	57__	58__	59__	60__	61__	62__	63__
	64__	65__	66__	67__	68__	69__	70__	71__	72__	73__
	74__	75__	76__	77__	78__	79__	80__	81__	82__	83__
	84__	85__	86__	87__	88__	89__	90__	91__	92__	93__
	94__	95__	96__	97__	98__	99__				

RoadMap™ Checklist #3: 12-Week

Timeline	Month 1 - Steps 1-30	Complete by:							
	Month 2 - Steps 31-53	Complete by:							
	Month 3 - Steps 54-99	Complete by:							

Month 1									
Week 1	**Steps 1-8**	1_	2_	3_	4_	5_	6_	7_	8_
Week 2	**Steps 9-13**	9_	10_	11_	12_	13_			
Week 3	**Steps 14-21**	14_	15_	16_	17_	18_	19_	20_	21_
Week 4	**Steps 22-30**	22_	23_	24_	25_	26_	27_	28_	29_	30_

Month 2								
Week 5	**Steps 31-35**	31_	32_	33_	34_	35_		
Week 6	**Steps 36-42**	36_	37_	38_	39_	40_	41_	42_
Week 7	**Steps 43-45**	43_	44_	45_				
Week 8	**Steps 46-53**	46_	47_	48_	49_	50_	51_	52_	53_

Month 3										
Week 9	**Steps 54-65**	54_	55_	56_	57_	58_	59_	60_	61_	62_	63_
		64_	65_							
Week 10	**Steps 66-80**	66_	67_	68_	69_	70_	71_	72_	73_	74_	75_
		76_	77_	78_	79_	80_				
Week 11	**Steps 81-89**	81_	82_	83_	84_	85_	86_	87_	88_	89_
Week 12	**Steps 90-99**	90_	91_	92_	93_	94_	95_	96_	97_	98_	99_

Business Start-up Checklist

Starting a business is a different process than planning the business. Here is a comprehensive list of tasks to help you with your start-up process.

Personal Readiness	Clarify personal vision and goals	
	Assess your personal suitability to business	
	Determine how much money you need or want to earn	
	Check your personal credit rating	
	Clean up any credit incidentals or negatives	
	Put your personal financial affairs in order (sell toys, tidy up debt, etc.)	
	Develop a personal net worth statement	
	Clarify why you want to go into business (lifestyle, financial, etc.)	
	Assess your business and trade skills and determine training needs	
Business Feasibility	Identify a need or a problem	
	Determine what products and/or services might fill the need	
	Determine how many clients will need the products and services	
	Research sources of suppliers for the products or services	
	Validate suppliers as to security, level of risk, stability	
	Determine how much money is required to start the business	
	Calculate how much of your own money or assets you can invest	
	Identify what kind of security or collateral you can offer to lenders	
	Identify potential sources of credit and financing	
	Roughly calculate whether or not your idea is feasible	
	Assess whether your background qualifies you to operate this business	
	Decide whether to pursue developing a business plan for this idea	
Business Planning	Complete market research	
	Conduct market survey(s)	
	Develop your business concept	
	Create your marketing strategy and plan	
	Determine how you will run your business operations	
	Calculate your business financial projections	
	Write draft of business plan	
	Review and revise business plan	
	Produce final copy of business plan	
Financing	Determine how much money you need to start your business	
	Determine how much money you need to operate your business	
	Identify sources and uses of funds	
	Select financial agencies and submit loan applications	
Regulatory	Complete business name search	
	Register business name	
	Establish business legal structure (proprietorship, corporation, etc.)	
	Determine your requirements and register where necessary	
	* Business License	
	* Other Licenses (Environmental, Forestry, Fish & Wildlife, Gaming)	
	* Goods and Services Tax (GST)	
	* Provincial Sales Tax (PST)	
	* Workers Compensation Board (WCB)	
	* Food Industry Regulators	
	Identify and acquire industry specific certification requirements	

Employees	Identify what you will require for employees	
	Clarify and write job titles and descriptions	
	Determine how and where to advertise to recruit employees	
	Interview and select employees	
	Identify needs and establish training for employees	
Subcontractors	Identify what you will require for subcontractors	
	Clarify and write job descriptions	
	Determine how and where to advertise to recruit subcontractors	
	Interview and select subcontractors	
	Identify needs and establish training for subcontractors	
Location	Assess what location will work best for your customers	
	Assess your location for its marketing strength	
	Observe or assess the flow of traffic at the location	
	Identify where the competitors are located	
	Talk with other business owners in the area	
	Identify any safety issues or concerns	
	Determine whether handicap access is necessary	
	Research public transportation services	
	Establish parking requirements	
	Check zoning requirements	
Utilities	Research costs and establish heating connection (gas, oil, propane)	
	Research costs and establish hydro/electrical connection	
Telephone	Establish business number and account	
	Establish business fax number and account	
	Establish Internet hookup (telephone)	
	Establish a cell phone number and account	
	Research and choose a long distance carrier	
	Set up an answering service or voicemail system	
Technology and Internet	Determine whether you will establish a web page	
	Research and set up account with Internet Service Provider	
	Research and register domain	
	Design and build website	
	Identify physical technical requirements	
	Create a system for making back-up copies of digital information	
Equipment	Determine computer requirements and identify sources	
	Determine printer requirements and identify sources	
	Determine industry specific equipment needs and identify sources	
	Vehicles	
	Other equipment	
Software	Research, select and purchase, as needed:	
	· Word processor	
	· Spreadsheet	
	· Internet browser and/or email program	
	· Graphics	
	· Database	
	· Inventory/sales	
	· Accounting	

Bank Account	Research and select a bank	
	Open a business bank account	
	Order business cheques	
	Set up debit account and machine	
	Visa / Master Card	
Security Systems	Physical (employees, customers, facility, parking lot)	
	Technical (heat control, back-up systems, lock-up, passwords)	
	Fire (extinguishers, evacuation plan)	
	Theft (alarm systems, monitoring by security company)	
	Money (cheque signing authority, transportation)	
Marketing Materials	Determine who will create marketing materials, images and graphics	
	· Business cards	
	· Signage	
	· Logo	
	· Letterhead	
	· Fax cover	
Communication and Credentials	Resumés for key personnel	
	Biographies for key personnel	
	Letters of support	
	Letters of reference	
	Business resumé or prospectus	
	Awards	
	Certificates, Diplomas, Accreditation, Degrees, Designation	
Advertising and Promotion	Research advertising options and costs	
	Research reciprocal and co-op advertising options	
	Organize and promote grand opening	
	Press release promotion	
	Ad in telephone directory (Yellow Pages)	
	Newspaper or magazine articles on your business	
	Interviews with the press	
	Identify networking opportunities	
	Call everyone you know and inform them you are in business	
Lawyer & Legal	Research and select a lawyer	
	Attend to legal requirements	
	Identify any variances for different jurisdictions	
	Define and map any requirements with regard to area of operation	
	Research and secure patent, trademark or copyright protection	
	Identify the need for and develop any pertinent agreements:	
	· Partnership	
	· Management	
	· Employee	
	· Subcontractor	
	· Lease	
	· Supplier	
	· Customer	
	· Confidentiality	

Bookkeeping and Accounting	Research and select bookkeeper	
	Set up bookkeeping system	
	Set up filing system	
	Research and select accountant	
	Set up chart of accounts	
	Identify what the bookkeeper and accountant need from you and when	
	Set up payroll systems	
Establish Employee Benefits Plan	Medical	
	Dental	
	Short-term disability	
	Long-term disability	
Policy Manual	Write draft copy of policy manual	
	Complete revisions	
	Produce final copy	
Operations Manual	Write draft copy of operations manual	
	Complete revisions	
	Produce final copy	
Set Up Office / Facility	Research office/facility supply needs and identify sources	
	Research office/facility furniture needs and identify sources	
	Research office/facility equipment needs and identify sources	
	Complete office/facility renovations	
	Set-up inventory and displays	
	Organize and set up work area	
	Organize and set up storage area	
	Organize and set up administration area	
Professional Affiliations	Chamber of Commerce	
	Trade Associations	
	Rotary Club	
	Professional Networking Groups	
Price Lists	Source suppliers	
	Confirm and compare prices	
	Create price lists for internal use	
	Create price lists for external use	
Insurance	Research insurance needs	
	General liability insurance	
	Product liability insurance	
	Errors & omissions liability insurance	
	Malpractice liability insurance	
	Automobile liability insurance	
	Fire & theft insurance	
	Business interruption insurance	
	Overhead expense insurance	
	Personal disability insurance	
	Key person insurance	
	Shareholders' or partners' insurance	
	Business loan insurance	
	Term life insurance	
	Medical insurance	
	Group insurance	

Suggested Reading

Abrams, Rhonda. *The Successful Business Plan: Secrets and Strategies*
3rd ed. Palo Alto, California. Running 'R' Media, 1991, 1993, 2000.

Allen, James. *As a Man Thinketh*.
Marina del Ray, California. DeVorss & Company

Alreck, Pamela L. Settle, Robert B. *The Survey Research Handbook*
United States of America. Irwin/McGraw-Hill, 1995.

Andrus, Carol. *Fat-Free Writing*
United States of America. Crisp Publications, Inc., 2000.

Bangs, Jr., David H. *The Business Planning Guide*
9th ed. United States of America. Dearborn Trade Publishing, 1995, 1998, 2002.

Beck, Nuala. *Excelerate*
1st ed. Toronto, Ontario, Canada. HarperCollins Publishers 1996.

Cameron, Julia. *The Artist's Way*
1st ed. New York, New York, USA. G. P. Putnam's Sons. 1992.

Chilton, David Barr. *The Wealthy Barber*
1st ed. Toronto, Ontario, Canada. Stoddart Publishing Co. Limited, 1995.

Clason, George S. *The Richest Man in Babylon*
New York. New American Library, Penguin Putnam Inc., 1955, 1988.

Cork, David. *The Pig and the Python*
1st ed. Toronto, Ontario, Canada. Stoddart Publishing Co. Limited. 1996.

Covey, Stephen R. *Principle-Centerd Leadership*
1st Fireside ed. New York, New York, USA. Fireside, 1992.

Covey, Stephen R. *The 7 Habits of Highly Effective People*
1st Fireside ed. New York, New York, USA. Fireside, 1990.

Cyr, Donald. Gray, Douglas. *Marketing Your Product*
3rd ed. Bellingham, WA, USA. Self-Counsel Press Ltd. 1998.

Doman, Don. Dennison, Dell. Doman, Margaret. *Market Research Made Easy*
2nd ed. USA and Canada. International Self-Counsel Press Ltd., 2002.

Dominguez, Joe. Robin, Vicki. *Your Money or Your Life*
1st ed. New York, USA. Penguin Books 1992.

Doyle, Denzil J. *Making Technology Happen*
5th ed. Ottawa, Ontario, Canada. Doyletech Corporation, 2001.

Dyer, Dr. Wayne W. *You'll See It When You Believe It*
1st Avon Books Printing. New York, New York, USA. Avon Books, 1990.

Falkenstein, Dr. Lynda. *Nichecraft*
1st ed. New York, New York, USA. HarperCollins Publishers. 1996.

Foot, David K. *Boom Bust & Echo*
1st ed. Toronto, Ontario, Canada. Footwork Consulting Inc. 1996.

Foot, David K. *Boom Bust & Echo 2000*
1st ed. Toronto, Ontario, Canada. Footwork Consulting Inc. 1998.

Frishman, Rick. Larsen, Michael. Levinson, Jay Conrad. *Guerrilla Marketing for Writers*
1st ed. Cincinnati, Ohio, USA. Writer's Digest Books. 2001.

Fulghum, Robert. *All I Really Needed to Know I Learned in Kindergarten*
1st Ballantine ed. USA. Ballantine Books, 1989.

Gerber, Michael E. *The E Myth Revisited*
1st ed. New York. HarperCollins Publishers, Inc., 1995.

Good, Walter S. *Building a Dream*
5th ed. Toronto, Ontario, Canada. McGraw-Hill Ryerson Limited, 2003.

Griffiths, Bob. *Do What You Love For the Rest of Your Life*
1st ed. New York and Toronto. The Ballantine Publishing Group, 2001.

Handy, Charles. *Beyond Certainty*
1st ed. Great Britian. Arrow Books Limited, 1996.

Hawken, Paul. *Growing a Business*
1st ed. New York. Fireside, 1988.

Hawken, Paul. *The Ecology of Commerce*
1st ed. New York, New York, USA. HarperCollins Publishers, 1993.

Helmstetter, Shad. *Choices*
1st Pocket Books ed. New York, New York, USA. Pocket Books, 1990.

Hendricks, Mark. Riddle, John. *Business Plans Made Easy*
2nd ed. Canada. Entrepreneur Media, Inc., 2002.

Hill, Napoleon. *Think and Grow Rich*
1st Ballantyne Books ed. New York, New York, USA. Ballantyne Books, 1990.

Hoffman, Helene & Larry. *Going Solo*
1st ed. Agincourt, Ontario, Canada. Authors' Marketing Services Ltd. And Freelance Writing Associates, Inc. 1983.

Jensen, Marlene. *The Everything Business Planning Book.*
Avon, Massachusetts, USA. Adams Media Corporation, 2001.

Kintler, David. Adams, Bob. *Adams Streetwise Consulting*
1st ed. Holbrook MA, USA. Adams Media Corporation, 1997.

Kiyosaki, Robert T. *Rich Dad Poor Dad*
1st ed. New York, New York, USA. Warner Books, Inc. 1998.

Kremer, John. *1001 Ways to Market Your Books*
5th ed. Fairfield, Iowa. Open Horizons, 1998.

Levinson, Jay Conrad. *Guerrilla Marketing*
1st ed. USA. Houghton Mifflin Company. 1984.

Levinson, Jay Conrad. *Guerrilla Marketing Weapons*
1st ed. USA. Penguin Group. 1990.

Magos, Alice H. Crow, Steve. *Business Plans That Work*
2nd ed. Chicago, USA. CCH Incorporated, 2003.

McCarthy, Michael J. *Mastering the Information Age*
1st ed. New York, New York, USA. St. Martins Press. 1990.

McCormack, Mark H. *What They Don't Teach You at Harvard Business School*
1st ed. New York, New York, USA. Bantam Book, Inc. 1986.

O'Hara, Patrick D. *The Total Business Plan*
2nd ed. New York and Canada. John Wiley & Sons, Inc., 1995.

Peters, Thomas J. Waterman, Js. Robert H. *In Search of Excellence*
1st ed. New York, New York, USA. Warner Book, Inc. 1982.

Peterson, Mark A. *The Complete Entrepreneur*
1st ed. Hauppauge, New York, USA. Barron's Educational Series, Inc. 1996.

Raab, Steven S. *The Blueprint for Franchising a Business*
1st ed. USA. John Wiley & Sons, Inc. 1987.

Ramu, S. Shiva. *International Licensing*
1st ed. New Delhi. Sage Publications Inc. 1997.

Ries, Al. Trout, Jack. *Marketing Warfare*
1st ed. New York, New York, USA. McGraw-Hill, 1986.

Ries, Al. Trout, Jack. *The 22 Immutable Laws of Marketing*
1st ed. New York, New York, USA. HarperCollins Publishers, 1994.

Sirolli, Ernesto. *Ripples in the Zambezi*
1st ed. Australia. Institute for Science and Technology Policy, Murdock University, 1995.

Small Business BC. *Business Development Concepts.*
Vancouver, British Columbia. Small Business BC, 2004.

Sun Tzu. *The Art of War*
USA. Oxford University Press. 1971.

Taylor, Harold L. Delegate: *The Key to Successful Management*
2nd Printing. Toronto, Ontario. Stoddard Publishing Co. Limited, 1984.

Tiffany, Paul. Peterson, Steven D. *Business Plans for Dummies*
1st ed. Foster City, California. IDG Books Worldwide, Inc., 1997.

Timmons, Jeffry A. Zacharakis, Andrew. Spinelli, Stephen. *Business Plans That Work*
New York. McGraw-Hill, 2004.

Touchie, Rodger D. *Preparing a Successful Business Plan*
2nd ed. North Vancouver, British Columbia, Canada. Self-Counsel Press, 1989, 1993.

Index

RiskBuster™

Business Planner

Digital Business Planner CD or Download

The RiskBuster™ Business Planner is a collection of business planning tools ready for you to use. This resource contains all of the necessary digital tools for you to successfully complete your business plan, including a Business Plan Shell™, a financial forecasting tool and sample business plans and financial scenarios.

What You Will Get

Biz4Caster™ 101: A printable step-by-step guide to forecasting your financial scenarios.

Business Plan Shell™: An empty business plan template formatted and ready for your input.

Biz4Caster™: A spreadsheet template that makes it easy for you to forecast your financial projections.

Sales and Cashflow Worksheets: A simple spreadsheet to forecast sales and build cashflow projections for your business.

Sample Business Plans: Includes business plans for Macrolink Action Plans Inc. and Mountain Mapping.

Sample Financial Forecast: Includes the Biz4Caster™ forecast for Macrolink Action Plans Inc.

Business Start-up Checklist: A comprehensive list of the necessary steps to successfully start your business.

System Requirements

You need to have a word processor (for The Shell™) and a spreadsheet (for the Biz4Caster™). For most people this will be Microsoft Office or OpenOffice. Some documents (Biz4Caster™ 101) require Adobe Reader, which can be downloaded for free from www.adobe.com.

Visit our website at www.riskbuster.com
or e-mail Dan at danb@riskbuster.com

RiskBuster™

Biz4Caster™

Digital Biz4Caster™ CD or Download

The Biz4Caster™ is a forecasting tool that gives you the opportunity to convert your market research efforts into meaningful numbers before taking any risks with your investment. Biz4Caster™ will transform your business planning experience into a safe and fun learning adventure while saving you time, money and energy.

Biz4Caster™ will:

1. Make the Financial Section of your business plan enjoyable and simple.
2. Enable you to efficiently build and test different financial scenarios for your business.
3. Reveal whether your financial case will earn you money and make a profit.

Biz4Caster™ Components

Introduction	Cash Flow Forecast
Springboard	Start-up Expenses
Assumptions	Use & Source of Funds
Loan Calculator	Bizplan Summaries 1
Owner's Drawings	Bizplan Summaries 2
Price Generator	Cashflow Copy Sheet
Sales Forecast	Projected Income Statement
Market Share Calculator	Pro Forma Balance Sheet
Cost of Goods Sold	Ratios
Labor Projections	Personal Net Worth Statement

System Requirements

You need to have a spreadsheet. For most people this will be Microsoft Office or OpenOffice. Biz4Caster™ 101: The Forecaster's Handbook will require either a word processor or Adobe Reader, which can be downloaded for free from www.adobe.com.

Visit our website at www.riskbuster.com

or e-mail Dan at danb@riskbuster.com

RiskBuster™

Trainer Kit

Teach others how to do business plans

The RiskBuster™ Business Planning Trainer Kit comes fully stocked and ready to use. Neatly packaged in a durable container, each kit includes a facilitator manual with overheads, supporting reference material, training aids and a reproducible learner workbook.

You'll find:

- High quality, proven curriculum
- Independent, stand-alone course units
- Mix and match activities to serve your learners
- Adaptable courses, easy to use by all trainers

What you will get...

- A course description
- Learning objectives
- Training plan
- Facilitator guide
- Facilitator manual
- Generic activities, icebreakers & energizers
- Macrolink activity plans
- Overhead transparencies
- Training aids
- Reproducible learner materials

This Course Kit is for you if...

- You have owned and operated a business
- You wish to start or expand your training business
- You wish to provide training as a part of your job

Marnie Perrier, Owner of People by Perrier, says, "Macrolink has thought of everything. They take the worry out of presenting valuable information."

Visit our website at www.riskbuster.com
or e-mail Dan at danb@riskbuster.com

RiskBuster™

Business Planner's Primer

Prove Your Business Case: Know Your Bottom Line

Workshop Length

12.0 hours

Description

The purpose of this workshop is to introduce you to the business plan as an opportunity to become an expert on your own business. The session will begin by highlighting the importance of market research and providing you with a process for researching your business idea. The business plan is a structure to help you organize your market research and enable you to prove or disprove your business case. All aspects of the business plan are covered, including developing a business concept, building a marketing strategy, planning business operations, and an overview of the Financial Section for a business plan.

The workshop is interactive, including a number of activities aimed at guiding you to draft Elements of your business plan. Small group learning activities are followed with time for questions and discussion. You will leave the workshop with a clear understanding of the next steps needed to complete your business plan. For this workshop, successful outcomes can include deciding to complete a business plan, deciding to hire a consultant, or moving on to pursue further education or training.

The workshop can be delivered in 2 days or broken into shorter segments.

Course Goals

At the end of this workshop, you will be able to:

- Identify the benefits of a business plan
- Define and plan your market research
- Discover a business plan structure and process
- Determine how to prove your business case
- Build draft Elements of your business plan
- Ease the fear of financials and forecasting
- Recognize where to find assistance and information
- Review and decide whether to finance a business plan

What You Will Learn

- What a business plan is and why it is necessary
- Where to get business planning tools
- How to organize your market research
- Where to access information and get help
- How to prove your business case
- How to do a financial forecast
- How to avoid business planning pitfalls
- How to identify and manage risk
- How to prepare a professional business plan
- Where to access related educational opportunities

(continued next page)

RiskBuster™

This Workshop is for you if...

- You have an opportunity to start, purchase or expand a business
- You want or need to develop a business plan
- You wish to transform your work experience or hobby into a business
- You have basic reading and writing skills

This Workshop is for...

- Anyone wishing to develop his or her own business plan
- Business planning facilitators, trainers, coaches
- New business start-ups
- Small or micro-business owners
- Workers who wish to become self-employed
- Non-profit organizations aspiring to develop a social enterprise
- Business owners who need to refocus or expand their business

What you can expect...

This workshop is learner-centered and designed for maximum participation and practice. You will fill your business planning tool chest with tricks and techniques in a safe and fun learning environment. You will leave the workshop with a clear idea of what a business plan is and how to go about developing one. Most importantly, you will know whether you are ready to develop your own business plan, take further training or hire a consultant to develop your plan for you.

What you will get...

Each participant will get a copy of the 99-Step Business Planner's RoadMap™ (over 200 pages) and the RiskBuster™ Business Planner's CD. The CD includes sample business plans and the Biz4Caster™, a Microsoft Excel based forecasting template.

Who will facilitate this Workshop?

Dan Boudreau, President and CEO, Macrolink Action Plans Inc.

Dan Boudreau

RiskBuster™

Business Coach

A Seasoned Entrepreneur in Your Corner!

Business Name: Macrolink Action Plans Inc.

Address: Box 101, Prince George,
                   British Columbia V2L 4R9 Canada

Phone: 250-612-9161

Email: danb@riskbuster.com

Website: www.riskbuster.com

Time Zone: Pacific Standard Time

Type of Coaching: Business Planning
                   Business Development
                   Business Start-up

Coaching Activities: One-on-one Coaching
                   Group Coaching

Language: English

Dan Boudreau

Profile:

Dan is the sole owner, President and CEO for Macrolink Action Plans Inc:

- Involved in small business development since 1980, as owner, coach, trainer and consultant.
- Worked in community economic development for 15 years.
- Served ten years on Finance and Lending Committee for a $5 million loan fund for entrepreneurs.
- Manages a $15 million fund that provides grants for economic development projects.
- Nominated twice as Entrepreneur of the Year — 1997 and 1999.
- Develops and delivers workshops for entrepreneurs (Business Planning, Train the Trainer).
- Published Dream Catcher Business Planning Toolkit and Scratchpad (since 1995).
- Published Business on a Shoe String e-zine — 1999 to 2003.

Visit our website at www.riskbuster.com
or e-mail Dan at danb@riskbuster.com
or Call Now 250-612-9161

ISBN 141209285-X